SUMMER JOBS BRITAIN 2002

Including Va Traineesl

GW00808311

EDITORS

Andrew James
David Woodworth

Distributed in the U.S.A.
by Peterson's, a division of Thomson Learning
2000 Lenox Drive, Lawrenceville, New Jersey 08648
www.petersons.com
800-338-3282

Published annually by
Vacation Work, 9 Park End Street, Oxford
www.vacationwork.co.uk

Thirty third edition

SUMMER JOBS IN BRITAIN

ISBN 1-85458-264-X (hardback)
ISBN 1-85458-263-1 (softback)

ISSN 0143 3490

Statement for the purposes of
The Employment Agencies Act 1973:
The price of *Summer Jobs in Britain*
is £15.95 (hardback) or £9.99 (softback) and is for the book and
the information contained therein; it is not refundable.

Cover design by Miller Craig & Cocking Design Partnership

Typeset by WorldView Publishing Services Ltd (tel 01865-201562)

Printed by William Clowes Ltd., Beccles, Suffolk, England

Preface

For the past few years every edition of **Summer Jobs in Britain** has contained more jobs than its predecessor, and this edition for 2002 is no exception. Whether you are looking for a job to occupy mind or body and whether your aim is to earn good wages, gain work experience or to help others, we hope that you will find what you are looking for in these pages.

The summer has always been a period when employers in Britain look for large numbers of additional staff. Even when the recession of the last decade was at its worst people still, for example, ate fruit and vegetables and went on holiday, so agriculture and tourism continued to provide a reliable source of short-term work. **Summer Jobs in Britain** is designed to help you in your search for a job, whether you wish to work near home or further afield. And while many of the jobs are in the fields of tourism and agriculture, this book lists a wealth of other opportunities, ranging from putting up marquees to joining archaeological excavations.

In this book we have collected details of job vacancies supplied to us by employers in England, Scotland, Wales and Northern Ireland. The jobs have been arranged in regional chapters under the following headings: Business & Industry, Children, Holiday Centres & Amusements, Hotels & Catering, Language Schools, Medical, Outdoor and Sport, Voluntary Work and Vacation Traineeships, the latter providing on-the-job work experience for students in business and industry.

Many employers in the book express a willingness to take on overseas applicants. While nationals of EU and EEA countries, young nationals of Commonwealth countries and American students can seek work in the UK without too much difficulty, it can be hard for most other foreign citizens. Nevertheless, there are a number of special schemes recognised by the Home Office which give non-EU nationals the opportunity to work for a limited period in this country. Detailed information is given about all such programmes in the introduction.

The companies and individuals listed in **Summer Jobs in Britain** are for job-seekers to apply to directly; the publishers cannot undertake to contact individual employers or to offer assistance in arranging specific jobs.

The Directory is an annual publication and is VALID FOR 2002 ONLY. A thoroughly revised edition will be published in November 2002.

Andrew James
David Woodworth
Oxford, October 2001

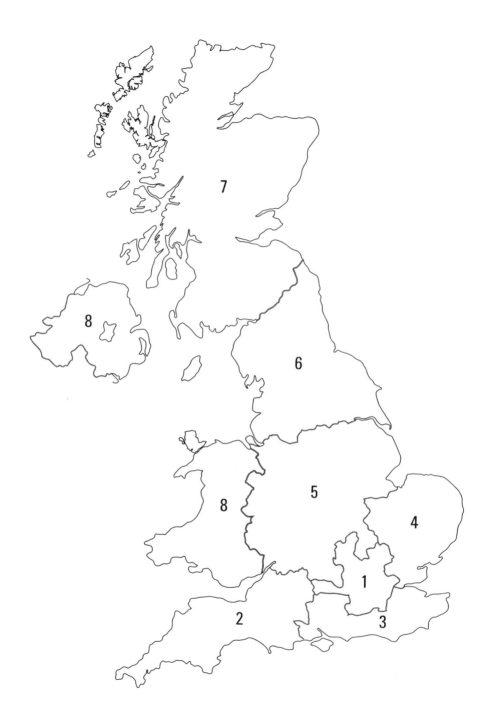

Contents

Working this Summer

Overview

This book goes to the printers as the lowest unemployment figures for over a quarter of a century have been announced. True, There are a few economic clouds on the horizon: manufacturing industry in the UK is contracting, and there is national and international talk of a possible recession. But the British economy is starting from a strong base, and the prospects are rosy for finding summer work for 2002: the job vacancies advertised in the windows of businesses down any high street bear witness to the fact that many employers are having problems finding enough staff.

Now that local authority grants for students have been phased out in Britain and university tuition fees have been introduced finding a holiday job to raise money is increasingly important for students. Figures published in *The Times* in September 2001 estimated that the average student graduated with accumulated debts of £10,095, or £12,215 if studying in London. Fortunately, as this book proves, there are plenty of jobs to be found to help you build up a nest egg.

CATEGORIES OF WORK

To make this book easier to use we have divided the jobs listed into the following categories.

Business and Industry

This category includes working as *Drivers, Temps, Office Workers, Labourers and Cashiers*, amongst others.

Temping. Work as a 'temp' involves covering for staff away on holiday, on sick leave etc., and is usually arranged through an agency. These positions are primarily for those with secretarial skills, though some clerical jobs require no qualifications. Since the job prospects are better for those with word processing skills, you may consider doing an evening course before the summer starts.

One of the advantages of temping work is that it is available at any time of year and can be found at short notice. The availability of this sort of work has increased greatly over the last decade and is likely to increase further as employers realise the importance of a flexible workforce; taking on a temp to meet an increase in demand saves those nervous about the arrival of another recession from having to commit themselves to taking on permanent staff. A private employment agency recently estimated that temporary staff now make up nearly 8% of the workforce.

Another bonus is that temping can be extremely lucrative, particularly if you have relevant qualifications. Good word-processing skills can earn £8 an hour, with more for higher-level computer work. Unskilled clerical work may bring in about £5 an hour. However, the advantages of temping work are not purely financial. It can also provide a valuable insight into different sectors of industry and the opportunity to develop computer and interpersonal skills, which according to graduate recruiters too many students lack.

In addition to the agencies listed in this book, most towns have a number of agencies specialising in temp work; to find them look under *Employment Agencies* in the Yellow Pages. Alternatively, the employment agencies' association *The*

Recruitment and Employment Confederation has the website www.rec.uk.com on which you can search for agencies in your area by type of work sought.

Shop Work. There is an extra demand for extra staff in the summer both to cover for regular staff who are away on holiday and to serve customers in tourist areas. The trend for late-night and Sunday shopping has created many extra jobs around the year. Most supermarkets now open until at least 8pm most nights of the week and many larger ones do not close at all between Monday morning and Saturday evening; they regularly require check-out staff and shelf-fillers, especially those willing to work antisocial hours. The demand is primarily for part-time workers. But if a full-time vacancy comes up, anyone already working for the company has a good chance of being chosen as a replacement. Large homecare and DIY stores such as B & Q and Homebase are another good source of this type of work.

For full-time jobs preference may be sometimes be given to those showing an interest in eventually joining permanently. This applies in particular to the more prestigious employers such as Marks & Spencer. Other department stores, including Littlewoods tend to be less fussy.

Sales. Employment as a sales person conjures up outdated images of traipsing from house to house trying to sell dusters or encyclopaedias. While this type of work still exists, telesales (which involves selling a product over the telephone) is a more popular method nowadays. *The Times* newspaper has predicted that by the next century one out of every fifty employed people will be performing this type of work. Call centre staff tend to be young, according to a member of BIFU, the bank and insurance union. Apparently there is a burn-out problem, as staff may be continuously monitored to assess their performance. Pay is often fairly good.

A good telephone manner may be all you need to get a sales job with a holiday tour operator, though the ability to speak a European language will give you the edge over monolinguists; work with holiday companies needs to be arranged early, in the spring. Some companies may offer pay solely on a commission basis; make sure the terms of employment are clearly stated before signing a contract.

Cleaning. Office and industrial cleaning is another area that offers temporary vacancies. Most cleaning companies prefer to employ staff for long periods, but they will occasionally take people on temporarily for jobs such as cleaning newly-built or refurbished office blocks, or for the annual deep-clean of those factories which still shut down for a couple of weeks each summer.

Factory Work. Spending the summer on a production line may not be your idea of fun, but the potential for work in this field is good. The factories most likely to require extra staff are those that are preparing for the Christmas rush (they usually start increasing production in August) or those which specialise in the packaging and processing of seasonal food. Huge quantities of fruit and vegetables, harvested between late spring and early autumn, must be preserved by canning or freezing. Factories in this business have an urgent need for line workers, packers and delivery drivers.

Be prepared for early mornings, shift work and high levels of boredom. While pay for production line work is not outstanding, nor is it the worst in the country.

Children

This category includes working as *Leaders, Nannies, Playworkers and Instructors* amongst others. In response to the desperation of parents trying to occupy their children during the long summer holiday, over the last decade there has been a boom in the American style of holiday centres and playschemes designed to amuse the younger generation. Anyone looking for work in such a centre will frequently not require qualifications unless their job involves some hazardous sport or activity – most employers are looking for people with energy, enthusiasm and an outgoing personality. But anyone looking for work with children can expect to be carefully vetted, as the safety of the children is paramount. With parents increasingly worrying about political correctness and safety, some centres are no longer offering more dangerous activities such as rifle-shooting.

Preference is likely to be given to those with experience of working with children. Trainee primary school teachers are particularly well suited.

Jobs on holiday camps can vary from teaching sports to organising discos. Since much of the work is similar to that in camps geared towards children and/or adults, more details are given below under *Holiday Centres* below.

Holiday Centres and Amusements

This category includes working as, amongst others, *Receptionists, Catering Staff, Retail Assistants, Ticket Sellers, Ride Assistants, Car Park Attendants, Supervisors, and Entertainers*

Tourism. Although most British families would now prefer a package holiday abroad to a fortnight at Blackpool, the British tourist industry remains huge. The industry provides jobs for about 1.5 million people. Although many British people may go elsewhere for their main holiday they are taking more additional short breaks in the UK than ever, with the West Country officially the most popular area. In addition some recent hot British summers have encouraged more and more people to stay at home as there has been no need to go abroad in search of the sun.

Sadly, in 2001 the British tourist industry was badly hit by foot and mouth disease, which for a time placed some of the most popular parts of the country including the Lake District, the Scottish borders and parts of the West Country out of bounds. Almost as bad as the direct restrictions caused by the disease was the fact that many people, especially visitors from abroad, were unnecessarily discouraged from visiting the countryside by the bad publicity. We have not dwelt on foot and mouth in the regional chapter introductions as severe measures have been taken to combat foot and mouth and it is hoped that by next year it will have been totally eradicated.

Television and films provide a major force in marketing different regions as more and more tourists want to follow in the footsteps of their favourite stars and literary characters. For example, Glen Nevis in Scotland attracted over a million visitors a year eager to experience the atmosphere of the film *Braveheart* which was filmed there. Testament to the lasting power of a kiss, Carnforth Railway Station in Lancashire, the setting for the embrace in *Brief Encounter* still draws more than 100,000 visitors a year.

Holiday Centres. One of the greatest recent trends in tourism in the UK has been the growth in the number of holiday camps, activity centres and theme parks. These centres are some of the largest seasonal employers in the country. Not only do they take on thousands of staff between them – the largest ones can employ hundreds of people each – but they also offer a wide range of jobs for both skilled and unskilled workers. Many chains of holiday centres have refurbished and updated their images, such as Butlins Skylines which has centres at Bognor Regis, Minehead, and Skegness. There may be vacancies for receptionists, lifeguards, bar and restaurant staff, car park attendants, shop assistants, cleaners, ride attendants, activities organisers, nurses, babysitters and so on. The work is often hard, with a high degree of participation in activities expected, but can also be very enjoyable.

Some holiday centre jobs do not require qualifications, though experience is an asset, and it depends which post you are applying for. As a result, this type of work is popular and competition for jobs is intense. It is essential to apply as soon as possible because many of the big employers start recruitment early in the year. Although extra people are hired later in the season, to cover bank holidays and particularly busy weeks, these are frequently selected from a reserve list compiled from the surplus of earlier applications.

If you fail to find a job with one of the centres listed in the book, try a speculative, personal approach. The British Tourist Authority (tel 020-8846 9000; www.travelengland.org.uk) can provide information on the major theme and leisure parks throughout England. Visit Scotland (tel 0131-332 2433; www.visitscotland.com) and the Wales Tourist Board (tel 0292-044 9909; www.visitwales.com) provide the same information for Scotland and Wales. The book *The Britain Guide* (AA Publishing, £9.99) also provides a comprehensive directory of attractions.

Hotels and Catering

Hotels and catering establishments offer a range of jobs including work as *Waiting, Bar and Chamber Staff, Receptionists, Chefs, Porters and Kitchen Assistants*. Many of the temporary hotel and restaurant jobs during the summer season are to be found in the country's main tourist resorts and beauty spots. If you are based in or near a big city, the best sources of work may well be the big hotel chains, such as Forte or Hilton UK. Their hotels employ large numbers of staff, have a comparatively fast turnover and can have vacancies at any time of year. The disadvantage is that they are less likely to provide accommodation and are more likely to want experienced and trained staff for particular duties.

Working in a large and impersonal hotel in the city is likely to be more regimented and therefore less fun than spending the summer in a family-run guest house in the South-West (unless you find yourself working for Basil Fawlty). If you choose a hotel in a remote area with a lower cost of living and/or fewer opportunities to spend, such as the Scottish Highlands or the Welsh Mountains, you will also find it easier to save money. Many hotels begin advertising for summer staff before Easter, and in general applicants who can work for the entire summer season are preferred.

Hotel work can be hard and tiring, and you are usually expected to work shifts, sometimes at unsociable hours. Hotel and restaurant kitchens are particularly hot and frantic, with chefs notorious for their short tempers. On good days, however, hotel work is lively and can be exciting.

Always ask for precise details about your duties. Many of the job titles do not provide a clear definition of the work: a 'kitchen porter', for example, may spend most of his or her time washing up and being a general dogsbody. Small hotels tend to employ general assistants for a range of duties that can go from cleaning toilets to working in reception.

Fast food restaurants generally have a high turnover of staff at any time of year; the main chains, including McDonalds and Pizza Hut, employ large numbers of people throughout the country. Motorway service stations and roadside restaurants such as Little Chef and Burger King also take on extra workers in summer.

Unless you want to be a chef, you will seldom require qualifications to work in a hotel or restaurant; and while experience is often preferred, it is by no means always essential. A neat appearance and a resilient nature may be all you need, although increasingly a knowledge of more than one language can be an advantage.

Wages. While the majority of hotels do not indulge in exploitative practices nor do they pay through the nose for their staff; but there can be perks to the job; for example, some hotels will allow staff to use their sporting and leisure facilities.

Anyone with silver service or other specialist experience can expect to earn more than the average wage for this type of work, as can restaurant staff in London. Tips can be a bonus to those serving the public directly, but remember that centrally organised tips may be included in the National Minimum Wage.

Youth Hostels. Seasonal Assistant Wardens are employed to help in the running of the YHA's 230 Youth Hostels in England and Wales. Work is available for varying periods, between February and October each year. For further information about working in a Youth Hostel see the entry at the end of the Hotels and Catering section in the *Nationwide* chapter.

Language Schools

The staff needs of language schools are principally for *EFL Teachers and Social Organisers*. Teaching English as a foreign language (TEFL) is perhaps not now the major growth industry it was a decade ago but it still remains a good source of well-paid summer jobs. During the summer months people of all nationalities and ages come to spend time in Britain to learn or improve their English. The language schools that cater for them are found for the most part in London, Canterbury, Brighton, Hastings, Eastbourne, Bournemouth, Oxford and Cambridge.

Most British language schools require a TEFL qualification of their teachers, though some will take on either graduates with an English or modern language degree, or students doing PGCE and teacher training courses. There are a vast number of TEFL courses and qualifications on offer, and these vary widely in length, location and cost. One of the most widely recognised, and most commonly asked for certificate is The Cambridge CELTA (Certificate in English Language Teaching to Adults), previously known as the Cambridge/RSA CELTA. Courses take place in a variety locations both British and worldwide, and usually last four weeks. (University of Cambridge Local Examinations Syndicate, Syndicate Buildings, 1 Hills Road, Cambridge, CB1 2EU; tel 01223-553355; e-mail efl@ucles.org.uk; www.cambridge-efl.org.uk).

The other major Certificate is awarded by Trinity College London, which stipulates a minimum of 130 hours of teaching, over a four-week period (or part-time over a much longer period: contact Trinity College London, 89 Albert Embankment, London SE1 7TP; tel 020-7820-6100; fax 020-7820-6161; e-mail tesol@trinitycollege.co.uk; www.trinitycollege.co.uk). Many of the courses advertised cost between £750 and £950, for some of which, examination and accommodation costs are included. For a full guide to TEFL courses, see the *ELT International Careers Guide* which includes tables comparing costs, duration, dates and locations.

Language schools that run residential courses may take on general staff to supervise day trips, visits and the more social side of the school's programme:

qualifications are rarely required for this type of work, though experience is desirable. There are also opportunities for sports instructors as many of the schools offer a wide range of outdoor activities.

Medical

This category consists largely of opportunities for *Carers and Nurses*. Britain is currently suffering from a shortage of health professionals, and anyone with valid nursing qualifications should have no difficulty finding work. There can also be shortages of care staff to look after the sick and disabled: often training is given, so previous experience is not always necessary. In addition to the opportunities listed in this book you could also look for specialist medical agencies on www.rec.uk.com.

Outdoor

The majority of vacancies in this category are for *Fruit Pickers, Farm Staff and and Marquee Erectors*.

Agriculture. While increased mechanisation has reduced the number of pickers required at harvest time, agriculture remains the second largest source of seasonal work after tourism. Soft fruit are still picked by hand; and since some other crops don't necessarily ripen at the same time machines can't always be used for them. Furthermore, fruit that goes to supermarkets must fit increasingly precise criteria in terms of size and shape, and extra staff are required to help in the selection process. The increasing number of pick-your-own farms has dealt another blow to fruit and vegetable picking in some areas.

But since food processing factories can't pick their own, pickers and packers will always be required. In fact, in some recent years tons of English strawberries, raspberries and cherries have been left unpicked because of a shortage of seasonal workers to pick them. Some farmers object to the fact that they are unable to bring in sufficient foreign students who are willing and able to work on the harvest because of the limited number of work permits allocated by the government for this work every year, and have asked for this quota to be doubled.

The best areas for looking for fruit and vegetable picking work in the summer are from the Vale of Evesham over to the River Wye (in the Midlands); Kent; Lincolnshire; East Anglia (particularly the Fens); and north of the Tay in Scotland (especially Perthshire). Harvest times differ between regions, so raspberries may ripen two weeks later in Scotland than in the South. Among the first fruits to ripen in southern Britain are strawberries and gooseberries, usually in June. Processing and packing work tends to be available in the Vale of Evesham after the main harvest season. Work involving harvesting outdoor salad crops is also available in the Hampshire and West Sussex area.

Kent and Herefordshire are the centres of hop picking in the UK, with the harvest taking place in September. There is now a high degree of mechanisation employed, but people are still required to drive tractors, strip hop flowers from vines, etc. Women can get landed with the indoor jobs, so if this doesn't appeal ask about the availability of outdoor work.

The apple harvest, which runs from August until mid-October, is traditionally one of the longer-lasting and most lucrative crops to pick. The industry is currently however in a state of flux; due to an increasing number of cheap imports from hotter climates, the apple orchards of southern Britain are fast disappearing.

The generous allowances for importing cheap wine from across the Channel and the easy accessibility of the French hypermarkets have similarly destabilised the young British wine industry. Despite falling farm-gate sales, some vineyards, found mainly along the South Coast, may still require local workers. Harvest times are difficult to predict as the sugar content of the grapes lies at the mercy of the sun. Out of the 400 vineyards in the UK, about 60 are commercial, and the rest are hobbies. For more information, contact the UK Vineyard Association (tel 01728-638080).

Over the last two decades the number of areas of farmland devoted to growing cherries has shrunk from over 4,000 acreas to under 800. But in 2001 the supernmarket chain Tescos began experimenting with a new variety of dwarf tree that may rejuvenate the industry and represent a source of employment in the future as cherries have to be picked by hand. One advantage of these dwarf trees is that you do not need to use a ladder to reach the fruit, unlike the traditional trees.

While fruit-picking work tends to be short-term, it is possible to string several jobs together by following the ripening crops around the country. It is a line of work in which on-the-spot applications are often productive (but note that most farmers like the first approach to be made by phone). Harvests are unpredictable and may turn out better or later than anticipated: the number of pickers a farmer has hired in advance may prove to be inadequate, or some workers may be unable to wait around for apples to ripen if they have other commitments.

Picking fruit can be exhausting and back-breaking (try to learn the best techniques from more experienced pickers), and you can't always look forward to a comfortable bed to sleep in as the accommodation offered by farmers is often basic. While some provide comfortable bunkhouses and meals, others require you to take your own tent and to prepare your own meals. Some will provide cooking facilities and others will not. Where they are provided they can sometimes be in a poor state of cleanliness as they may be used by large numbers of people and yet it is no-one's responsibility to keep them clean. The Food and Farming Information Service advises that workers take out insurance to cover their own personal belongings, and that where possible it is best to visit the farms in advance.

Farmers can recruit students from any part of the EEA. In addition, some farms take part in the Seasonal Agricultural Workers scheme which enables them to recruit student pickers from outside the EEA. This is done through the organisations Concordia (YSV) Ltd (Heversham House, 2nd Floor, 20/22 Boundary Road, Hove, East Sussex BN3 4ET; tel 01273-422293; fax 01273-422443) and HOPS(GB) (YFC Centre, NAC, Stoneleigh Park, Kenilworth, Warwickshire CV8 2LG (tel 02476-857206; fax 02476-857229). These organisations accept only overseas applicants for fruit-picking, and all participants must pay a registration fee. In return Concordia exercise control over participating farms and expect certain standards. The farms take from one up to as many as two hundred workers at one time, of many different nationalities, often largely from southern and eastern Europe. Further information about the Seasonal Agricultural Workers scheme is given under *Work Permits and Special Schemes.*

In addition to harvesting work, there are also opportunities for other types of farm work, as a general assistant on a family farm or as a groom, for example. Both these and picking jobs are listed in the *Outdoor* sections of the regional chapters in the book. Some organic farms take on volunteers: for details of one scheme see the entry for WWOOF in the *Voluntary Work* sction of the *Nationwide* chapter.

Wages. Pay varies according to the fruit and the difficulty involved in the picking process. Many farmers pay piece work rates, which means that you are paid according to the quantity you pick. This method can be very satisfactory when a harvest is at its peak but when fruit is scarce earning more than the minimum can be much more difficult. However, even if you are paid on a piece work basis the amount you earn for each hour worked must average the rates set out in the

Agricultural Wages Order. Before starting work you should obtain a copy of the current order from the Agricultural Wages Board. If you have any queries about the rate you are being paid the Agricultural Wages Board Regional Office staff should be able to advise you. Be prepared to cope with frustration when three days of rain means no picking and therefore no wages.

The Agricultural Wages Board (Nobel House, 17 Smith Square, London SW1P 3JR) sets minimum weekly and hourly rates for agricultural workers in England and Wales. For standard workers aged 19 and over in England and Wales (different rates apply in Scotland and Northern Ireland) the minimum wage with effect from October 1st 2001 is £4.77 an hour and £7.16 for overtime. For casual workers who are engaged by the hour or the day the minimum rate for workers aged 19 is £4.10 (£6.15 for overtime). The rates for younger workers are lower. It is anticipated that a new Wages Order will come into force on July 1 2002.

Many farmers calculate wages by a combination of piece work and hourly rates of pay. Remember that the farmer is legally obliged to pay you at least the appropriate minimum rate for your age for the hours worked. Ask exactly how much you will be paid before accepting a job: some people have been paid as little as 12p for picking a pound of strawberries. The Department for Environment, Food and Rural Affairs has a helpline for both employers and employees who want to know more about the Agricultural Wages Order: the number for England and Wales is 0845-0000134.

Gangmasters. Gangmasters can be involved in the recruitment of seasonal summer staff on farms. While most gangmasters treat their workers fairly, a significant minority could exploit their workers in some way. This exploitation can take different forms and might involve underpayment of wages, unsafe working conditions, use of illegal workers, and illegal deductions from pay for transport and accommodation. If you have any concerns or are unaware of your rights, you should ask for a copy of the leaflet *Planting, Picking or Packing Agricultural Produce? Your Rights Explained* from MAFF Publications (tel 0645-556000; Website www.maff.gov.uk) or ring their Helpline on 0645-335577.

Useful Addresses. Many farmers have entries in this book, but you may find a farm near you which is too small to need to advertise nationally. Economic pressures have forced farmers to diversify, and an increasing number of farms are being opened to the public, sometimes generating a need for extra help. Temporary jobs are sometimes advertised in *Farmers Weekly*, though prospective employers are likely to require some experience.

Organic farms often rely on voluntary assistance too. EU volunteers should send a s.a.e. to WWOOF (World Wide Opportunities on Organic Farms), PO Box 2675, Lewes, Sussex BN7 1RB for details of membership and the opportunities available on organic farms in the UK and worldwide throughout the year. In return for hard work, workers receive free meals, accommodation, the opportunity to learn and transport to and from the local station.

Removals and Marquee Work. While manual jobs with removal firms are available at any time of year, the summer is a real boom time for marquee erectors. During the sunny season there is a never-ending round of agricultural shows, wedding receptions and so on. And while a village dog show may require just one marquee, a music festival will require a whole range of tents plus large amounts of furniture and other equipment. All this has to be loaded and unloaded from lorries, as well as driven to and from a depot; for this and other driving work possession of an HGV driving licence will make you of more interest to employers. Overtime is often available, so marquee work can be lucrative. The disadvantage for women is that most employers take on only men for loading work.

Sport

The range of jobs under this category includes amongst others *Instructors, Coaches, Boat Crew, Stable Staff, Lifeguards, Riding, and Walk Leaders.*

Sports holiday centres often specialise in sea, river or mountain activities and as such are often found in remote and beautiful places such as Scotland and the Lake District. They almost always need to recruit live-in workers. While there are opportunities for unskilled staff, most vacancies are for sports instructors, teachers and camp managers. Applicants will normally require governing-body qualifications and a reasonable amount of experience; growing concern about insufficient supervision and instruction at activity centres in the past has resulted in tougher new controls.

Sources of information for anyone choosing to approach an outdoor activity centre independently, on the off-chance of finding a vacancy, include the *RAC Activity Holiday Guide* (RAC) and *The Action Guide to Britain* (Harvill Pres, London).

Anyone with life-saving qualifications could consider working as a lifeguard at a leisure centre. Several local authorities advertise such vacancies in this book.

Riding: Riding schools and trekking centres (which are particularly common in Wales) take on experienced riders. Since a lot of the work is dealing with groups, the ability to get on well with people is also important.

There might be a riding school or holiday centre in your area where you could ask about the possibility of a temporary job. The British Horse Society (tel 08701-202244; fax 01926-707800; e-mail enquiry@bhs.org.uk; www.bhs.org.uk) publishes a register of approved riding centres called *Where to Ride*, price £6.50 including postage and packing. This is available by mail order from the BHS Bookshop, Stoneleigh Deer Park, Kenilworth, Warwickshire CV8 2YX (tel 08701-201918); the list is also available on the above website.

The Association of British Riding Schools produces a directory of its 500 members which is available for £5 including postage and packing from Queen's Chambers, Office No. 2, 38-40 Queen Street, Penzance, Cornwall TR18 4BH (tel 01736-369440; fax 01736-351390; e-mail office@abrs.org; www.equiworld. abrs.org). You should also contact them for information about trekking holidays and centres.

Also check the adverts in *Horse & Hound* magazine: stable staff and riders are sometimes needed to work on stud farms and in racing establishments.

Voluntary Work

The category of voluntary work encompasses a large range of activities including *Archaeology, Children, Conservation and the Environment, Heritage, Physically/Mentally Disabled, Social and Community Schemes and Workcamps.* Many organisations throughout the UK need volunteers to help with a host of different types of work, from caring for people with disabilities or the elderly to taking part in conservation and archaeological projects.

This type of job experience is strongly recommended if you are contemplating a career in any of these fields. In addition, a survey in 2001 by the recruitment company Reed International found that almost three quarters of employers preferred to recruit candidates with experience of voluntary work listed on their CVs. Most of the voluntary organisations in this book do not require specific skills; willingness and enthusiasm are the most important attributes.

Working with people with special needs is demanding: you are expected to work hard physically and to give a lot of time and commitment. However, many volunteers find the challenge to be both a rewarding and maturing experience. Most organisations provide free board and lodging, and sometimes a small amount of pocket money and help with travel expenses. Many social or community projects need volunteers all year round, but there is always a demand in the summer for extra staff to help with outings and holidays.

Conservation and archaeological projects are increasingly popular. The drawback is that such projects tend to be only short-term and most require volunteers to make a contribution towards their board and lodging.

Museums, stately homes and gardens frequently operate on a very tight budget and may be pleased to receive offers of voluntary help; some may even pay a small wage. *Historic Houses, Castles and Gardens,* price £4.95, and *Museums and Galleries,* £8.95, are both published by Johansens. Both books are crammed full of addresses. *The National Trust Handbook,* which lists all the UK properties open to the Public, is free with membership or available from all good bookshops for £4.50. The Trust also produces a variety of free leaflets about properties in certain areas.

Sources of Information. *The International Directory of Voluntary Work* (£11.95, published by Vacation Work, 9 Park End Street, Oxford OX1 1HJ) includes information on both short and long-term opportunities. The National Council for Voluntary Organisations (Hamilton House Mailings, Earlstrees Court, Earlstrees Road, Corby NN17 4AX; tel 01536-399016; fax 01536-399012) publishes the *Voluntary Agencies Directory,* price £25 plus £5 postage and packing, which lists over 2,500 organisations countrywide.

The National Centre for Volunteering (tel 020-7520 8900; www.volunteering.org.uk; e-mail Volunteering@thecentre.org.uk) is a national database of local volunteering opportunities that is updated annually, and is an excellent source of contact names and addresses of organisations requiring help in your area. It also provides details of Volunteer Bureaux which are found in most big towns and dispense information about, and do some of the recruiting for, local voluntary organisations.

Information on voluntary work in Wales can be obtained from *The Wales Council for Voluntary Action:* Baltic House, Mount Stuart Square, Cardiff Bay CF10 5FH (tel 029-2043 1700; fax 029-2043 1701; e-mail enquiries@wrva. org.uk; www.wcva.org.uk). Offices also in Colwyn Bay (tel 01492-539800) and Welshpool (tel 01938-552379).

Vacation Traineeships

Vacation traineeships are schemes which aim to provide young people with an opportunity to gain on-the-job training during their holidays. These vocational positions may not appeal to those wanting a summer job simply to have fun or to earn enough money to finance a holiday or keep the bank manager at bay. Against this, in the long run they can prove to be a most valuable long-term investment of your time.

The jobs listed in the *Vacation Traineeships* section of each regional chapter in this book share a number of basic characteristics. They are short-term placements open to students from both schools and institutes of higher or further education. Jobs usually arise during the summer vacation, and last for two to eight weeks. Some short-term positions are also available over the Easter and Christmas breaks.

The degree of actual training varies enormously from one firm to another, with the highest levels offered generally by companies involved in science, engineering and computing. Traineeships are also most numerous in these fields since students are increasingly reluctant to choose a career in Engineering or

Science – and therefore have to be actively encouraged. The competition for placements is likely to be greater in other areas such as law and accountancy, both of which are now well established in the vacation training field. In recent years, the big retailers have also marked a new growth area in the field of on-the-job training schemes.

Some companies offer work shadowing schemes, which are ideal for students who are undecided about their future career. They usually involve the student observing a chosen person at work for a period of one to five days. Although these schemes are generally unpaid, students may receive free meals and travel expenses.

The Advantages of Vacation Training. Since students in higher education are no longer eligible for income support or housing benefit during the holiday periods, the financial rewards of doing a traineeship have become increasingly alluring: many trainees are paid a weekly wage of £150-£200. Even so, for many the value of the experience gained far outweighs that of the salary. Note that accommodation is rarely supplied with a traineeship, though assistance may be given in looking for a room.

The very principle of training is helpful even before the work starts, since it encourages you to consider your eventual career in good time before the end of your course. Then, once you have begun the traineeship, you can assess the working environment without having to make any commitments to a certain branch or employer. You also gain an insight into what will be expected of you later on, and can test your own capabilities.

The greatest benefits of taking part in a training scheme, however, come when you are applying for full-time work. Firstly, it gives you the chance to gain experience at interviews and to develop important skills; secondly, an employer is more likely to consider seriously an application from someone who spent their previous summer on a vacation traineeship than someone who worked in the local pub. And once at the interview, your experience as a trainee is likely to become a central subject of discussion, since it will be the main guide your prospective employer has for assessing your ability to do the job being advertised.

Another major advantage of vacation training is that a substantial number of companies treat traineeships as extended assessment periods and the best trainees either by-pass the preliminary interviews or are offered full-time positions after graduation. Even if the company doesn't give you a permanent job, by giving you a good reference they may indirectly help you find work elsewhere. In professions in the Media or the Arts where jobs are rarely advertised a work placement, whether paid or unpaid, is often the only way to find out about a vacancy or gain valuable contacts.

Experience and Qualifications. Many employers specify a preferred field of study relevant to the job. Not surprisingly, candidates reading English or Philosophy are unlikely to be employed on projects involving structural analysis calculations or computer programming.

Certain companies say they consider only university students, but these are an increasingly small minority. Others stipulate that candidates should be in their second undergraduate year. Where such information has been forthcoming, the entries specify which stage of their academic careers candidates should have reached.

More generally, employers are looking for self-motivated students with a positive attitude, the ability to work well in a team and an aptitude to analyse and solve problems quickly and effectively. If you give the impression that you really want just a holiday job, you are unlikely to be considered for a post.

Au Pairs, Home Help and Paying Guest Agencies

Amongst the types of job to be found in this category are positions for *Au Pairs, Mother's Helps, Nannies, Playscheme Leaders and Paying Guests.*

Playschemes. Most local authorities organise playschemes for children during the summer holidays. Throughout the country dozens of playleaders and assistants are needed to run activities for children of all ages. Cash limits mean that some councils ask specifically for volunteers.

Domestic Work. Anyone preferring closer contact with children should consider working in a family as a mother's help or (for applicants from overseas) as an Au Pair. This work usually requires some experience and involves light housework and looking after children.

There are many agencies in the UK which specialise in placing home helps. Details of these and other au pair opportunities are listed in the *Au Pair, Home Help and Paying Guest* chapter towards the end of the book. If you prefer to find work independently, job advertisements appear in *The Lady* magazine and occasionally in *Horse and Hound*, both available from newsagents.

Further Sources of Information and Employment

Jobcentres. These state employment agencies are run by the government's Employment Service and usually have at least one board devoted to temporary vacancies. Some, mainly in London, have a special Temporary Desk. Others run registration schemes, enabling you to put your name down on a list – but in order to do this you may be required to have a specific skill, and you will be advised to still check the boards regularly. Or check the internnet: Jobcentre Plus, the new Government Executive Agency responsible for the network of over 1,000 Jobcentres in Great Britain, advertises all of its vacancies at www.worktrain.gov.uk.

To find the address of your nearest Jobcentre either look in the telephone directory under Employment Service or look at the Website www.employmentservice.gov.uk. Jobcentre vacancies can be accessed by telephone through Employment Service Direct on 0845 6060 234.

Employment Service Direct (0845-6060-234) is a phone service designed to help you find a full or part-time job. Telephone advisors have access to jobs nationwide and can help match your particular skills and requirements to vacant positions. Anyone without a job can use the service whether or not they are claiming Jobseeker's Allowance, students and others looking for seasonal work can also benefit from the service particularly if they are looking for work in other parts of the country.

The employment service website www.employmentservice.gov.uk also advertises nationwide vacancies, particularly those in more specialised fields: it has access to all the jobs currently available to Employment Service Direct.

Big companies such as Butlins Skyline like to recruit early and advertise vacancies through their local Jobcentre in the spring. In the summer many jobs are available on the spot too. The organisers of big local events and farmers, for example, sometimes use Jobcentres to recruit staff.

Employment Agencies. While the number of agencies dealing with temporary work in London can be positively daunting, outside the capital the range is much more narrow. It is worth registering with as many agencies as possible in order to enhance your chances of finding work. The jobs offered are frequently office-based, though some specialise in hotel and catering or manual work. Brook Street

Bureau and Alfred Marks, which have branches all over the UK, both tend to concentrate on clerical work. Manpower, also with offices nationwide, has information on labouring and warehouse jobs. You can find their addresses in the Yellow Pages.

Under the Employment Agencies Act it is illegal for an agency to charge a fee for finding someone a job: agencies make their money by charging the employers.

The Internet. The Internet can be an invaluable aid to the jobseeker. Details of new vacancies are posted on www.vacationwork.co.uk, which also has links to other relevant sites.

National Institutes. One way of finding out more about Vacation Training opportunities within a specific field is to contact the relevant national professional body or institute. Institutes do not themselves offer traineeships, but may be able to offer general advice and/or give names and addresses of companies within their field.

Insurance and Related Financial Services N.T.O.: Careers Information Service, 20 Aldermanbury, London EC2V 7HY (tel 020-7417 4793; fax 020-7726 0131; Website www.cii.co.uk).

Hotel & Catering International Management Association: 191 Trinity Road, London SW17 7HN (tel 020-8772 7400, fax 020-8772 7500).

Institute of Chartered Accountants in England and Wales: Gloucester House, 399 Silbury Boulevard, Central Milton Keynes MK9 2HL (Student Recruitment Section: tel 01908-248108; www.icaew.co.uk/careers).

Institute of Chartered Accountants of Scotland: Head Office: CA House, 21 Haymarket Yards, Edinburgh EH12 5BH (tel 0131-347 0100; fax 0131-347 0105; Website www.icas.org.uk).

Royal Town Planning Institute: 41 Botolph Lane, London EC3R 8DL (tel 020-7929 9494; fax 020-7929 9490; www.rtpi.org.uk). This organisation runs a Vacation Employment Register which is designed to put prospective employers in touch with planning students on RTPI accredited courses who are looking for work over the summer vacation. It has nothing to do with formal vacation traineeships, although the work experience may be useful.

Tax and the Minimum Wage

Income Tax. Single people are entitled to a personal tax allowance, which means that you don't pay income tax until your yearly earnings exceed £4,535. Few people are likely to earn this much over the vacation.

To avoid paying tax you need to fill out the right form; new employees will usually be taxed under an 'emergency code' until the Tax Office receives this form from your employer. Students in higher education should fill in form P38(S) which effectively makes them exempt from paying tax, and school and college leavers a P46. Ask your employer to send the form to the Tax Office as soon as possible after you start work. You should be put on the right code within a month or so, after which time you will get a rebate. If you have not been put on the right tax code by the time you leave your job, send a tax rebate claims form to the Tax Office together with your P45, which you will get when you finish work.

National Insurance. National Insurance contributions are compulsory for employees over 16 years of age if they earn over a certain limit. The rate you pay is calculated according to your wages. Currently, anyone who earns less than £88 a week pays nothing.

If you require information in addition to that given above, contact the Contributions Agency or the Tax Office (as relevant), or else your local Citizens Advice Bureau.

The National Minimum Wage

The UK now has a national minimum wage which as of October 2001 is £4.10 for those aged 22 and over and £3.50 an hour for those aged 18-21. But there are a small number of cases in which the minimum wage does not apply, notably if a worker is aged under 18 but also in other cases such as, for example, for people living with and working for a family business or if a worker is aged under 26 and in the first year of an apprenticeship; in addition if an employer provides accommodation he can also deduct up £22.75 a week of a worker's pay against the cost of providing it. All this means that a low wage that appears at first sight to be breaking the law may in fact be legal.

This is a complicated subject. Those wanting more detailed information, leaflets or to register a complaint should call the National Minimum Wage Helpline on 0845-6000-678. There is also a new interactive Website on which people can check to see if their wage complies with the law; it can be found at www.tiger.gov.uk.

Creating Your Own Job

Some people may not want to spend time sending off speculative letters or phoning around potential employers asking for a job that may not exist. The alternative is to make a job for yourself, by creating a service which people in your local area might be willing to pay for. A company called Shell LiveWire produces a free essential business kit and expert advice for anyone aged 16-30 wishing to start up a business. For a copy of this call 0845-757 3252 or write to LiveWire, FREEPOST NT805, Newcastle upon Tyne NE1 1BR. Window cleaning, car-washing, housework and babysitting are a few of the most obvious odd-jobs, and there are many more. Below are some questions to ask yourself before turning self-employed:

1. What do people want? You can find this out by (a) asking neighbours, (b) reading local papers and (c) looking at advertisements in local shops.

2. What can I offer? It is surprising how many different things most of us can turn our hands or minds to. It may well be that a hobby or spare-time activity can be turned into a moneyspinner. Some suggestions:
carpentry: simple woodwork, mending gates, making/putting up shelves.
cooking: lunch and dinner party catering or sandwich-making.
cycling: bicycle repairs (highly recommended), courier work (suitable for those with a mountain bike who live in a big city).
gardening: grass-cutting, weeding or pruning.
knitting: making jumpers, cardigans, etc. on commission.
music: busking, playing in pubs or being a disc jockey.
sewing: dressmaking, repairs and alterations, cushion-making.
walking: dog exercising, tourist guiding or shopping for the elderly.

3. Who wants me? After you have identified the job you can do and for which you think there will be a demand, you need to publicise your services. The best way to start is with advertisements in local shop windows (which are very cheap) and, if you can afford it, in your local newspaper. It will also be useful to run off a handbill and distribute it locally.

The principal feature of successfully creating a job for yourself is your reputation. If you impress someone with your hard work, promptness and efficiency, they will tell others.

Tips on Applying for a Job

1. Most employers like to make their staff arrangements in good time, so apply early and according to the dates mentioned in the job details.

2. Before applying for a position, check that you fulfil all the requirements, such as age and qualifications. Employers are normally able to find someone who meets all their needs, so you are wasting your time (and the employer's) if you apply for a job for which you are clearly not suitable.

Period of work: employers generally prefer to take on one person for the whole season. If you are able to work for longer than the minimum period quoted, you are more likely to get the job.

Accommodation: it is particularly important to note whether or not lodging is provided, especially for those who are coming from abroad. In areas which attract a lot of tourists over the summer, temporary rented accommodation can be either difficult to find or prohibitively expensive. Some employers can recommend lodgings in the area or be of more positive help, but often they are reluctant to recruit those who have no pre-arranged accommodation.

3. Prepare an application. This will normally be in the form of a covering letter and a *curriculum vitae* (CV). The point of the application is to show (i) that you want the job, (ii) that you want to work for that organisation, and that (iii) you have had the appropriate experiences and demonstrated the relevant skills and qualities so that the employer wants you.

In order to achieve these three objectives it is firstly necessary to consider why the specific job interests you and secondly what are the key qualities and skills needed - typically these may include social/interpersonal skills, organisational abilities, leadership, verbal and written communication skills, numeracy, intelligence, diligence, conscientiousness, thoroughness, work processing, etc. Once these factors have been worked out, it is time to write a complementary CV and covering letter to show that you are the best person for the job.

Curriculum Vitae: This should be typed on one A4 sheet in note form and include the following details, ordered in titled groups of information:

(a) Personal details (name, address, telephone number, nationality, age, marital status);

(b) Educational qualifications and subjects you are currently studying if you are a student, otherwise your present occupation;

(c) Relevant Experience which may include such things as organising social events, captaining a football team or any work experience;

(d) Skills such as computing, word processing, other languages, driving licence;

(e) Interests and Hobbies;

(f) Referees - preferably one from work and one personal.

Covering Letter: this should be fairly short (again one side of A4) and tidy, and preferably typed. This is your chance to explain why the job must be given to you in terms of points (i), (ii) and (iii) above, using the information on the CV to support your argument. Use positive, enthusiastic language and include the following information, possibly in separate paragraphs:

(a) Which exact position you have chosen and why it appeals to you (and also make it clear which geographical region you have chosen if there are several to choose from);

(b) Why you have chosen that particular organisation – here it is worth being extremely complementary in your praise of them;

(c) Why they should employ you - and use your CV to prove that your claims are true.

4. Address the letter to the person specified in the entry, whether this gives an actual name or merely the title, e.g. Personnel Manager, Student Training Officer, etc.

5. Always enclose a stamped addressed envelope (s.a.e.) or, if you are applying from abroad, an International Reply Coupon (IRC). IRCs are available from any post office. It can be both expensive and inconvenient for employers to reply to a large number of applicants, especially once the positions have been filled. Some employers simply won't respond to applications without a s.a.e. or IRC.

6. When an interview is necessary, and this applies in particular to firms offering vacation traineeships: you should be able to show a basic knowledge of, and interest in, the activities of the company in question, as well as demonstrate that you are seriously considering a career in that particular field. In other words, you must demonstrate premeditated enthusiasm for the work and the organisation. It is also essential to realise that how you say it is as important as what you say - be positive, friendly and enthusiastic.

7. If you receive a job offer, check all the relevant information: the job details given in this book are supplied by the employer, but it is wise to obtain confirmation of them before accepting the position. Things to check include: wages, board and lodging, hours and the conditions of work. Some staff have ended up working unpaid overtime, others have been sacked without warning, so clarify **all** terms and conditions in advance.

Ask your employer to put the relevant details in writing (though for these to become legally binding, both parties must sign a contract).

8. If you are offered more than one job, decide quickly which you prefer and inform all employers of your decision as soon as possible.

9. Many young people regard their summer job as a holiday, but this is seldom the attitude taken by the employer. If the job details indicate that a hotel needs an assistant to serve three meals a day six days a week, or a hop farmer needs pickers to work seven days a week in all weathers, then you should be warned that there will be far more work than holiday.

10. Finally, ask for a reference when you leave your job, since this should enhance your chances of finding work in the future. In some fields, such as retail, the ability to produce a reference is considered important.

Work Permits and Special Schemes

Before writing letters to prospective employers, overseas applicants should clarify the terms under which they may visit and work in Britain. Anyone arriving at UK Immigration without the necessary visa, letter of invitation or other required documentation, could be sent back home on the next available flight. An outline of the regulations is given below. For further information, contact the nearest British Consulate or High Commission.

Visa Requirements

You may need a visa to enter the UK irrespective of the reason for your visit. Citizens of Western Europe, most Commonwealth countries and of the USA do not need a tourist visa to enter Britain. Since the fall of communism in the Eastern Bloc, many Eastern Europeans – including Poles, Czechs, Slovaks and Hungarians – no longer need visas either.

Nationals of the former Soviet Union and most Asian and African countries are required to obtain a visa. Exceptions include Israel, Japan, South Africa and Zimbabwe. It is advisable to check visa requirements at the nearest UK Diplomatic Post.

Work Permits

Wherever relevant, entries in this book specify if the company or organisation in question welcomes applications from overseas. Unfortunately, this does not mean that all foreigners can legally work for them in this country. It is an offence under the Immigration Act of 1971 to take employment in breach of conditions of stay, and a person found to be working illegally may be fined and may also be liable to deportation. An employer employing overseas nationals whom he or she knows to be working in breach of their landing conditions may also be liable to prosecution and a fine of up to £5,000.

Having studied the section below carefully, if you believe you are eligible for some kind of permit, make enquiries with the consulate or relevant organisation as soon as possible: preparing the necessary documentation may take some months.

EEA Citizens Nationals of the European Economic Area are free to enter the United Kingdom to seek employment without a work permit. At present this applies to citizens of EU countries and Norway, Iceland and Liechtenstein. However, EEA nationals still require a permit for the Channel Islands and the Isle of Man.

EEA nationals intending to stay longer than six months may apply for a residence permit, although there is no obligation on them to do so.

Non-EEA Citizens. The general position under the Immigration Rules is that overseas nationals (other than EEA nationals) coming to work in Britain must have work permits before setting out. The employer (**not** the employee) has to apply to Work Permits (UK) which administers the scheme. Permits are issued only for specific jobs requiring a high level of skill and experience for which resident or EEA labour is not available. In other words, a British employer cannot apply for a work permit for a non-EEA citizen unless it is for a job that no EEA National can do.

There are, however, a few exceptions to these rules:

Citizens of Commonwealth Countries: nationals of Commonwealth countries (including Australia, New Zealand, Canada and South Africa) between the ages of 17 and 27 are permitted to visit the UK as a 'Working Holiday Maker'. This allows them to take up casual employment which will be incidental to their holiday, but not to engage in business or to pursue a career. The total period which can be spent in the UK is two years. A six-month period may be granted initially, but this can then be extended.

Prior entry clearance is mandatory and must be obtained from the British High Commission in your home country.

Commonwealth citizens with at least one British-born grandparent may wish to apply for 'UK Ancestry employment entry clearance' from the British High Commission: this eliminates altogether the need for a work permit. Married couples must apply for separate entry clearance before travelling.

Students from North America: US students seeking temporary work in the UK can benefit from the 'Work in Britain Program'. This allows full-time college students and recent graduates over the age of 18 to look for work in Britain, finding jobs through programme listings or through personal contacts. Jobs may be pre-arranged, though most participants wait until arrival in Britain to job hunt. They must first obtain a 'British Universities North America Club (BUNAC) Card', which is recognised by the British Home Office as a valid substitute for a work permit ; this 'BUNAC Card' must be obtained before leaving the US for Britain, as it acts as an entry document. It allows the holder to work for a maximum of six months at any time of year: extensions are never granted. For information on the BUNAC card is call toll free tel 1-888-GO BUNAC.

A similar programme, called the Student Work Abroad Programme (SWAP), is organised for Canadian students, graduates and young people, with varying age restrictions applying. It is administered by the Canadian Universities Travel Service, which has over 40 offices in Canada. For details see www.swap.ca.

Seasonal Agricultural Work Scheme: farm camps under this scheme are authorised by the Home Office and are the main hope for non-EEA and non-Commonwealth nationals wishing to work in this country. Special 'entrance authorisation cards' are issued to a certain number of non-EEA nationals each year, taking the place of otherwise impossible-to-obtain work permits.

Most of the recruitment for these farms is handled by two agencies, the Harvesting Opportunity Permit Scheme or HOPS and Concordia (for address see *Agriculture* above). Between them they recruit pickers for over 160 farms between April and October. While you can contact the farmers directly, you are advised to apply through the above-mentioned agencies. Prospective participants should be aged 18 to 25 and should be full-time students in their own country.

Voluntary Work. Overseas nationals may be admitted for up to 12 months for the purpose of voluntary work without requiring a permit, providing he or she will be working for a registered charitable organisation and receiving no remuneration other than pocket money, board and accommodation. The work which they do must be closely related to the aims of the charity i.e. working with people, and they must not be engaged in purely clerical, administrative or maintenance work (for which a work permit is required). Volunteers are expected to leave the United

Kingdom at the end of their visit.

Traineeships. Permission can be given for overseas nationals with pre-arranged work placements to obtain permits for professional training or managerial level work experience for a limited amount of time. The UK employer offering the placement has to apply for a permit to the Overseas Labour Service at the address below.

Practical training places in the UK for US nationals are available through the Career Development Programme administered by the Association for International Practical Training (AIPT), 10400 Little Patuxent Parkway, Suite 250, Columbia, Maryland 21044-3510 (410-997-2200; aipt@aipt.org/ www.aipt.org). To be eligible you must be aged 18-35 with relevant qualifications and/or at least one year of work experience in a career field. A good starting place is AIPT's online placement system (www.pinpointtraining.org). Temporary UK work permits are available through the Training & Work Experience Scheme; details are available from the Overseas Labour Service (www.dfee.gov.uk/ols).

While many companies in the book are happy to employ overseas students as trainees, since most of them run their schemes in order to try out potential employees, they may not be keen to take on anyone who cannot return to them after their studies.

Work Permits (UK) issues permits under its Training and Work Experience Scheme for limited periods of pre-arranged on-the-job training to gain a professional qualification, or for short periods of managerial level work experience. This can include students on recognised exchange placements through AIESEC, or the International Farm Experience Programme.

Non EEA Students Studying in the UK. Overseas students studying in Britain who wish to take up vacation work no longer have to obtain permission to do so. As long as they do not pursue a career by filling a full-time vacancy or work for more than 20 hours per week during term time, except where the placement is a necessary part of their studies with the agreement of the educational institution.

Au Pairs. For details of regulations affecting au pairs see the chapter *Au Pair, Home Help and Paying Guest* at the end of the book.

Further Information
Once in the UK, general information about who needs work permits and other immigration matters can be obtained from the Home Office Immigration and Nationality Directorate, Block C, Whitgift Centre, Croydon CR9 1AT (tel 0870-6067766; www.homeoffice.gov.uk/ind): be prepared to wait in line for your call to be answered, it will be eventually. Guidance leaflets are also available from the Correspondence Unit of the Foreign and Commonwealth Office and Home Office Joint Entry Clearance Unit, 89 Albert Embankment, London SE1 7TP (www.fco.gov.uk). Work Permits (UK), Moorfoot, Sheffield S1 4PQ (tel 0114-2594074; www.workpermits.gov.uk) can advise employers on the rules of the work permit scheme.

ABBREVIATIONS

approx.	approximately	max.	maximum
a.s.a.p.	as soon as possible	min.	minimum
B & L	board and lodging	p.a.	per annum
CV	curriculum vitae	s.a.e.	stamped addressed envelope
IRC	International Reply Coupon	w.p.m.	words per minute

Glossary of Qualifications

The following list of qualifications (often the name of the institute or association which issues them) are listed in alphabetical order.

ACA/ACCA – (Chartered) Association of Certified Accountants
BASI – British Association of Ski Institutes
BCU – British Canoe Union
BHSIC – British Horse Society Instructor's Certificate
BTEC – Business and Technology Education Certificate
CIMA – Chartered Institute of Management Accountants
City and Guilds 706/1, 706/2 – catering qualifications
GCSE – General Certificate of Secondary Education
GNAS – Grand National Archery Society
HGV – Heavy Goods Vehicle driving licence
HND – Higher National Diploma
LGV – Light Goods Vehicle driving licence
LTA – Lawn Tennis Association
MLTB – Mountaineering Leadership Training Board
NAMCW – National Association for Maternal and Child Welfare
NNEB – National Nursery Examination Board
OND – Ordinary National Diploma
PCV – Passenger Carrying Vehicle
PLG – Pool Life Guard
RGN – Registered General Nurse
RLS (S) – Royal Life Saving (Society)
RSA – Royal Society of Arts (Examinations Board)
RYA – Royal Yachting Association
SEN – Senior Enrolled Nurse
TEFL/EFL – (Teaching) English as a Foreign Language

N.B. The author and publishers have every reason to believe in the accuracy of the information given in this book and the authenticity and correct practices of all organisations, companies, agencies etc. mentioned; however, situations may change and telephone numbers can alter, and readers are strongly advised to check facts and credentials for themselves. Readers are invited to write to Andrew James and David Woodworth, Vacation Work, 9 Park End Street, Oxford OX1 1HJ with any comments, corrections and first hand information. Those whose contributions are used will be sent a free copy of the next edition or any other Vacation Work publication of their choice.

NATIONWIDE

Organisations which have branches in various parts of Britain

Business and Industry

BETTERWARE: Headquarters, Stanley House, Park Lane, Castle Vale, Birmingham B35 6LJ (freephone 0800-0565646).
Distributors to deliver and collect Betterware's Household Products brochure to existing customers. Vacancies exist in all parts of the UK at all times of the year. Positions are full or part-time. Successful applicants can expect to earn £40-£200 per week dependent on the hours available, but must do a minimum of 8 hours per week. Full-time career opportunities in sales management also exist for the right candidates.

For more details or to make *applications* write to Mrs L. Rushton, Recruitment Advertising Manager, at the above address.

BLUE ARROW LIMITED: 800 the Boulevard, Capability Green, Luton, Bedford LU1 3BA (tel 0800-0855 777; www.bluearrow.co.uk).
Temporary/Permanent Staff (500,000 per year) to work in offices, catering, industry and construction around the UK. Contracts may be of any length of time from a day onwards. Relevant previous experience may or may not be required. Minimum age 16.

Those interested should *contact* the above freephone number or can visit one of Blue Arrow's 250 branches around the country.

FOCUS: Komtech House, 255/257 London Road, Headington, Oxford OX3 9EH (tel 01865-308488; fax 01865-742235; e-mail headoffice@focus-charity.co.uk). Branches in Oxford, Nottingham, Leicester and Cambridge. FOCUS runs personal development programmes to help people develop their skills and self-confidence and to achieve the goals in life that are important to them. As part of a longer-term programme, Focus runs 10 day long Residentials during the Easter and Summer Holidays.
Administrators (8) are required to help prepare for these projects, working full-time for up to 3 weeks before each residential, with the possibility of accommodation. National Minimum Wage. 2 administrators are required for each of the four Focus branchs. Those filling these poste are then encouraged to attend, on a voluntary basis, the Residentials, during which room and board are provided. (See Voluntary Work for more information on volunteering for Residentials). Administrators must be flexible, well organised and enthusiastic and aged 18+ with a good grasp of the English language.

Applications by March for the Easter Residentials and by June for the summer Residentials to Denise Barrows at the above address. Interview and references required and able to have a check for criminal convictions.

HORIZON HPL: Signet House, 49-51 Farringdon Road, London EC1M 3JB (tel 020-7404 9192-3; fax 020-7404 9194; e-mail horizonhpl.London@ btinternet.com). A training centre established in 1991 which organises paid work placements hotels and companies in the UK and in France for EU citizens, including English and French tuition and preparation to sit British and French examinations.

Company Staff. Placements are available all year round (in a variety of fields) from 3 months to 1 year. They receive a trainee wage and accommodation if working in a hotel. Applicants from 17-50 years. An interview is necessary.

Applicants should contact the agency 2 months before the intended work date.

MAJESTIC WINE WAREHOUSES: Majestic House, Otterspool Way, Watford WD25 8WW (tel 01923-298200; fax 01923-819105; www. majestic.co.uk). Majestic is the UK's foremost by-the-case retailer of wines, beers and spirits. There are 96 stores throughout England, Scotland and Wales and expansion plans for another 8-10 stores a year.

Temporary Drivers to help with delivery driving, merchandising and dealing with customers. The job is physically demanding and wages vary according to location (£4.45-£4.75 per hour). Vacancies available in most holiday periods, particularly at Christmas and during the summer. Applicants should enjoy working with the public, must have held a driving licence for at least a year and be over 19. No accommodation is provided.

Application forms can be obtained by phoning 01923-298210 or by writing to the Recruitment Manager at the above address.

PROMOTIONAL SUPPORT LTD: 276 Chase Road, Southgate, London N14 6HA (tel 020-8886 7009; fax 020-8886 0078). A promotional company that organises roadshows, exhibitions and events and supplies promotional staff for clients such as Walkers, Robinsons, Pepsi and other blue chip clients.

Temporary Promotional Contracts available. Wage varies from £40-£60 per day. To work 8-10 hours a day. No accommodation available. Min. period of work 1 day at any time of year.

Applicants should have bubbly, outgoing, attractive personalities. Overseas applicants considered. Interview preferred, but not necessary.

Applications at any time to Louise at the above address. E-mail louise@promotionalsupport.co.uk or post a CV and photograph with sae.

Children

ARDMORE LANGUAGE SCHOOLS: Berkshire College, Burchetts Green, Maidenhead, Berkshire SL6 6QR (tel 01628-826699; fax 01628-829977; e-mail mailbox@ardmore.org.uk; www.ardmore.org.uk). Ardmore Language Schools offers summer junior vacation courses in English to overseas juniors. Residential centres located throughout Britain.

Centre Directors, Assistant Centre Directors, Centre Administrators, Head Teachers, English Language Teachers, Senior Sports Leaders, Sports Leaders. Those aged 20+ preferred. Period of work 2-8 weeks during June, July and August. Further details from and *applications* to Ardmore Language Schools at the above address.

BARRACUDAS SUMMER ACTIVITY CAMPS: Bridge House, Bridge Street, Saint Ives, Cambridgeshire, PE27 5EH (e-mail info@barracudas.co.uk; www.barracudas.co.uk). Barracuda recruits staff to work at children's multi-activity day centres in Greater London, Essex, Berkshire, Surrey, Kent, Cheshire, Norfolk and Cambridgeshire. Activities include go-karting, video-making, archery, swimming, arts and crafts and drama. Monday to Friday, 8.30am-5.00pm.

Activity Co-ordinators (300). To supervise groups of 20-30 children. To work as

Instructors, Assistants and Co-ordinators. Must have experience of working with children. £140-£160 per week
Lifeguards (30). To supervise swimming pools, RLS National Pool Lifeguard Qualification necessary. £160-£180 per week.
Soccer Coaches And Sports Instructors (50) to plan, implement and supervise children on specialised progressive courses. Enthusiasm and relevant experience/qualifications necessary.

Accommodation is available if required at some centres. The accommodation is available for the duration of the camps. Training Courses leading to National Governing Body qualifications are organised prior to the camps. This includes Club Fencing Award, National Pool Lifeguard and First Aid courses, as well as extensive in house training. All costs are met by Barracudas if staff work the full season of four to six weeks.

Applications to the above address. All staff must speak fluent English. All staff are police checked and DoH checked. Barracudas is an equal opportunities employer.

EAC ACTIVITY CAMPS: First Floor, 46 Bavelaw Road, Balerno, Edinburgh EH14 7AE (tel 0131-449 7036; fax 0131-538 7407; e-mail afisher@ activitycamps.com; www.activitycamps.com). Multi activity day and residential camps in Edinburgh, Glasgow, Oxford, Canterbury, York, Manchester, London and Taunton. For children aged 5-16.
Camp Directors (7) must be over 21, wages £230-£250 per week with accommodation available.
Assistant Camp Directors (7) must be over 21, wages £180 per week.
Qualified Instructors required for canoeing, wall climbing/abseiling, archery and swimming. £150 per week. Relevant qualifications essential: BCU Instructor, EFL, MLTB/SPSA, GNAS, or Bronze Medallion/PLG.
Group Captains (8). £150 per week.
Group Monitors (16). £140 per week.
Activity Leaders (40) must be at least 18, wages £135 per week.
Senior Activity Leaders (12) must be over 21, wages £220 per week.
Accommodation and food provided. Must have all round sporting ability and be enthusiastic. Sporting qualifications and coaching awards preferred.
All staff to work 40 hours per week. Min. period of work 5 weeks between June and September. The work is hard but good fun. Overseas applicants welcome. All applicants must be available for interview.
Applications from January to Andrew Fisher, EAC Activity Camps.

EF INTERNATIONAL LANGUAGE SCHOOLS: 74 Roupell Streeet, London, SE1 8SS (tel 020-7401 8399; fax 020-7401 3717; www.ef.com).
Summer Teachers required for July and August to work full-time. Wages vary according to location and experience. Candidates should have at least a first degree and CTEFLA.
Applications with CVs should be sent to the Director of Studies at the above address. Vacancies are also available at schools in Brighton, Bournemouth, Cambridge and Hastings.

EF LANGUAGE TRAVEL: EF House, 1-3 Farman Street, Hove, Sussex BN3 1AL (tel 01273-822777; fax 01273-729561). Language courses with free time programmes for international students in locations in the UK and Ireland.
Group Leaders And Teachers (650 nationwide). Salary varies depending on region and experience. Min. age 20 years. Teaching or leadership experience

preferred. Applicants must have a standard of English as high as that of a native speaker. Both residential and non-residential staff required, accommodation available for residential appointments only.

Activity Organisers (40 nationwide) to plan an activity programme for all students in one particular town or residential centre. Salary varies depending on region and experience. Min. age 20 years. Previous organisational experience essential.

All staff to work flexible hours, 6 days a week. Min. period of work 3 weeks between late May and late August. All applicants must be available for interview. *Applications* as soon as possible to the Recruitment Officer at the above address.

ISIS EDUCATIONAL PROGRAMMES: 259 Greenwich High Road, Greenwich, London SE10 8NB (tel 0208-293 1188; fax 0208-293 1199; e-mail Katie@isisgroup.co.uk). ISIS runs Language/Activity Centres in summer at 15 locations around England including Oxford, Bath, Stamford, Winchester and York and also at Edinburgh.

EFL Teachers (150) to teach mainly teenagers on courses from 18 June to 27 August. 3 hours teaching mornings and 3 hours of repeat lessons in the afternoon (i.e. 30+ hours a week but lesson preparation for only 15 hours). Teaching qualification needed. Pay of £160 p.w.

Activity Leaders (150) from 18 June to 27 August. To lead sixteen sessions (mornings and afternoons) per week. Hours are guaranteed. No special qualifications. Appointments are personality based. Wages start from £120 p.w.

The above wages include full board and lodging, but non-residential arrangements also possible with slightly higher wages.

Applications to Katie-Anne Ray, HR Manager, at the above address

PGL TRAVEL: Alton Court, Penyard Lane (874), Ross-on-Wye, Herefordshire HR9 5GL (tel 01989-767833; www.pgl.co.uk/personnel). Over 1,500 staff needed to assist in the running of children's activity centres throughout the UK. Europe's largest provider of adventure holidays for children has offered outstanding training and work opportunities to seasonal staff for over 40 years.

Group Leaders required to take care of small groups of children and ensure that they get the most out of their holiday. Min. age 18. Previous experience of working with children necessary.

General Staff. To help with stores, site cleaning, kitchen, driving (car, PCV or LGV), administration, coffee bar, nurses (RGN or SEN), etc. Min. age 18.

Pocket money from £50-75 per week, with B & L provided. Vacancies available for short or long periods between February and October. Overseas applicants eligible to work in the UK welcome.

Requests for application forms to the Personnel Department at the above address.

PRIME LEISURE: 56 Spareacre Lane, Eynsham, Oxon OX8 1NP (tel 01865-884200; fax 01865-884300; e-mail prime.leisure@btinternet.com). Runs multi-activity Easter and summer day camps for children aged 4-14 in centres in Oxfordshire, Berkshire, and Hertfordshire. Prime Leisure is committed to providing safe and fun-packed activities (including art/craft and sports) for all children attending its camps.

Site Leaders (8). £200+ per week. Qualified teachers with camp experience.

Second In Charge (8). £140 per week. Qualified/trainee teachers or individuals with substantial children's camp experience.

Swimming Pool Lifeguards. £90-£140 per week. Must have experience and hold a recognised and up-to-date life-saving/coaching qualification (RLSS, Bronze Medallion etc).

Activity Instructors. £60-£100 per week. To teach a range of activities to children aged 4-14 years. First aid and relevant childcare qualifications/camp experience are an advantage. Training is provided, therefore enthusiastic individuals with an interest in sports or arts and crafts and a genuine interest in working with children are welcome to apply.

Staff needed for April and from the end of July and August. Free board & lodging provided. Good experience for those wishing to go into a teaching, childcare or recreation/leisure profession. Overseas applicants considered subject to language ability and relevant qualifications.

Applications all year round to Personnel at the above address.

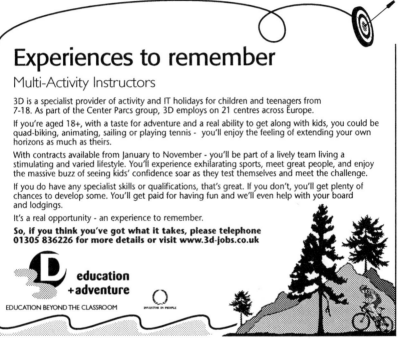

Experiences to remember

Multi-Activity Instructors

3D is a specialist provider of activity and IT holidays for children and teenagers from 7-18. As part of the Center Parcs group, 3D employs on 21 centres across Europe.

If you're aged 18+, with a taste for adventure and a real ability to get along with kids, you could be quad-biking, animating, sailing or playing tennis - you'll enjoy the feeling of extending your own horizons as much as theirs.

With contracts available from January to November - you'll be part of a lively team living a stimulating and varied lifestyle. You'll experience exhilarating sports, meet great people, and enjoy the massive buzz of seeing kids' confidence soar as they test themselves and meet the challenge.

If you do have any specialist skills or qualifications, that's great. If you don't, you'll get plenty of chances to develop some. You'll get paid for having fun and we'll even help with your board and lodgings.

It's a real opportunity - an experience to remember.

So, if you think you've got what it takes, please telephone 01305 836226 for more details or visit www.3d-jobs.co.uk

education +adventure

EDUCATION BEYOND THE CLASSROOM

3D EDUCATION AND ADVENTURE LTD: Business Support, Osmington Bay, Weymouth, Dorset DT3 6EG (tel 01305-836226; fax 01305-834070; e-mail darren@3d-education.co.uk). 3D is a specialist provider of activity and educational experiences for young people. Owned by Center Parcs, 3D has been operating since 1991 and gone from strength to strength year on year.

Activity Instructions (500) Employed and trained as either multi-activity instructor, field studies instructor, specialist watersports instructor or IT instructor, staff will work with children at specialist holiday centres across the south of England as well as across the UK and Europe with Pontins and Center Parcs.

Field studies instructors must hold or at least be gaining a relevant degree. IT instructors need to have a broad range of IT skills. Any sports coaching awards or national governing body awards are advantageous, if applying for Activity instructor and Watersports instructor postitions, although those with relevant experience will be considered. Training courses are held from late January through to July, so there is plenty of opportunity to develop your skills and qualifications.

Most important is an applicant's enthusiasm, personality and energy, coupled with a true desire to work in the outdoor leisure industry. Excellent accommodation and catering packages are offered with payment and working hours as covered by minimum wage and working time legislation. Minimum period of work 14 weeks.

Applicants should telephone 01305-836226 for a recruitment pack between September and June. Before employment all applicants must complete a residential training programme in the UK.

Holiday Centres and Amusements

BOURNE LEISURE LIMITED

With 40 holiday parks situated in coastal locations throughout England, Scotland and Wales, we are looking to recruit team members who are available for a minimum period of 8 weeks, March - October, for the following positions:-

❖ **BAR TEAM MEMBERS**   ❖ **CATERING TEAM MEMBERS**

❖ **COOKS**   ❖ **SHOP ASSISTANTS**

Previous experience is not essential. Applicants must possess an outgoing personality, smart appearance and be willing to work flexible hours. Minimum age 18. Accommodation is available at a small charge. Competitive wages with incentives offered and full training given. In the first instance, visit our websites for further information on the Company and our locations, then submit an on line application form. Full details of position applied for, dates available, preferred location and references must be included.

www.british-holidays.co.uk

www.havenholidays.co.uk

BOURNE LEISURE LIMITED: Park Lane, Hemel Hempstead, Hertfordshire HP2 4YL. Owns and operates 40 holiday parks in resorts throughout England, Scotland and Wales.

Bar Team Members, Catering Team Members, Cooks And Shop Assistants. Competitive wages and full training given. Accommodation available at a small charge. Applicants must possess an outgoing personality, smart appearance and be willing to work flexible hours. Vacancies exist between the months of March and October for team members who are available to work for a minimum of 8 weeks.

For more information on Bourne Leisure's parks and details on how to *apply* see the advertisement above.

OCTAGON MOTOR SPORTS LTD: Fawkham, Longfield, Kent DA3 8NG (tel 01474-872331; fax 01474-879259; e-mail vickiclaxton@octagon.com; www.octagon.com) Octagon Motor Sports Ltd is now recognised as the largest and most successful motor sports leisure business in Europe and operates a major British motor sport leisure venues. Seasonal staff are always needed to work at a number of venues around England, but especially at Brands Hatch, near Dartford, Kent and Silverstone in Northamptonshire.

Marshals Includes some weekend work. To marshal track activities. Must be flexible and able to work as part of a team.

Bar Assistants Variable hours to include evening work and weekends. To work behind busy bar. Experience in cash handling and stock rotation an advantage. Must be flexible and able to work long hours.

Catering Assistants Variable hours to include evening work and weekends. Cash handling and food production experience essential. The duties will include some cooking, serving, cash handling, general hygiene and maintenance.

General Assistants Variable hours to include evening work and weekends. To provide assistance to the Catering Department, and help ensure that all services are provided to the highest standard.

Cleaning Operatives To ensure that all areas are maintained in a clear, tidy safe and hygienic manner.

Wages are available on application. Staff are required from March to November. To work as and when required on a fixed term contract. Overseas applicants must have a valid work permit.

Applications to Vicki Claxton, Human Resources Administrator, from March at the above address.

Hotels and Catering

ANGLO CONTINENTAL PLACEMENTS AGENCY: Dial Post House, Dial Post, Nr Horsham, Sussex RH13 8NQ (tel 01403-713344; fax 01403-713366; e-mail sharon@anglocontinental.fsnet.co.uk; www.anglocontinentalplacement. co.uk). A friendly agency established in 1988 who operate throughout the UK. The office is open from 8.30 to 5.30 Mon-Fri. Hotel and Catering staff placed all over the UK. They wish to work with new agencies abroad.

CHEFS, WAITING STAFF, RECEPTIONISTS, COMMIS CHEFS, CHEFS DE PARTIES, PORTERS, ETC required. Positions available in all aspects of the hotel industry.

Live-in positions available. Staff wanted from New Zealand, Australia and South Africa and EEC. Previous work experience not essential. Min. period of work 6 months.

Applications **including CV and references to Sharon Wolfe at the above address.**

CHEF CENTRE LTD: 1 Kingly Street, London W1B 5PA (tel 020-7439 0771; fax 020-7287 3576; e-mail info@chefcentre.com). A recruitment agency established 30 years ago with a long-standing client base and contacts.

Temporary/Seasonal Chef Work. Wages negotiable, often living-in; to work as required. Must have a City and Guilds 706.II or equivalent NVQ and food hygiene certificate. Accommodation is frequently available as part of the package. Staff required from March to December. Overseas applicants with relevant experience, qualifications and a work permit if from outside the EU are welcome.

Applications at least one month before intended work date to Alison, Suzi, Emily or Mike at the above address.

CHOICE HOTELS EUROPE: 112 Station Road, Edgware, Middlesex HA8 7BJ (tel 020-8233 2001; fax 020-8233 2080; e-mail FBernardon@

ChoiceHotelsEurope.com). Owns, manages and franchises over 400 hotels in 13 European countries. Guidance can be offered with finding jobs in Europe, but posts are primarily for the UK.

Receptionists, Chefs, Waiting Staff, Bar Persons. Minimum period of work: 6 months, 1 year in Front Office. 39 hours per week spread over 5 days. Salary in accordance with Minimum Wages Regulation. Applicants are considered all year round and in all parts of the UK. Applicants must be over 18, customer orientated, smart and pleasant. Priority given to those with hotel qualifications and/or experience of the business.

Applications in writing to Francoise Bernardon, Human Resources Officer, at the address above.

CIP RECRUITMENT: 195 Victoria Street, London SW1E 5NE (tel 020-7630 9993/0123; fax 020-7630 0170).

Agency specialising in **Catering Recruitment** throughout the UK. Short-term assignments are available, particularly during the summer months, for all grades of qualified chefs, catering managers, front-of-house staff, catering assistants, kitchen porters, housekeepers and chambermaids. Assignments and wages vary but, for example, a castle in Scotland providing five star catering for shooting-parties from June to November will offer full board for the period of employment. Salaries offered range from £200-£500 per week, depending on the grade of chef.

Contact CIP on the above number, overseas applicants should wait until they are in the UK to call.

DE VERE & VILLAGE HOTELS: The Malt Building, Greenhalls Avenue, Warrington WA4 6HL (tel 01925-232244; fax 01925-403185). Opportunities exist in the De Vere & Village Hotels group at ten hotels throughout the UK: De Vere Swindon, Wiltshire; De Vere Royal Bath, Bournemouth; De Vere Slaley Hall, Northumberland; De Vere Cameron House; Loch Lomond.

Waiting Staff, Room Attendants, Porters, Bar Staff, Commis Chefs And Casual Banqueting Staff. Must be over 18. Staff needed for a minimum of 2 weeks between May and October. Accommodation may be available at some locations, although it is not guaranteed. Overseas applicants who speak English are considered, subject to work permits.

Applications from February to the Personnel Manager at the relevant hotel. Contact the Personnel Department at the head office, address above, for addresses of individual hotels.

GREAT ADVENTURES: Grafham Water Centre, Perry, Huntingdon, Cambridgeshires PE18 0BX (tel 01480-810521; fax 01480-812739). Provides activity and special interest holidays with centres in Cambridgeshire, Derbyshire and Gloucestershire.

Catering Assistants (10). £170 per week plus food and accommodation. Must have food hygiene certificate. To work 40 hours per week from May to July; min. period of work 2 months. Work also available for 10 months. Overseas applicants welcome.

Applications from January to Mr Ian Downing at the above address.

HATTON HOTELS GROUP: Hatton Court, Upton Hill, Upton St Leonards, Gloucester GL4 8DE (tel 01452-617412; fax 01452-612945; e-mail res@hatton-court.co.uk; www.hatton-hotels.co.uk). A privately owned collection of character hotels located in Gloucestershire, Wiltshire, Somerset and Jersey. Accredited Investors in People who operate high quality service-orientated hotels.

Bar Staff, Restaurant Staff, Housekeeping Staff. Good rates of pay plus board and lodging and tips. 5 days working week on rota. Excellent training and incentives provided.

Applications should be send to Personnel at the above address.

HORIZON HPL: Signet House, 49-51 Farringdon Road, London EC1M 3JB (tel 020-7404 9192-3; fax 020-7404 9194; e-mail horizonhpl.london@ btinternet.com). A training centre established in 1991 which organises paid work placements in hotels and companies in the UK and France for EU citizens, including English and French tuition and preparation to sit British and French examinations.
Hotel Work. Placements are available all year round (in a variety of fields) from 3 months up to 1 year. They receive a trainee wage and free accommodation. Applicants from 17-50 years. An interview is necessary.

Applicants should contact the agency 2 months in advance of intended work date.

HOSPITALITY DIRECT RECRUITMENT: 1 North Pallant, Chichester, West Sussex PO19 1TL (tel 01243-787003; fax 01243-787694; e-mail aminto@hdrecruit.com; www.hdrecruit.com). A recruitment agency in direct contact with top hotels and restaurants throughout the UK and Channel islands.
All Chefs and Front-of-House Management Personnel positions. Wages on application. Permanent and temporary positions, variable hours. Accommodation is available at a charge of up to £40 per week. Staff required for a minimum of 4 months between March and December.

Applications from November to Andrew Minto at the above address.

MILL HOUSE INNS LTD: Barclay House, Falcon Close, Quedgeley, Gloucester GL2 4LY (tel 01452-887222; e-mail info@millhouseinns.co.uk; www.millhouseinns.co.uk). Owns a current estate of 50 managed houses all over the UK. Most are located in wonderful countryside settings with a focus on casual family dining.
Bar Staff (20), Waiting/Table Service Staff (20), Kitchen Porters (10), Chefs (20, Receptionists/Administration Staff (5). Wages depend on site location. Flexible working hours.

Accommodation available, but not always at places of work, at a cost already deducted from pay. Full training is provided. Min. period of work 8 weeks between March and October. Overseas applicants are considered, but must be proficient in written and spoken English and have necessary work authorisation. Applicants should have a neat appearance and a pleasant personality.

Applications from March to Personnel at the above address; they will provide further information on positions available at individual establishments.

MONTPELIER EMPLOYMENT AGENCY: 34 Montpelier Road, Brighton, Sussex BN1 2LQ (tel 01273-778686; fax 01273-220359; e-mail info@themontpelieremploymentagency.co.uk). Specialises in positions away from Brighton, and runs a full countrywide service. The agency has been established for 37 years and particularly seeks experienced hotel staff such as chefs and restaurant and reception staff.
All Types Of Catering Staff required for positions in hotels and restaurants throughout Britain. Wages negotiable. Usually 5 days per week. Previous hotel and catering experience essential. Overseas applicants must already be resident in the UK with valid work authorisation. Min. period of work 12 weeks from May/June to September/October.

Applications from April/May to the Montpelier Employment Agency.

SHEARINGS HOLIDAY HOTELS: Carlton Chambers, Vaughan Parade, Torquay, Devon TQ2 5E6 (tel 01803-290029; fax 01803-213989). Shearings Hotels is one of the UK's largest hotel groups comprising nearly 40 hotels from Ullapool in the Northern Highlands to St. Ives in Cornwall. Most hotels operate 48 weeks of the year with a season which extends from February to December, including Christmas and the New Year.

Housekeeping, Restaurant And Kitchen Staff. Wages typically £3.70 per hour or £3.20 if live-in; to work 39 hours per week. Live-in accommodation is available. Minimum period of work 3 months. Experience in hotel work valuable but not essential. Foreign applicants need to have English of at least an intermediate standard.

Applications to the Personnel and Training Manager at the above address.

THISTLE HOTELS PLC: Gillian Ong, Recruitment Manager, Thistle Hotels plc, Capital house, 25 Chapel Street, Marylebone, London NW1 5JJ (tel 020-7723 8383; fax 020-7724 9899; e-mail careers@thisltle.co.uk; www.thistlehotels.com). With over 56 hotels within the UK, mainly 4 star and country house, vacancies exist in **Most Departments**. Some live-in accommodation is provided but is not available in all hotels. Wages are calculated on an hourly basis and vary from hotel to hotel. Applicants must be available for a minimum of three months and non-European nationals must possess a work permit before applying. Fluent English is essential.

All *Applications* should be sent to the above address.

TOWNGATE PERSONNEL LTD: 3 Alum Chine Road, Westbourne, Bournemouth, Dorset BH4 8DT (tel 01202-752955; fax 01202-752954; e-mail enquiries@towngate-personnel.co.uk). A recruitment agency which specialises in the hospitality industry, but also recruits permanent management staff and experienced operational staff for seasonal positions (March-October).

Short-term Live-in Assignments also in hotels throughout England.

Silver Service Waiting Staff (50). £180-£200 per week.

Chefs: All Grades (50). £200-£400 per week.

To work in various hotels throughout the UK mainland, the Channel Islands and the Isle of Man. To work a 5 to 6 day week. Previous experience essential.

Hotel Receptionists (20) for hotels on the Channel Islands. £150-£220 per week. To work 5 to 6 day week. Hotel reception experience a must. All staff required for a minimum of 6 months between April and September. Accommodation included. Overseas applicants welcome.

Applications from March to James Tucker, Operations Manager, at the above address.

YHA: National Recruitment Department (Hostel Staff) PO Box 11, Matlock, Derbyshire DE4 2XA (www.yha.org.uk). The YHA, a registered charity, is the largest budget accommodation provider in Britain with 240 youth hostels in diverse locations throughout England and Wales.

General Assistants needed to help run the YHA's youth hostels throughout England and Wales. Work is available for varying periods, between February and October each year. Preferred min. age 18 years. Assistants undertake a variety of tasks including catering, cleaning, reception and general maintenance. Experience in one or more of the above areas is desirable, customer service experience and enthusiasm are essential. Non-EU nationals require a valid work permit.

All posts are subject to an interview, usually at the hostel where the vacancy is. For an *application form* call the YHA National Recruitment line on 07626-

939216 between November and June or send a large s.a.e. to the above address. Alternatively visit the YHA website at www.yha.org.uk

Language Schools

ANGLO EUROPEAN STUDY TOURS LTD.: 8 Celbridge Mews, London W2 6EU (tel 020-7229 4435; fax 020-7792 8717). Runs summer courses for 10-18 year olds all over the UK, offering general English plus sports, entertainments and excursions.

Teachers Of English As A Foreign Language to teach overseas students for 16 hours a week, Monday to Friday, at centres all over the UK. Wages £190-£220 per week. Mainly non-residential posts available. To work June, July-August.

No age limits but applicants need a TEFL qualification (RSA or Trinity) and a degree. *Applications* to Claire Woollam, Director of Studies, at the above address.

ARDMORE LANGUAGE SCHOOLS: Berkshire College, Burchetts Green, Maidenhead, Berkshire SL6 6QR (tel 01628-826699; fax 01628-829977; e-mail mailbox@ardmore.org.uk).

Centre Director, Assistant Centre Director, Centre Administrator, Head Teacher, English Language Teacher, Senior Sports Leader, Sports Leader.

For further details *contact* Ardmore Language Schools at the above address.

EMBASSY CES: Lorna House, 103 Lorna Road, Hove, East Sussex BN3 3EL (tel 01273-322353; fax 01273-322381; e-mail vacjobsuk@embassyces.com; www.embassyces.com). Organises summer schools for international students, combining English lessons and an activity/excursion programme at schools and universities around the UK.

Activity Leaders (200) to organise a variety of daytime, evening and weekend activities. Experience of working with children or in the leisure or tourism industry is desirable but full training will be given. All applicants must speak fluent English, have enthusiasm and initiative and be hardworking.

Teachers of English (300) as a Foreign Language to teach and participate in the activity programme. Applicants must be 18+ and have RSA, CELTA or Trinity cert. TESOL. Previous experience is desirable.

Wages dependent on experience. 6 days work per week. Positions are available from June to September. Full board accommodation is available at residential centres.

Apply from February onwards either online (click on the 'Summer Jobs in the UK' link) or contact the Recruitment Department for an application pack. Interview necessary, usually by telephone.

ENGLISH LANGUAGE AND CULTURAL ORGANISATION: Lowlands, Chorleywood Road, Rickmansworth, Herts WD3 4ES (tel 01923-776731; fax 01923-774678; e-mail efl@elco.co.uk; www.elco.co.uk). Three centres based in Rickmansworth in Hertfordshire, Newland Park in Buckinghamshire, and Ardingly College in Sussex.

EFL Teachers (20-30). To work from July 2-August 26; min. period of work three weeks. Must have either a degree, PGCE, RSA or Trinity qualifications. Salary £250-£350 per week. Accommodation is provided free of charge at Newland Park and Ardingly centres. Applicants should normally be available for an interview.

Contact Tony Thompson at the above address from February 2002.

INTERNATIONAL QUEST CENTRES: Idun House, 9 Stradbroke Road, Southwold, Suffolk IP18 6LL (tel/fax 01502-722648). Work available in language centres in Cardiff, Edinburgh, Hertford, London, Medway, Oxford, Southampton, Winchester and Loughborough. The agency has been established for 23 years, and only offers work if vacancies actually exist.

EFL Teachers (200). Must speak English to the level of a native. Wages in 2001 were £10.50 per hour for certificate holders and £9.25 for undergraduates. 18 hours per week. Accommodation is provided in some centres where local recruitment is difficult. Undergraduates studying modern languages or primary scholll teachers welcome; EFL an advantage but not essential.

Min. period of employment 2 weeks. Interviews are carried out in Cardiff, Edinburgh, London, Loughborough and Southampton. Successful candidates must attend an induction session for which they are paid.

Applications from April to Anna Maria McCarthy, Director of Studies, at the above address.

ISIS EDUCATIONAL PROGRAMMES: 259 Greenwich High Road, Greenwich, London SE10 8NB (tel 0208-293 1188; fax 0208-293 1199; e-mail robin@isisgroup.co.uk). ISIS runs Language/Activity Centres in summer at 15 locations around England including Oxford, Bath, London, Stamford, Winchester York and Edinburgh.

EFL Teachers (150+) to teach mainly teenagers. 3 hours teaching mornings and 3 hours of repeat lessons in the afternoon (i.e. 30 hours a week but lesson preparation for only 15 hours). Teaching qualification needed. Pay starts from £160 p.w.

Activity Leaders (40+) To lead sixteen two and a half hour sessions (mornings and afternoons) over six days. Hours are guaranteed. No special qualifications. Appointments are personality based. Wages start from £120 p.w.

The above wages include full board and lodging, but non-residential arrangements also possible with slightly higher wages. Available from June to August. *Applications* the H.R. Manager, at the above address

PGL TRAVEL: Alton Court, Penyard Lane (874), Ross-on-Wye, Herefordshire HR9 5GL (tel 01989-767833; www.pgl.co.uk/personnel). Europe's largest provider of adventure holidays for children has offered outstanding training and work opportunities to seasonal staff for over 40 years.

EFL Teachers required during March, April, July and August to work at children's activity holiday centres throughout the UK. Free B & L is supplied plus a wage of £100 per week.

Full *details* and application forms from the Personnel Department at the above address.

STAFFORD HOUSE STUDY HOLIDAYS: 19 New Dover Road, Canterbury, Kent, CT1 3AH (tel/fax 01227-787730; e-mail studyholidays@ staffordhouse.com;).

EFL Teachers required for residential and non-residential posts at various locations in Britain. To teach English and supervise activities. Period of work by arrangement between July and August. Residential tutors are paid from £210 per week plus full board and lodging depending on experience, non-residential tutors are paid £220 per week depending on experience. Applicants should have a minimum of RSA/CELTA/TESOL/Trinity Certificate in EFL teaching.

Centre Managers, Activity Leaders. Details available on application.

A full job pack including *application form* is available from the above address, unsolicited CVs are not accepted.

TWIN GROUP: 24 Clarendon Rise, Lewisham, London SE13 SEY (tel 020-8297 1132; fax 020-8297 0984; e-mail m.borley@twinschool.co.uk; www.twinschool.co.uk).

EFL Teachers. Wages from £210 to £275 per week. Involves both teaching and running activities, with groups of up to 15 students. Must hold at least Cert. TEFL qualifications.

Activity Organisers, Administration Officers and Welfare Officers. Wages of £250 per week.

Work is available in July and August in schools mainly in the south of England with a few in the Midlands and East Anglia. Some centres require applicants to be residential and some do not.

Applications to Marcus Borley at the above address as soon as possible.

YES EDUCATION CENTRE: 12 Eversfield Road, Eastbourne, East Sussex BN21 2AS (tel 01323-644830; fax 01323-726260; e-mail dos@yeseducation. co.uk). A friendly, independent school commmitted to high academic and professional standards.

EFL Teachers. Wages £175-£400 per week for adult and junior schools in Eastbourne, and junior schools in Abingdon, Brighton, Hastings, Oxford and Seaford. Staff required in July and August. No accommodation provided. Relevant teaching qualifications required.

Applications to Mr Paul Atkins, Director of Studies for Eastbourne, and Mrs Brigid Simcox, Course Director External Centres, for the other towns.

Medical

ACTIVE ASSISTANCE: Mill House, Staveley Mill Yard, Staveley, Kendal, Cumbria LA8 9LS (tel 01539-822212; fax 01539-822201; www.active assistance.com)). Active Assistance provides live-in carers to spinally injured clients in their own homes.

Care Assistants required for live-in positions. Wages from £45 per day worked. Must be 21 or over and have a driving licence. Minimum period of work 3 months at any time of year. Suitably qualified foreign applicants with good spoken English are welcome.

Applications at any time to the Personnel Department at the above address or please complete the on-line form on the above Website address.

ALL CARE SOUTH WALES: 228 Holton Road, Barry CF63 4HS (tel 01446-701020; fax 01446-722788).

Home Care Workers (6) needed between July-September to work various hours and days for wages of £3.80 per hour. Applicants must be over 21.

Applications to Anne Payne at the above address.

CHRISTIES CARE LTD: The Old Post Office, High Street, Saxmundham, Suffolk IP17 1AB (tel 01728-605000; fax 01728-605026; e-mail recruitment@christiescare.com; www.christiescare.com). Founded in 1987, the company provides live-in care to people in their own homes nationwide.

Carers (50) for live-in positions with clients in their own homes. Clients are all dependent adults with many different ailments who need varying degrees of care such as incontinence management, hoist work for paraplegics, experience with dealing with dementia and the bedridden; all need home help with cooking, shopping and housekeeping. Salary up to £400 per 7 days. Staff required all year round; minimum period of work 7 full days. Applicants with experience preferred

but training provided, be over 18, and able to work legally in the UK.
Applications to the Recruitment Department at the above address.

CONSULTUS: 17 London Road, Tonbridge, Kent (tel 01732-355231; fax 01732-360693; e-mail info@consultuscarers.co.uk; www.consultusagency.co.uk). Founded in 1962 by the present Managing Director, consultus is now one of the major providers of live-in care in Britain. Their aim is to help the elderly remain in their own homes for as long as possible.
Live-in Carers (20) needed nationwide to perform domestic duties and some personal care for elderly clients. Duties may include cooking, cleaning, housekeeping, shopping and a varying degree of personal care of the client. Wages from £40+ per day, with own room in client's house. To work on two-week live-in assignments. Positions are available all year. Over 21 only. Some experience with care of the elderly/disabled necessary. Foreign applicants with correct permits and able to speak clear English are welcome.
Applications should be made at any time to the Residential Care Department at the above address. Interview necessary.

CURA DOMI-CARE AT HOME: 8 North Street, Guildford, Surrey GU1 4AF (tel 01483-302275; fax 01483-304302).
Carers required to care for elderly and disabled people in their own homes. Positions are either residential (nationwide) or non-residential (local to Guildford, Surrey). Wages vary according to the position being offered but are typically £255-£321 a week, plus accommodation and travel expenses, as relevant and paid annual leave. Period of work by arrangement. Applicants are given an interview and training session. Qualified Handling and Moving courses available free to all carers plus 24 hour office support. Overseas applicants with fluent English and the necessary documents to work in the UK welcome.
Applications to the above address.

FOCUS: Komtech House, 255/257 London Road, Headington, Oxford OX3 9EH (tel 01865-308488; fax 01865-742235; e-mail headoffice@focus-charity.co.uk). Branches in Oxford, Nottingham, Leicester and Cambridge. FOCUS runs personal development programmes to help people develop their skills and self-confidence and to achieve the goals in life that are important to them. As part of a longer-term programme, Focus runs 10 day long Residentials during the Easter and Summer Holidays.
Qualified Nurses will be needed to work on these Residentials during 2002. Based at locations across England, each Residential will require 2 nurses and will provide a week of fun, challenging team-based activities for mixed teams of disadvantaged young people and adults with a physical or learning disability. Current UKCC registration or overseas equivalent is required. Room and board plus a small honorarium are offered per 10 day Residential, although wages and terms of employment may change. Please check current terms with FOCUS. Good grasp of English required.
Applications by March for the Easter Residentials and by June for the summer Residentials to Denise Barrows at the above address. Interview and references required and able to have a check for criminal convictions.

NURSES DIRECT: 26 Harmer St, Gravesend, Kent DA12 2AX (tel 0800-376 6154; fax 0870-124 8146; e-mail k.may@nursesdirect.co.uk). Nurses Direct has 14 offices serving South London, Kent, Surrey, Sussex, Hampshire and Dorset. They employ trained nurses and experienced carers to work for various organisations.

Trained Nurses (50); Care Assistants (75) Learning Disability Support Workers (35). Wages are competitive. To work weekdays or weekends. No min. period of work. All applicants should be over 18. Required qualifications depend on the position sought. Positions are available all year. Foreign applicants are welcome if they are authorised to work in the UK and have a good standard of English.

Applications should be made as early as possible to Kevin May at the above address. An interview will be necessary.

PGL TRAVEL Alton Court, Penyard Lane (874), Ross-on-Wye, Herefordshire HR9 5GL (tel 01989-767833; www.pgl.co.uk/personnel). Europe's largest providers of adventure holidays for children have offered outstanding training and work opportunities for seasonal staff for over 40 years.

Nurses (RGN, EGN. or equivalent) to work at residential children's activity holiday centres throughout the UK. Vacancies available for short or long periods between February and October. Free B & L supplied plus £100 per week. Suitably qualified overseas applicants who are eligible to work in the UK welcome.

Full *details* and an application form can be obtained from the Personnel Department at the above address.

Outdoor

EVENTS STAFF LTD: 25 York Road, Northampton NN1 5QA (01604-627775; fax 01604-627004). A recruitment company that supplies staff to events such as the British Grand Prix, large scale outdoor events and shows, and various horse racing fixtures across the country.

Stewards, Programme Sellers, Ticket Sellers, Car Park Attendants (1000+ at peak of summer).

Applications welcome any time. Applicants must be over 16, and willing to work long hours outdoors. Call the above number for an information pack.

FIELD AND LAWN (MARQUEES) LTD: Southlands, Leeds Road, Thorpe Willoughby, YO8 9PZ (tel 01757-210444). A young and enthusiastic company which takes a pride in its product and employees. Work hard, play hard atmosphere.

MARQUEE ERECTORS (10-20) required to work long hours erecting marquees throughout England and Wales. Wages starting at £4.50 per hour. The work is very strenuous so fitness is essential. Overseas applicants,

particularly from New Zealand, South Africa and Australia, welcome. Positions are available from May to November.

Applications from 1 April through to end of November to the Operations Manager at the above address or telephone number.

LEAPFROG INTERNATIONAL LTD: Riding Court Farm, Datchet, Berkshire SL3 9JU (tel 01753-589328; fax 01753-580881; e-mail aimee@leapfrog-int.co.uk).
Event Crew (Up To 100) Ages 18-40, needed to help set up and run outdoor activities such as team-building challenges, family fun days and 'Its a knockout' tournaments. Events take place all around the UK and there may also be the opportunity to work on events around the world. Period of work June-September. Hours of work vary per day and wages are a set amount per event. Travel to events is organised by Leapfrog International from their headquarters in Datchet. Applicants should be enthusiastic, outgoing, enjoy working with people and like to travel. A clean driving licence is an advantage; previous experience not essential as full training will be given.

Please call Aimee Carver, Human Resource Manager, for an *applications* pack.

Sport

GREAT ADVENTURES: Grafham Water Centre, Perry, Huntingdon, Cambridgeshire PE18 0BX (tel 01480-810521; fax 01480-812739). Run special interest and activity holidays and courses with centres in Cambridgeshire, Derbyshire and Gloucestershire.
Activity Instructors (20) wanted for canoeing, windsurfing, sailing, archery, climbing and mountain biking. Must have N.G.B. qualifications. £170 per week plus food and accommodation. To work 40 hours per week from May to July; min. period of work 2 months. Positions also available for 10 months. Overseas applicants welcome; note interview is required.

Applications from January to Mrs Ian Downing at the above address.

HF HOLIDAYS LIMITED: Imperial House, Edgware Rd, London NW9 5AL (tel 020-8905 9556 quoting LEA1). The UK's leading walking holiday company is a non-profit seeking organisation which owns 19 Country House Hotels based in some of the most scenic parts of Britain.
Walk Leaders are required to lead walks catering for all levels of walker. Applicants may choose where, how often and when they want to lead the walking holidays (from 2-30 weeks per year). Full board accommodation, travel expenses and £15 per week equipment allowance will be provided. This is an excellent opportunity to improve leadership skills and for ML logbook experience.

Applicants should be experienced walkers with leadership potential, fully competent in the use of map and compass, considerate and tactful. Residential assessment courses are held during the winter and spring(difficult for applicants living abroad) so application by February is essential.
For *applications* or an information pack contact the Walking Department at the above address.

PGL TRAVEL: Alton Court, Penyard Lane (874), Ross-on-Wye, Herefordshire HR9 5GL (tel 01989-767833; www.pgl.co.uk/personnel). Over 1,500 staff needed to assist in the running of children's activity centres throughout the UK. Europe's largest provider of adventure holidays for children has offered outstanding training and work opportunities to seasonal staff for over 40 years.

Qualified Instructors required to teach canoeing, sailing, windsurfing, pony trekking, hill walking, fencing, archery, judo, rifle-shooting, fishing, motorsports, arts and crafts, drama, English language and many other activities. Pocket money £36-£85 per week with full B & L provided. Min. age 18. Vacancies available for short or long periods between February and October. Overseas applicants eligible to work in the UK welcome.

Requests for application forms to the Personnel Department at the above address.

Websites

anyworkanywhere.com: e-mail info@anyworkanywhere.com; www.anywork anywhere. com

This organisation provides a free source of information to people looking for casual, seasonal and temporary work in the UK and worldwide through the site www.anyworkanywhere.com. It lists a variety of employment including work in 16th century pubs, forestry conservation in the Caledonian mountains, hotel work, fruit and vegetable picking, jobs in activity centres, care work and childcare.

The site also provides other useful information on work and travel such as directories of hostels, cyber cafés and embassies and links to other useful and relevant sites. For those who are a little more adventurous and just want to turn up and see what jobs are available further afield it includes a guide to the main locations and times of ski seasons and harvests worldwide.

Voluntary Work

Archaeology

COUNCIL FOR BRITISH ARCHAEOLOGY: Bowes Morrell House, 111 Walmgate, York YO1 9WA (tel 01904-671417; fax 01904-671384; e-mail info@britarch.ac.uk; www.britarch.ac.uk).

The CBA works to promote the study and safeguarding of Britain's historic environment, to provide a forum for archaeological opinion, and to improve public interest in, and knowledge of, Britain's past.

Details of **Excavations** and other fieldwork projects are given on the Council's website and in the Council's publication *British Archaeology*. The magazine appears six times a year. An annual subscription costs £23; however, it also forms part of an individual membership package which is available for £24 per year and brings extra benefits.

Having studied the magazine you should make *applications* to the Director of the projects which interest you. The min. age for many projects is usually 16.

Children

NATIONAL ASTHMA CAMPAIGN: Providence House, Providence Place, London N1 ONT (tel 0207-704 5892; fax 020-7704 0740). Runs PEAK (Project for Eczema and Asthma Kids).

Volunteer Helpers, Doctors And Nurses to work with children and young people with asthma and eczema on five one-week adventure and activity holidays at Easter and in July and August. The young people are aged 6-9, 10-13, 14-17 and the camps take place in locations throughout the UK.

Board and accommodation are provided; those accepted must take part in a training weekend, with travel and board paid. Applicants must be aged at least 18 and are expected to stay for the duration of a camp; relevant medical or sporting and childcare experience are essential. Volunteers will also be needed for a camp next Easter.

Applications should be sent to the Peak Manager at the above address.

SCRIPTURE UNION: 207-209 Queensway, Bletchley, Milton Keynes, Bucks MK2 2EB (tel 01908-856152; fax 01908-856111; e-mail holidays@ scriptureunion.org.uk; www.scriptureunion.org.uk).

An International non-denominational Christian movement that has been running residential holidays for children and young people throughout England and Wales for over 100 years

Volunteers to help as team members on Scripture Union residential holidays around the UK lasting 7-10 days for young people aged from 8-18+. Volunteers are expected to be on site 24 hours a day to help organise activities during the holiday as part of a team; training is given before the beginning of the holiday.

Volunteers pay for their own accommodation and meals, but a Volunteer Grant Fund may assist with some of the costs. Minimum period of work one week. Applicants must be committed Christians in sympathy with the aims of Scripture Union and aged 18 or over; there are particular needs for people with qualifications in catering, first aid, life-saving, sports, mountaineering and working with disabled people.

Applications should be sent to the Holidays Administrator at the above address.

Conservation and the Environment

BTCV: 36 St. Mary's Street, Wallingford, Oxfordshire OX10 0EU (tel 01491-821600; e-mail information@btcv.org; www.btcv.org).

BTCV is the UK's leading practical conservation charity. Every year it involves over 130,000 volunteers in projects to protect and enhance our environment.

BTCV offers a programme of over **500 Conservation Working Holidays** each year in the UK and overseas. These last from 3 to 10 days, and include wetland management in the Norfolk Broads, dry stone walling in Cumbria, wolf tracking in Slovakia and turtle protection on the Island of Rhodes.

No experience is required, just plenty of enthusiasm and energy. Prices start at £25 for a weekend and £50 for a week to cover food, accommodation and training in conservation skills (£200 plus for international holidays). Volunteers typically work from 9am-5pm with evenings free and a day off during the week. Accommodation ranges from village halls to youth hostels and field centres.

For further information *contact* the above address or visit the BTCV website.

BRITISH TRUST FOR ORNITHOLOGY (BTO): The Nunnery, Thetford, Norfolk IP24 2PU (tel 01842-750050; fax 01842-750030; e-mail general@ bto.org; www.bto.org).

The BTO promotes and encourages the wider understanding, appreciation and conservation of birds through scientific studies using the combined skills and enthusiasm of its members, other birdwatchers and staff. In pursuit of these aims, the Trust seeks to maintain high **Scientific And Professional Activities** in all its activities; co-operate with others engaged in relevant research; work constructively with those whose activities impinge upon the conservation of birds and their environment; ensure that its projects widen participants' experience, knowledge and understanding of birds and their environment.

BTO does not normally offer paid vacation work but does sometimes take on a limited number of volunteers for work at Thetford. For further details and *applications*, contact the Director of Services at the above address.

CATHEDRAL CAMPS: 16 Glebe Avenue, Flitwick, Bedfordshire MK45 1HS (tel 01525-716237; e-mail admin@cathedalcamps.org.uk; www.cathedralcamps. org.uk). Registered Charity No. 286248.

Volunteers required to work in groups of 15-25 people undertaking maintenance, conservation and restoration of cathedrals and their surroundings all over the country. Hours normally 8.30am-5.30pm, 4^1/2 days a week. The one-week camps take place from July to September. A contribution of approx. £55 is asked to go towards the cost of the camp and board and lodging. Min. age 16, most are aged 17-25.

For further details and an *applications* form contact Shelley Bent at the above address.

EARTHWATCH: 57 Woodstock Road, Oxford OX2 6HJ (tel 01865-318831; fax 01865-311383; e-mail vp@earthwatch.org.uk; www.earthwatch.org/europe).

Earthwatch recruits **Paying Volunteers** to help research scientists in fields from archaeology to zoology on short term research projects in over 50 countries throughout the year. Around 4,000 volunteers each year take part in the projects, which last from 2 days to 3 weeks. Team volunteers in the UK may take part in an otter survey, help scientists on a badger watch, monitor raptors, or participate in the ever-popular sapling survey in South Wales.

All English speaking volunteers are welcome, and no technical skills are needed as training, when needed, is given on site. Some projects may also have minor health restrictions if, for example, they take place in remote areas. Volunteers pay a share of the project costs, ranging from £75 to £360 for these UK projects(with reductions for members). Prices include food and accommodation, although volunteers on projects in London usually find their own B & B accommodation.

Those interested should send *applications* to Earthwatch Volunteers at the above address.

THE NATIONAL TRUST: Working Holidays, PO Box 84, Cirencester, Glos., GL7 1RQ.

A charity dependent on volunteers which cares for 240,000 hectares of outstanding countryside, almost 600 miles of unspoilt coastline, and over 300 historic houses.

The National Trust organises **Working Holidays** in outdoor conservation work, biological surveying, archaeology, construction and various other interests. These take place on National Trust properties in England, Wales and Northern Ireland throughout the year. Each project involves 12-20 volunteers and lasts for 1 week to 10 days. There are also some weekend projects.

Volunteers pay from £51 per week to help cover the cost of board and lodging, and are responsible for their own travel expenses. Accommodation varies from purpose-built hostels to converted barns; volunteers supply bedding or sleeping bags. Min. age 17. Overseas applicants welcome but must be over 18 and have good conversational English.

For a brochure, please telephone 01603-739543, e-mail workingholidays@smtp.ntrust.org.uk or write to Opencontact Direct Marketing, Stalam Road, Wroxham, Norwich NR12 8DH.

WWOOFUK (World Wide Opportunities on Organic Farms): PO Box 2675, Lewes, Sussex BN7 1RB. (tel/fax 01273-476286; e-mail hello@wwoof.org; www.wwoof.org).

An opportunity to help the organic growers, get into the countryside (UK and worldwide) and meet like-minded people to learn and share in an atmosphere of mutual trust.

Volunteers are needed to spend time working on organic farms, gardens and smallholdings around the UK: organic farming avoids the use of artificial fertilisers and pest killers, and can be labour intensive. Simple accommodation and food are provided. Short and long stays available. Applicants must have a genuine interest in furthering the organic movement. Applications welcomed from students/individuals of any nationality all year round. EU applicants do not need work permits, Australians, New Zealanders and Canadians need vacation work permits, all others need work permits.

For further information and *applications* send a s.a.e. to the above address.

Heritage

WATERWAY RECOVERY GROUP LTD: PO BOX 114, Rickmansworth, Herts WD3 1ZY (tel 01923-711114; fax 01923-897000; e-mail enquiries@wrg.org.uk; www.wrg.org.uk).

The National co-ordinating body for voluntary labour on the inland waterways of Great Britain.

Volunteers needed to restore Britain's derelict canals: work may involve restoring industrial archaeology, demolishing old brickwork, driving a dumper truck, clearing mud and vegetation and helping at a National Waterways festival. To work either on weekends or weeklong canal camps. Work is available year round; minimum period of work 1 day. No experience or qualifications are necessary but applicants should be at least 17 years old. Accommodation and food are available in a village hall for £35 per week and £10 per weekend. Overseas applicants welcome.

Apply to The Enquiries Officer at the above address.

Physically/Mentally Disabled

THE CAMPHILL VILLAGE TRUST: Delrow House, Hilfield Lane, Aldenham, Watford, Herts WD25 8DJ (tel 01923-856006).

The Association of Camphill Communities runs working communities for mentally handicapped adults and children throughout Britain. They are based on anthroposophy, as founded by Rudolf Steiner. **Voluntary helpers** are required for the household, workshop or on the land. There are a limited number of summer jobs available, otherwise the min. period of work is 12 months. Free B & L is provided and a small personal allowance. Min. age 20. Overseas applicants welcome.

For a list of the addresses of Camphill Village Trust centres, *apply* in writing to the Secretary at Delrow House.

FOCUS: Komtech House, 255/257 London Road, Headington, Oxford OX3 9EH (tel 01865-308488; fax 01865-742235; e-mail headoffice@focus-charity.co.uk). Branches in Oxford, Nottingham, Leicester and Cambridge. FOCUS runs personal development programmes to help people develop their skills and self-confidence and to achieve the goals in life that are important to them. As part of a longer-term programme, Focus runs 10 day long Residentials during the Easter and Summer Holidays.
Volunteers will be needed to work on these Residentials during 2002. Each Residential will require up to 40 volunteers and will provide a week of fun, challenging team-based activities for mixed teams of disadvantaged young people and adults with a physical or learning disability. Volunteers will join these teams to help supervise and support these participants. Previous experience with young people or people with special needs is an advantage but all necessary training is provided at the start of each Residential. Volunteers must be 18 or over with a good grasp of the English language. Accommodation and food is provided. Donations towards the cost of the accommodation etc. are welcome.
Volunteer Cooks are also needed. Each Residential will require 2 cooks. A UK Basic Food Hygiene Certificate or equivalent, plus experience of catering for 30+ people is required. Room and board provided.

Applications by March for the Easter Residentials and by June for the summer Residentials to Denise Barrows at the above address. Interview and references required and able to have a check for criminal convictions.

LEONARD CHESHIRE: Central Office, 30 Millbank, London SW1P 4QD (tel 020-7802 8200; fax 020-7802 8250; e-mail a.mckenzie@london.leonard-cheshire.org.uk).
Leonard Cheshire is the UK's leading charity providing support services for people with physical and learning disabilities. Many of the 80 residential homes offer **Opportunities For Volunteers**, who assist with the day-to-day care and social activities of physically disabled residents.

Boards and lodging and pocket money is provided. Period of work from 6 to 12 months. Volunteers must be able to speak good English. *Enquiries* to Head of Volunteer Support c/o the above address.

RADAR (Royal Association for Disability and Rehabilitation): 12 City Forum, 250 City Road, London EC1V 8AF (tel 020-7250 3222; fax 020-7250 0212; minicom 020-7250 4119; e-mail radar@radar.org.uk; www.radar.org.uk). A national organisation run by and working with disabled people to remove architectural, economic and attitudinal barriers. Areas include civil rights, holidays, mobility, employment and social services. RADAR publishes a list, *Voluntary and Paid Opportunities* giving details of organisations and various clubs which run holidays for disabled people. **Volunteers** are needed to help on these holidays (which last for at least one week), providing personal assistance to the holidaymakers. Free B & L is generally provided. Min. age usually 18.

For further details and *applications* write to RADAR at the above address, sending a SAE.

RIDING FOR THE DISABLED ASSOCIATION: Lavinia Norfolk House, Avenue R, National Agricultural Centre, Stoneleigh Park, Warwickshire CV8 2LY (tel 024-7669 6510; fax 024-7669 6532; e-mail rdahq@riding-for-disabled.org.uk; http://www.riding-for-disabled.org.uk).
The RDA is a registered charity consisting of some 615 member groups throughout the UK. Providing holidays for disabled people is one of the many services it offers to its members.
Volunteer Helpers are required to help on RDA holidays throughout the summer months, providing 24 hour care and supervision for between 3 and 7 days. Living expenses are provided along with free accommodation at some venues. Volunteers are needed for a minimum of 3 days between May and September. Applicants must be 16 or over, a knowledge of horse riding is preferable along with a First Aid/medical qualification and work experience with disabled people. Suitably qualified foreign applicants are welcome.
   Applicants should contact the above address from January for details of the holidays being run and to make *applications*.

SUE RYDER CARE: PO Box 5736 Sue Ryder Care, Cavendish, Sudbury, Suffolk CO10 8RN (tel 01787-282591).
A Christian based charity. This international organisation runs more than 20 care centres in Britain, providing care for the sick, disabled and physically handicapped, as well as palliative care. **Volunteers** are needed throughout the year to do essential duties at the Home in Cavendish or at the retreat house at Walsingham, Norfolk, or at certain Sue Ryder Centres in Britain: this may include helping with patients, doing domestic or a variety of other jobs.
   Minimum period of work is normally 8 weeks. Simple accommodation, meals and pocket money are provided free of charge. Min. age 18. Send *Applications* (enclosing s.a.e./IRC) to the above address.

THE 3H FUND: 147a Camden Road, Tunbridge Wells, Kent TN1 2RA (tel 01892-547474; fax 01892 524703).
Carers (around 100) required to assist with one-to-one care for physically disabled people on holiday. In 2002 3H Fund is holding six holidays in Majorca and the UK, including an adventure holiday on a canal boat on the Norfolk Broads. Holidays are usually for one week to 10 days and take place between May and September.
   B & L are provided, but a contribution of £175 is requested for the overseas holidays: advice can be given on raising this by sponsorship. Applicants should have a sense of humour, a strong back, great patience and a sense of responsibility. Experience is an advantage but not essential. Volunteers can enjoy a working holiday with much fun and laughter whilst enabling the people with disabilities to also enjoy a holiday. Applicants should be aged between 18 and 60.
   Applications to Peggie King, Holiday Organiser, from November at the above address.

WINGED FELLOWSHIP TRUST: Angel House, 20-32 Pentonville Road, London N1 9XD (tel 020-7833 2594; fax 020-7278 0370; e-mail admin@wft.org.uk; www.wft.org.uk).
WFT provides holidays for disabled people and breaks for carers. **Volunteers** are needed for one or two weeks at a time, to help trained staff enhance the holiday atmosphere for the guests. Holidays are available at purpose-built centres in Essex, Nottingham, Surrey, Merseyside and Southampton, where guests can enjoy a break with or without their regular carer.

Volunteers are provided with free accommodation and meals in exchange for their time. Overseas applicants with good English welcome. For an *application* form please contact Marina or Karen at the above address.

Social and Community Schemes

CSV (COMMUNITY SERVICE VOLUNTEERS): 237 Pentonville Road, London N1 9NJ (freephone 0800-374991; fax 020-7837 9318; e-mail volunteer@csv.org.uk; www.csv.org.uk).
Volunteers go away from home for 4-12 months and volunteer on a range of social care and community projects in Britain. You could support children with special needs, homeless people or enable someone with a disability to lead an independent life. You gain valuable work experience by volunteering with CSV.

All volunteers receive free accommodation and food (or a food allowance of £32.50 per week), all expenses and a living allowance of £26.50 per week. You can start a placement at any time of the year. Support is provided to all volunteers. No qualifications are required and volunteering with CSV is available to everyone aged 16-35.

Further details from the above address or from freephone number. *Applications* are welcome at any time but preferably submitted at least 2 months prior to starting date.

COTTAGE & RURAL ENTERPRISES LTD.: 36D Newgate Street, Morpeth, Northumberland NE61 1BA (tel 01670-511157; fax 01670-511080; e-mail carefund.north@freeuk.com).
CARE provides support to people with a learning disability through the provision of residential accommodation work and other daycare facilities which offer each person the opportunity to live a full and purposeful life.
Volunteers work alongside staff in assisting people with learning disbilities in CARE's communities around England. Around 40 hours work a week; volunteers receive an allowance and board and lodgings.

A minimum commitment of 4 weeks is expected at any time of the year. Minimum age 18; must have good communication skills.

Applications to Mr Gary Richardson, Assistant Director of Fundraising, at the above address.

THE PRINCES TRUST VOLUNTEERS: 18 Park Square East, London NW1 4LH (tel 020-7543 1234; fax 020-7543 1200; www.princes-trust.org.uk).
A **Personal Development Programme** open to all 16-25 year olds, whether employed or unemployed. Certificates in skills, including team-working and communication are awarded on completion. The majority of unemployed people who take part go on to jobs or education after finishing. The programme lasts 12 weeks including a week of outdoor activities as well as various tasks in the community. It takes place at approximately 150 centres throughout the UK. Each year there are places for about 10,000 participants. No qualifications or experience are necessary and anyone claiming benefit can still do so while taking part. To find out where the nearest Prince's Trust Volunteers programme is call 0800-842 842 (in the UK).

TOC H: 1 Forest Close, Wendover, Aylesbury, Buckinghamshire HP22 6BT (tel 01296-623911; fax 01296-696137; e-mail info@toch.org.uk; www.toch.org.uk).
Toc H runs short-term residential projects throughout the year in Britain and Belgium, lasting usually from a weekend up to two weeks. **Project work**

undertaken can include: work with people with different disabilities; work with children in need; playschemes and camps; conservation and manual work; study and/or discussion sessions. These projects provide those who take part with opportunities to learn more about themselves and the world we live in.

Minimum age 16, but there is no upper age limit. The Toc H events programme is published yearly. There is no closing date for *applications*, but you are advised to apply early. Annual recruitment is over 500.

Workcamps

ATD FOURTH WORLD: 48 Addington Square, London SE5 7LB.
ATD Fourth World is an international voluntary organisation which adopts a human rights approach to overcome extreme poverty. It supports the effort of very disadvantaged and excluded families in fighting poverty and taking an active role in the community. Founded in a shanty town on the outskirts of Paris in 1957, it now works in 27 countires on 5 continents.

ATD Fourth world organises workcamps, street workshops and Family Stays in London and Surrey in the UK and other European countries. The workcamps are a combination of **Manual Work** in and around ATD's buildings, conversation and reflection on the lives and hopes of families living in extreme poverty and on the aims and objectives of the organisation.

The street workshops bring a festival atmosphere to underprivileged areas. **Voluntary Artists, Craftsmen Etc** share their skills with the children and their parents. These street workshops for painting, crafts, computing and books etc. take place in the streets of deprived areas and make it possible to break down barriers allowing freedom of expression and building confidence.

The family stays allow families split up by poverty, perhaps with children in care, to come together for a break. The volunteers assist ATD Fourth World workers to give the families a holiday to grow together and learn new skills. The camps, Street Workshops and Family stays take place from July to September. Most last two weeks. Participants pay their own travel costs plus a contribution to the cost of food and accommodation. ATD is willing to take on foreign applicants.

For further information volunteers should *contact* ATD Fourth World at the above address enclosing a s.a.e.

CONCORDIA: Heversham House, 20-22 Boundary Road, Hove BN3 4ET (tel/fax 01273-422218; e-mail info@concordia-iye.org.uk; www concordia-iye.org.uk).
Concordia is a small not-for-profit charity committed to international youth exchange. Its International Volunteer Programme offers young people the opportunity to join an international team of **Volunteers Working On Community-Based Projects** ranging from nature conservation, restoration, archaeology and construction to more socially based schemes; they last for 2-3 weeks with a main season running June-September, although there are some spring projects.

In general no special skills or experience are required but real motivation and commitment are essential. Volunteers pay a registration fee of approx. £60 for these UK schemes and must fund their own travel.

Volunteers aged 20 or over are also required to act as group co-ordinators, for which training is required and expenses are paid.

Details of projects will be available from March/April; for further information send an s.a.e. to the Volunteer Programme Manager or consult the above Website. Please note that foreign applicants must apply through a voluntary organisation in their own country; if necessary Concordia can pass on details of partner organisations.

Applications should normally be made to the above address.

INTERNATIONAL VOLUNTARY SERVICE: IVS-GB South, Old Hall, East Bergholt, Colchester CO7 6TQ (tel 01206-298215; fax 01206-299043); IVS-GB North, Castlehill House, 21 Otley Road, Leeds LS6 3AA (tel 0113-2304 600); IVS-Scotland, 7 Upper Bow, Edinburgh EH1 2JN (tel 0131-226 6722).

International Voluntary Service (IVS) is the British branch of Service Civil International (SCI). It organises about 40 workcamps in Britain each year as well as sending volunteers to workcamps in over 35 countries overseas. **Volunteers** work for two to four weeks in an international team of 10-20 people, sharing domestic and social life as well as the work. The projects include work with children, work with people with physical or mental disabilities and manual work, often connected with ecology or conservation. The projects are not holidays: the work can be hard and demands commitment.

Most workcamps are between June and September. Volunteers pay membership plus a registration fee (£35-£115) and their own travel costs, and must be 16 or over (or 18 for workcamps overseas). Free B & L is provided on the project. IVS is working toward equal opportunities and welcomes applications from women, black people, people with disabilities, people from ethnic minorities, gay men and lesbians. Applicants from overseas should apply for IVS Schemes through partner voluntary organisations in their own country. Americans should contact SCI, Innisfree Village, Route 2, Box 506, Crozet, Virginia 22932, USA.

Write for more information to one of the regional addresses above, enclosing £4 for the listing of summer workcamps (available from April). Enquiries from January will be put on a mailing list to receive the listing when it is ready.

PILGRIM ADVENTURE: 120 Bromley Heath Road, Downend, Bristol BS16 6JJ (tel 0117-957 3997; fax 0117-9521 180). An ecumenical Christian organisation founded in 1987.

Volunteer Team Members (3) to help lead all age groups of 10-25 people taking part in Pilgrim Adventure's annual programme of Pilgrim Journeys within the UK, Spain and Ireland. Staying in hostels, monasteries, tents and small hotels. Duties include assisting with worship and chores. Volunteers receive a clothing allowance plus full board, accommodation and travel. Minimum period of work 2 weeks between May to mid-October. Help is occasionally required at other times, including opportunities to join a year round team of volunteers who plan and recce Pilgrim journeys. Each Pilgrim Journey lasts for between 5 and 15 days, with usually 2 or 3 days off between trips.

Applicants must be aged at least 18, with an interest in outdoor activities. *Applications* to Mr David Gleed at the above address.

QUAKER VOLUNTARY ACTION: Friends Meeting House, 6 Mount Street, Manchester M2 5NS (tel/fax 0161-819 1634; e-mail qva@quakervolaction. freeserve.co.uk; www.qva.org.uk).

QVA runs short-term (2-3 weeks) volunteer projects in Britain and Northern Ireland each year which mainly take place in the summer. Some medium-term and long-term **Opportunities** are now being developed. Please phone or e-mail for details.The topics include manual projects, work with adults or children who have mental or physical disabilities, playschemes, youth work or community art events. All projects meet a particular need in a local community which could not be met without the help of QVA volunteers.

Food and accommodation (usually basic) is provided free of charge.

Volunteers pay for their own travel to the project and their own pocket money, and a small registration fee is also charged.

Special experience is not required. Volunteers with disabilities are welcome to apply. through an organisation in their own country. QVA can only deal with *Applications* from UK residents. There are opportunities to go on projects in other countries (Western and Eastern Europe, USA and Japan). Min. age 18. The new Summer Programme is available in April; to obtain a copy please send a large s.a.e. with a 33 pence stamp to the above address.

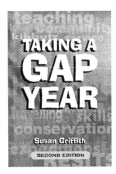
Vacation Traineeships

Accountancy, Banking and Insurance

ANDERSEN: 1 Surrey Street, London WC2R 2PS (tel 020-7438 3000; fax 020-7438 3150).

Andersen's **Summer Vacation Programme** aims to provide penultimate-year university students with an insight into a global professional services firm and the various opportunities that it can offer. The firm offers approximately 40 students the opportunity to work in their offices for 8 weeks during the summer vacation. Vacancies exist throughout the UK. The programme consists of a two-week residential course in bookkeeping, auditing, tax and microcomputer skills followed by two three-week placements in both the Assurance and Business Advisory (A&BA) and Tax Consultancy practice. Limited vacancies are also available in Business Consulting and Global Corporate Finance. Trainees are paid weekly and expenses are covered. Salaries are set on an annual basis, the summer 2001 salary was £312 per week (London). Successful performance during the placement will result in students going straight to final interview stage should they wish to apply for a full-time position in their final year.

For **penultimate-year university students** there also exist the following programmes: International Leadership Conference - four days; UK Leadership Challenge - five days; Art of Business: five days; Workshadow Programme - one week; Insight Courses - two to three days;

For **all university students** there also exists the Summer Experience - 3 days. Applicants should have a strong academic record.

There also exists the **Andersen Scholarship Programme for gap year students** which is one of the most successful and well-established programmes around. You will receive invaluable paid work experience at one of the world's leading professional services firms, a generous travel bursary and an annual academic scholarship throughout your time at university. Approximately 80 scholarships are offered each year.

The structure of the programme is as follows: Gap Year/Year 1 - You receive 35 weeks of paid work and training at one of our UK offices, the programme starts in September and ends in May - you will receive £1,500 as a travel bursary in May; Years 2 & 3 - you receive an annual £1,500 academic scholarship whilst you are at university, we also provide you with paid work experience - a minimum of six weeks a year, if you wish, you can work in a different area of the firm; Year 4 - You receive your scholarship and, if all goes well, there is also the potential offer of a full-time position after graduation.

For information on how to *apply* please refer to the website: www.anderson.com/ukcareers or call the freephone number

BARCLAYS BANK PLC: Graduate Recruitment, 54 Lombard Street, London EC3P 3AH (www.summer.barclays.com).
Barclays operates in over 60 countries, and its global reach extends to all the worlds' major financial centres. With a variety of e-commerce initiatives the company is a leading e-enabled bank in the UK. Barclays offers summer business placements to honours degree undergraduates who are in their penultimate year and considering a career in the financial services industry.

Summer Business Placements offer an exceptional opportunity to gain real business experience in the summer before beginning the final year of a Honours degree. Additionally, if trainees prove that they have the potential to make a valuable contribution to the business, Barclays will offer places on their graduate programme for September 2002.

The **8 Week Summer Programme** gives the chance to gain practical commercial experience and develop skills at the heart of an international organisation. Once the placement starts trainees are a member of an established team, with the scope to make a genuine contribution to the business with real responsibility for a piece of work and an invaluable insight into the way a global business operates. Trainees are given a broad range of support and advice that will enhance their experience and add to their commercial understanding.

Application is on-line only and the closing date determined by the number of successful *applications*. Overseas applicants should be eligible to live and work in the UK.

DELOITTE AND TOUCHE: Hill House, 1 Little New Street, London EC4A 3TR (tel 0800-323333; e-mail gradrec.uk@deloitte.co.uk; graduates.deloitte.co.uk).
Professional services firm with offices in Aberdeen, Belfast, Birmingham, Bristol, Cambridge, Cardiff, Crawley, Edinburgh, Glasgow, Isle of Man, Guernsey, Jersey, Leeds, Liverpool, London, Manchester, Newcastle, Nottingham, Southampton and St Albans.

Deloitte and Touche offer **100 Vacation Trainee Placements** each year throughout the UK primarily for work within Chartered Accountancy areas, though experience within other service lines may be possible. Placements are open to penultimate year students with 24 UCAS points and grade B at Maths and English Language GCSE, and the expectation of a 2:2 from any degree discipline. Placements are offered during Christmas, Easter and Summer vacations with a competitive salary paid. Overseas applicants are welcome but must have a valid work permit.

For *applications* an EAF should be sent to the office of the applicants choice addresses available from the above address.

ERNST & YOUNG: Graduate Recruitment, Becket House, 1 Lambeth Palace Road, London SE1 7EU (freephone 0800-289208; www.ey.com/uk/graduate).
Ernst & Young is one of the world's largest professional services firms dedicated to helping their clients identify and capitalise on business opportunities throughout the world. They serve clients from 675 offices in over 130 countries. From most of their 20 offices in the UK the firm offers **Students** in their penultimate year at university the opportunity to work for a period of up to six weeks in the summer vacation. The scheme consists of a one week induction course followed by around five weeks practical work experience in a number of their departments. The scheme provides an excellent insight into a career with Ernst and Young.

Applicants should have a minimum of 22 UCAS points, excluding general studies, and possess the determination to build a successful business career. For further information and an *application* form contact your careers service or ring the above freephone number.

KPMG: 8 Salisbury Square, Blackfriars, London EC4Y 8BB (tel freephone 0500-664655; www.kpmgcareers.co.uk).
KPMG is one of the world's big five firms of business advisers, providing solutions to clients' business problems right across the globe. They have offices in 159 different countries staffed by over 110,000 people worldwide.

KPMG runs **Vacation Programmes** offering an insight into the workings of a leading business advisory firm; it shows both the opportunities available to graduates and how a major international firm operates. KPMG offers on a national basis vacation experience to students of any degree discipline in their penultimate year at university. The length of the programmes vary and they may include workshadowing partners, managers and both qualified and trainee business advisers.

KPMG also offer a *Leading Edge* programme for those in their first year of study which involves a two day residential course aiming to provide a series of both personal and professional skills to aid career development; these are run at a variety of universities from late September.

For further details *contact* the Graduate Recruitment department at the above address or apply on line to the above website address.

PRICEWATERHOUSECOOPERS: No. 1 London Bridge Street, London SE1 9QL (tel 0808-100 1500; fax 020-7804 3030; www.pwcglobal.com).

PricewaterhouseCoopers is the world's largest professional services organisation, providing a full range of business advisory services including auditing, business advisory, tax and actuarial services.

The **Summer Vacation Programme** gives students an insight into what the company does, the way it works and its company culture. The programme runs in London and regional offices, in a range of business areas – Assurance and Business Advisory Services, Tax and Legal Services, Actuarial, Corporate Finance and Recovery, and Management Consulting Services. Students are given a combination of business training and work experience similar to that of a graduate. Working with teams, students are able to make a direct contribution to the work of the firm while developing their own personal skills.

Pricewaterhousecoopers are looking for outstanding penultimate year undergraduates of any degree discipline. As competition for places is fierce you will need a strong academic record, expecting at least a 2:1, and should be able to demonstrate excellent communication and interpersonal skils.

For more information call into your careers service, telephone Freephone 0808-100 1500, or visit the Website at www.pwcglobal.com/uk/bridges. Apply before Easter.

SAINSBURYS SUPERMARKETS: 169 Union Street, London.
For **Finance Positions** see Sainsburys under *Business and Management* below.

WATSON WYATT WORLDWIDE: Terra Firma, 86 Station Road, Redhill, Surrey (tel 01737-241144; fax 01737-274312; e-mail graduate.recruitment@ en.watsonwyatt.com; www.watsonwyatt.com/graduate).
Actuarial, Investment and HR Consulting Summer Scheme (approx. 20).
Wages of approx. £250 per week. To work in a 6 week placement. Applicants should be penultimate year students, expecting a 2(i) degree or have 24 UCAS points. No accommodation is available but assistance may be given in finding some.

Applications should be made by 31 March on line using the above website address.

Business and Management

DIALOGUE DIRECT LTD: www.jobs.dialoguedirect.co.uk; jobs@dialoguedirect. co.uk; tel: 07966 343039. A successful international fundraising agency working on behalf of charities and NPOs. Currently raising donations for Greenpeace in the UK Dialogue will be working with other charities in the near future. Work available year-round with main campaign in the summer months.
Dialoguers. Expenses plus an average of. £250 per week. All candidates start as face-to-face fundraisers, communicating directly with the public. Minimum period of work 5 weeks. Work is in small, live-in, UK mobile teams. Hrs: Flexible working hours, 6 days per week for 5 weeks.
Team Guides. Fast progression for the right candidate to Team Guide. Dialogue has an in-house training and certification programme (4 modules including self-management, negotiation and team management).

Candidates must be prepared to work away from home, have a positive and flexible attitude towards work and team-life, excellent communication skills and a commitment to the aims of the organisation. Overseas applicants with fluent English and a working visa welcome, particularly those from New Zealand, Australia, America and South Africa.

Applications should be made to the above e-mail address or telephone number.

JOHN LEWIS PARTNERSHIP: 171 Victoria Street, London SW1E 5NN (tel 020-7592 6339; fax 020-7592 6301; e-mail careers@johnlewis.co.uk; www.johnlewis.co.uk).

The John Lewis Partnership offers around **8 Placements**, lasting 6 weeks, to penultimate year university students of any discipline. Successful candidates gain an overall view of trading in a department store. They gain experience of the different presentation, stock control and selling techniques applicable to a wide assortment of products. This is backed up by attachments in selling support departments and a project on a commercial aspect of the business. Trainees receive £220-£240 per week; no accommodation is provided.

You should have good written and verbal communication skills as you will be working with senior management, colleagues on the shop floor and customers and you will also make a presentation based on your project. Foreign applicants with work permits are not considered.

Applications should be sent to the Recruitment Manager by 5 April 2002.

SAINSBURYS SUPERMARKETS: 169 Union Street, Southwark, London SE1 ONL (tel 020-7695 7944; fax 020-7695 2927; e-mail wjcetau.sainsburys.co.uk; www.sainsburys.co.uk/fresherthinking).

15 Vacation Traineeships are available in the Finance Division, the Food Technology Division and the Buying Division. The positions are open to university students only. Wage is £13,495 per annum pro rated. The placement last for 6 weeks during the summer months and is located at the Head Office, Holburn, London. Accommodation will be provided for the Finance position. Suitably qualified foreign applicants may apply if they plan to work in the UK after graduation.

Applications should be made online via the above website.

THISTLE TOWER HOTEL: St Katharine's Way, London E1 1LD (tel 020-7481 3745; fax 020-7680 0256; e-mail hrtower@thistle.co.uk; www.thistlehotels.com)

Student Vacation Traineeships are offered in the following areas;

Human Resources Trainee; work will involve recruiting, selecting and interviewing.

Kitchen Staff; to work with a team of chefs preparing food. **Housekeeping;** work will involve supervising, cleaning and the maintaining of bedrooms to hotel standard. Receptionist/Cashier; a customer service position, checking guests in and out of the hotel.

The placements are paid or unpaid depending on the department worked in and last from 3 months to 1 year. Experience is not always necessary as training is provided. Applicants from overseas with proper work documents are welcome.

Applications should be sent to Claire Porter, Assistant Personnel Manager or Sarh How, Assistant Training Manager, at the above address.

The Law

BEVAN ASHFORD SOLICITORS: 35 Colston Avenue, Bristol BS1 4TT(tel 0117-9751690; fax 0117-9291865; e-mail j.brierley@bevanashford.co.uk; www.bevanshford.co.uk).

Bevan Ashford solicitors offer student **Vacation Traineeships** to 2nd year law students or 3rd year non-law students who are considering applying for training contracts with the firm after graduation. The placements consist of 1 week unpaid work experience with a day spent in a different department work shadowing and some case study work to test ability and aptitude. The placements are based in Bristol, Exeter, Taunton, Tiverton and Plymouth.

Applications should be sent to Jean Brierle, Joint Office Administrator by 21 March, by *application* form only, availaible from the website.

EVERSHEDS: Senator House, 85 Queen Victoria Street, London EC4V 4JL (tel 020-7919 4500; fax 020-7919 4919; e-mail gradrec@eversheds.co.uk).
A European law firm, Eversheds has over 1,750 legal and business advisors in Amsterdam, Birmingham, Brussels, Cambridge, Cardiff, Copenhagen, Derby, Ipswich, London, Manchester, Monaco, Newcastle, Norwich, Nottingham, Paris, Sofia and Teeside. Each office provides a wide range of services to the business and financial community and to the public sector. Its distinctive approach gives clients access to a large team of lawyers who combine local market knowledge with an international perspective.

Two week **Summer Placements** at all UK offices to penultimate law and non-law final year students expecting a 2:1 degree.

Apply on an EAF to the National Graduate Recruitment Officer at the above address by the end of January.

MASONS: 30 Aylesbury Street, London EC1R OER (tel 020-7490 4000; fax 020-7490 2545; e-mail graduate.recruitment@masons.com; www.masons.com).
Masons is internationally recognised as one of the foremost legal advisers to the IT, Construction and Engineering, Energy and Infrastructure Industries. Their strategy is to remain the premier legal adviser to these industries whilst remaining a leading provider of specialist skills.

Masons offers **40 Students A Year** the opportunity to partake in their summer vacation traineeship, working with fee earners and trainees on various projects including attending client meetings, going to court hearings and carrying out research.

Applicants should be law students in their 2nd year or non-law students in their final year. Placements last for 2 weeks and take place between June and August. Salary is £225 per week. No accommodation is provided but Masons provide a list of hostels and student halls in London to assist students.

Applications should be sent to Kelcy Davenport by 15th February.

NABARRO NATHANSON: Lacon House, 84 Theobalds Road, London. WC1X 8RW (tel 020-7524 6000; fax 020-7524 6524; e-mail graduateinfo@nabarro.com; www.nabarro.com).
Nabarro Nathanson offer **60 Vacation Traineeship** placements each year to final year non-law students, penultimate year law students, CPE and LPC students seeking a training contract two years on. The placements last for three weeks between mid June and late August and trainees are paid £200 per week. Placements are available at their London, Sheffield and Reading offices. No accommodation is available. Suitable foreign applicants looking for a training contract in the UK who are authorised to work there are welcome.

Applicants should call the freephone number 0800-0564021 from November for a copy of their brochure and *applications* form.

Public Sector

THE ARMY: Freepost, CV37 9GR (tel 0345-300 111 www.army.mod.uk).
Although the Army does not offer vacation training as such, it does run the Gap Year Commission, which is open to students who wish to take a year out after leaving school and before taking up a firm place at University. It is aimed at students of high academic ability who demonstrate a responsible and mature

attitude and show leadership potential.

Successful candidates attend a 3 week course at Sandhurst and are commissioned into their chosen Corps or Regiments as 2nd Lieutenants, on a special rate of pay of £1000 per month. They serve for a minimum of four months and a maximum of 18 months. There is no subsequent obligation to serve in the Army.

Applicants must undergo a rigorous selection procedure, which begins with an advisory interview with an Army Career Advisor. This can be arranged through the Schools Careers' Staff or by writing to the above address. Applicants should have a guaranteed place at University.

THE CIVIL SERVICE:

More than 60 departments and over 100 executive agencies, employing around 480,000 people making the Civil Service on of the largest employers in the UK.

A number of Government Departments and Agencies will offer vacation **opportunities for students** in 2002; details are published in a booklet – *Vacation Employment for Students 2002* available from your Careers Service, or Civil Service Careers from March (tel 0117-982 1171; note that this number is for despatch of copies only; please do not call it for further information on vacation work).

Students are advised to apply early as most opportunities have deadlines for *Applications* early in the year. Further information on careers in the Civil Service is available from Careers Services and also via the internet: www.civil-service.gov.uk/jobs.

LOCAL GOVERNMENT NATIONAL TRAINING ORGANISATION

(LGNTO): LGNTO, Careers & Learning, Layden House, 78-86, Turnmill Street, London, EC1M 5LG (tel 020-7296 6600; fax 020-7296 6666). Part of the LGNTO's remit is to provide promotional and careers information about local government in the UK. They answer general careers enquiries about local government as well as running a summer placement scheme and two websites. www.LGcareers.com provides comprehensive local government careers information and www.LGjobs.com advertises hundreds of vacancies every week in local authorities all over the country.

The Training Opportunities Placement (TOP) scheme offers structured paid work experience placements to higher education students who are in the penultimate year of their first degree. These are specifically designed to introduce individuals to **The Management of a Local Authority** while they undertake a worthwhile project for at least five weeks during the summer.

Applications are invited from committed students who are able to demonstrate a genuine interest in working in local government. Although no specific degree discipline is required for many of the opportunities on offer, the competition for places is extremely high. To ensure success, candidates will have to demonstrate a good understanding of the challenges currently facing local government and identify the skills and experience they could bring to the projects.

Students will receive a minimum training allowance of £150 per week and are given the opportunity to compete for further cash prizes when they submit a management report at the end of the placement. The application period is October 2001-April 2002. For an *applications* form and further details, either telephone the TOP scheme Co-ordinator on 020-7296 6508, email topscheme@lg-employers.gov.uk or check the information and application forms on the LGNTO website: www.LGnto.gov.uk.

POST OFFICE: The Assessment Centre, Coton House, Rugby, Warwickshire CV23 0AA.

The Post Office Finance Vacation Scheme offers 10 traineeships for 8 weeks over the summer. It gives penultimate-year undergraduates, who are hoping to pursue a career in Accountancy, an opportunity to gain career-related work experience and training, whilst completing a 'real-life' project.

Vacancies occur nationwide, and in all of the Post Office businesses. Students studying any degree subject will be considered, although good A level grades (24 UCAS points) or equivalent qualifications are asked for. Overseas applicants eligible to work in the UK will be considered. The salary is approximately £200 per week, plus London weighting if applicable.

Written enquiries should be made to the above address enclosing a current cv. *Applications* for any other vacation work in The Post Office should be made to the Personnel Manager at local Royal Mail or Post Office Counters offices.

Science, Construction and Engineering

CORUS: Ashorne Hill Management College, Leamington Spa CV33 9PY (tel 01926-488025; fax 01926-488024; e-mail recruitment@corusgroup.com; www.corusgroupcareers.com).

Corus is a customer-focused, innovative, solutions-driven company which manufactures, processes and distributes steel and aluminium products as well as providing design, technology and consultancy services.

Every year Corus offers **30 summer placements and 100 12 month placements** around the UK in their engineering, research and development, supplies management, logisitics, finance, human resources, commercial, customer technical services, manufacturing and operations management departments. These positions are suitable for final year A level students or students in their first or second year at university. Salary based on £10,000 per year pro rata. Help can be given in finding accommodation.

Applications should be made on line only after consulting www.corusgroupcareers.com.

ESSO & EXXON MOBIL GROUP: Recruitment Centre, MPO2, ExxonMobil House, Ermyn Way, Leatherhead, Surrey KT22 8UX (tel 0845-120 0292; e-mail recruit.cuk@esso.com; www.esso.co.uk) .

ExxonMobil offer around **35 eight-week summer placements** during July and August for degree students. **Production Department.** Aberdeen, London. Studying any Engineering discipline. **Manufacturing & Distribution.** Fawley. Studying Chemical Engineering. **Fuels Marketing.** Leatherhead. Any degree subject. **Finance.** London. Any numerate degree. **Information Technology.** Fawley, Leatherhead. IT or Business related degree.

The summer placements are open to penultimate year students and salaries will be a minimum of £14,250 (pro-rata). All students will be given a project to complete (based on a real business scenario), receive some skills training and attend a two day outward bound type course. At the end of the placement students will have the opportunity to go through the graduate recruitment process where hopefully Esso can make a mutually informed decision as to whether they would be suitable for a graduate position.

Closing date is 18 January. Please *apply* via www.exxonmobil.com/ukrecruitment or call 0845-120 0292 for an application form.

FORD MOTOR COMPANY LIMITED: Head Office, Eagle Way, Warley, Brentwood, Essex CM13 3BN (tel 01277-251467; fax 01277-251186; e-mail lbenne17@ford.com; www.ford.co.uk/recruitment).

Positions are available in most areas of the business, including HR, Finance, IT an Engineering. The job descriptions for each of these roles will vary substantially. However, the student will play a large part in the day-to-day routine of the company and will undertake certain projects. They will have significant responsibility. Positions are open to undergraduates.

Wages are approx. £1,000 per month plus various benefits. Terms of employment are for 8 weeks to 3 months and can be taken at any time of the year. What is specifically offered at different times can be seen more clearly on the company website. The location of the traineeships will be decided by Ford. They will be either in Essex (Dagenham, Dunton, Warley, Frafford House), Southampton, Halewood, South Wales, Coventry or Daventry. Accommodation is not provided nor is help in finding lodgings, other than the provision of a list of letting agents in the local area.

Foreign applicants who do not need a working visa to be arranged are welcome. *Applications* will only be accepted if made online at www.Ford.co.uk/recruitment.

IMI PLC: PO Box 216, Witton, Birmingham B6 7BA (tel 0121-332 22628; fax 0121-356 2877; e-mail grad.recruit@imi.plc.uk; www.imi.plc.uk).
IMI is a major international engineering group operating in the field of fluid control. It is organised in four business areas; Hydronic Control, IMI Cornelius, IMI Norgen and CCI. Each business area is focused on market requirements and linked by common technology and manufacturing techniques. IMI has offices in over 60 countries worldwide but predominantly in the UK, USA and Germany.

Each year IMI offers a number of **Vacation Placements (approx 12)** to penultimate year students who are studying for a degree in Mechanical, Manufacturing or Electronic and Electrical Engineering. The salary for the placement is £770 per month. During their placement students are required to attend a 2 day management skills training course. On completion of a successful placement students wil be offered sponsorship through their final year at university and a place on the IMI Graduate Engineering Training Scheme. Placements can be overseas depending on individual language skills and availability. Successful candidates should be able to work for a period of 8-12 weeks.

Application forms available from above address and on company website. Closing date for applications 22 February .

LOGICA: Freepost 21, London W1E 4JZ (tel 020-7446 2333).
Logica is one of the leading IT companies in the FTSE 100, bringing together around 8,500 people from offices in 23 countries. They are in business to help leading organisations worldwide achieve their business objectives through the innovative use of information technology.and they develop and support many of the world's most complex IT projects.

Logica offer a number of **Summer Vacation Oportunities** across the UK and are interested in applicants in their penultimate year who are studying a computer science related degree. Accommodation is not provided.

Please *apply* online at www.logica.com/ukgraduates.

MARS: Dundeee Road, Slough, Berks SL1 4JX (tel 01753-514999; fax 0173-215559; e-mail mars.graduate@eu.effem.com; www.mars.com/university).
Offices in Berkshire, Hampshire, Yorkshire, Anglia and Worcestshire.
Student Vacation Traineeships are offered in the following areas; Commercial; Engineering; Finance; IT; Logistics; Marketing; Personnel;Production

Manufacturing; Research and Development; Sales and Software Engineering. Traineeships are offered for 8 weeks in the Summer vacation and a £290 salary is paid per week. There are 25-40 vacancies and the placements are aimed at penultimate year students. Overseas applicants are welcome and Mars assists in the finding of accommodation.

Applications should be addressed to Mars Graduate Marketing and received by 13 March 2002.

MOTT MACDONALD: Demeter House, Station Road, Cambridge CB1 2RS (tel 01223 463658; fax 01223 461007; e-mail graduaterecruitment@ mottmac.com; www.mottmac).

The firm is a multi-disciplinary consultancy engaged in development touching many facets of everyday life from transport, energy, water and the environment to the building and communications industries. Traineeships are offered in Croydon, Cambridge, Newcastle, Manchester, Birmingham and Winchester.

Placements are offered within the design office for civil, mechanical and building services engineering students. There are 50 vacancies per year and preference is given to penultimate year university students. Placements take place during the summer vacations and last for 8-12 weeks; trainees receive £170-£200 per week. Overseas applicants are welcome. Assistance is given in helping trainees find local accommodation.

Applications should be addressed to Marion Pass at the above address between January and February.

NIAB (National Institute Of Agricultural Botany): Huntingdon Road, Cambridge CB3 0LE (tel 01223-342234; fax 01223-342206; e-mail jobs@Niab.com; www.niab.com).

Vacation Work involving working in fields, laboratories, etc. is offered to about 30 applicants a year, at regional trial centres and the head office. £151.40-170.33 per week according to contract terms and experience. Accommodation not provided although lists of accommodation are available.

Applications from April/May for summer work to the Personnel Office at the above address.

RICARDO: Bridge Works, Shoreham-by-Sea, West Sussex BN43 5FG (tel 01273-794614; fax 01273-794580; e-mail jastevens@ricardo.com; www.ricardo.com).

Various Traineeship Positions are offered each year throughout Ricardo's engineering business. Positions are open to those studying or intending to study any of the following disciplines: Automotive, Control, Electronic, Electrical, Mechanical, Software Or Engineering Sciences. Wages vary depending on age, experience and the type of placement. Placements ideally last between 6 weeks and 3 months, at any time of the year subject to business requirements, and at any of Ricardo's sites in the UK. Some assistance can be provided in arranging lodgings. Foreign applicants welcome.

Applications should ideally be made by 31 December for the following year to Julia Stevens, Graduate Recruitment and Development Officer at the above address. Further information on Ricardo is available on their website.

ROLLS-ROYCE PLC: P.O. Box 31, Derby, DE24 8BJ (tel 01332-269286; fax 01332-513929; e-mail Graduates@rolls-royce.com).

Rolls-Royce plc is a global company providing power on land, sea and air. The company has established leading positions in civil aerospace, defence marine and

energy markets. Its core gas turbine technology has created one of the broadest ranges of aero engines in the world, with around 50,000 in service in over 150 countries. Customers include more than 500 airlines, 2,400 corporate and utility operators and 160 armed forces, using both fixed wing and rotary wing aircraft.
Vacation Trainees for attachments in engineering, commercial, manufacturing, procurement, marketing, human resources and logistics. Ten weeks are spent in a department that is of relevance to the course the applicant is studying. Training takes place during the summer vacation that precedes the final academic year. Students complete an individual project or contribute towards a major piece of work within the department.
Industrial Trainees for placements usually during the final training period of a sandwich course. The number of attachments will be influenced by business requirements. Twelve month placements in finance usually include three attachments within the company. Attachments in manufacturing or research may last 6 or 12 months and trainees may be required to undertake one major project in one department.

Help is given in finding accommodation and placements are in the Midlands, South West and Scotland. *Applications* online at www.rolls-royce.com or call us on the above telephone number, quoting CRO/0249.

SCOTT WILSON: Scott House, Basing View, Basingstoke, Hampshire RG21 4JG (tel 01256-461161).
A dynamic multi-disciplinary international consulting group involved in engineering, transportation planning and environmental planning projects throughout the UK, Europe, and world markets.

The company has a regular requirement for Civil Engineering students who have completed at least one year of their University course to undertake **Summer Vacation Work** based in their Basingstoke offices. Opportunities are available within their Maritime, Highways and Transportation sections.

Applicants should have a genuine interest in their subject, be adaptable, and show initiative. Duties and duration of placement may vary considerably depending on the workload at the time. *Applications* should be made in April to Mr A. Morton, Head of Personnel, at the above address.

SKANSKA CONSTRUCTION: Maple Cross House, Denham Way, Maple Cross, Richmansworth, Hertforshire WD3 5AS (tel 01923-423571; fax 01923-423242; e-mail robert.dunn@skanska.co.uk; www.skanska.co.uk).
Trainee Positions (20) working in the positions of engineer, civil engineer, quantity surveyor or land surveyor. Placements are nationwide and site-based. Wages are subject to previous experience. Ideally to work over the summer vacation and for a min. period of 8 weeks. University or College degree students (HNC or HNA) or pre-university gap year students considered. Some assistance with accommodation available.

Applications should be made before June to Mr R.W. Dunn at the above address. Interview required.

London and the Home Counties

Prospects for Work.

London: if you want to move to London to work during the summer season think first about where you are going to live. While rented accommodation is not difficult to find the price is likely to be high and staying for only a short period may prove difficult. However, there are several youth hostels, and you may be able to find a cheap deal among the 'Accommodation to Rent' columns of the city's many newspapers and magazines. In addition to numerous local papers there are several publications which are not associated with any particular area. The main ones to look out for are: *TNT* and *Southern Cross* (both free), the *Evening Standard* (daily), *Time Out* and *Loot*. These publications also carry job advertisements. Vacancies arise most commonly in retail, secretarial, hotel, restaurant and domestic work. The chance of finding a job will be increased if you are flexible as to where you can work, so consult the local paper in several different districts.

Various Jobcentres in London have special Temporary Sections. The Hammersmith Jobcentre (Glen House, 22 Glenthorne Road, W6 0PP; tel 020-8210 8100; fax 020-8210 8181) offers a wide range of temporary work, including retail, administrative and construction jobs. Their vacancies are not just for Hammersmith, but also for W6, W14, SW13, SW14. They also keep lists of vacancies with the local

Borough Council – these tend to be clerical and administrative posts.

There are also hundreds of private employment agencies, especially along Oxford Street. The South of the River Agency (128c Northcote Road, SW11; tel 020-7228 5086) recruits staff for any jobs private householders might require, from babysitting to barbecue staff. Drake International (branches at 20 Regent Street SW1, tel 020-7437 6900; 44 South Molton Street, W1Y; 62-63 Fenchurch Street, EC3; 43 Maiden Lane, WC2E) covers a range of fields, including secretarial, industrial, driving and catering, for both permanent and temporary positions. Many such agencies advertise in *TNT* magazine.

In terms of vacation traineeships, prospects are particularly good for anyone interested in accountancy or law. In addition, many big companies have their head offices in London, so a variety of other opportunities are also available.

Home Counties: in the comparatively prosperous Home Counties job prospects can be fairly good over the summer. In particular, there is a demand for staff among marquee erectors and events organisers. The Jobcentre in Reading (0118-980 8200) has access to jobs at the Ascot and Windsor racecourses, Henley Regatta, music festivals and other events both in the city and elsewhere in the region. Epsom, Newbury and Sandown are the other main racecourses in the area; it is worth contacting these at any time of year.

Reading is a major source of longer-term summer employment in the Home Counties. Finding rented accommodation here is surprisingly easy too. Office, domestic, retail and packing work tends to be the most common, though it is worth approaching the local authority, which runs various summer programmes. Vacancies tend to be most numerous in the earliest months of the year. Try looking in the *Reading Evening Post* (daily), the *Reading Chronicle* (weekly) and the *Newbury Weekly News*.

Windsor is a busy tourist town all year round, but especially over the summer. Temporary work may be available at the Leisure Pool as well as at the local hotels and river boat companies. McDonalds are among the largest employers of temporary staff. The Jobcentre in Maidenhead (tel 01628- 844900) has a temporary work board with a wide range of vacancies, both full-time and part-time, permanent and temporary, and in a variety of occupations. The weekly *Maidenhead Advertiser* (on Fridays) has job pages.

In Luton, north of London, there is some demand for factory workers, who may need forklifting qualifications. In addition a large number of vacancies exist within the service centre, including retail work which is steadily increasing due to the expansion of the airport. Various other types of work are also available, including manual labour, caring, and catering.

Business and Industry

ADVENTURE BALLOONS: Winchfield Park, London Road, Hartley Wintney, Hants RG27 8HY.
Office Staff (1/2) to work from 8.30am-5.30pm Monday-Friday. Wage £200 per week; no accommodation available. Period of work from March to October. Applicants need computer experience and a good telephone manner.
Applications to the Manager at the above address.

ANGEL HUMAN RESOURCES PLC: Angel House, 4 Union Street, London Bridge, London SE1 1SZ (tel 020-7940 2000; fax 020-7940 2018; e-mail hq@angelhr.org; www.angelhr.org). Angel was founded in 1965 and adheres strictly to the codes of practice laid down by its professional bodies. Open 7am-

6pm Monday to Friday with branch offices throughout London and the South East. **Chefs, Cooks, Waiting and General Catering and Kitchen Assistants;** work may be offered in **Catering Environments**, throughout the year. Work also available for **Administrators**. Work may also be offered to experienced **Office Staff**; to **Warehouse and Factory** staff; to experienced or qualified **Nurses and Carers**. Pay may vary between £3.50 and £16 per hour dependent on experience. Work may also be offered to experienced office staff with 50wpm typing; to warehouse and factory staff; and to experienced or qualified nurses and carers.

Applicants from abroad should note that placements can only be made after arrival in the UK; Angel cannot enter into correspondence prior to arrival in the UK. Work can usually be offered within 2-3 days of arrival. Angel cannot assist with accommodation. *Apply* to the office in person or by phone on arrival in London.

BLUE ARROW: Blue Arrow Construction, Refuge House, 2nd Floor, 9-10 Riverfront, Enfield EN1 3SZ (tel 0208-367 9541; e-mail enfield148@ bluearrow.co.uk).
Shopfitters. Minimum wage £10.50 per hour. Previous experience necessary.
Labourers. Minimum wage £5 per hour. Minimum age 18. Site experience required.
Trade Mates. Minimum wage £6.50 per hour. Minimum age 18. Site experience necessary.
Electricians. Minimum wage £10 per hour. JIB approved.
Plumbers. Minimum wage £10 per hour. Previous experience required.

Hours vary for all positions. Staff required all year round to work in the Home Counties; minimum period 1 week. Overseas applicants with work permits welcome.

Applications can be made by phone at any time on 0800-328 6890.

CARRON MARQUEES: Holt Farm, Old Lane, Dockenfield, Farnham, Surrey GU10 4HG (tel 01252-795252; fax 01252-794120). Marquee hire company catering for local parties and weddings.
Drivers (2) to drive a 7¹/₂ ton lorry. Wages £7 per hour, free accommodation. To work a minimum of 40 hours per week, including weekends. Min. period of work of 1 month. Position is available from May to September. Applicants should be strong and fit and aged over 25. Overseas applicants welcome.

Applications to Richard from early May onwards. Interview necessary.

CATAMARAN CRUISERS: Embankment Pier, Victoria Embankment, London WC2N 6NU (tel 020-7695 1824; fax 020-7839 1034; e-mail nicola. gilbert@bateauxlondon.com or sally.elsdon@bateauxlondon.com). London pleasure boat company operating between central London and Greenwich, providing river cruises with commentary and refreshments.
Pier Supervisors (5). Wages £4.66 per hour, 5 or 6 days per week.
Retail Assistants(15) to work on board boats. Wages £4.22 per hour, 5 or 6 days per week.
Retail Assistants (5) for the shop. Wages £4.66 per hour, 5 or 6 days per week.
Ticket Agent (1). Wages £35 per day, 5 days per week.
Additional pay may include a 5% loyalty bonus at end of contract, supplementary pay of extra hours, and commission in retail jobs.

Applicants should be 18+, able to swim, have experience with dealing with the public in front line situation, a positive attitude and a happy smile. Second language an advantage. Min. period of work 2 months. Positions are available from April to October. Foreign applicants with reasonable English welcome. No accommodation available.

Applications to Nicola Gilbert or Sally Esldon at the above address from

March onwards. Interview necessary.

CATCH 22: 199 Victoria Street, London SW1E 5NE (tel 020-7821 1133; www.c22.co.uk). Employment agency covering the whole of the London area.
General Industrial Staff for temporary jobs such as furniture moving, driving, warehouse and message-running. Flexible hours but usually 8 hours a day and preferably 5 days a week. Possibility of overtime.

No accommodation available. Min. age 18. Must be adaptable to different environments and have a good level of English. Work available all year round. Min. period of work 3 months.

Apply by phone when in the UK to the above number.

FRED (UK) 2000 LIMITED: Copthall House, Victoria Road, Aldershot, Hampshire   (tel   01252-315544;   fax   01252-342727;   e-mail freduk2000@hotmail.com). Specialised recruitment agency.
Industrial and Technical Staff (10). Wages from £5 per hour. To work Monday to Friday. Min. period of work of 1 week. Positions are available all year. Positions open depend on qualifications. Foreign applicants entitled to work in the UK and with acceptable spoken English welcome. Accommodation available for some positions.

Applications should be made at any time to a Recruitment Consultant at the above address. Interview necessary, by telephone is sufficient.

HARRODS LTD: Knightsbridge, London SW1X 7XL (tel 020-7893 8793; www.harrods.com).
Sales Staff, Clerical Staff, Selling Support Staff to work in August and from October through to January to cover the Christmas and January Sale. Applicants must be a minimum of sixteen years old, be eligible to work in the UK. Fluent spoken English is essential.

Interested applicants should *visit* the Harrods Recruitment Centre, 11 Brompton Place, SW1. Opening hours Monday-Saturday 10am-7pm.

MARGARET HILTON TRAVEL INN: Oakley House, Oakley Road, Luton (tel 01582-567972; fax 0870-2419000; e-mail margaret.hilton@whitbread.com). Part of the largest budget hotel brand in the UK.
Call Centre Team Members (10-15). Wages £6.14 per hour. To work within the hours of operation, 8am-8pm. Positions are available from August. Applicants should be 16+. Prior experience helpful but not essential but communication and keyboard skills are necessary. Foreign applicants welcome. No accommodation available.

Applications should be made to Nichola Ashby, Team Leader, from November 2001. Interview necessary.

MONTHIND CLEAN: 91 London Road, Copford, Colchester, Essex C06 1L9 (tel 01206-215300; fax 01206-212126; e-mail info@monthindclean.co.uk; www.monthind-clean.co.uk). The company provides contract cleaners for various businesses.
Cleaners. Wages to be arranged. To work mainly during evenings. Minimum age 18. No experience necessary. Work available during any vacation. Applicants must understand English and be able to comply with Health and Safety Rules. No accommodation available. Foreign applicants with work permits and acceptable spoken English welcome.

Applications can be made all year round to Penny Cander at the above address.

SATURDAY VENTURE ASSOCIATION: PO Box 9, Chichester, West Sussex

PO20 7YD (tel/fax 01243-513464; e-mail SVA2@btinternet.com;) SVA2@talk.com. A small charity founded to support young disabled people, their siblings and friends. Currently setting up a project to form nationwide support and a club for young disabled people.

Project Work (2) involving research, correspondence and fund raising. Wages from £5 per hour. To work 15-20 hours weekly. Min. period of work of dependent of exact position. Positions are available from October 2001 to September 2002. A-levels or postgraduates. Mobile if possible. Good English essential. No accommodation available.

Applications should be made as soon as possible to the Chairman at the above address. Interview may be required.

VAUXHALL AFTERSALES: Griffin House, Osborne Road, Luton LU1 3YT (tel 01582-426477; fax 01582-426446).

Warehouse Operatives (80); duties include manual function shift work. Wages were £6.79 per hour in 2001, plus shift premium if applicable. To work 38 hours a week. Staff needed from July for 6-10 weeks. Work may also be available at Christmas. No accommodation is available. Applicants must be over 18.

Applications to the Personnel Dept. TW4 from October onwards.

WETHERBY STUDIOS: 23 Wetherby Mansions, Earls Court Square, London SW5 9BH (tel 020-7373 1107).

Male Photographic Models. Wages £100 cash for 2-hour sessions. Dozens needed throughout the year. No accommodation available. Should be aged 18-40 years, but physique is more important than age. While more than half the models used are slim, it can be difficult to find men who have worked on their chest and arm definition, which is required if picture sessions promoting leisure wear are planned. Moustaches and beards permissible. No modelling experience necessary. Applicants must supply snapshots to show how they photograph facially and physically. Follow-ups are frequent, depending on the photographers' reactions to the first test shots. Overseas applicants and all colours more than welcome, but must speak fluent English.

Applications to Mr Mike Arlen, Director, Wetherby Studios.

WILLIAM HILL ORGANIZATION LTD: 1-5 Morris Place, Finsbury Park, London N4 3JG (tel freephone 0800-917 8210; e-mail achandler@ williamhill.co.uk). One of the largest betting organisations in the country with over 1,500 branches; summer opportunities may lead to a career.

Cashiers to work various flexible hours in betting shops during the summer (days and evenings), including Saturdays. Positions in London only. Min. age 18. Training will be given. Period of work 10-16 weeks between April and August.

Applications between January to March to the Recruitment Office, William Hill Organisation.

Children

ADVENTURE & COMPUTER HOLIDAYS LTD: PO Box 183, Dorking, Surrey RH5 6FA (tel 01306-881299). A small, friendly company with 19 years experience in running activity holidays for children aged 4-13. Based in a school in Surrey, with an activity centre in Cornwall.

Camp Leaders, Teachers required for day and residential camps. £155-£185 per week. Day camp staff to work 9am-5pm; on residential camps staff work longer hours, depending upon requirements. Min. age 20. Qualifications or experience with children preferred. Period of work April to August (mostly July-August), min. period one week. Free accommodation is provided on residential camps. Day camp staff need to live in London or Surrey area. All applicants should be able to attend an interview.

Applications any time to Ms Sarah Bradley, Director, at the above address.

CAMP BEAUMONT: Kingwood House, 11 Prince of Wales Road, Norwich NR1 1BD (tel 01603-284284; E-mail adventures@kingswood.co.uk). Non-residential day camps are located around Greater London in Kent, Essex, Surrey etc. Residential camps are located in Surrey, Norfolk, Isle of Wight and Normandy.

Group Leaders for summer camps. Leaders instruct in non-specialist activities, assist activity instructors and help to run camps. Minimum age 18. Previous experience of working with children and interest in sports, arts & crafts, music and drama essential. Group leaders are responsible for the welfare of the children in their group at all times,

Activity Instructors to lead specialist activities for 3-7 sessions per day at camps. Appropriate recognised qualifications must be held e.g GNAS Instructor for Archery.

Period of employment July and August. Wages £144-£167 per week less £70 for food and accommodation.

To *apply* write or e-mail to the Recruitment Department at the above address.

CROYDON PLAY PLUS: 2nd Floor, Day Lewis, 324-340 Bensham Lane, Thornton Heath CR7 7EQ (tel 020-8239 7189; fax 020-8239 7196).

Holiday Playworkers (10+) needed for the summer (5 hour shipfs per day for 3-6 weeks in Croydon area). Wages £4.25 per hour. To assist with play activities and to accompany children on outings. The many duties include preparing play activities and clearing away, preparing and clearing snacks, helping with collection of children from school and generally participating in all the activities involving children and supervising safety. Children aged 4-11 years. Age 18+ with childcare experience.

For *applications* contact Jean Bellinfantie, Accounts Officer at the above address. Must be police checked, give two references and be able to attend interview in June.

THE GROVE: Stone Court Carshalton, Surrey SM5 3AL (tel 020-8770 6616/7; fax 020-8770 6655). Six playschemes for 4-12 year olds run by the London Borough of Sutton.

Assistant Playleaders (30). Up to £6.32 per hour. To work approximately 36 hours a week, Monday to Friday. Relevant experience plus a knowledge and understanding of children's play and care needs aged $4^1/_2$-12 years. Staff required throughout school holidays, approx. 6 weeks in summer (July to September) (also Easter and half term holidays). Min. period of work is the duration of the holiday playscheme. No accommodation provided. Applicants must be available for interview during the 2nd week of April.

Applications asap to Personnel, Learning for Life Group, at the above address or ring 020-8770 6528/9.

HORNIMANS ADVENTURE PLAYGROUND: c/o 1 Bosworth Road, London, W10 5EG (tel 020-8969 5740).

Summer Playworkers (2) to work from 23rd July to 31st August. Playworkers work from 11am-6pm, with some variations, to a total of 36 hours per week, for a wage of £245. Applicants should be over 18 and ideally have skills in drama, arts and crafts and sports.

Applications should be made to Jane Marshall, Joint Playleader at the above

address.
JIGSAW GROUP LTD: 600 Thames Valley Park (tel 0118-9266 277; fax 0118-9662 949; e-mail TVP@jigswaw.com). Jigsaw is a private nursery group providing childcare for children aged 3 months to 5 years. There are 30 units with vacancies for the childcare sector.
Early Years Practitioners (Nursery Nurses). Wages from £10,500-16,000 p.a. pro rata. To work 40 hours per week Monday to Friday.
Early Years Support Worker (Assistant). Wages from £7,500-9,500 p.a. pro rata. To work 40 hours per week or 1-6pm Monday to Friday. Min. period of work of 1 week. Positions are available all year. Appropriate qualifications required (NNEB, NVQ3 or B-Tec equivalent). No accommodation available. Suitably qualified foreign applicants welcome.
Applications should be made as soon as possible to Lesley Hornby at Jigsaw central office (tel 020-8343 8008). Interview necessary.

M. LEVENE: 13 Anthony Road, Borehamwood, Hertfordshire WD6 4NF (tel 020-8386 5912; fax 020-8207 6417; e-mail jollytots2@aol.com).
Au Pair required for July to carry out general au pairing duties. Pocket money of £60 per week, applicants must be at least 18 years old.
Applications should be made to the above address.

LONDON BOROUGH OF HAMMERSMITH AND FULHAM: Education Department, The Town Hall, King Street, London, W6 9JU (tel 0208-8748- 3020 ext 3641; fax 020-8576 5505).
Part time Youth Workers to work in evening youth clubs during term times. Wages approx £9.74 per hour to work Monday to Saturday. Child related qualification or experience of work with children helpful but not essential. Overseas applicants with a work permit welcome. All applicants will be subject to a check for criminal convictions.
Applications can be made at any time to Personnel at the above address.

MRS J. MARBER: 27 Ham Farm Road, Ham Common, Richmond, Surrey TW10 5NA (tel 020-8546 9457).
Au Pair required for an adult family. Duties to include light housework, ironing, washing up and walking the dog. Own bedroom and bathroom provided. Period of work May to October. Minimum stay 3 months. To work 5 hours a day/5 days a week. Position most suitable for a female student: aged 17-25, non-smoker and with a good knowledge of English. Public transport is available in the area.
Applications, including a recent photograph and s.a.e. or IRC, to Mrs J. Marber at the above address.

NORTH HERTFORDSHIRE DISTRICT COUNCIL: Council Offices, Gernon Road, Letchworth, Hertfordshire SG6 3JF (tel 01462-474333; fax 01462-474500).
Playworkers for summer playschemes. Pay rates range from £145 to £200. Duties include general supervision, health and safety, planning of activities and creating a fun and happy environment to play in. All staff work 35 hours a week, Monday to Friday. To work 21 July-27 August, depending on summer holidays. Applicants must be over 18. Experience of working with children aged 5-11 is essential. Teacher/Nursery nurse training/qualifications are an advantage.
Applications to Rebecca Coates.

MRS ROSA PEREIRA: 511 Activity Club, Tottenham Sports Centre, 701-703

Tottenham High Road NI7 8AD (tel 020-8801 1400; fax 020-8801 9360). After school and school holidays programme for supervising and entertaining children; club caters for 45-52 children aged 4-11.

Child Supervisors (2). Duties include local school pick-up, art and craft activities, some cleaning, and child supervising.

Wages start from minimum national wage. To work Monday to Friday; 20 hours per week in term time and 25 to 30 hours in holidays. Min. period of work negotiable. Positions are available around the year. No accommodation available. Applicants need any childcare qualification or a first aid certificate.

Applications to Miss Liz O'Brien at the above address from November 2001. Interview necessary.

PGL TRAVEL LTD: Alton Court, Penyard Lane (874), Ross-on-Wye, Herefordshire HR9 5GL (tel 01989-767883; www.pgl.co.uk/personnel). Over 100 staff needed to assist in the running of activity centres in Surrey. Europe's largest provider of adventure holidays for children has offered outstanding training and work opportunities to seasonal staff for over 40 years.

Qualified Instructors in canoeing, sailing, windsurfing, pony trekking, hill walking, fencing, archery, judo, rifle shooting, fishing, motorsports, arts and crafts, drama, English language and many other activities. Min. age 18 years.

Group Leaders to take responsibility for small groups of children and ensure that they get the most out of their holiday. Min. age 18 years. Previous experience of working with children necessary. From £50-85 per week pocket money and full B & L provided. Vacancies available for short or long periods between February and October.

Requests for application forms to the Personnel Department at the above address.

RUNNYMEDE BOROUGH COUNCIL: Civic Offices, Station Road, Addlestone, Surrey KT15 2AH (tel 01932-425693; fax 01932-855135).

Splash Co-Ordinators (2) to take overall responsibility for organising activity scheme, including managing staff, for a group of 280 children aged 11-16. To work for 3 weeks in August. No accommodation. Hours: 8.45am-5pm Mon-Fri. Supervisory experience preferable.

Splash Instructors (18) to organise activities and supervise off-site coach trips. Dates and hours as above.

Playscheme & Play Plus Scheme Directors (12) to be responsible for organising schemes for 30-60 5-7 year olds and up to 40 8-11 year olds. To work for 4 weeks in August. Hours 9am-4pm Monday to Friday.

Instructors (37) to organise activities on above playschemes and supervise coach trips. 9am-4pm Monday to Friday.

Assistants (20) for the above playschemes. Same hours as for instructors and to assist with same duties.

All posts above are non-residential. No overseas applicants.

Applications to Leisure Development Officer at the above address.

STONY STRATFORD CHILDRENS CENTRE: London Road, Stony Stratford, Milton Keynes MK11 1JQ (tel/fax 01908-562485).

Playworkers (4) to work from July 23rd until 1st September. Hours of work are a minimum of 39 hours spread over various shifts between 8.30am and 6pm, for a wage of £4.60 per hour. Playworkers will set up, organise and supervise a summer playscheme for children aged 4^1/$_2$ to 14. Applicants must be over 18 and enjoy arts and sports activities. Training will be given; Food Hygiene

Certificate, First Aid training and some experience with children are desirable but not essential.

Applications in writing to Tamasine Redman, Playleader at the centre.

WATFORD AREA YOUTH SERVICE: c/o Watford Council, Leggatts Youth Centre, Leggatts Way, Watford WD24 0DT (tel 01923-460538; e-mail stephf44@hotmail.com). Working with young people aged 10-16 from a variety of backgrounds, this local government organisation offer arts, crafts, sports, and leisure-based activities, and issue-based projects.
Staff (10) for summer youth drop-ins. Wages approx. £6.77 per hour. To work Monday to Friday, 12 to 4:30pm for between 4 and 6 weeks. Positions are available from July to August. Applicants should have some experience of working with young people aged 10-16 years. Fluent English essential. Minimum age 18. No accommodation available.

Applications should be made from April onwards to Stephanie Fitzgerald and Ann Shearly at the above address. Interview required. Since police checks are required, it is regretted that only UK applicants may apply.

WOKING LEISURE CENTRE AND POOL IN THE PARK: Woking Park, Kingfield Road, Woking, Surrey GU22 9BA (tel 01483-771122; fax 01483-776005) **Children's Holiday Activity Staff (20)** Wages £4.75 to £5.77; to work from 8.30am to 4.30pm Monday to Friday. Staff needed from 27 July to 31 August. Must be over 18.
Pool Lifeguards (10) Wages £5.19 to £6.31 per hour; to work from 20 June to 10 September. Hours variable over a 7 day period. Must have a national pool lifeguard qualification.

Applications to Jacki Wikeley, Children's Activities Co-ordinator, or the Duty Manager, Pool in the Park.

Holiday Centres and Amusements

BEALE PARK: Lower Basildon, Reading, Berkshire RG8 9NH (tel 0118-9845172; fax 0118-9845171). A non profit-making charitable trust which offers many leisure activities and birdwatching, set in a Thames-side family park in an area of outstanding natural beauty.
Ticket Sellers (2). Wages approx. £4 per hour. To work full and/or part-time over the summer months. No accommodation is available. Period of work May-September. Min. period of work July/August. Some experience in working with the public and handling cash is preferred. Interview necessary.

Applications from May to Andrew Howard.

CHESSINGTON WORLD OF ADVENTURES: Leatherhead Road, Chessington, Surrey KT9 2NE (tel 01372-729560; fax 01372 725050; jobs@chessington.co.uk; www.chessington.com). One of the top theme parks in the South, located off Junction 9/10 of the M25 and accessible via trains from Waterloo to Chessington South.
Ride Operators, Retail Staff, Cleaners, Guest Services, Photography, Catering, Admissions, Security. All staff to work approx. 8-12 hours a day, 5 days a week, overtime available. Wages competitive. Benefits include free uniform, free parking, discounted canteen and possibly 10 free tickets to Tussaud's attractions.

No experience is necessary but you must be enthusiastic and enjoy working as part of a team. EU and Commonwealth nationals welcome. *Apply* to the above address from January.

GREENWICH LEISURE LIMITED: Middlegate House, The Royal Arsenal, Woolwich, London SE18 6SX (tel 020-8317 5000 ext. 4020; fax 020-8317 5021; e-mail gll.hrm@greenwich.gov.uk). The largest leisure centre operator in London, with 26 centres. As a worker-owned and controlled organisation GLL offers opportunities and benefits that far exceed the rest.

Leisure Assistants (many). National Pool Lifeguard qualification an advantage but not essential.

Catering Assistants (20). Experience required.

Kids Activity Instructor (40). No experience required.

Assistant Receptionists (20). Experience required.

Wages of £5.10 per hour for up to 48 hours work per week. Min. period of work of 7 weeks. Positions are available from June to September. Foreign applicants welcome with appropriate permits. Minimum age 18. No accommodation available but can help locate some. Subsidised training courses are also offered to those who want to build a career in the leisure industry.

Applications should be made from early June onwards to Lorraine Patrick, Personnel Department, at the above address. Interview necessary.

LEGOLAND WINDSOR: Winkfield Road, Windsor, Berkshire SL4 4AY (Human Resources Department tel 01753-626150; fax 01753-626143; e-mail jobs@legoland.co.uk). Legoland Windsor is a theme park dedicated to the imagination and creativity of children, where the kids are king. It draws on the inspiration of the world-famous Lego toys and models. The operating season lasts from June to October during which staff are employed in the following positions: **Admission Assistants (20), Food and Beverage Assistants (100), Retail Assistants (50), Rides and Attractions Assistant (100), Environmental Services Assistant (20), Secutity Guard (10), First Aiders (5).** Wages are £4.60 per hour.

To work an average of 40 hours over 5 days (including weekends). Min. period of work of work 6 weeks. Help is available to find accommodation. Fluent English essential. Minimum age 16. No previous experience necessary.

Applicants must have a passion for serving others, an exuberant personality and a natural affinity with children. To be part of the Legoland team staff need to be willing to work hard and have fun whatever the weather (many positions involve working outside).

Applications should be made to Jenny Webb or Lesley Carrothers from February. Interview necessary.

THE LONDON AQUARIUM: County Hall, Westminster Bridge Road, London SE1 7PB (tel 020-7967 8010; fax 020-7967 8029). The biggest aquarium in the UK.

Ticket Office Staff (4), Customer Service Staff (4) required to work between June and September selling entry tickets and dealing with members of the public, including conducting tours and talking about the marine life exhibits. No experience required, just enthusiasm.

Education Assistant to provide administrative support to the Education manager and to supervise the visitor information assistants (guides).

Wages £4.50 per hour. *Applications* to Human Resources at the above address.

MOTIVACTION PLC: Church Farm, Ardeley, Stevenage, Herts, SG2 7AH (tel 01438-861192; fax 01438-861170; e-mail catiem@motivaction.co.uk; www.motivaction.co.uk).

Part Time Casual Event Instructors needed from May to September by this hospitality, incentive and motivational event company. The work involves providing excellent events for client groups and may include quad bike instructing, working with children, and role-playing in themed events. Ideally applicants will be able to work for the entire period (although shorter periods are possible) and the ability to make their own way to Ardeley near Stevenage (Hertfordshire) sometimes as early as 6am is helpful. Pay varies between £40-£100 per day according to skills, ability and level of responsibility, plus a bonus day is paid for every 10 days worked after a 3 month qualifying period.
Contact Catie Muirhead for further details.

THE SHERLOCK HOLMES MUSEUM: 221B Baker Street, London NW1 6XE (tel 020-7738 1269; fax 020-7224 3005; e-mail sherlock-holmes.co.uk; info@sherlock-holmes.co.uk).
Victorian Maids (2) to receive visitors attending the museum. Minimum age 24; knowledge of other languages would be an asset.
Sherlock Holmes Lookalike to dress up as Sherlock Holmes and give out promotional literature to tourists. Must be slim, at least 6' tall and well spoken.
Wages £5 per hour; no accommodation available. Period of work from May to September. *Applications* to Grace Riley, Manager, at the above address.

THORPE PARK: Staines Road, Chertsey, Surrey KT16 8PN (tel 01932-569393; fax 01932-566367; e-mail personnel_thorpe_park@thorpe-park.com; www.thorpepark.com). One of the top theme parks in the South, located off junction 11/13 of the M25 and accessible via British Rail from Waterloo to Staines, a short bus ride will take you to the park.
Staff for shops, rides and attractions, photography, cleaning, catering, admissions, guest services and security. Benefits include a competitive hourly rate and bonus scheme, free uniform, free parking, discounted canteen and after a qualifying period 10 free tickets to most Tussaud's attractions. Period of work by arrangement. Assistance may be given in finding accommodation.
Applications to Human Resources at the above address.

THE TUSSAUDS GROUP, LONDON SITES: c/o Madame Tussauds, Marylebone Road, London NW1 5LR (tel 020-7487 0289; fax 020-7465 0860; www.madame-tussaurds.com). The Tussaud's Group is one of Europe's largest operators and developers of visitor attractions with over 10 million guests a year. The London sites incorporate Madame Tussaud's and the London Planetarium.
Guest Services Assistants, Catering Assistants, Retail Assistants, and Photographers. Positions are available from late June to mid September. Experience in a customer focused environment will be an advantage.
For *applications* please send your CV and covering letter to Human Resources at the above address.

Hotels and Catering
THE BERKELEY: Wilton Place, Knightsbridge, London SW1X 7RL (tel 020-7201 1645; fax 020 7201 1643; e-mail info@the-berkeley.co.uk). The Berkeley is a five star deluxe hotel situated on the corner of Knightsbridge and Wilton Place and has achieved the 'Investor in People' status. It opened in 1972 and has 210 bedrooms, all fully air-conditioned and luxuriously furnished.
Day Room Attendants (5). Wages are approximately £11,000 per annum, pro

rata; to work 40 hours per five-day week. Maids clean 8-11 rooms a day. Good command of English and experience as a room attendant is desirable.

Commis Chefs (4). Wages are approximately £9,000 per annum pro rata; to work 45 hours per five-day week. Duties include assisting other chefs in preparation and service of food, maintaining high standards of hygiene and ensuring tidiness and cleanliness of designated sections.

Minimum period of work is 3 months. Overseas applicants with a good level of spoken English are welcome. An interview is required.

Applications from March to David Naish at the above address.

BLOOMSBURY PARK HOTEL: 126 Southampton Row, London WC1B 5AD (tel 020-7430 0434; fax 020-7242 0665; e-mail HR.Bloomsbury@thistle.co.uk). A 95 bedroom hotel with a restaurant and 2 bars.

Waiting Assistant, Bar Person & Receptionist. Wages £175 per week gross. To work 39 hours a week. Accommodation maybe provided for a short period. Min. period of work 6 months between January and December. Applicants must be over 18. No experience is necessary.

Uniform, meals on duty and on/off-the-job training are provided. Selected staff will attend training courses. Overseas applicants with good English considered.

Applications from February to the Personnel Manager. Interview necessary.

BRIGGENS HOUSE HOTEL: Briggens Park, Stanstead Abbotts, near Ware, Herts. SG12 8LD (tel 01279-829955; fax 01279-793685).

Casual Waiting, Bar And Banqueting Staff. £4.25 per hour. Period of work May to October. Min. age 18 and experience essential. Overseas applicants welcome. Very important; minimum period of work is 6 months.

Applications to the Gail Needham at the above address.

BROCKWELL LIDO LTD: Brockwell Park, Dulwich Road, London (tel 020-7274 3088; fax 020-7924 0232; e-mail evianlido@aol.com or thelido@dial.pipex.co.uk; www.thelido.co.uk). An open-air swimming pool in South London, providing a service to customers 24 hours a day during the summer months.

Chefs and Caterers (6). Wages £6 per hour, limited accommodation available at no charge. To work 30-40 hours per week. Positions are available from June to September. Relevant experience required. Foreign applicants welcome.

Applications should be made from April onwards to Patrick Castledine. Interview necessary.

THE BULL HOTEL: Oxford Road, Gerrards Cross, Bucks SL9 7PA (tel 01753-278804; fax 01753-880116; e-mail kfindlay@saroua.co.uk). 111 bedroom busy hotel. Frequent weddings and functions. Tranquil and picturesque. Many live-in staff. Community spirit.

Housekeeping Staff (5). Wages of £4.08 per hour. 40 hours per week and overtime to be considered. Prefer 18+.

Night Porter. Wages of £5.22 per hour. 40 hours per week and overtime to be considered. Prefer 21+.

Receptionist (2). Wages of £10,500 pa. 40 hours per week. Prefer 18+.

Restaurant Staff (4). Wages of £4.08 per hour. 40 hours per week. Prefer 18+.

Bar Staff (2). Wages of £4.74 per hour. 40+ hours per week. Prefer 21+.

Conference Assistant. Wages of £4.08 per hour. 40 hours per week. 16+.

Duties are various and hotel is very busy. Board and accommodation available for

£35 per week. Min. period of work 3 months. Positions available from April onwards.

Applications should be made to Katherine Findlay from March onwards. Interview required, by telephone if necessary.

CANAL CRUISES: 250 Camden High Street, London NW1 8QS (tel 020-7485 4433; fax 020-7485 9098).

Boat Trip Crew (2) needed from May/June to October for the maintenance, crewing and guiding of canal trip boats. Five hour shifts including evenings and weekends.

Restaurant Boat Waiting Staff (2) same dates and hours as boat trip crew.

Pay by arrangement dependent on age, position and experience. No accommodation provided. Minimum age 18; relevant experience preferred.

Apply to Anne Bodie, Administrator.

CATAMARAN CRUISERS: Embankment Pier, Victoria Embankment, London WC2N 6NN (tel 020-7695 1824; fax 020-7839 1034; e-mail nicola.gilber@bateauxlondon.com or sally.elsdon@bateauxlondon.com). London pleasure boat company operating between central London and Greenwich, providing river cruises with commentary and refreshments.

Hosts/Hostesses (15). Wages £4.66, 5 or 6 days per week. Additional pay may include a 5% loyalty bonus at end of contract and supplementary pay of extra hours. Applicants should be 18+, able to swim, have experience with dealing with the public in front line situation, a positive attitude and a happy smile. Second language an advantage. Min. period of work 2 months. Positions are available from April to October. Foreign applicants with reasonable English welcome. No accommodation available.

Applications to Nicola Gilbert or Sally Esldon at the above address from March onwards. Interview necessary.

THE CROWN HOTEL: 7 London Street, Chertsey, Surrey KT16 8AP (tel 01932-564657; fax 01932-570839). The hotel dates back to Queen Victoria's reign.

Chefs (2), Bar Staff (4), Waiting Staff (3), Receptionist. Pay is negotiable depending on experience. Possibility of accommodation. Work is 5-days split shifts, 39 hours per week.

Applications to D. Fiddes, General Manager.

DOWN HALL HOTEL: Hatfield Heath, Bishop's Stortford, Herts. CM22 7AS (tel 01279-731441; fax 01279-730416; e-mail personnel@downhall.co.uk). A Victorian mansion brimming with charm, style and elegance, with 100 bedrooms.

Waiting Staff (5/6) to work in one of two restaurants; casual work in conference and banqueting also available. Staff needed at any time of year; to work five out of seven days, 8 hours per day. Salary at the equivalent of £8,000 p.a. There is a charge for accommodation. Overtime is paid at the basic rate.

Room Attendant (1-2) to work from June to September. Same terms as waiting staff (see above).

Minimum age for work is 16 years and training will be provided. *Applications* to the Personnel and Training Manager.

EURO PAIR AGENCY: 28 Derwent Avenue, Pinner, Middlesex HA5 4QT (tel 020-8421 2100; fax 020-8428 6416; e-mail europair@btinternet.com; www.euro-pair.co.uk). The agency takes great care in the selection of posts available and has a back-up service if things do not work out.

Hotel Work (50+). Wages of £150 for approx. 8 hours work over five days plus free board and accommodation. Min. period of work of 12 weeks. Positions are available from June to September. Applicants should be 18+, have service industry experience and speak reasonable English. EU applicants are welcome.

Applications should be made from March onwards to Mrs C Burt at the above address. Telephone interview possibly required.

FMC: All England Lawn Tennis and Croquet Club, Church Road, Wimbledon, London SW19 5AE (tel 020-8947 7430; fax 020-8944 6362; e-mail resourcing@fmccatering.co.uk). FMC have grown to be one of the larger outdoor event caterers in Europe. Their portfolio has to contain a full and varied agenda covering some of the most prestigious events in the society calendar including the Volvo PGA Golf Tournament, Wimbledon, the Farnborough Air Show, Cartier Polo, Rugby at Twickenham and numerous other events.

Managers, Chefs, Porters, Food Service Assistants, Silver Service, Plate Waiting & Bar Staff (1,500 In All) needed to work at the Wimbledon Tennis Championships between Saturday 22 June to Sunday 7 July inclusive. There are also spaces on the set up project throughout May. Hours of work and rates of pay are by arrangement. Applicants must be aged at least 18 and have either a National Insurance number or the relevant work permit documents if coming from abroad. For all events applicants should be people who are outgoing and fun loving with good communication skills.

Applicants should contact the Personnel Department at the above address for an *applications* pack.

FRED (UK) 2000 LIMITED: Copthall House, Victoria Road, Aldershot, Hampshire (tel 01252-315544; fax 01252-342727; e-mail freduk2000@ hotmail.com). Specialised recruitment agency.

Catering Staff (5-10). Wages from £5-£18 per hour. Hours vary. Positions are available all year. Positions open depend on qualifications. Foreign applicants entitled to work in the UK and with acceptable spoken English welcome. Accommodation available for some positions.

Applications should be made at any time to a Recruitment Consultant at the above address. Interview necessary, by telephone is sufficient.

GARFUNKELS: 103 Charing Cross Road, London WC2H 0QZ (020-7440 5501; fax 020-7440 5503; e-mail 106404.3075@compuservecom). A restaurant chain with branches in Bath, Cambridge, Sutton, Edinburgh, Glasgow, Heathrow Airport, Gatwick Airport, and all over London.

Waiting Staff and Kitchen Staff. Flexible hours; wages to be arranged. Staff required throughout the year, mainly between June and September. Minimum period of work 3 months. Accommodation not available. Kitchen staff must have good knowledge of food hygiene. Foreign applicants with high standard of spoken English considered. All applicants should be available for interview.

Applications all year round to the Manager of the appropriate branch.

HILTON LONDON METROPOLE: Edgware Road, London W2 1JU (tel 020-7616 6474; fax 020-7616 6471). One of the largest conferencing and banqueting centres in Europe. A cosmopolitan four star hotel with 1,073 bedrooms and 37 meeting rooms in central London.

Waiting Staff (4). £200 per week. Min. age 18. Must have a good command of the English language.

Luggage Porters (2). £170 per week. Must have good customer care skills, smart appearance and a good command of the English language.

Sales Researcher (1). £170 per week. Intelligent and studying for a degree in sales and marketing.

To work 39-50 hours per week. Staff required all year round. No accommodation available. Minimum period of work 6 months.

Applications at any time to the Personnel Department.

HILTON COBHAM: Seven Hills Road South, Cobham, Surrey KT11 1EW (tel 01932-864471; fax 01932-867067). A 155 bedroom busy 4 Star hotel, set in 40 acres of woodland, with 11 conference rooms and leisure club facility.

Food and Beverage Servers to work in the Caffe Cino bar, restaurant and for conferences and banquets. Wages £4.12 per hour (live in), £4.64 per hour (live out). Some experience preferred.

Room Attendants. Wages £3.91 per hour (live in), £4.41 per hour (live out).

All applicants must be 18 over, with a good level of English. All positions are based on 39 hours per week and for a minimum of 6 months. Live in accommodation is subject to availability. Telephone interview sufficient if applicants enclose a photo with their CV

Applications should be addressed to Rachel Holland, Human Resources Manager.

HILTON ST ANNE'S MANOR HOTEL: London Road, Wokingham, Berkshire RG40 1ST (tel 0118-977 2550; fax 0118-977 2526). A four star 180 bedroom luxury conference based hotel, set in 25 acres of gardens.

Bar Persons, Room Attendants, Banqueting/Restaurant Waiting Staff. Wage for all positions approx. £4.50-£5 per hour. To work hours as required. Accommodation may be available for £20 per week, inclusive of bills and food. Min. period of work 6 months. Staff should be at least 18 years old; training will be given. Overseas applicants with good knowledge of English considered.

Applications to Michaela Cassa, HR Manager. An interview is necessary.

HOLIDAY INN BRENT CROSS: Tilling Road, Brent Cross, London NE2 1LP (tel 020-8201 8686; fax 020-8967 6372). Owned by Bass, the hotel is part of the Holiday Inn chain.

Food And Beverage Assistants (2/3) to perform bar and waiting work. Wages £4.25 per hour.

Receptionist (1) to greet and check in guests. Wages £4.25 per hour. Must have hotel reception experience.

All staff work 30-40 hours a week depending on business. Accommodation is available at a cost of £70 per week inclusive. Min. period of work 4 months.

Overseas applicants who are suitably qualified and speak English well are considered. Interview may be necessary if applicants are in the UK. *Applications* to Helen Condell from January.

HOLIDAY INN MAYFAIR: Berkeley Street, London W1J 8NE (tel 020-7493 8282; fax 020-7412 3008). A busy 4 star hotel situated in Mayfair that caters for business and leisure clients.

Room Attendants (5) to clean 14 rooms a day to a high standard. Wages £9,400 per annum. To work 5 days a week according to a rota. No accommodation is available. Min. period of work 6 months all year round.

Commitment and enthusiasm are more important than experience. Overseas applicants with work authorisation are considered. *Applications* should be made after arrival in the UK to the Personnel Department. Interview necessary.

HOTEL INTER-CONTINENTAL: One Hamilton Place, Hyde Park Corner, London (tel 020-7409 3131; fax 020-7495 0973). This 458 bedroomed hotel is considered one of the world's finest five star hotels; situated in the very heart of London, it has impressive views of the Royal Parks.

Food and Beverage Servers. Wages £5 per hour. To work approx. 40 hours per week. Positions are available all year round. Previous experience helpful. Foreign applicants with appropriate qualifications and acceptable spoken English welcome. No accommodation available.

Applications should be made at any time to the Personnel Department at the above address from June. Interview necessary.

THE IMPERIAL LONDON HOTELS LTD: 6 Coram Street, Russell Square, London WC1N 1HA (tel 020-7278 3922; fax 020-7278 9318; e-mail info@imperialhotels.co.uk; www.imperialhotels.co.uk). Group of 6 prestigious hotels based in central London.

Chamber Staff Wages from £165 per week. Shared accommodation and full board available for £117 per week . To work 34 hours per week. Min. period of work of 3 months. Positions are available from June to August. Intermediate English essential. Minimum age 18. No previous experience necessary. Foreign applicants with correct work permits are welcome.

Applications should be made from April onwards to the Personnel Departmnet. References essential.

JARVIS ELCOT PARK HOTEL: Elcot, Newbury, Berkshire RG20 8NJ (tel 01488-658100; fax 01488-658288). A 75 bedroom hotel with 9 conference rooms and a leisure club set in 16 acres of countryside.

Restaurant Attendants (1-2). Wage £3.70 per hour if living in, £4.23 if living out. To work 39 hours over 5 days a week. Accommodation subject to availability at a cost of £20.67 per week (2000 figure). Meals and uniform provided. Paid overtime. Min. period of work 2 months between May/June and August/September.

Applicants must be over 18 with some experience of restaurant work. Interview necessary, but can be conducted over telephone. Overseas applicants entitled to work in the UK considered.

Applications from March to the Personnel and Training Manager.

KENSINGTON POSTHOUSE: Wrights Lane, Kensington, London W8 5SP (tel 0870-400 9000; fax 020-7937 8289). A 550 bedroom hotel serving international professional clients located in central London.

Housekeeping and Waiting Staff. Wages on application for 36^1/2 or 39 hours a week or hours to suit. No accommodation available. Min. period of work 3 months between June and September. Overseas applicants welcome.

Applications from May to the Personnel Officer. Interview necessary.

KENTCHOICE SITE SERVICES: 58 Park Road, Hampton Hill, Middlesex TW12 1HP (tel/fax 020-8941 8900; e-mail kentchoice@aol.com)

Waiting Staff, Bar Staff, Contract Cleaners, Labourers, Chefs And Kitchen Staff aged over 17; details of work by arrangement.

Applicants should contact Mr G. Povey at the abovce address.

LONDON HOSTELS ASSOCIATION LTD: 54 Eccleston Square, London SW1V 1PG (tel 020-7834 1545; fax 020-7834 7146; www.london-hostels.co.uk). Established in 1940, recruits residential staff for 10 London hostels run for young employed people and full-time bona-fide students.

General Domestic Staff to do housework and help in kitchens. Wages by arrangement, paid weekly with B & L provided. Opportunities to attend courses and improve English skills. Hours: average of 30-39 hours per week (mornings and evenings). Min. period of work 3 months throughout the year. Jobs available all year round, long stays welcome. Voluntary jobs also available, working only 20 hours per week in exchange for board and lodging.

Min. age 18 years. Common sense and willingness to tackle variety of jobs required. EC applicants eligible to work in the UK welcome. *Applications* should be sent 2 months before date of availability to the Personnel Manager, London Hostels Association, at the above address.

MAYDAY TEMPORARY CATERING STAFF: See below for addresses. Arranges temporary and permanent catering jobs to suit all levels of experience. Excellent benefits.
Chefs. From £7 per hour.
Waiting Staff. From £5 per hour.
Bar Staff. £5.25 per hour.
Deli Assistants. From £5 per hour.
Kitchen Porters. From £4.75 per hour.
Catering Assistants. From £4.75 per hour.
Silver Service From £6.00 per hour.
Temporary and permanent positions available all year round. Overtime is available for evening and weekend work and employees are paid weekly.

Applicants should telephone any of the offices listed below or come directly to their nearest office from Monday to Thursday between 10am and 12pm: 2 Shoreditch High Street, London E1 6PG (tel 020-7377 6416) (City); 21 Great Chapel Street, Soho, London W1F 8FP (tel 020-7439 3009) (West End). All applicants must have a valid work permit and references.

MAYFAIR INTER-CONTINENTAL HOTEL: Stratton Street, London W1A 2AN (tel 020-7629 7777; fax 020-7629 7504). A 5 star deluxe hotel in London's West End with 290 bedrooms. Part of the Inter-Continental Hotels and Resorts chain.
Waiting Staff (10). Wages £5 per hour plus tips. To work 40 hours a week.

No accommodation is available. Min. period of work 1 month between June and September. All applicants must be over 18 and have a minimum of 6 months previous experience. Overseas applicants with work permits considered. Interview necessary.
Applications to the Personnel Department.

MELIA WHITE HOUSE HOTEL: Albany St, Regents Park, London, SW8 4TX (tel 020-7387 1200; fax 020-7872 0087; e-mail vida.macdermott@ solmelia.com). Sol Media is an international hotel group which has adopted an approach of 'Everything is Possible'.
Waiting and Catering Staff (25), Porters (3), Room maids. Wages from £4.04 to £5.09 per hour. Hours of work vary. Min. period of work is 1 week. Positions are available from April to September. Waiting experience may be required. Accommodation is available for £45 per week.
Applications should be made to the HR Officer at the above address from April onwards.

NATIONAL TRUST ENTERPRISES: c/o Polesden Lacey, Dorking, Surrey RH5 6BD (tel 01372-455033/4; fax 01372-452023; e-mail sensak@

smtp.ntrust.org.uk)
Catering Assistants to work in 15 National Trust properties catering to the general public in West Sussex, Hampshire and Surrey. Wages vary from property to property but will be at least £4.20 per hour. Accommodation not available. Please do not apply if accommodation is required. Working hours vary but may include working over weekends and bank holidays. Experience of working in the catering industry and basic food hygiene are desirable but not essential; full training will be given.

Those interested should *contact* Sue Knevett, Regional Catering Manager or Sylvia Raynor at the above address who will refer them to an appropriate property.

THE NATIONAL TRUST: Regional Office, Hughenden Manor, High Wycombe, Bucks HP14 4LA (tel 01494-755515; fax 01494-463310).
Tea-Room Catering Manager to work for the National Trust at Greys Court, near Henley-on-Thames, Oxfordshire. Wages on application. Position available from March until 30th September. Hours are based on a contracted 39 hours per week including Wednesday to Saturday and Bank Holidays. Relevant cooking experience for preparing home-made cakes and biscuits, but formal cooking qualification not essential.

Apply to Lynn Hamilton, Personnel, at the above address.

NORFOLK PLAZA HOTEL: 29/33 Norfolk Square, London W2 1RX (tel 020-7723 0792; fax 020-7224 8770; e-mail enquiries@norfolkplazahotel.co.uk). An 87 bedroom, 3 Star hotel by Paddington Station in London W2. The majority of clients are Europeans on short leisure breaks in London, with a mixture of local UK Corporate customers. The hotel employs approx. 40 staff.
Hotel Receptionists. Wages £50 (gross) per 8-hour shift, with 5 shifts per week, plus weekly tips. Uniforms and other benefits provided free but no accommodation available. Period of work June to end of September. Min. age 20. Applicants must be able to speak fluent English; knowledge of another Western European language would be an advantage. Experience of working on a computer database system and telephone switchboard essential. Overseas applicants welcome. Two weeks' training will be provided for successful applicants.

Applications should be sent to Mr Ali Muttawa, General Manager, at the above address.

ROYAL GARDEN HOTEL: 2-24 Kensington High Street, London, W8 4PT (tel 020-7361 1944; fax 020-7361 1914; e-mail emmabailes@royalgdn.co.uk).
Room Attendants (10) to clean 12 rooms a day between 8am-4.30pm, 5 days a week on a rota basis. Wages £150 per week. Staff are required from June until the end of September.

Applications should be sent to Emma Bailes, Personnel Administrator, at the above address.

SAVOIR FAIRE (MARQUEES) LTD: Essex Place, Finings Road, Lane End, High Wycombe, Bucks. HP14 3EY (tel 01494-883663; fax 01494-883553; e-mail party@savoirfaire.co.uk; www.savoirfaire.co.uk).
Marquee Erectors (Up To 10) needed from April to September. To work Monday to Friday from 8am to 5 or 6pm plus occasional weekend work at time and a half. Wages from £4.30 p.h. with occasional tips. Must be sociable, work well in a small team, preferably strong and at least five feet eight inches in height. No accommodation available.

Applications to Richard Hall, Managing Director, at the above address.

SELFRIDGE HOTEL: Orchard Street, London W1H 6JS (tel 020-7408 2080; fax 020-7493 7590; e-mail hr.selfridge@thistle.co.uk; www.thistle.com).
Waiting Staff (2) to work in the hotel's busy Orchard Terrace brasserie-style restaurant; plate service. Wages of £170 per week plus gratuities. To work 6.30am-3pm or 3-11.30pm, 5 days out of 7. Applicants should have 6 months' previous waiting experience, good social skills and be smart and presentable. Must be available for 6 months minimum. No accommodation available.
Applications to Human Resources at the above address.

THAMES LUXURY CHARTERS Ltd: on board HMS Belfast, Tooley Street, London, SE1 2JA (tel 020-7378 1211; fax 020-7378 1359; e-mail belinda@livetts.co.uk).
Silver Service And Bar Staff (20) required to work on board vessels on the Thames for corporate hospitality events. Hours of work are variable, but mostly evening work; wages from £6.25 per hour plus tips.
Applicants must have previous experience, a good command of English and like boats. *Applications* to Belinda Livett, Company Secretary.

THISTLE MARBLE ARCH HOTEL: Bryanston Street, Marble Arch, London W1A 4UR (tel 020-7629 8040; fax 020-7629 0628).
Waiting Staff. Experience in catering essential.
Bartender. Min. age 18 years. Bar experience essential.
All staff to work 20-40 hours a week in shifts. Wages approx. £4.70 gross per hour. Some uniform provided, all meals on duty provided. Work offered at all times of the year. Must have excellent presentation. Overseas applicants considered, provided they speak fluent English. All applicants must be available for interview.
Applications at any time to Human Resources Manager at the above address.

THISTLE VICTORIA: 101 Buckingham Palace Road, London SW1W 0SJ (tel 020-7834 9494; fax 020-7868 6293). An elegant 364-bedroomed hotel with 7 conference rooms, restaurant and bar located near London's West End.
Front of House and Food and Beverage Staff (5) who are excellent customer-orientated team players. Wages from £5 to £8 per hour, working a 39 hour week. Applicants must be 18 with leisure and tourism experience with accommodation available for the right candidates. Minimum stay is 1 year with NVQ Qualifications being offered and all nationalities welcome.
Applications to the the Human Resources Department at the above address.

THISTLE WESTMINSTER HOTEL: 49 Buckingham Palace Road, London SW1W 0QT (tel 020-7834 1821; fax 020-7931 7542; e-mail westminster@thistle.co.uk). A four star central London hotel, with 134 bedrooms, a brasserie style restaurant and a popular bar.
Waiting Staff (2) to wait at tables. Wage £175 per week plus tips. To work 39 hours over 5 days a week. Shared accommodation available at a cost of approx. £47.50 per week. Min. period of work 3 months between end of June and end of September.
Applicants must be over 18. Experience not necessary, but interview required. Overseas applicants with excellent English considered.
Applications in March/April to the Human Resources Department.

VINCENT HOUSE: 5 Pembridge Square, London W2 4EG (tel 020-7229 1133). Residential club for business people.
General Assistants required to help with housekeeping, restaurant and porterage. Wages £93.70-£115.20 per week, dependent on age, plus free B & L. To work average of 32 hours per week. Applicants should be 18 or over. Work available all year round but employment is for a minimum period of 4 months. Overseas applicants welcome.
Applications to Mr R. Tomkins, Vincent House.

WOODLANDS PARK: Woodlands Lane, Stoke D'Arbernon, Cobham, Surrey KT11 3QB (tel 01372-843933; e-mail gm.woodlands@arcadianhotels.co.uk).
Hotel Staff to work 40 hours a week. Wages from £4.30 an hour; company discounts. Uniform provided. Minimum period of work 6 months all year round. All positions are live-in. Overseas applicants with a high standard of English welcome.
Applications at any time to Human Resources Department at the above address.

Language Schools

ANGLOSCHOOL: 146 Church Road, London, SE19 2NT (tel 020-8653 7285; fax 020-8653 9667; e-mail english@angloschool.co.uk).
Part Time Guides (1 or 2) to work in July and August. 3 or 4 hours of work per afternoon for 7 weeks. The work involves showing adult students around London and helping with leisure activities, wages are £130-£140 per week. Guides must know London well and be confident; good organisers and keen sportspeople preferred.
Applications to John Adams, Principal, at the above address.

EJO Ltd: Passfield Business Centre, Lynchborough Road, Passfield, Liphook GU30 7SB (tel 01428-751993; e-mail ed@ejo.co.uk)
Course Directors, Senior Teachers, Teachers required for residential and non-residential courses. Course Directors and Senior Teachers need teaching experience, an MA or a TEFL/TESOL diploma (RSA or Trinity). Teachers need to have CELTA/Trinity TESOL qualification.
Activity Staff required for non-residential and residential courses to work 5-6 days per week. Applicants should be studying towards or graduates in a sports qualification.
Staff are required for Easter, June, July and August, with pay varying according to qualifications and experience.
Applications to The Education Department, at the above address.

EUROACCENTS/YOUTH SERVICE SCHOOLS: 16/20 New Broadway, London W5 2XA (tel 020-8566 2188; fax 020-8566 2011; e-mail languages@euroaccents.co.uk). Organises language courses (mainly English) for foreign students. In addition to accommodation and tuition, students are offered a full programme of daily activities.
Social Organisers (1/2). Wages £150-£230 per week. To work long hours. Min. period of work 8-10 weeks between April/mid May and the end of August. Accommodation available.
Applicants should be aged 20-25. Experience is useful but not necessary. Overseas applicants with good English considered. Interview necessary.
Applications from January/February to Mr G. Gerosa.

FRANCES KING SCHOOL OF ENGLISH: 5 Grosvenor Gardens, London SW1W 0BB. A large language school located on 4 sites in Central London. Their Students come from all over the world, particularly Italy and Spain during the summer months.

English Language Teachers (30) to teach up to 30 hours per week at various centres, plus optional leading of groups and taking part in activities with students; residential centres may require extra duties. Pay on an hourly basis, with accommodation included at centres outside London. Period of work from the first week of July-last week of August. Must hold RSA/Cambridge TEFL certificates plus a minimum of one years experience.

Applications to R. Stewart, Director of Studies, at the above address.

HAMPSTEAD SCHOOL OF ENGLISH: 553 Finchley Road, Hampstead, London NW3 7BJ (tel 020-7794 3533; fax 020-7431 2987; e-mail info@hampstead-english.ac.uk). The school has an average of 350 foreign students, and enjoys a reputation for excellence. Staff pride themselves on treating each student as an individual.

Student Group Leaders (6-8) to guide foreign language students around London and take care of them while on route to and during their evening engagements. Wages of £6.00 per hour (negotiable); flexible hours ranging from 15 to 40 hours over mainly afternoons and evenings. Work would suit undergraduates aged 19 and over who have successfully completed at least one year of a university course. Work is available from last week of June to the end of August, to early September 8. Applicants should be energetic, enthusiastic and like dealing with people. No accommodation provided.

Applications to Kevin McNally, Principal, at the above address. Applicants must be available for interview.

HARVEN SCHOOL OF ENGLISH: The Mascot, Coley Avenue, Woking, Surrey GU22 7BT (tel 01483-770969; fax 01483-740267; e-mail harven.school@btinternet.com). A private organisation providing full-time intensive courses in English as a foreign language with a comprehensive social programme for adults and juniors in pleasant surroundings.

Qualified EFL Teachers (10), Sports/Social Assistants (2) to work for an English language school in June, July and August. Salary according to qualifications and experience; no accommodation provided. To work from Monday-Friday or Saturday from 9.30am-4pm approx. and some evenings for the social programme. Applicants should have relevant qualifications and experience.

Applications to the Director of Studies, at the above address.

INTERNATIONAL COMMUNITY SCHOOL: 21 Star Street, London, W2 1QB (tel 020-7402 0416; fax 020-7724 2219; e-mail bmurrayskola@aol.com).

EFL Teachers (10-15) to work between the start of June and the end of August. Hours of work are full-time, 9am-4.30pm, for wages of £290-£340 per week. Staff should have CELTA/DELTA/PGCE and preferably experience of teaching young learners.

Social Organiser (1-2) required for full-time work in July and August. Wages are £300 per week and applicants must have experience of organising social activities for teenagers.

Applications to Chrys Zisimov-Cowley, Director of Studies, at the school.

KING'S SCHOOL OF ENGLISH (LONDON): 25 Beckenham Road, Beckenham, Kent BR3 4PR (tel 020-8650 5891; fax 020-8663 3224; e-mail info@kingslon.co.uk; kingslon.co.uk). The only all year round recognised school in Beckenham. Takes around 150-250 students from all over the world. Established in 1966.

EFL Teachers (Approx 10) to work from mid June to end of August for 16-32 lesson per week programmes (min 4 weeks) mainly for learners aged over 16. Only RSA Cambridge qualified applicants to apply from January.

Travel Manager & Assistant for the organisation of leisure programme including evening work and weekends, and airport transfers. Must have a good knowledge of attractions in London and South East England. Knowledge of Italian or Spanish or Russian an advantage. Suitably qualified overseas applicants with good English considered. Interview essential.

Salaries by negotiation. Applicants must be EU Citizens or have work permits. *Applications* to the Principal at the above address.

LANGUAGE LINK: 21 Harrington Road, London SW7 3EU (tel 020-7225 1065; fax 020-7584 3518; e-mail languagelink@compuserve.com). Language Link is accredited by the British Council and is a member of ARELS.

EFL Teachers (5). Pay is dependent on qualifications and experience. Monday-Friday. To work from end of June to the end of August. Applicants must be Cambridge, Trinity or equivalent TEFLA certified. No accommodation is available.

Applications from June to the Director of Studies at the above address. An interview is required.

MARBLE ARCH INTENSIVE ENGLISH: 21 Star Street, London W2 cQB(tel 020-7402 9273/4; fax 020-7724 2219). Long established language school; also runs CELTA teacher training courses.

EFL Teachers to teach classes of 15 adults or 20 children. Wages starting at £11.55 per hour. To work Monday to Friday, 15 hours (part-time) or 25 hours (full-time). Min. period of work of 4 weeks. Positions are available from late June to early September. CELTA or TRINITY certificate required. Experience preferred but not essential. No accommodation available.

Applications to David Riddell at the above address from Easter onwards. Interview necessary.

OISE YOUTH LANGUAGE SCHOOLS: OISE Youth Language Schools, Newbury Hall, Enborne Road, Newbury RG14 6AD (tel 01635-36891; fax 01635-48400; e-mail yloise@btclick.com). Work available throughout Britain.

Teachers to teach English as a foreign language to small groups of foreign students. Must be qualified EFL teachers with experience.

Academic Directors. Qualified EFL teachers with organisational ability.

Leisure Directors to run a pre-planned leisure programme and teach half a timetable.

Period of work Easter and July/August. Applicants must be graduates and native English speakers. Some residential courses available. *Details* from the Recruitment Administrator, OISE.

OXFORD HOUSE COLLEGE: 28 Market Place, Oxford Circus, London W1W 8AW (tel 020-7580 9785; fax 020-7323 4582; e-mail fiona@oxfordhouse.co.uk). A leading British Council accredited college in central London providing English, Computing, Travel and Tourism and teacher training courses.

EFL Teachers And EFL Teacher/Trainers required to work for a minimum period of 2 weeks or throughout the year. Applicants must be TESOL/TEFL certified.

Applications at any time to Fiona Balloch at the above address.

SELS SCHOOL OF ENGLISH: 64 Long Acre, Covent Garden, London WC2E 95X (tel 020-7240 2581; fax 020-7379 5793; e-mail english@sels.co.uk; www.sels.co.uk). Located in fashionable Covent Garden near the Opera House, the school teaches English at all levels to foreign adults in groups of 5-9 and on a one-to-one basis.

Assistant to work in the tea room and clean premises. Wages £4.50 per hour. To work 5-9 hours per day, Monday to Friday and alternate weekends. Period of work by arrangement. Ages: 18-30 years. Knowledge of Portuguese, Spanish or Italian useful.

Clerks/Secretaries. £6+ per hour. To work approx. 20-40 hours per week. Must have typing and word processing experience.

Long period of employment preferred. *Applications* to Mr Y. Raiss, Sels School of English, at the above address.

SUPERSTUDY UK: 1-3 Manor Parade, Sheepcote Road, Harrow HA1 2JN (tel 020-8861 5322; e-mail superstudy.london@btinternet.com; www.superstudy.uk). Teaches all levels of English to all nationalities, specialising in general English and conversation in a friendly atmosphere. Five minutes walk from Harrow-on-the-Hill Underground station.

EFL Teachers (2-4). from £12.23 per hour, exact hours of work to be arranged. Minimum period of work 2-4 weeks between 1 July and 31 August. Accommodation not available. RSA/UCLES, CTEFLA and first degree required.

Applications as early as possible to Iain Tebb at the above address.

TASIS ENGLAND AMERICAN SCHOOL: Coldharbour Lane, Thorpe, Surrey TW20 8TE. Set in 35 acres; approx. 30 minutes train journey from London, the school runs a summer programme for American and International students.

Counsellors. To supervise sports and activities such as visits and trips all over England, and act as teaching aides. Driving licence necessary.

Teachers. To teach English as a foreign language and traditional high school maths and English courses. Must be familiar with the American educational system. Wages according to relevant experience. Room and board provided. Applicants must have a standard of English as high as that of a native speaker and have completed at least one year at university.

Applications, including CV, should be sent by 15 March to Mr David West, Director of Summer Programmes, at the above address.

YOUTH SERVICE SCHOOL: 16/20 New Broadway, Ealing, London W5 2XA (tel 020-8566 2188; fax 020-8566 2011; e-mail cristina@euroaccents.co.uk).

EFL Teachers (15) wanted to work from mid-June to the end of August. Teaching duties are for 3 hours per day Monday-Friday, with the possibility of helping with the social programme in the afternoons. Wages of £8.50-£10 per hour. Applicants must have RSA, CTEFLA/CELTA, or Trinity College TESOL.

Applications to Cristina Hyde, Principal, at the above address.

Medical

ALLIED HEALTHCARE GROUP: Hollytree Cottage, Bryants Bottom Road, Great Missenden, Buckinghamshire HP16 OJS (tel 01494-488040/1; fax 01494-488650; e-mail highwycombe@alliedhealthcare.com). Nursing agency.
Health Care Assistants (100) needed for work in the community, hospitals and nursing homes. Wages £6.75 per hour. Positions are available all year.
Applications should be made to Mrs Vanessa Cracknell. Interview necessary.

ANCHOR CARE ALTERNATIVES: 206 Worple Road, Wimbledon, London SW20 8PN (tel 020-8946 8202; fax 020-8944 7431). Cares for the elderly and disabled in their own homes throughout the UK.
Live-In Care Workers. Wages from £5.78 per hour.
Daily Care Workers. Wages from £262.80 per week.
Staff required all year round to care for mainly housebound people. Minimum period of work 1-3 months. Duties include personal care, cooking, housekeeping, laundry, shopping and companionship. Overseas applicants authorised to work in the UK welcome. Applicants must be friendly with a caring attitude.
Applications 2-3 weeks before work is required to the Senior Area Manager at the above address.

EUROPEAN NURSING AGENCY LTD: Smallford Works, Smallford Lane, St Albans AL4 O5A (tel 01727-825000; fax 01727-825005; e-mail jobs@ena.co.uk).
Live-in Care Assistants. to work one-to-one at home for busy young adults disabled by car accidents etc. The clients lead busy lives and enjoy going to the cinema, pub etc; help also needed with personal care, washing, dressing etc. Wages from £318-£400, board and accommodation included. To work various hours. Min. period of work of 3 months around the year. Positions are available all year. Applicants should be 21+; previous experience and a clean driving licence are advantages.
Applications should be made at any time to Recruitment at the above address.

FRED (UK) 2000 LIMITED: Copthall House, Victoria Road, Aldershot, Hampshire (tel 01252-315544; fax 01252-342727; e-mail freduk2000@ hotmail.com). Specialised recruitment agency.
Care and Nursing Staff (17). Wages from £6.45-£50 per hour. To work shifts. Min. period of work of 1 week. Positions are available all year. Positions open depend on qualifications. Foreign applicants entitled to work in the UK and with acceptable spoken English welcome. Accommodation available for some positions.
Applications should be made at any time to a Recruitment Consultant at the above address. Interview necessary, by telephone is sufficient.

KELLS NURSES BUREAU: 43 The Grove, London N13 5LP (tel 020-8886 6589; fax 020-8886-6168).
Care Assistants (30-40) needed from May to September to work with elderly and frail people in local authority residential homes in North and Central London. Shifts are from 7.30am-2pm and from 1.30-9pm. Wages are from £6 p.h. (£7 at weekends). Minimum age is 20 and experience of working in a similar post for at least 6 months is essential; the work is particularly suitable to nursing and medical students.
Applications should be sent to Michael Ganeski, the Manager.

Office Work

STRATEGY RESEARCH AND ACTION: Parkway house, Sheen Lane, London SW14 8LS (tel 020-8878 1482; fax 020-8876 1204; e-mail robinbirn@cs.com) An international marketing and research consultancy concerned with publishing and food distribution.
Research Assistants (2) Wages by negotiation. To work 7 hours a day, 7 days a week. Applicants must have studied/be studying business. Research assistants are needed all year round.
Applications should be addressed to Robin J Birn and sent to the above address. An interview is required.

Outdoor

ALRESFORD MARQUEES: Ashdell Farm, Headmore Lane, GU34 3ES (tel 01420-587444; fax 01420-587444).
Marquee Labourers (3) needed from May onwards. £55 per day. Long hours, hot work, good laughs. Must be over 17 years old.
Applications to the above address.

BUCKS WIGWAMS: Ibstone, near High Wycombe, Buckinghamshire HP14 3XT (tel 01491-638227).
Marquee Erectors (5) wanted for the summer period until the end of November to put up marquees in the Thames Valley area. Working hours are 8am-5pm with some overtime and weekend work, for wages of between £4.50-£6 per hour according to age and experience. Employees must be over 18 with own transport and physically fit.
Applications should be made in writing to Mr W.M. King, Manager.

CAM VALLEY PLUMS: 39 Chiswick End, Meldreth, Royston, Herts. SG8 6LZ (tel 01763-262964/260332; fax 01763-260332; e-mail camvalley.plums@ virgin.net).
Fruit Pickers (6) for work in September. Wages at piece-work rates; to work 5-7 days per week. Caravan accommodation available. Applicants must be aged 18 and over. Applicants must be students authorised to work in the UK.
Applications to T.J. Elbourn, Manager, at the above address.

DIALOGUE DIRECT LTD: www.jobs.dialoguedirect.co.uk; email: mailto: jobs@ dialoguedirect.co.uk; tel: 07966 343039. A successful international fundraising agency working on behalf of charities and NPOs. Currently raising donations for Greenpeace in the UK, Dialogue will be working with other charities in the near future. Work available year-round with the main campaign in summer months.
Dialoguers. Expenses plus an average of £250 per week. All candidates start as face-to-face fundraisers, communicating directly with the public. Minimum period of work 5 weeks. London-based. Flexible working hours, 6 days per week.
Team Drivers: Fast progression for the right candidate to Team Guide. Dialogue has an in-house training and certification programme (4 modules including self-management, negotiation and team management).
Candidates must have a positive and flexible attitude towards work and team-life, excellent communication skills and a commitment to the aims of the organisation.
Overseas applicants with fluent English and a working visa welcome, particularly those from New Zealand, Australia, America and South Africa. (Also live-in, UK

mobile teams).

Applications should be made by e-mail or to the above telephone number.

INTENTS MARQUEES CO: Laplands Farm, Brill, Aylesbury, Bucks HP18 9T2 (tel 01844-238466; fax 01844-238870) A family run group operating up to around 50 miles from the base.

Marquee Erectors (6) Wages £5 per hour, minimum £40 per week. Applicants must be over 18, strong and fit, preferably with a driving licence. Foreign applicants are welcome but must speak good English. Accommodation is available.

Staff are needed from Easter to September for a minimum of 1 week.

Applications to Mr James Borgnis from January 1st at the above address.

MAIN EVENTS: MPR House, Island Farm Avenue, West Molesey Trading Estate, West Molesey, Surrey KT8 0UZ (tel 020-8941 2411; fax 020-8941 4710). **Staff (up to 10)** required to set up and man inflatable equipment including bouncy castles at events, activity days etc. £5 per hour. Work is on an ad hoc basis; hours and dates cannot be guaranteed but depend upon company's contracts at a particular time. Min. age 21. Must be able to deal with people and have a sense of fun. First-aid qualification an advantage. No accommodation available; applicants should ideally live locally. Overseas applicants with a good level of English welcome. If possible applicants should be able to attend an interview.

Applications at any time to Mr James Feary, Main Events.

MERIDIAN MARQUEES: Avoca, Church Lane, Three Mile Cross, Reading, RG7 1HB (tel 0118-988 7660; fax 0118-988 7661; e-mail meridian@ankerbold.co.uk).

Marquee Erectors (6) wanted between June and September for wages of £5.50-£6 per hour, extensive overtime offered. Hours and other details by arrangement.

Applications to M. James, Partner.

E.W. MORRIS Home Bush, Brox Lane, Ottershaw, Surrey KT16 0LN (tel 01932-873050). Small scale herb grower.

Harvesting Staff(2). Piecework. To work 5^1/2 days per week including Sunday morning. Positions are available from June to October. No accommodation available.

Applications should be made from mid-May onwards to Jane Morris at the above address. Interview necessary.

Sport

BRAY LAKE WATERSPORTS: Monkey Island Lane, Windsor Road, Maidenhead, Berks SL6 2EB (tel 01628-638860; fax 01628-771441; e-mail braylake@msn.com). Set next to a 60 acre lake ideal for beginners and intermediate windsurfers, sailors and canoeists. This popular centre caters for adults and juniors. The centre has a good range of equipment for teaching, hire and demo.

Seasonal Watersports Instructors (8) to teach windsurfing, sailing and canoeing. Required from June/July to September to instruct adults and juniors in windsurfing, sailing and canoeing 5 days a week. Wages dependant on qualifications. Instructors should hold RYA Windsurfing, RYA Sailing or BCU Canoeing Instructor's Certificates.

Applications should be sent to Simon Frost, Director.

BROCKWELL LIDO LTD: Brockwell Park, Dulwich Road, London (tel 020-7274 3088; fax 020-7924 0232; e-mail evianlido@aol.com or thelido@dial.pipex.co.uk; www.thelido.co.uk). An open-air swimming pool in South London, providing a service to customers 24 hours a day during the summer months.

Lifeguards (12). Wages £5/£6 per hour, limited accommodation available at no charge. To work 30-40 hours per week. Positions are available from June to September. NPLQ or equivalent qualification required. Foreign applicants welcome.

Applications should be made from April onwards to Patrick Castledine. Interview necessary.

CHARLIE MANN RACING LTD: Whitcoombe House Stables, Upper Lambourn, Hungerford, Berkshire RG17 8RA (tel 01488-71717; fax 01488-73223; e-mail charlie.mann@virgin.net).

Stable Lads/Girls (2) wanted between May and September. Work entails mucking out, riding, grooming and leading up at races. Hours of work are Monday-Friday 6am-12pm, 4-6pm and Saturday 6am-12pm, alternate weekends are Sat 4-5.30pm, Sun 8am-10.30am, 4-5pm. Wages are between £200-£235 per week before tax.

Applicants must be over 18, competent riders and experienced with horses.

Applications should be sent to Nicole Rossa, Secretary at the above address.

CONTESSA RIDING CENTRE: Willow Tree Farm, Colliers End, Ware, Hertfordshire SG11 1EN (tel 01920-821 792/496; fax 01920-821496; e-mail contessariding@c.s.com; www.contessa-riding.com). A riding school and competition yard with a particular interest in dressage. Set in a rural area 30 miles north of London, with easy access to Cambridge and Stansted Airport. Has a large indoor and outdoor school and highly qualified staff.

Stable Helpers to perform general yard duties including mucking out, grooming, tack cleaning and horse handling. Horses range from novice to grand prix standard. Pocket money, riding and self-catering accommodation are provided. To work from 8am-5pm (beginning at 8.30am on two days) over 5 1/2 days per week. Applicants must be aged 17; qualifications and experience preferred.

To work throughout the year, especially around the holiday periods. Minimum period of work two months. Applicants preferably should be available for an interview and must apply with references. Brochures available.

Applications are welcome year round to Tina Layton at the above address.

EXSPORTISE INTERNATIONAL LTD: PO Box 402, Redhill, Surrey, England RH9 8YQ (tel 01342-892899; fax 01342-892898; email info@exsportise.co.uk; www.exsportise.co.uk). Founded by Olympic gold medallist Steve Batchelor, Exsportise runs specialised sport and language holidays for children aged 8-18.

Hockey, Tennis, Cricket, Golf, Swimming, Football And Rugby Coaches. £100-£300 per week plus B & L. Qualifications essential. Applicants must be willing to work all hours and organise evening entertainment. Opportunity to make extra money by doing airport pick-ups.

Pastoral Carers And Administrative Staff needed. £120-£500 per week.

Period of work 6 weeks between July and August, and during the Easter and Christmas holidays. Interviews will be held.

Applications to the Course Co-ordinator at the above address.

FRENCH BROTHERS LTD: The Clewer Boathouse, Clewer Court Road, Windsor, Berks SL4 5JH (tel 01753-851900; fax 01763-832303; e-mail info@boat-trips.co.uk). French Brothers are a prestigious Thames passenger boat operator with 14 all-weather vessels operating on the Upper Thames from Windsor to Runnymede and to Henley, Maidenhead, Staines and Hampton Court. This family run business incorporates a well-established outside catering company.

Boat Crew (6) to keep boats clean and tidy and work with skipper handling boats and customer care. Five to six days work a week and some nights.

Catering Assistants and Bar Staff (6) for food preparation and serving, five to six days and some nights. Duties to include outside catering and waiting. Cash handling experience preferred.

Applications should be made to the above address.

GREAT FOSTERS HOTEL: Stroude Road, Egham, Surrey TW20 9UR (tel 01784-433822; fax 01784-472455; www.great.fosters.co.uk). A four star privately owned historic hotel with period bedrooms and superb banqueting facilities. Close to London with excellent train links.

Swimming Pool Attendants (2) to work 5 days per week, 9am-6.30pm, between May 1st and September. Wages to be negotiated, with accommodation available. Candidates should be over 18, good swimmers and holders of Bronze Medallion in Life Saving.

Hall Porter(1) to work 5 days per week, shift work. Wages negotiable, accommodation available.

Applications to Angela Collins, Assistant Manager, at the above address.

GREEN LANE RIDING STABLES: Green Lane, off Garth Road, Lower Morden, Surrey SM4 6SE (tel 020-8337 3853; fax 020-8337-8383; www.greenlaneriding.co.uk). A BHS approved riding school. Majority of pupils are children, lots of school riding activities and the opportunity to ride young horses.

Riding Teacher (1) Work involves mostly teaching and general yard duties; riding is available. Wages are according to experience; to work either full-time or part-time. Applicants must either have BHSAI qualification or be very experienced with children.

Staff are required from mid July to end of August and must work during the school holidays. Suitably qualified applicants are welcome to apply. *Applications* should be sent to Natalie Donald from mid June onward. Interview is necessary.

LEE VALLEY WATERSPORTS CENTRE: Banbury Reservoir, Harbet Road, London E4 8QB (tel 020-8531 1129; fax 020-8527 0969; e-mail watersports@leevalleypark.org.uk). The centre runs a schools programme in conjunction with a commercial watersports operation.

Seasonal & Relief Instructors (2-4) to teach windsurfing, dinghy sailing and waterskiing. Wages and working hours by arrangement. Needed for work between May 1-October 31st. Applicants must be aged at least 18 and need a relevant national governing qualification and knowledge of first aid.

Applications to Peter T. Stephenson, Site Manager, at the above address.

QUADRON RUSHMOOR LTD: Aldershot Pools Complex, Guildford Road, Aldershot, Hampshire GU12 4BP (tel 01252-322750; fax 01252-316499).

Lifeguards (15) needed from 24th May-10th September. Wages are currently £4.33-£4.60 per hour but a pay award is pending. Potential employees must have National Pool Lifeguard Qualification or Bronze Medallion, and First Aid skills

would be helpful.
Applications should be made in writing to A.P. Dudley at the above address.

Voluntary Work

Children

CHILDREN'S COUNTRY HOLIDAYS FUND (CCHF): 42-43 Lower Marsh, London SE1 7RG (tel 020-7928 6522; fax 020-7401 3961; e-mail clare@childrensholidays-cchf.org).
CCHF is a registered Charity that has been providing holidays for London children in need since 1884. One of the aspects of CCHF's work is to run residential summer activity holidays. These activity holidays provide a variety and balance of activities designed to meet the needs of all the children on them.
Volunteers (Aged 18 Upwards) needed during the school summer holidays to work as Camp Supervisors, looking after small groups of children (aged 8-12) under the guidance of an experienced Camp Leader. Relevant experience desirable although full training will be given. Supervisors are responsible for the care and welfare of children in their group for the duration of the camp. A camp lasts for 7 days, on a variety of dates in July and August and are held in residential centres in the south of England.
Accommodation, board, insurance, travel and pocket money are provided. To ensure the safety of the children, applicants must have been residents of England or Wales for five years to enable Police and Social Service checks to be made of them. *Applications* by May at the latest.

THE CHILDREN'S TRUST: Tadworth Court, Tadworth, Surrey KT20 5RU (tel 01737-365038-9; fax 01737-373848).
Offers care, treatment, and education to approx. 80 children with exceptional needs and profound disabilities, and gives support to their families.
The Trust requires **Volunteers** to work on a residential summer scheme for profoundly disabled and exceptional needs children. The services are provided in a number of specialised nursing and therapeutic child care units and at a residential school. The work involves acting as a friend to the children, carrying out basic personal care, organising games, encouraging them to take an active part in daily activities, escorting them on outings and organising evening activities.
Previous experience with children or handicapped children is preferable, but not essential. Only those wishing to go into the caring profession should apply. Creative skills, handicraft or musical ability welcomed. The work is very rewarding but is also physically and emotionally tiring. 9 volunteers are appointed each year. Minimum age 18. To work a $37^1/2$ hour week with 2 days off per week. Mid July to first week in September. Students are expected to stay for the duration of the scheme. Accommodation is provided free of charge and an allowance of £51 per week is paid. Travel expenses within mainland England will be paid. Apply before 31 March to Rachel Turner at the above address.
The Residential School also requires volunteers for 6 to 12 months to assist with the daily routine of physical care and education of the children in both the residential home and school. Under the guidance of teachers, therapists and senior care staff, work as part of an interdisciplinary team on the individual planned programmes for the children. Minimum age 18, to work a $37^1/2$ hour week, 2 days

off per week. Accommodation is provided free of charge and an allowance of £51 per week is paid. Travel expenses within England can be reimbursed.

Applications to Rachel Turner, Voluntary Services Manager.

Conservation and the Environment

CORAL CAY CONSERVATION LTD: The Tower, 13th Floor, 125 High Street, Colliers Wood, London, SW19 2JG (tel 0870-750 0668; fax 0870-750 0667).

Recruits paying volunteers to help alleviate poverty through research, education, training and alternative livelihood programmes worldwide.

Assistant Science Co-Ordinators are required to assist with management, analysis and synthesis of scientific data collected from coral reef and tropical forest conservation expeditions to the Caribbean and Southeast Asia.

Fund-Raisers are required to assist with fund-raising campaigns on behalf of the Coral Cay Conservation Trust, a UK-registered charity which supports conservation education and training projects in developing countries.

Administration Assistants are required to help manage Volunteer recruitment campaigns.

The above are needed to work for Coral Cay Conservation (CCC), a non-profit organisation established in 1986 to provide support for the conservation and sustainable use of coastal and marine resources. CCC maintains full-time expedition projects in the Philippines and Honduras.

To work 8 hours a day, 5 days a week at CCC's London offices. Work is available all year round. Board and lodging is not provided, but travel and subsistence costs are included. The jobs are essentially voluntary but in some cases a basic wage can be negotiated. Volunteers are provided with full training so no previous experience is required.

Applications at any time to Alex Page at the above address.

LONDON AND WEST MIDDLESEX NATIONAL TRUST VOLUNTEERS: c/o Hughenden Manor, High Wycombe, Buckinghanshire HP14 4LA (www.lwmntb.org.uk).

The largest regional volunteer group of the National Trust, with over 250 members from all over the UK. Members carry out practical conservation all over the country.

Volunteers to repair paths, build bridges, clear scrub, repair dry stone walls and carry out other general land management and access work. Volunteers participate in weekend programmes, staying in Basecamps, converted outbuildings on estates, usually dormitory style accommodation with basic facilities. Volunteers work all day Saturday, until lunchtime on Sunday.

Basecamps are supervised by National Trust wardens who provide safety equipment and tools. The group is open to anyone over 16. Volunteers need enthusiasm and old clothes. The weekends have leaders who organise catering and travel. Membership of the group costs 6 per year. A typical weekend will cost around 10 for food, accommodation and travel.

Contact the above address for an information pack.

THE LONDON AQUARIUM: County Hall, Westminster Bridge Road, London SE1 7PB (tel 020-7967 8010; fax 020-7967 8029). The biggest aquarium in the UK.

Volunteers to study a specialised field of the housed waterlife and provide information on this to the public. Any applicants with a proven **Interest In**

Biology are welcome at any time.
Applications to Human resources at the above address.

SAVE THE RHINO INTERNATIONAL: 16 Winchester Walk, London SE1 9DG (tel 020-7357 7474; fax 020-7357 9666; e-mail save@rhinos.demon.co.uk; www.savetherhino.co.uk).
A London based charity raising funds for projects protecting rhinos and other endangered wildlife in Africa and Asia, through endurance challenges, marathons and donations.
Office Volunteers (5) needed to carry out general office work including data entry, managing mailings, leafleting and money collections. Volunteers work 10am-5pm with lunch and travel expenses provided. Must be over 18 with some office and financial administration experience. Volunteers are required all year round for a minimum period of two weeks. Foreign applicants with good spoken and written English are welcome.
Applications to Jo Shaw at the above address.

Heritage

ALEXANDER FLEMING LABORATORY MUSEUM: St. Mary's Hospital, Praed Street, London W2 1NY (tel 020-7886 6528 fax 020-7886 6739; e-mail Kevin.Brown@St-Marys.nhs.uk).
Volunteer Guides needed all year round to conduct visitors around the Alexander Fleming Laboratory Museum, which is based on a reconstruction of the laboratory in which Fleming discovered penicillin. The job includes making a short presentation and retail duties in a small museum shop. Full training will be supplied: knowledge of the subject matter is not required. Hours from 10am to 1pm from Monday to Thursday. Minimum age 16. The museum lacks disabled access.
Applications to Kevin Brown, Trust Archivist and Museum Curator.

THE ALICE TRUST: Waddesdon Manor, Aylesbury, Bucks HP18 0JH (tel 01296-651282; fax 01296-651293).
Waddesdon Manor is a magnificent French Renaissance-style chateau, home to the Rothschild Collection of superb 18th century French furniture and decorative arts. The gardens are considered to be one of the finest examples of Victorian flamboyance in Britain and contain a broad range of both formal and informal areas including a parterre, large parklands with many mature trees, splendid walks and a rococo-style aviary.
Volunteer Gardeners (2) required for a diverse range of maintenance tasks, alongside a team of eleven other professional gardeners. Full time work for a minimum period of one month (if residential), although a three month period is preferred. Some travel expenses may be met; rent free accommodation may be available. Age range 17-60. No experience necessary but commitment and reasonable fitness are required. Overseas English speaking applicants are considered.
Volunteer Gardeners for the Sunday Task Groups to work one Sunday per month undertaking varied project and maintenance work.
There are also opportunities for other volunteers within the collection and the gardens; applicants for these areas of work are also welcomed. Please contact to find out more.
Applications with CV and references to Marian Ridgway (ref SJ2) at the above address.

APSLEY HOUSE, WELLINGTON MUSEUM: Hyde Park Corner, London W1V 9FA (tel 020-7493 6376).

The museum is the historical residence of the Duke of Wellington of Waterloo fame and is part of the Victoria and Albert Museum.

Administrative Assistant needed around the year; lack of space dictates that only one assistant works at a time. This is an unpaid position though there is a possibility of being reimbursed travel expenses. Hours are from 10am-5pm full-time or part-time. Duties are varied and include dealing with marketing, database, public enquiries. Volunteers can work short term (2-3 weeks) or longer if they prove suitable and interested. Need to be cheerful, bright and willing to muck in.

   Applications to Eleanor Appleby, Administrator.

THE FORGE MUSEUM AND VICTORIAN COTTAGE GARDEN: High Street, Much Hadham, Hertfordshire SG10 6BS (tel/fax 01279-843301; e-mail cristinaharrison@hotmail.com).

The Forge Museum is owned by the Hertfordshire Building Preservation Trust. It is situated in the picturesque village of Much Hadham, and houses displays about blacksmithing and village life.

Volunteer Museum Assistants (2) These positions are aimed at those interested in gaining museum work experience. To work at least 2 days a week and up to 5 days a week. Applicants must be over 16. No previous experience is necessary.

Volunteer Conservation Assistants (10) These positions are aimed at anyone interested in gaining experience of conservation work in museums. No previous experience is necessary as training will be given. To work between 1 and 5 days per week.

   Volunteers are required from July to the end of August for a minimum period of 1 week. *Applications* should be addressed to Cristina Harrison and sent to the above address from May onwards.

LEIGHTON HOUSE MUSEUM: 12 Holland Park Road, London W14 8LZ (tel 020-7602 3316).

The house was built between 1864-79 to designs by George Aitchison. It is the expression of Leighton's vision of a private palace devoted to art.

Volunteers to work at the home of Frederic, Lord Leighton (1830-1896), the great classical painter and president of the Royal Academy. Duties include office work and helping mount exhibitions. Hours are flexible. Applicants must be interested in museums and be graduates or currently studying. No accommodation is available. Min period of work 1 month at any time of year. Overseas applicants with good communications skills are considered. Interview necessary.

   Applications at any time to Reena Suleman.

Physically/Mentally Disabled

HERTFORDSHIRE ACTION ON DISABILITY: The Woodside Centre, The Commons, Welwyn Garden City, Herts AL7 4DD (tel 01707-324581; fax 01707-371297; e-mail herts_action@dial.pipex.com).

Hertford House Hotel is a 22 bedded seaside hotel which is fully accesible to people with physical disabilities.

Volunteers (6 per fortnight) are required to assist with holidays for people with disabilities . Helpers work, aiding the mobility of guests, to give companionship and assist them in dressing, transferring from wheelchair to bed/bathroom/toilet, pushing guests in wheelchairs to shops, church, the seafront etc. and escorting them on outings in hotel minibus.

Free return transport to hotel from Welwyn Garden City provided. Period of work all year round. Volunteers usually work for a two-week period. Min. age 20. Experience of working with disabled people would be helpful.

Write a.s.a.p. for an *applications* form, enclosing two character references, to the Manager at the Hertford House Hotel, 11 Parkway, Clacton-on-Sea, Essex CO15 1BJ (tel 01255-475994)

INDEPENDENT LIVING ALTERNATIVES: Trafalgar House, Grenville Place, London NW7 3SA (tel 020-8906 9265; e-mail ILA@cwcom.net; ILA.mcmail.com).

Volunteers required to provide support for people with disabilities, to enable them to live independently in their own homes. The work involves helping them get dressed, go to the toilet, drive, do the housework, etc. Volunteers receive £63.50 a week plus free accommodation, usually in the London area or in Cumbria. ILA offers a chance to learn about disability issues and see London at the same time. No qualifications required, except good English. Vacancies arise all year round.

Applications should be sent to Tracey Jannaway at the above address.

INDEPENDENT LIVING SCHEMES: Lewisham Social Care and Health, Louise House, Dartmouth Road, London SE23 3HZ (tel 020-8314 7239 (24 hours); fax 020-8314 3014; e-mail kensmith@lewisham.gov.uk).

Part of a local government body which assists disabled people.

Volunteers (8 At Any One Time) to help disabled people living independently. Duties include dealing with the personal care and assisting with the leisure and social activities of independent people with severe disabilities (lifting is involved). Allowances of £60 per week and an additional £15 per month are paid, plus free, shared accommodation with all bills covered. To work on a rota basis with other volunteers; usually 24 hours on (sleeping in) followed by 48 hours off.

Volunteers are needed around the year; those who can make a six month commitment are preferred. Applicants should be aged 17 or over and should have a commitment to civil rights for disabled people.

Applications to Kenneth Smith, Project Worker, at the above address. An interview in London is required before an offer can be made, UK travel expenses will be paid.

KITH & KIDS: Attention Dan Cary c/o Haringey Irish Centre, Pretoria Road, London N17 8DX (tel 020-8801 7432; e-mail projects@kithandkids.org.uk; www.kithandkids.org.uk).

A family support group meeting the needs of people with learning, physical and/or sensory disabilities. Minimum age is 14.

Volunteers (50-60) to work with disabled students (two volunteers to one student) on a non-residential social training project lasting two weeks. Travel expenses will be reimbursed. Period of work from the end of July or early August.

Volunteers (50 or more) to work on a similar scheme held on a summer camp in the Guildford area from late August. Accommodation will be provided. Min. age 16. Training given.

Applications to Kith & Kids at the above address.

SHAD (BALHAM): The Volunteer Development Officer, SHAD Wandsworth, 5 Bedford Hill, Balham, LW12 9E2 (tel 020-8365 8528; e-mail shadwand@aol.com).

SHAD (Support and Housing Assistance for people with Disabilities) enables people with physical disabilities to live independently in their own homes. **Volunteers** are required to act as 'arms and legs' for disabled people. Volunteers receive £60 per week, free furnished accommodation, training, adequate support and expenses, 2-3 days off per week, social networking in London, excellent experience, advice on career prospects and insight into disability. No experience is necessary but a minimum commitment of 4 months or more is required. All nationalities are welcome but a good standard of the English language is essential.

For more *details* and an application form, please contact the above address.

WOODLARKS CAMP SITE TRUST: Tilford Road, Lower Bourne, Farnham, Surrey GU10 3RN (tel 01252-716279; e-mail woodlarks1@aol.com).
The Trust provides camping facilities for organisations interested in running summer camps for people with disabilities, particularly children. Several of the camps require volunteers to act as **Carers/Enablers** to the disabled participants. Camps normally last for one week each and a small fee is usually paid by volunteers to the camp leader to cover the cost of food. All camping equipment is provided.

Anyone interested should make *applications* in writing, enclosing s.a.e., to the Honorary Secretary, Kathleen Marshall House, at the above address.

Social and Community Schemes

THE GRAIL CENTRE: 125 Waxwell Lane, Pinner, Middlesex HA5 3ER (tel 020-8866 0505; fax 020-8866 1408; e-mail WAXWELL@compuserve.com).
The Grail is both a conference centre and the home to a community of Christian women. The Elizabethan house has modern extensions and is set in 10 acres of wooded garden.
5-6 Volunteers are needed throughout the year to live alongside the resident community and help to maintain the house and garden and assist in running the centre. Much of the work is household/manual. Duties are arranged on a flexible basis and volunteers are required to be available for $7^1/2$ hours daily. There is one full day off a week and one day's holiday per 2 weeks worked. Those who need a well defined timetable/ fixed hours would find this pattern unhelpful.

Volunteers are offered board, their own room and an allowance for necessary expenses. Min. age 20; no upper limit. No special skills are required, but goodwill and sense of humour essential. Overseas applicants pay their own fares and arrange the correct immigration clearance but an invitation letter is provided on request. EU applicants should be familiar with the medical cover between their country and the UK. Others should be insured or prepared to pay the cost of any treatment they may require. Applicants must have enough spoken and written English to function in this very busy household. In-house lessons can be arranged for those interested. Religious observance is not a requirement.

Send a letter (to the Volunteer Co-ordinator), CV and a recent photograph to the above address. Early *Applications* are likely to be more successful. All applications must include a s.a.e. or an IRC.

HACKNEY INDEPENDENT LIVING TEAM: Richmond House, 1a Westgate Street, London E8 3RL (tel 020-8985 5511 volunteer hotline ext. 227; fax 020-8533 2029; www.hilt.org.uk).
Supports adults with a learning difficulty in Hackney to live in the community as independently as possible, and to continue to develop their independence and

personal identity.
Independent Living Support Volunteers (12). Volunteers may be involved in all projects and activities of HILT. Some of the ways in which volunteers have supported service users include sports, leisure and social activities, arranging and accompanying on holidays sand assessing education and training opportunities. Volunteers support service users in achieving goals, and support in personal development. Wages £55 per week, plus weekly zones 1-2 Travelcard. To work 35 hours a week.

Applicants must be over 18 and must be committed to enabling people with learning difficulties to have as much control over their lives as possible. They should also help provide a service which reflects the cultural, racial and religious needs of service users, and promote anti-discriminatory practice. They should have a willingness to understand service users' emotional needs, and attend regular supervision and communicate ideas and suggestions.

Min. period of work 6 months at any time of year. All volunteers have their own furnished room, including all bills apart from telephone. Food allowance is incorporated into weekly allowance. Overseas applicants must have a good level of conversational English, and the right to enter the UK. Interview necessary.

Applications as far in advance of intended start date as possible to the Volunteer Co-ordinator.

HEALTHPROM: Star House, 104-108 Grafton Road, London NW5 4BD (tel 020-7284 1620; fax 020-7284-1881; e-mail healthprom@healthprom.org; www.healthprom.org).
Healthprom works in partnerships to improve healthcare for the most vulnerable in the former Soviet Union.
Voluntary Administrative Assistant to perform general office administration and desktop publishing. Must be able to type and use computers, preferably Microsoft Word for Windows.
Translater/Interpreter fluent in Russian.
The above are needed to assist a charity which works to enhance healthcare in the former Soviet Union through partnership project work, postgraduate education and advocacy. No pocket money paid but local travel expenses will be refunded.

Applications to Catherine Hine, Business Manager, at the above address.

HOLY CROSS CENTRE: Holycross Church, The Crypt, Cromer Street, London WC1H 8JU (tel/fax 020-7278 8687; e-mail cmt@hcct.org.uk).
This centre in the Kings Cross area of London is a social centre for people with mental health issues and drug/alcohol problems.
Full-Time (2) and Part-Time (40) Volunteers needed to run the centre, catering and befriending clients and offering peer support in a friendly and informal atmosphere, with the possibility of teaching arts and crafts and computing. P/T volunteers work 5 hours per week, F/T 37 hours, minimum commitment 3 months. In return P/T volunteers receive travel expenses and a meal for each session. F/T are provided with free accommodation, meals and a £55 allowance.

Applications to P.Byczek, Centre Management Team, at the above address.

SIMON COMMUNITY: PO Box 1187, London NW5 4HW (tel 020-7485 6639; fax 020-7482 6305; e-mail simoncommunity@ic24.net).
Living and working in the Simon Community is a unique and challenging way of life offering the chance to meet people and situations as never before while doing vital and rewarding work.

The Simon Community is a community of volunteers and homeless people living and working with those of London's homeless for whom no other provision exists. **Volunteers** are expected to help run its night shelter or one of two residential homes, as well as participate in group meetings, regular outreach work, campaigning and fund raising. The community also has a farm near Canterbury, and conducts tea runs round London and other outreach work.

B & L are provided plus £27 per week pocket money. Volunteers are required throughout the year for a minimum of 3 months. All applicants should be aged 19 or over, have a mature and responsible attitude and a good command of the English language. *Initial enquiries* to the above address.

SOUTHWARK HABITAT FOR HUMANITY: PO Box 14284, London SE22 8ZH (tel 020-7701 2631; fax 020-7701 2391; e-mail southwarkhfh@ zetnet.co.uk).
Volunteer Construction Workers to work with an innovative community self-help group building houses to provide affordable housing for people with low incomes. Southwark HFH is part of HFH Great Britain, an ecumenical Christian housing ministry working to provide high quality affordable housing to those on low incomes and in need of housing.

The construction programme is continuous throughout the year so help is needed on weekdays and at weekends; volunteers can help for as little as one day. Volunteers must pay for their own transport and provide their own lunch. Applicants should be aged over 16; no building skills or experience are needed as skilled supervisors direct the work.

If interested in making *applications* call the above telephone number.

Vacation Traineeships

Accountancy, Banking and Insurance

BARING ASSET MANAGEMENT: 155 Bishopsgate, London EC2H 3XY (tel 020-7214 1403; fax 020-7214 4163; e-mail jane.quilter@baring-asset.com; www.baring-asset.com).
Trainee Fund Administrators will be responsible for the daily collation and distribution of information relating to the administration (valuing and pricing) of funds (UK and overseas).
Trainee Registration Administrators will be responsible for maintaining the register in respect of each unit trust and OEIC Management group. **6 positions in total.**

Wages from £200 per week (GCSE educated) to £250 per week (A level educated). Positions are available for the Summer Vacation only, typically for 6 weeks. These positions are not open to university students and relevant qualifications include GCSE and A level passes at Maths and English or BTEC general or nationals in relevant subjects such as business, finance, economics and statistics. No accommodation available. Foreign applicants with valid work permits and able to arrange their own travel and accommodation are welcome.

Applications should be made by 31 March to Jane Quilter, Human Resources Manager, at the above address.

BARNES ROFFE: 16-19 Copperfields, Spital Street, Dartford, Kent DA1 2DE (tel 01322-275335; fax 01322-287177; e-mail m.moran@brdartford.co.uk;

www.barnes-roffe.co.uk).
An accounting firm based in Dartford but trainees will spend most of the time at clients' premises.
Two Traineeships are offered for audit/accounting assistants. The work involves assisting with the preparation and audit of clients' financial statements. Suitable candidates would be considering taking up ICAEW training contracts on graduation. A wage of £150 per week is paid (2000 summer rate). Placements are primarily aimed at second year university students and take place during the summer vacations, although Christmas and Easter may be considered for strong candidates.

Applications should be sent to M.J. Moran at the above address.

BLOOMBERG L.P.: City Gate House, 39-45 Finsbury Square, London EC2A 1PQ (fax 020-7661 5809; e-mail Recruitment@Bloomberg.net; www.careers. Bloomberg.com or www.Bloomberg.co.uk).
Approx. 60 Internships in most areas of the business including Sales, Broadcast and Broadcast Operations, HR, IT Support, Networks, etc.

The internships would suit university students or graduates but anyone can apply. Looking for people with proven interest in Finance. A fluency in a second European language is a bonus. Interships last 12 weeks and the wage is dependent on experience. No accommodation is provided. Overseas students with a UK working permit are welcome.

Applications should be sent to Human Resources, c/o Amanda Isaacs, at the above address.

EUROMONEY INSTITUTIONAL INVESTOR PLC: Nestor House, Playhouse Yard, London EC4V 5EX (tel 020-7779 8524; fax 020-7779 8513; e-mail jlewington@euromoneyplc.com; www.euromoneyplc.com).
Euromoney Institutional Investor plc is an international publications and events company. Although it has no formal vacation scheme, it often has work available for university undergraduates or gap year students with excellent grades. Students of any subject are considered but economics, law and languages are particularly useful. **Positions** available include researchers, telesales executives, administrators and data inputters. Periods of employment depend on vacancies as does the wage. No accommodation is provided. Qualified applicants from abroad with excellent English and the relevant work permits are considered.

Applications by e-mail only to Julie Lewington at jlewington@euromoneyplc.com

INSTITUTE FOR FISCAL STUDIES: 7 Ridgmount Street, London WC1E 7AR (tel 020-7291 4800; fax 020-7323 4780; e-mail mailbox@ifs.org.uk).
IFS is an independent research institute which specialises in the economic analysis of public policy, especially the field of taxation policy. It aims to bridge the gap between purely academic research and issues of practical policy. The research is largely orientated towards microeconomic analysis, and has a strong quantitative flavour.

The institute makes use of major UK surveys of households, individuals and firms in order to analyse the impact of taxation and other public policies on individuals' and companies' behaviour. Research is disseminated through conferences, publications, the journal *Fiscal Studies* and other journals. IFS aims to provide impartial information from a politically independent standpoint.

IFS offers approx. **5 Placements** which last for 6 weeks in the summer in London. Trainees can expect to work with a research team on a particular project.

Tasks involve the preparation and analysis of data, the conducting of literary searches, and writing up search results. Applicants should have a minimum of 2 years undergraduate experience in Economics or a closely related subject. The salary in 2001 was £230 per week. No accommodation is provided, paid travel expenses to interview within the UK only.

Overseas applicants entitled to work in the UK are considered, interviews take place in London. *Applications* including a CV and covering letter should be sent to Robert Markless by the middle of March.

MERRILL LYNCH EUROPE PLC: MERRILL LYNCH FINANCIAL CENTRE, 2 King Edward Street, London EC1A 1HQ (www.ml.com/careers).
Approx. 150 Internships are available within the following business areas: Debt Markets, Equity Markets, Investment Banking, Investment Managers, Research, Securities Services, Financial Operation, Human Resources and Technology.
Internships are aimed at penultimate year university students. There are no required degree disciplines but students should have outstanding academic achievement and be able to demonstrate quantitative and analytical problem solving skills. Internships start in early July and last 10 weeks.

All *applications* must be made online at www.ml.com/careers by mid-February 2002. Applications are dealt with on a first come, first serve basis so early application may be advantageous.

Law

ADDLESHAW BOOTH: 60 Cannon Street, London, EC4N 6NP (tel 0113-209 2000; fax 0113-209 2060; e-mail grad@addleshawbooth.com).
Addleshaw Booth is a leading UK law firm with an international capability. Their client portfolio features a spectrum of high profile companies that chose them because of their high quality, bespoke service; these include J. Sainsbury plc, Airtours plc, BT Cellnet, Rugby Football League and AstraZeneca. Addleshaw also has a well regarded private client department. The firm has experienced significant growth in size, client base and profitability over the past few years. The firm currently employs over 1,200 staff, including 128 Partners and more than 600 Fee earners
Addleshaw offer a **2 Week Vacation Scheme**. The scheme provides opportunities to experience work within legal departments and is supplemented by a number of presentations and exercises. The scheme is open to all those who would be in a position to commence a training contract with the firm in September 2004 or March 2005. The scheme is currently remunerated at a rate of £150 per week and assist with accommodation can be given if required.

Placements are located in the company's Leeds, London and Manchester offices. *Applications* will only be considered if our own employer's application form is completed and which is available online or can be requested by telephone. Applications must be received by 22 February 2002.

Send your application to Mrs Simran Foote, Graduate Manager, Addleshaw Booth, 100 Barbirolli Square, M2 3AB.

ALLEN & OVERY: One New Change, London EC4M 9QQ (tel 020-7330 3000; fax 020-7330 9999; e-mail graduate.recruitment@allenovery.com; www.allenovery.com).
Founded in 1930, Allen & Overy is one of the UK's leading law firms. It has over 300 partners and over 4,000 staff working in 25 major centres on three continents, with an international reputation for serving business, financial institutions,

government and private individuals wherever there is a need for decisive legal advice on complex transactions.

Allen & Overy offers **90 Three Week Placements** to penultimate year students (law and non-law) interested in a career in law. Students spend time in two departments, becoming fully involved and making genuine contributions to the work. They will be treated as one of the team; sometimes attending meetings and observing, at other times carrying out research and helping to check documents, but at all times getting an insight into how law is practised in the firm.

Salary is £250 per week in London and £280 outside, with positions also available in Brussels, Frankfurt, London and Paris. Assistance may be given in finding accommodation.

Application forms are available from 1 November and before 28 February. Completed *Applications* should be sent to Graduate Recruitment at the above address.

ASHURST MORRIS CRISP: Broadwalk House, 5 Appold Street, London (tel 020-7638 1111; fax 020-7972 7800; e-mail gradrec@ashursts.com; www.ashursts.com).

International City law firm with 126 partners, around 390 solicitors and a total staff of 1,400. Main areas of specialism include Company/Commercial, Litigation, International Finance, Real Estate and Tax.

Offers **70 Placements** in the Summer and **30 at Easter**. During the schemes, students are placed in a different department each week and share an office with a solicitor or partner. The main aim is that students become involved in the solicitor's daily workload by completing 'real' tasks such as letter writing, drafting, legal research and attending client meetings. In addition a series of lectures, workshops and social activities are arranged.

Penultimate year law degree students and final year non-law degree students are eligible. Wage is £250 per week. No accommodation is provided but help in finding some can be given. Foreign applicants who speak fluent English are welcome.

Applications should be made online to Stephen Trowbridge, Graduate Recruitment, by 25 January, including CV and covering letter.

BAKER & MCKENZIE: 100 New Bridge Street, London EC4V 6JA (tel 020-7919 1000; fax 0207-919 1999; e-mail london.graduate.recruit@bakernet.com; www.ukgraduates.bakernet.com).

A city law firm offering **25 Student Vacation Traineeships** for 3 weeks during the summer vacation. These 3 week placements are for students in their 2nd year (or 3rd of a 4 year course) of an undergraduate course, law or otherwise. Students can expect a high degree of responsibility, being involved in working with, and for, clients. With appropriate supervision students will also participate in various commercial transactions. Training sessions and social events are part of the programme. The salary for 2001 was £250 per week.

No accommodation is provided, however details of suitable accommodation are given to help students find their own.

Applications should be sent to Natalie Stacey at the above address or students can apply on-line by January 31.

S.J. BERWIN: 222 Grays Inn Road, London WC1X 8XF (tel 020-7533 2222; fax 020-7533 2000; e-mail info@sjberwin.com; www.sjberwin.com).

S.J. Berwin offer up to **60 Placements** on their vacation training schemes, each one lasting 2 weeks. The placements are open to second year law students (and above) and third year non-law students (and above) who are expecting or have gained a 2:1 degree. Trainees spend 2 weeks working in a department ideally suited to them, gaining hands-on experience in a wide range of legal tasks during the summer. Attendees receive £225 per week and whilst accommodation is not provided suggestions on good hostels and university halls can be made. Suitably qualified applicants from abroad who do not require a work permit are considered.

Applications should be sent to Graduate Recruitment by 31 January 2002.

CAMERON McKENNA: Mitre House, 160 Aldersgate Street, London EC1A 4DD.
Cameron McKenna, an international city law firm, offers **two-week placements to students during Easter and Summer and Christmas**. Positions are open to second and final year law students or final year non-law graduates who expect to achieve at least a 2:1 degree. The firm is distinctive, unstuffy and approachable, and is looking for creative, bright, commercially aware, committed people who have the potential to contribute to its future success.

For an application form and further details please call 0845-3000 491. The closing date for *Applications* is Friday 28th February.

DENTON WILDE SAPTE: Five Chancery Lane, Clifford's Inn, London EC4A 1BU (tel 020-7242 1212; fax 020-7320 6555; e-mail trainingcontracts@ dentonwildesapte.com; www.dentonwildesapte.com). Denton Wilde Sapte is a large international commercial law firm.
Their vacation schemes are targeted to penultimate/final year law students or final year non law students, looking to make a career in law. **Christmas open days (35/40)** are specifically for non-law students, **Easter Open Days (35/40)** and **Summer Information Weeks (80/90)** are open to both law and non law students. These comprise skills workshops and departmental talks designed to give an overview of the firm.

Wage for summer information week is £250. Positions are open to current university students or graduates from any discipline. Graduates need to have a minimum 2i degree result or show a good indication of achieving this. Fluent English essential. Minimum age 16. No previous experience necessary. No accommodation is provided

Applications to the vacation schemes should be made using the firm's application form and addressed to Emma Hooper, Recruitment Officer (Trainee Solicitors). This is available on the website or can be requested by telephone. Deadlines are as follows: Christmas open day, 7 December 2001; Easter and Summer schemes, 15 March 2002. Overseas candidates are considered.

MACFARLANES: 10 Norwich Street, London EC4A 1BD (tel 020-7831 9222; fax 020-7831 9607; e-mail gs@macfarlanes.com; www.macfarlanes.com).
Macfarlanes is a leading firm of solicitors based in the City. Areas of work include corporate, property, litigation and private clients.
Macfarlanes run a summer student scheme which offers those seeking a training contract the opportunity to gain hands-on experience of life in a city law firm. There are **40 Positions** available for the 2 week scheme, open to University students with a strong academic record at both A-level and degree level. Students receive a wage of £250 per week and help can be given in finding accommodation. Suitably qualified applicants from overseas are welcome.

Applications by 25th February to Graham Stoddart, Graduate Recruitment Officer, at the above address.

RICHARDS BUTLER: Beaufort House, 15 St. Botolph Street, London EC3A 7EE (tel 020-7247 6555; fax 020-7247 5091; e-mail gradrecruit@ richardsbutler.com; www.richardsbutler.com).
Richards Butler is a premier international law firm with its head office in the City of London and 10 other offices worldwide.
Richards Butler offer **Vacation Traineeships** during the summer to both law and non-law students in their 2nd Year or above. Traineeships last for 2 weeks in which students partake in work shadowing and research for one week and one week of lectures. Trainees receive £200 per week and are expected to arrange their own accommodation. Foreign applicants eligible to work in the UK are welcome.
Applications between November and February should be submitted online via the website www.richardsbutler.com.

SINCLAIR ROCHE AND TEMPERLEY: Royex House, 5 Aldermanbury Square, London EC2V 7LE (tel 020-74524000; fax 020-7452 4001; e-mail recruitment@srtlaw.com ; www.srtlaw.com).
Sinclair Roche and Temperley is an international commercial Law firm founded in the City of London in 1934; today it also has offices in Hong Kong, Shanghai and Bucharest and provides high quality, specialised legal advice to the international business community, with a particular focus on shipping, international trade, aviation, energy and finance.
The firm runs a two week summer **Vacation Programme** for up to twelve students in July each year. Students sit with a Partner or a Senior Lawyer and are allocated a trainee to act as their mentor. The aim of the placement is to provide as much hands-on experience as possible including going to court, arbitrations, client meetings, research, assisting in the preparation of documents for court and generally assisting with the work of the department to which they have been assigned. Preference is given to undergraduates in their final or penultimate years of study. Students receive a wage of £200 per week and overseas applicants are welcome, subject to work permits being granted.
The firm's application form can be obtained from www.srtlaw.com. The deadline for *applications* for placements in 2002 is 28 February, subject to availability.

STEPHENSON HARWOOD: One, St Paul's Churchyard, London EC4M 8SH (tel 020-7329 4422; fax 020-7606 0822).
Stephenson Harwood is a City law firm with five overseas offices and an international practice. Their main areas of work are: corporate, commercial litigation, property, private capital and shipping.
Stephenson Harwood offer **21 Students** the opportunity to spend 2 weeks work-shadowing solicitors. Students spend 1 week each in 2 different departments. Applicants must be 2nd year Law undergraduates or 3rd year non-Law undergraduates. Salary is £200 per week.
Placements last 2 weeks and take place from the last fortnight in June to the end of July in the firm's St Paul's Office. No accommodation is provided but help can be given in finding it.
Applications by form only by 15 February 2002 to the Graduate Recruitment Department.

Media and Marketing

INDEPENDENT TELEVISION:

A limited number of work experience placements are sometimes available with the 19 regional ITV companies. Vacancies are rarely known in advance and demand constantly outstrips supply.

Applicants must be students on a recognised course of study at a college or university; their course must lead to the possibility of employment within the television industry (ideally, work experience would be a compulsory part of the course); and the student must be resident in the transmission area of the company offering the attachment, or in some cases, attending a course in that region. However, opportunities may occasionally exist for students following computing, librarianship, finance, legal, administrative or management courses. Suitably qualified applicants from overseas are considered.

Placements vary in length from half a day to several weeks or months, depending upon the work available and the candidate's requirements. Students do not normally receive payment from the company, although those on courses of particular relevance to the industry are paid expenses. Students from sandwich courses who are on long-term attachments may be regarded as short-term employees and paid accordingly.

Applications should be sent to the Personnel Department of the applicant's local ITV Company. General information on working in the television industry can be obtained from Skillset, the National Training Organisation for Broadcast, Film, Video and Multimedia, on 020-7534 5300 and ask for *Skillset Careers Handbook; or call recruitment on 020-7843 8058 for basic guidance.*

MERIDIAN RECORDS: PO Box 317, Eltham, London SE9 4SF (tel 020-8857 3213; fax 020-8857 0731; e-mail meridian-records@supanet.com).
Meridian Records is a small record company specialising in the recording and production of classical records.

In 2002 the company will be seeking **One Or Two Candidates** who can demonstrate motivation and a keen interest in music. No other particular qualifications are required, although applicants should have a general interest in all aspects of running a record company. An ability to read music is useful but not essential. The successful candidate(s) will participate in a wide variety of tasks including the preparation of artwork, accounting, recording, editing and the maintenance of machines, buildings and grounds.

The traineeships are unpaid, though the company may be able to offer accommodation on its premises. The placements run for a varying number of weeks during any of the three main vacations. Overseas applicants will be considered. It is the policy of Meridian Records to only employ non-smokers.

Applications should be sent to Mr John Shuttleworth, Director, at the above address.

SKI CLUB OF GREAT BRITAIN: The White House, 57-63 Church Road, Wimbledon Village, London SW19 5SB (tel 020-8410 2000/2016; fax 020-8410 2001; e-mail skiers@skiclub.co.uk; www).
An independent non-profit snowsports club with 27,500 members which produces own magazine and holiday brochures.
Marketing Junior(s) (1-2) with a good knowledge of English and an interest in marketing. Tasks will include, copy writing, proof reading, small project work, event organisation and database management.
To work for $37^1/2$ hours per week. Min. period of work of 3 weeks. Positions are

available from July to September. University students are mostly sought. No accommodation available.

Applications should be made from March onwards to the Marketing Department at the above address. Interview required, by telephone if necessary.

Science, Construction and Engineering

BINNIE, BLACK & VEATCH: Grosvenor House, 69 London Road, Redhill, Surrey RH1 1LQ (tel 01737-774155; fax 01737-772767).

Binnie, Black & Veatch is an engineering consultancy specialising in water supply, public health, environmental engineering, power, telecommunications and energy services.

Each year the firm takes two **Pre-University Trainees** for up to twelve months. These students will normally have Mathematics and Science A-levels and will be preparing to read Electrical, Electronics or Mechanical Engineering, Mathematics, Physics or Applied Science. The firm also offers placements over the summer to two or three undergraduate students of Civil Engineering. These traineeships last for up to ten weeks and take place in the firm's Consultancy Services, Water Infrastructure, water process and energy service, Business Units. Suitably qualified applicants from abroad will be considered.

In 2000 those on summer placements were paid £180 per week and pre-university trainees about £8,500 p.a.

Applications should be sent to Celia Morris, Learning and Development Manager, by Easter.

CADOGAN TIETZ LTD: 14 Clerkenwell Close, Clerkenwell, London EC1R 0PQ (tel 020-7490 5050; fax 020-7490 2160).

An independent civil and structural engineering consultancy based in lively Clerkenwell.

Cadogan Tietz offers **Summer Placements** to students from university or college who are studying Civil Engineering or related disciplines. All trainees will gain first-hand experience of structural and civil engineering. Suitably qualified applicants from abroad, preferably from Germany and France, will be considered. Salary will be discussed at interview.

Applications should be sent by April to S. Grindley, Director, at the above address.

DATA CONNECTION LTD: 100 Church Street, Enfield, Middlesex EN2 6BQ (tel 020-8366 1177; e-mail recruit@dataconnection.com; www.dataconnection.com).

Founded in 1981, Data Connection is one of the world's most successful computer technology companies with a worldwide reputation for developing complex high quality products. Customers include the development laboratories of organisations such as Cisco, Hewlett Packard, IBM/Lotus, Microsoft and Sun. The company has over 200 employees and is based in North London, with satellite offices in Edinburgh, Chester, San Francisco and Washington DC. They offer outstanding students the chance to develop their computing skills at the cutting edge of technology.

Vacation Work is offered to exceptional students with an interest in the development of complex software. Applicants typically have all A grades at A level. Data Connection provides complex and challenging programming assignments, with help and support. A salary of £1,100 per month and subsidised accommodation in the Company House is offered. Many vacation students go on to join Data Connection as full-time employees; some receive sponsorship while still at University.

Interviews are held all year round. However, as vacancies are limited it is best to apply in the autumn term. For more details *contact* Denise Crisp at the above address, or apply on-line following the links from the Website.

M.W. KELLOGG LTD: Kellogg Tower, Greenford Road, Greenford, Middlesex UB6 0JA (tel 020-8872 7000).
M.W. Kellogg Ltd is a world leader in the design, engineering, procurement, constuction and project management of process plants within the oil, gas and petrochemical industries.

It offers traineeships during the summer vacation mainly for **Engineering And IT Positions.** Main degree subjects of interest are chemical engineering, mechanical engineering or computer science or other related degree. Other possible areas include, Purchasing and Supply, Construction, Civil and Structural, Business, CAD, Electrical, Instumentation, Process Control and Materials. Excellent facilites and a work environment condusive to enthusistic innovative team players are offered.

Trainees will be paid around £6 per hour. Placements take place at the head office in Greenford. Help is usually given with finding accommodation, but students must pay for their own board and lodging.

Applications should be sent from April to the Recruitment Officer at the above address.

SIR ROBERT MCALPINE LTD: Eaton Court, Maylands Avenue, Hemel Hempstead, Herts HP2 7TR (tel 01442-233444; e-mail a.scarth@sir-robert-mcalpine.com; www.sir-robert-mcalpine.com).
Sir Robert McAlpine is one of the UK's major building and civil engineering contractors, undertaking projects such as industrial plants, marine works, power stations, hospitals, offices, theatres, leisure and retail complexes.

University Students reading degrees in construction-related subjects, or **'A' Level Students** considering degrees, are offered employment lasting a minimum of 8 weeks during the summer. Students assist site engineers and quantity surveyors working on various major construction sites throughout the country. The salary varies according to experience and qualifications and assistance in finding lodgings is provided. Approximate number of vacancies will be between 20 and 50.

Applications should be made to the Human Resources Department, at the above address.

MADGE NETWORKS LTD: Wexham Springs, Framewood Road, Wexham, Slough SL3 6PJ (tel 01753-661749; e-mail recruit@madge.com).
Madge is a global provider of advanced Internet-centric network services and products, and mission-critical enterprise solutions. The company's strategy is based on optimizing voice, video and data convergence via Internet Protocol (IP) solutions.

Madge runs a vacation training and **Work Experience Scheme** for students in a variety of disciplines, including software/hardware development and testing, marketing, finance and aministration. Details of summer placement vacancies are posted on the websites at the folowing address: www.madge.com/careers/graduate opportunities/summer placements. The Research and Development Centre in South Buckinghamshire provides placement involving programming and design work and the student is given specific projects to complete under supervision. The company is therefore looking for students from reputable universities who are reading Computer Programming, Computer Sciences or Electronic Engineering and are at the top of their academic field.

Chosen candidates for any summer positions will be expected to work for a minimum of two months over the summer vacation and will earn a salary in the region of £300 per week.

Applicants should contact a member of the Human Resources team at the above address or send details to recruit@madge.com. Many students who participate in the summer placement scheme return to Madge for successful careers on completing their academic qualifications.

THE MET OFFICE: Room 603, London Road, Bracknell, Berkshire RG12 2SZ (tel 01344-856018; fax 01344-856021).

The Met. Office provides the National Meteorological Service including weather forecasts, observations and climatological data. Scientists also carry out research into the improvement of weather forecasting and the consequences of long-term climate change. Over the summer the company offers **Placements** to university students entering their third year of Mathematics, Physics, Computing or a related subject. Students work at the Bracknell HQ for a period of 8-12 weeks, the salary is £12,740 pro rata. The deadline for this year's scheme is the 31st of January 2002.

To receive a summer placement *applications* form or for any other specific queries regarding placements then call the above number or visit the www.metoffice.com.

The West Country

Prospects for Work.

The coasts of Dorset, Devon and Cornwall are scattered with hotels which need staffing during the summer season. The largest employers of temporary staff are the many holiday camps in the region: Pontins has several centres in the South West, Butlins Skyline has its refurbished Family Entertainment resorts and there are a further two camps in St Ives and Hayle. The Jobcentre in Penzance recruits for local caravan parks during both Easter and summer, as well as for employers on the Scilly Isles. Recruitment for the Scilly Isles' particularly long season begins in January. In and around Penzance there are often vacancies for chefs and kitchen/service staff.

There may well be a demand for agricultural workers and fruit pickers at the strawberry farms around Camborne or in Penzance, home to one of the largest bulb farms in the area.

There is a Hotel and Catering Jobshop, with vacancies ideal for students, within Bournemouth Jobcentre. Its Catering Bank provides a useful service for experienced waiting staff. The Jobcentre, which deals with the West Dorset area and the Channel Islands, also advertises a variety of other summer jobs, including work as gardeners and beach workers as well as retail and clerical work.

Vacancies in Taunton in Somerset are mainly for administration, retail and the hospitality and leisure industry. There is also a need for temporary fruit pickers and production workers, mainly recruited through employment agencies. It is important to apply early because the demand is high among students. Some temporary jobs are advertised in the *Somerset County Gazette* and vacancies in the region and nationwide can also be accessed on the Employment Service website www.employmentservice.gov.uk or phone Employment Direct on 0845-6060 234. Temporary jobs are also advertised in the town's two Colleges. Bristol is one of the few other areas away from the coast where there is an extensive demand by retailers for more staff over the summer.

Business and Industry

ROCHESTERS EVENT HIRE LTD: Deer Park Farm, Marshwood Vale, Bridport, Dorset, DT6 5PZ (tel 01308-868743; fax 01308-868086).
Delivery Drivers (2) needed June to August/September. Hours to be agreed with applicant. Up to 60 hours a week if wanted. Clean driving licence essential.
Loaders (3) of washing machine, check orders and pack from June to September. Common sense and sense of humour required.
  Wage for all jobs is £5 per hour. *Apply* to Trevor Richards, Director.

Children

ADVENTURE AND COMPUTER HOLIDAYS: P.O. Box 183, Dorking, Surrey RH5 6FA (tel 01306-881299).
Camp Leaders needed to work on children's residential activity holidays in Cornwall. Wages £185 per week, accommodation provided. Min. age 21. Driving licence required. To work July and August. Must have qualifications or experience of working with children.
  Applications to Sarah Bradley, Director, at the above address.

3D EDUCATION AND ADVENTURE LTD: Business Support, Osmington Bay, Weymouth, Dorset DT3 6EG (tel 01305-836226; fax 01305-834070; e-mail darren@3d-education.co.uk). 3D is a specialist provider of activity and educational experiences for young people. Owned by Center Parcs, 3D has been operating since 1991 and gone from strength to strength year on year.
Activity Instructors (500) Employed and trained as either multi-activity instructor, field studies instructor, specialist watersports instructor or IT instructor, staff will work with children at specialist holiday centres across the south of England as well as across the UK and Europe with Pontins and Center Parcs.
  Field studies instructors must hold or at least be gaining a relevant degree. IT instructors need to have a broad range of IT skills. Any sports coaching awards or national governing body awards are advantageous, if applying for Activity instructor and Watersports instructor postitions, although those with relevant experience will be considered. Training courses are held from late January through to July, so there is plenty of opportunity to develop your skills and qualifications.
  Most important is an applicant's enthusiasm, personality and energy, coupled with a true desire to work in the outdoor leisure industry. Excellent accommodation and catering packages are offered with payment and working hours as covered by minimum wage and working time legislation. Minimum period of work 14 weeks.
  Applicants should telephone 01305-836226 for a recruitment pack between September and June. Before employment all applicants must complete a residential training programme in the UK.

Holiday Centres and Amusements

ALLNATT CENTRE: Ulwell Road, Swanage BH19 1LG (tel 01929-422122; fax 01929-422123). A residential activity centre for young people in a beautiful

seaside resort, offering outdoor education, climbing, and kayaking.
Kitchen Staff, House Keepers, Teachers, and Duty Staff with suitable qualifications, live-in. Period of work February to October. Overseas applicants welcome. An interview will be conducted by telephone.

Applications from January to the Manager at the above address.

CREALY PARK: Clyst St. Mary, Exeter, Devon EX5 1DR (tel 01395-233200; fax 01395-233211; e-mail employment@crealy.co.uk).
Receptionist (1) needed from April to September. Monday to Friday; working alternate weekends with a fixed week day off. Ideal first job. £4.50 p.h. Excellent telephone manner, computer literate, friendly personality all essential.
Retail Assistants (10-15) for the Easter and summer holidays.
Pay depends on age and experience. Flexible hours to suit. Retail experience an advantage. Friendly and enthusiastic. Minimum age 16 years.
Catering Assistants for the summer holidays. Wages depend on age and experience. Flexible hours. Experience not essential. Age 16+.
Play & Ride Operators (several) for the summer holdidays (July to September). Flexible hours. Must be level-headed and enthusiastic. Minimum age 17 years.

Some staff also needed for the Easter holidays. *Apply* to Karen Stacey, Personnel Officer.

DURSLEY POOL: Castle Street, Dursley, Gloucestershire GL11 4BS (tel 01453-546441; fax 01453-548629; e-mail dursley.pool@dial.pipex.com).
Recreation Officers (4) to run children's activities between 20th July and 19th August. Work involves looking after and supervising children during themed activity days. Wages up to £5.92 per hour. Applicants should have a knowledge of childcare or a childcare qualification such as NVQ, Take 10 for Play, or First Aid.
Assistant Recreation Officer/Lifeguards (4) to work supervising swimmers in the pool. Wages up to £5.11 per hour, National Pool Lifeguard Qualification essential.

Applications to Angela Gillingham, Manager, at the above address.

EXMOUTH FUN PARK: Queen's Drive, The Seafront, Exmouth, Devon EX8 2AY (tel 0797-0482 236; e-mail chriswrighty@lineone.net). Family-based amusement park, situated opposite the beach. Friendly holiday atmosphere.
Assistant Fun Park Manager (1), Fun Park Assistant (2). Negotiable wage depending on age and experience. These seasonal positions are paid for hours worked which may mean less hours than expected as the site is weather dependant. To work 30-50 hours per week. Min. period of work of July and August. Positions are available from April to mid-September. Reasonable English required. Accommodation not available.

Applications should be made from March onwards to Mr C. Wright. Interview necessary.

FARMER PALMER'S FARM PARK LTD.: Organford, Poole, Dorset BH16 6EU (tel 01202-622022; fax 01202-632111; e-mail farmerpalmers@ bigfoot.com). A professional farm park with 60,000 visitors per year, aimed primarily at children 8 years and under. The farm also includes a cafe, shop, play areas etc.
Waitresses (2) Potwashers (1) Kitchen Assistants (1). Wages £3.60- £4.50 per hour; to work 5 hours a day, 5 days a week, possibly more, from Easter to October. Applicants must be over 16. Experience is not essential as skills will be

taught, what is more important is a positive and happy attitude.

Shop Assistant (1) £4-£4.50 per hour; to work from 10am to 6pm, 3 days a week, Easter to September.

Uniforms are supplied and rolls are provided for lunch breaks. All staff working for over 4 hours must have half an hour break. Accommodation may be available. Staff are required to work for a minimum of 8 weeks. Foreign applicants are considered but must have a reasonable command of English in order to communicate with the other members of staff.

Applications should be sent to Miss Sandra Palmer from February onwards at the above address. Interview necessary.

PARK RESORTS: Bideford Bay Holiday Village, Bucks Cross, Bideford, Devon EX39 5DU (tel 01237-431331; fax 01273-431649).

Lifeguards. £3.80 per hour. Must hold National Pool Lifeguard qualification.

Catering Assistants, Bar Assistants. Wages on application.

All staff to work 39 hours a week. Posts occur between Easter and end of October. Min. age 18 years. An ability to deal with people is essential. Accommodation available at a small charge. Anglophone overseas applicants will be considered.

Applications from January to the Personnel Manager, Park Resorts.

HB LEISURE INTERNATIONAL LTD: c/o Butlins Fer, Minehead, Somerset TA24 5SH (tel 0771-505 2009; fax 01643-709932; e-mail minehead@hbLeisure.co.uk). International leisure company specialising in games and amusements.

Games Operators (10+). to work on prize-giving midway games. Wages and hours by arrangement. Some accommodation available at £20 per week. Min. period of work of 8 weeks. Positions are available at all times. Minimum age 18.

Applications should be made Tim North at the above address. Interview necessary.

HENSON & NEAVE: Cotswold Farm Park, Guiting Power, Cheltenham, Glos. GL54 5UG (tel 01451-850307; fax 01451-850423).

Farm Park Assistant needed until mid-October to work with small animals and the general public.

Cafe Staff to work until 1 October to prepare and serve food, clear tables etc.

Shop Staff needed until 1 October to serve in the gift shop and look after school parties and the farm park entrance.

All staff must be aged 18 plus and offer a high standard of customer service.

Apply to A.J. Henson, Partner at the above address.

OCEANARIUM: Pier Approach, West Beach, Bournemouth (tel 01202-311993; e-mail oceanarium@reallive.co.uk).

Front Of House/Retail Assistants (5-10) to serve customers, operate tills, stock up and for light cleaning, selling guide books, and leafleting.

Catering Assistants (5-10) to prepare food, work tills, clean, serve customers and clean tables.

Welcome Hosts/Hostesses (5-10) to greet customers, entertain, give talks and for face painting.

All positions are from July to September. Wages £3.70 to £4.00 p.h. Minimum age is 16.

For *applications*, contact, the Personnel Manager at the above address.

SUDELEY CASTLE: Winchcombe, Gloucestershire GL54 5JD (tel 01242-602308; fax 01242-602959).
Waiting Staff (15-20), Shop Assistants (2), Visitor Centre Assistants (3), Cleaning Staff (2), Plant Centre Assistant (1), Cooks (3) required to work 8-9 hours per day. Wage by arrangement. Experience preferred for shop, visitor centre and cooking positions. Staff required from Easter to September. Minimum period of work is 2 months.
Applications from late February to the Secretary at the above address.

WESTERMILL FARM HOUSE: Exford, nr Minehead, Somerset TA24 7NJ (tel 01643-831216). Campsite, six self-catering cottages and farmhouse cottage on 500-acre working hill farm by a river in the middle of Exmoor National Park. **Farm Campsite Assistants (2).** Wages specified on application. Long hours, with 1 day off a week. Large caravan provided, meals with family. Duties include signing people in and out, cleaning shower and loo block, working in the shop, grass cutting and weeding, checking and cleaning cottages, log cottage painting and some domestic jobs including cooking.
    Must be non-smokers, conscientious, intelligent and hard working, with a practical nature. One assistant needed from the end of June, the other from the end of July; to work until early September. Overseas applicants welcome.
Applications and further details (enclosing s.a.e./IRC, c.v and small photo) from January to Mrs O.J.C. Edwards at the above address.

Hotels and Catering

ABBOTSBURY OYSTERS: Ferrymans Way, Ferrybridge, Weymouth, Dorset DT4 AYU (tel 01305-788867; fax 01305-760661). A friendly, busy seafood bar connected to a working oyster farm.
Waiting Staff (3) will also involve some kitchen work. Wages £3-£4 per hour; to work 6-25 hours a week. Applicants must possess empathy, responsibility, consistency and efficiency.
Staff are required from Easter to September. Accommodation is not available.
Applications should be sent to Matthew Rodwell at the above address from 1st March.

**ANCHOR HOTEL AND SHIP INN: Porlock Harbour, Somerset TA24 8PB (tel 01643-862753; fax 01643-862843). Attractive hotel 10 yards from water's edge in a small picturesque harbour set in the beautiful scenery of Exmoor. BAR STAFF. Min. age 18. Experience preferred. Min. period of work July to September.
KITCHEN ASSISTANTS, SILVER SERVICE WAITING STAFF. Min. age 17. Min. period of work July to September.**
    All staff receive around £155 a week for 5 days' work. Split shifts including weekends. B & L available for £25 per week. *Applications* **in writing, enclosing s.a.e., from January to the Personnel Department, The Anchor Hotel and Ship Inn.**

AZTEC HOTEL: Aztec West, Almondsbury, Bristol BS32 4TS (tel 01454-201090; fax 01454-201593). A busy 4 star hotel with 128 bedrooms and 16 meeting/syndicate rooms. Old-style design and philosophy aims to make guests feel welcome.
Bar Staff (2). Must be over 18.
Waiting Staff (2). Must be over 17.

Wages on application. No accommodation is available. Full and part-time work available from April until October. Overseas applicants with good language skills considered.

Applications from January to Sandra Hart. Interview necessary.

BATH HOTEL: Lynmouth Street, Lynmouth, North Devon EX35 6EL (tel/fax 01598-752238). A family run seasonal hotel with approximately 14 members of staff during the season.

Chamber Person (1). Wages £128 per week, live-in; to work 39 hours over 6 days. Must be over 18.

Waiting Staff (2), Bar Person (1), Kitchen Porter (1). Wages £120 per week, live-in; to work 39 hours per week over 5^1/2 days. Must be over 18.

Staff required from April-October for a minimum period of 2 months. Foreign applicants with a good level of English are welcome.

Applications, from March to June, to Sharon Hobbs at the above address.

BOURNEMOUTH HIGHCLIFF MARRIOTT HOTEL: St Michael's Road, Westcliff, Bournemouth, Dorset BH2 5DU (tel 01202-557702; fax 01202-293155; e-mail HR.Bournemouth@marriotthotels.co.uk). Following £5.6 million of refurbishment by Whitbread, they consider this the premier hotel in Bournemouth.

Restaurant Staff (5), Pool Bar Staff (3), Leisure Club Pool Staff (2), Gardener (1). Wages from £4.05 per hour. Limited accommodation available. Full training, leisure club membership and excellent staff facilities are provided. Limited accommodation available for £45 per week. To work 39 hours over 5 days per week (30-40 for pool attendant, 20 over 3 days for gardener). Min. period of work of 2 months between June and September. Good level of English required: pool staff should be RLSS qualified.

Applications should include a referee and be made to the HR Manager at the above address from March onwards. Interview in person or by phone will be required.

COLLAVEN MANOR HOTEL: Sourton, Devon EX20 4HH (tel 01837-861522; fax 01837-861614; e-mail collavenmanor@supanet.com). A small 4 Crown, AA two star country house hotel with 9 bedrooms. Situated in a rural location admidat lovely scenery, the hotel is recommended in the *Good Hotel Guide*.

Waiting Staff (1). Wages £4.00 per hour.

Kitchen Assistant (1). Wages £3.50 per hour.

Sous Chef (1). Wages £4.50 per hour.

All staff must be adaptable and flexible, and prepared to assist in the general running of the hotel. Applicants must be over 16. Accommodation is provided. Period of work June to September. Overseas applicants who speak English considered

Applications from December to Mrs J. Mitchell. References must be provided if an interview is impossible.

THE CHINE HOTEL: 25 Boscombe Spa Road, Bournemouth BH5 1AX (tel 01202-396234; fax 01202-391737; e-mail reservations@chinehotel.co.uk).

Waiting Staff (4) needed mid-July to early September for restaurant and pool service; some silver service. 40 hours per week; some casual work available. 5-day week. £4.20 per hour plus tips. Live out. Food hygiene certificate, previous experience and references needed.

Chamber Staff (3) needed mid-July to early September to clean bedrooms and public areas. 30-40 hours work. 5-day week. £4.20 per hour. Live out. Previous experience and references required.

Apply to Mr. C Duley, Hotel Manager.

THE COTTAGE HOTEL: Hope Cover Kingsbridge, South Devon TQ7 3HJ (tel 01548-561555; fax 01548-561455; e-mail info@hopecover.com).
General Assistants (1-2) needed to work for as long as possible over the summer and around the year. Duties may include working in the restaurant or beach café, housekeeping, portering, depending on suitability. Wages at the national minimum wage (possibly more for experienced staff) plus tips and meals. To work a 39 hour week with 1½ or 2 days off per week depending on rota. Applicants should be aged at least 17, must speak excellent English and have previous experience of hotel work.

Applications to Sarah Ireland, Director, at the above address.

THE CROWN HOTEL: Exford, Somerset TA24 7PP (tel 01643-831554; fax 01643-831665; e-mail info@crownhotelexmoor.co.uk: www.crownhotelexmoor.co.uk) A relaxing, high-quality hotel located near moorland and wooded valleys and the picturesque Exford village.
General Assistants for waiting in the restaurant, bar work, chambermaiding and washing up duties. Wages £150 per week plus board and lodging. To work 39 hours a week. Staff required from April to September (inclusive); minimum period of work 2 months. Minimum age 19. Suitably qualified foreign applicants welcome.

Applications as soon as possible to Mr Hugo Jeune, at the above address.

THE CROWN HOTEL: Blockley, Gloucester GL54 5UG (tel 01386-700245; fax 01386-700247)
Dining Room Staff (2), General Assistants (2) for the summer period June to October. £4 per hour plus tips and accommodation. 40 hour week split shifts. Some experience preferred. Minimum age 18 years.

Applications to Virginia Piper, Manager.

EARLE HOTELS LTD: Whitsand Bay Hotel, Portwinkle, Cornwall PL11 3BU (tel 01503-230276; e-mail earlehotels@btconnect.com; www.cornish.golf.hotels.co.uk)
Restaurant And Housekeeping Staff required all year round.

Apply to J. da Rosa, Manager.

FAIRHAVEN SEA FRONT HOTEL AND RESTAURANT: 40 The Esplanade, Weymouth, Dorset DT4 8DH (tel 01305-760200).The Hotel is part of a family owned group of hotel and restaurants in Weymouth. Weymouth is a holiday resort on the South coast with a sandy beach and 17th century harbour.
Waiting Staff (5), Chefs And Grill Cooks (3), Kitchen Assistants (2). Wages by arrangement plus tips. To work 6 days a week. Meals provided and accommodation may be available. All staff must be available from the end of May to September. Some jobs are suitable for overseas students wishing to perfect their English.

Send *Applications* (with photograph) from March onwards to the Manager, Fairhaven Hotel.

HOOPS INN: Horns Cross, Bideford, Devon EX39 5DL (tel 01237-451222; fax 01237-451247). A 13th century 2 star historic inn and hotel with 12 rooms, close to the coastal path. Renowned for its cooking and traditional coaching inn atmosphere.

General Assistants for duties including waiting, housekeeping, kitchen and bar work. 40-45 hours per week. Minimum age 18. Experience preferred.
Chefs also needed. Experience essential.

Staff required for spring, summer and winter seasons. Accommodation available. *Applications* including recent photograph to Mrs Gay Marriott at the above address.

HUNTSHAM COURT: Huntsham Valley, near Tiverton, Devon EX16 7NA (tel 01398-361 365; fax 01398-361 456; e-mail andrea@huntsham.co.uk; www huntsham.co.uk). A country manor hotel that specialises in group parties, conferences and weddings. A gothic Victorian house set in a countryside location, it has a reputation for being different, unique and special.
Waiting Staff (2-4), Chamber Staff (2-4), Experienced Chefs/Cooks (2), Carpenter/Tradesman. Wages from £100 to £130 a week inclusive of accommodation and meals. Applicants must have knowledge of English, a neat appearance, and be a team worker.

Min. period of work 12 weeks, staff required all year round. *Applications* with photo and s.a.e./IRC to Andrea Bolwig, Director, Huntsham Court.

KNOLL HOUSE HOTEL: Studland Bay, near Swanage, Dorset BH19 3AH (tel 01929-452233/450450; fax 01929-450423; email staff@knollhouse.co.uk; www.knollhouse.co.uk). A country house holiday hotel superbly located in a National Trust Reserve overlooking Studland Bay. Independent and family run, it has a reputation for service and care of its guests, many of whom return annually.
Waiting Staff (6-10) for dining room including wine service. £4.20 per hour.
Housekeeping Staff (6-10). £4.20 per hour. No experience required.
General Assistants (2-3) to care for children. £4.20 per hour.
Kitchen Assistants (2-3) washing up and helping in kitchens. £4.20 per week.
Chefs (4). Salary dependent on experience. 706/1 or equivalent not always necessary.

All staff to work 38 hours with two days off per week. Deduction made for board and lodging, available in single rooms. A happy disposition and a good attitude are more important than experience. Min. age 17 years. Positions available for a min. 6 weeks between March to October. Easter and summer vacation positions also available, as well as further positions not mentioned here but only available for the entire season. EU applicants with good spoken English welcome.

Interview is not always necessary. *Applications* from the start of the year to the Staff Manager, Knoll House Hotel.

LAND'S END AND JOHN O'GROATS COMPANY: Land's End, Sennen, Penzance, Cornwall TR19 7AA (tel 01736-871501; fax 01736-871812). A leading tourist attraction in Cornwall located in a spectacular setting. It comprises various exhibitions and trading units which operate throughout the year. In winter the operation is reduced.
Catering Personnel, Retail Staff for various jobs at Land's End from spring to early autumn. Wages by arrangement; hours depend on the level of business. Applicants should be aged over 16, those with previous experience preferred.

Applications to Rob Tanner at the above address.

LIMPLEY STOKE HOTEL: Lower Limpley Stoke, Near Bath BA3 6HZ (tel 01225-723333; fax 01225-722406).

Waiting Staff (3), Cleaner, Chamber Staff (3), Bar Staff (3), Night Porter, General Assistants (2). Wages to be discussed depending on position applied for and previous experience. Period of work by arrangement.

Applications to Nick Gray, Managing Director at the above address.

LUCKNAM PARK HOTEL: Colerne, Chippenham, Wilts SN14 8AZ (tel 01225-742777; fax 01225-743536; e-mail personnel@lucknampark.co.uk; www.lucknampark.co.uk). A four star hotel with a 2 rosette restaurant, set in 500 acres of parkland, 7 miles from the historic town of Bath.

Restaurant Staff (2-4). Restaurant experience essential.

Chefs. must be qualified and experienced.

All staff to work full-time, shift hours. Min. age 18 years. Min. period of work 6 months between April and December. Accommodation available. All staff are entitled to use the hotel's extensive leisure spa facilities. Overseas applicants with good spoken English welcome; applicants in England will be required to attend an interview. Personality and appearance of the staff should reflect the high class nature of the hotel.

Applications to Claire Randall at the above address.

LUNDY COMPANY: The Lundy Island Shore Office, The Quay, Bideford, Devon EX39 2LY (tel 01237-470074; fax 01237-477779; e-mail info@ lundyisland.co.uk). Lundy is an island off the North Devon coast owned by the National Trust with 23 letting properties, a pub and a shop.

Tavern Staff (4) to help run the pub. Wages are variable; to work a 5 day week. Board and accommodation are provided free of charge. Applicants must have previous bar/kitchen experience.

Staff are required from April to September. *Applications* from January to Paul Roberts at the above address. Interview necessary. Also see under *Heritage* in the Voluntary Work section.

MR & MRS I.S. MACDONALD: The Flat, 1 Barton Road, Woolacombe, North Devon (tel 01271-870752). Fish and chip takeaway in a popular resort, a few minutes' walk from the sea.

Counter Assistants (3). £175-£180 per week, on an hourly basis. Serving takeaway food, plus some general cleaning when preparing food and shutting shop. Need little training but lots of sympathy.

Assistant Fryer. Training given. £200-£210 per week, on an hourly basis.

All staff to work 48 hours per 6-day week. Free B & L in comfortable flat with excellent facilities. Min. period of work 6 weeks between May and September. Must have pleasant appearance and sense of humour. Excellent English essential.

Applications (enclosing s.a.e. and photograph) from March to Mr & Mrs I. S. MacDonald at the above address.

MILL ON THE BRUE ACTIVITY CENTRE: Trendle Farm, Bruton, Somerset BA10 0BA (tel 01749-812307; fax 01749-812706; e-mail millonthebrue@compuserve.com). An outdoor activity centre (2 hours from London, 1 hour from Bath and Bristol) offering activities such as canoeing, climbing, archery etc. and with many young, energetic staff.

Housekeeping Assistants (1/2) for cleaning rooms and dining room duties. £142.20 per week. Staff work $7^1/2$ hours per day, $5^1/2$ days a week. Residential post, deductions made for accommodation. Full training provided. Min. period of work 2 months.

Group Leaders needed from June/July until end of August. First Aid Qualifications an advantage. Must be available for 24 hour selection process in March and a training week. Minimum age 19 years.

Long Term Instructors employed from January to November. Residential post, 44 hour week with deductions for board and lodgings.

Overseas applicants welcome. All applicants for Group Leader/Instructor positions should be available for interview. *Applications* from Ruth Braithwaite at the above address.

MOUNTAIN WATER EXPERIENCE: Countlands, Kingsbridge, Devon, TQ7 4BN (tel/fax 01548-550675; e-mail mwe@mountainwaterexp.demon.co.uk). **General Assistant** needed for June-October. Only female applicants accepted due to the accommodation available (shared). The work involves general kitchen and housework duties plus bar work. No qualifications are required, but candidates need to be over 18 and have a good sense of humour.

For *applications* and for details of wages and hours please contact Mark Agnew, Operations Manager, at the above address.

NARRACOTT GRAND HOTEL: Beach Road, Woolacombe, Devon EX34 7BS (tel 01271-870418). 100 bedroom hotel with extensive leisure facilities situated in a small coastal village near a surfing beach surrounded by National Trust land, and overlooking Woolacombe Sands.

Waiting Staff, Porters, Kitchen Staff And Room Staff. Wages specified on application. Short period of work between February and January. Longer periods possible.

Applications, including details of work experience and photo, to Mr Wyld, Narracott Grand Hotel.

NORFOLK ROYALE HOTEL: Richmond Hill, Bournemouth, Dorset BH2 6EN (tel 01202-551521; fax 01202-299729). A luxury 4 star hotel owned by the English Rose Hotels Group.

Bar Staff, Waiting Staff. Wages on application. Part-time and full-time work available for both positions. Previous experience helpful.

Kitchen Porters. Wages on application. Full-time positions only.

No accommodation is available. Staff are required for periods of 6 weeks or longer (although shorter time will be considered). Overseas applicants with work permits are considered.

Applications at any time to Personnel. Interview necessary.

OLD STOCKS HOTEL: The Square, Stow on the Wold, Glos GL54 1AF (tel 01451-830666; fax 01451-870014; e-mail theoldstocks@btinternet.com). A small 18 bedroom family run hotel with a friendly team of caring staff. Located in the highest point of the Cotswolds, a Grade II listed building.

Housekeepers (2), Waiting Staff (2), Kitchen Assistants (2), Bar Staff (2). Wages approximately £170 per week for 40 hour, 5 day week. Minimum period of work one month between April and November. Accommodation available. Previous experience not necessary as full training will be provided.

Applications should be sent to Julie Rose, Proprietor at the above address.

PENKERRIS: Penwinnick Road, St. Agnes, Cornwall TR5 0PA (tel/fax 01872-552262; e-mail info@penkerris.co.uk; www.penkerris.co.uk). Attractive detached house with garden.

Guesthouse Assistant required, to work on an *au pair* basis. Afternoons free to visit the beach or explore the cliff walks. Accommodation provided. Pocket money according to duties and season. The guesthouse is open throughout the winter. Min. work period 3 months; much longer preferred, but 3 weeks acceptable over Christmas and Easter. Overseas applicants welcome: the job is ideal for students wishing to perfect their English as they can study at Truro college nearby.

Applications a.s.a.p. to Mrs Dorothy Gill-Carey at the above address.

RISING SUN HOTEL: Harbourside, Lynmouth, North Devon EX35 6EG (tel 01598-753223; fax 01598-753480; e-mail: risingsunlynmouth@easynet.co.uk; www.risingsunlynmouth.co.uk) An award-winning historic smugglers inn overlooking a tiny picturesque harbour and Lynmouth. Internationally renowned cuisine.
General Assistant (1) for waiting in the restaurant, bar work, chambermaiding and washing up duties. Wages £150 per week less board and lodging. To work 39 hours a week. Staff required from April to September (inclusive); minimum period of work 2 months. Minimum age 19. Suitably qualified foreign applicants welcome.

Applications as soon as possible to Mr Hugo Jeune, at the above address.

RIVIERA HOTEL: Burnaby Road, Alum Chine, Bournemouth, Dorset BH4 8JF (tel 01202-763653; fax 01202-768422). A large family holiday orientated hotel based 20 minutes walk from the centre of Bournemouth and 2 minutes walk from the beach.
Waiting Staff (2). Wages on application, plus tips. To work 36 hours/6 days per week. Experience required.
Chamberperson. Wages on application, plus tips. To work 36 hours over 6 mornings per week. Experience preferred.
Wages may be increased depending on experience. Accommodation is available. Min. work period 3 months between March and November. Min. age 18. All applicants must have a friendly personality. Previous experience preferred. Overseas applicants eligible to work in the UK welcome.
Send *applications* with s.a.e. in February to the General Manager, Riviera Hotel.

ROSKARNON HOUSE HOTEL: Rock, Wadebridge, Cornwall PL27 6LD (tel 01208-862785/862329).
General Assistant (1/2). Min. of £80 for working 45 hours basic a week, plus overtime. To work 6 days per week. Any catering or housekeeping knowledge useful.
Assistant Cook, Kitchen Porter. Wages and hours negotiable.
Free B & L provided. Min. period of work 6 weeks from 25 May to 12 October. Work also available for 2-4 weeks at Easter. Overseas applicants eligible to work in the UK welcome. *Applications* in late March to Mr Veall at the above address.

ROYAL BEACON HOTEL: The Beacon, Exmouth, Devon EX8 2AF (tel 01395-264886; fax 01395-268890). Georgian Coaching House overlooking the sea, known for its old world charm and high standard of service. Two minutes walk from the beach.
Chamber Staff (2), Receptionists (2), Bar Staff (2), Kitchen Assistants (2), Porter (1), Waiting Staff (2). Pay by arrangement. To work 38 hours per 5-day week. Deductions made for B & L. Min. work period 4 months between 1 April

and 31 October. Also vacancies at Christmas, lasting 3-4 weeks. French, Spanish and German applicants welcome. *Applications* to Bill Ellis, Royal Beacon Hotel.

THE ROYAL CASTLE HOTEL: 11 The Quay, Dartmouth, Devon TQ6 9PS (tel 01803-833033; fax 01803-835445). A busy three star hotel which employs around 40 staff, Investors in People awarded.
Waiting Staff (4-6), Bar Staff (4-6). Wages from £4.40 per hour. To work 40 hours over 5 days a week. Accommodation is available at a cost of £35.50 per week. Work available all year round.
An interview is not always necessary. Staff do not need experience, just a bright personality, the right attitude, and the ability to work and play hard.
Applications about 3 weeks prior to desired start to the Duty Manager.

THE ROYAL YORK AND FAULKNER HOTEL: The Esplanade, Sidmouth, South Devon EX10 8AZ (tel 01395-513043; fax 01395-577472; e-mail yorkhotel@eclipse.co.uk; www.royalyorkhotel.co.uk). Regency resort hotel occupying a superb position on the Esplanade of Sidmouth, a charming coastal resort. 70 rooms. Family business.
Waiting Staff. To work 40 hours per week. £4.25 per hour.
Bedroom Cleaners/Dining Room Relief. To work approx. 39.25 hours per week. £4.40 per hour.
Accommodation and full board available for £25 per week. Staff all year round. Min. period of work 3 months.
Applications to Mr Peter Hook, Managing Director.

SUNNYDENE HOTEL: 11 Spencer Road, Knyveton Gardens, Bournemouth, Dorset BH1 3TE (tel 01202-552281). A family run hotel with 11 bedrooms situated midway between Boscombe and Bournemouth and catering for a wide range of customers.
General Assistant. £60 a week plus free B & L. To work 6 days a week in mornings: 8am-1pm. Assistants must be prepared to help with any aspect of hotel work including cooking, cleaning, waiting on tables, and bedroom work. Must like children, and have a very even temper, lots of patience and a lively sense of humour.
Min. period of work 10 weeks between mid July and mid September. Must be prepared to stay at least until 11 September. Overseas applicants welcome.
Applications from March enclosing a recent photograph and s.a.e./IRC, to Mrs L.H. Hackett, Proprietor, Sunnydene Hotel.

TORS HOTEL: Lynmouth, North Devon (tel 01598-753236; fax 01598-752544; e-mail Torshotel@torslynmouth.co.uk; www.torslynmouth.co.uk). A 3 star 4 crown 33 bedroom hotel situated on the North Devon coastline with stunning sea views across the Bristol Channel to Wales.
Silver Service Waiting Staff. £125 a week. Experience or the ability to learn required. 39 hours, 5¹/₂ days; split shifts. Wages dependent on experience.
Chamber Person, Porters, Kitchen Porters. £125 a week. To work 39 hours a week. No experience needed. Wages dependent on experience.
All staff work 6 days a week. Free B & L provided. Season lasts from March to January. Period of work must be for the whole period from April until September, applicants only available for summer vacation need not apply. Bonus paid on completion of season. Send *Applications* with details of previous experience and photograph a.s.a.p. to the Manager, the Tors Hotel.

TRALEE HOTEL LTD: West Hill Road, Bournemouth BH2 5EQ (tel 01202-556246; fax 01202-295229; e-mail personnel@tralee.co.uk). A busy 84 bedroom holiday and conference hotel.

Waiting Staff (1). Overtime available. Must have experience and be over 18

Kitchen Porter (1). Overtime available. Must be over 18. No experience necessary.

Room Attendant (1). No overtime. Must be over 18. Experience preferred.

Bar Attendant (1). Overtime available. Must have qualifications and experience and be over 18.

General Assistant (1). Must be over 16. Experience preferable.

All positions wages on application, work 40 hours a week over 5 days. Accommodation is available at a cost of £37.50 per week. Min. period of work 4 months. Staff should be professional, courteous, co-operative and flexible. Overseas applicants considered.

Applications to the Personnel Department 4 weeks prior to intended arrival. Interview necessary.

TREYARNON BAY HOTEL: Treyarnon Bay, St Merryn, Padstow, Cornwall PL28 8JN (tel 01841-520235; fax 01841-520239).

Kitchen Porter to work 6-8 hours per day providing general kitchen clean-up and help with preparing vegetables and starters. Applicants must have a basic hygiene certificate.

Chef/Cook to work 8-10 hours per day preparing, breakfast, lunch, dinner and for the overall running of a clean kitchen. Must have a Basic/Intermediate food hygiene certificate and NVQ.

Bar Staff (3-4) for general bar duties 6-8 hours per day, experience preferred but not essential.

Housekeeper/Room Cleaner (1-2) to clean rooms and some hotel areas for 5-6 hours per day, there is also some laundry work (although most of it is sent out).

All staff are required from July to September, and must be over 18, wages are between £3.75-£4.50 per hour according to experience, except for the chef whose wages will be £4-£5.50 per hour with accommodation available.

To apply *contact* Jennifer Kenley at the above address.

TWO BRIDGES HOTEL: (Warm Welcome Hotels) Two Bridges, Dartmoor, Devon PL20 6SW (tel 01822-890581; fax 01822-890575). A 29 bedroom hotel in the middle of Dartmoor with a busy pub trade restaurant and function suite for weddings, dinners and conferences. Friendly working atmosphere.

Bar Assistant, Waiting Staff (4), Reception Assistant to work a 5 day week of approx. 40 hours, with extra time available.

Housekeeping Staff (2) to work approx. 30 hours per week.

Required from the beginning of July to the end of October. Wages of £3.70 per hour if living out (or some limited opportunities for living in, wages negotiable) plus tips. Previous experience and qualifications not necessary, but bar assistant must be aged over 18.

Applications with recent photograph to the Personnel Manager, at the above address.

THE VICTORIA and BELMONT HOTELS: The Esplanade, Sidmouth, Devon, EX10 8RY (tel 01395-512555/512651; fax 01395-579101; e-mail info@victoriahotel.co.uk /info@belmonthotel.co.uk). These 4 star hotels have an excellent reputation for personal attentive service in a relaxed atmosphere provided by a young and enthusiastic team. Located on the beautiful Devon coastline in Sidmouth, famous for its International Folk Festival.

Room Attendants (2) required for a minimum of 3 months between June and October. Servicing of guest's rooms, working 5 days per week, mostly straight shifts 7am-3pm. Wages £135 per week, to include all meals and accommodation. Full training given.

Silver Service Waiting Staff (2) required for a minimum of 3 months between June and October. Servicing of guest's rooms, working 5 days per week, plus tips, to include all meals and accommodation. Full training given.

Candidates should be of smart appearance with a pleasant outgoing personality and sense of humour and ideally be between 18-26 years old. Must be EU citizens or possess UK work permit.

Applications to Mr M. Hext, Personnel and Training Manager, at the above address.

SANDBANKS HOTEL: 15 Banks Road, Poole, Dorset, BH13 7PS (tel 01202-707377; fax 01202-708885; e-mail personnel@sandbankshotel.co.uk). AA 3 star hotel. 116 bedrooms. Situated on beautiful Blue Flag beach. Excellent service and food.

Waiting Staff (8). Wages from £4.50-£5.00 per hour. To work 5 days out of 7, split shifts, 40 hours or casual, overtime available. Good level of English.

Room Attendants (8). Wages from £4.25-£4.75 per hour. To work 5 days out of 7, straight shifts, 37¹/₂ hours or casual.

Board and accommodation available for £30 per week. Min. period of work of 2 months. Positions are available from July to September. Applicants should be 16+, no previous experience necessary. Overseas applicants welcome as long as they have a good understanding of English.

Applications should be made to the Human Resources Manager. Interview necessary.

WATERSMEET HOTEL: Mortehoe, Woolacombe, Devon EX34 7EB (tel 01271-870333; fax 01271-870890). A 3 star high quality country house hotel with 25 bedrooms set on the National Trust's North Atlantic Coastline and overlooking a sandy beach.

Restaurant/Bar Staff (2), Housekeeping Staff (2), Kitchen Staff (2). 40-42 hours per week over 6 days. Wages £110 a week including B & L. Min. age 18 years. Experience an advantage. Min. period of work 3 months between May and October.

Applications, with CV and photograph, from January to Mr Neil Bradley at the above address.

WOOLACOMBE BAY HOTEL: Woolacombe, Devon EX34 7BN (tel 01271-870388; fax 01271-870613). A family hotel situated near 3 miles of golden sands and a surfing beach.

Waiting Staff, Room Staff, Kitchen Staff, Bar Staff, Porters. £3.70 per hour (live-in). To work 44 hours per week. B & L provided. Min. age 18. Min. work period 4 months between Easter and October. Staff are also required over Christmas and New Year (22 December to 2 January approx.).

Applications from March to The Manager, Woolacombe Bay Hotel.

Language Schools

ANGLO-CONTINENTAL EDUCATIONAL GROUP: 33 Wimborne Road, Bournemouth BH2 6NA (tel 01202-557414; fax 01202-556156; e-mail english@anglo-continental.com).

Teachers Of English (up to 100) for English language summer courses for adults. To teach 20, 25 or 30 lessons per week. Cambridge CELTA/Dip. TEFL or equivalent qualifications required, plus experience of TEFL.

Teachers Of English (20) for 8-16 year olds in residential and non-residential schools. TEFL or equivalent qualifications preferable, but candidates with enthusiastic and outgoing character may also be considered.

House Staff (6) for residential junior centre. To work 6 days per week, mostly in the afternoons and evenings. Experience with children needed.

Sports Staff (8) on both residential and non-residential junior courses. Cert.Ed/PGCE preferable; experience with children essential.

Salaries approximately £140-£240 per week according to qualifications and experience. No accommodation, except on some residential junior courses. Min. age 20. Period of work between 10 June and 24 August.

Applications from the beginning of March to Ms J. Haine, Anglo-Continental Educational Group.

BOURNEMOUTH TEACHING SERVICE LTD: 139 Charminster Road, Bournemouth, Dorset BH8 8UH (tel/fax 01202-521355). A small language school with 9 members of staff; established in 1980.

EFL Teachers (2). Wages £240-£290 per week. To work 22¹/2 hours per week. Min. period of work of 4 weeks. Positions are available from late June to end of August. RSA cert TEFL or RSA DIP TEFL required. Accommodation not available.

Applications should be made from April onwards to Stephen Laughton. Interview necessary.

CHANNEL SCHOOL OF ENGLISH: Country Cousins Ltd., Bicclescombe, Ilfracombe, Devon EX34 8JN (tel 01271-862834; fax 01271-865374; email help@country-cousins.com; www.country-cousins.com). Situated on the beautiful North Devon coast the school offers a range of English courses with 12, 15 or 21 hours of lessons per week to those aged 7 to adult.

EFL Teachers (3) to work July-August. Wages £9.70 per hour; to work 24 hours per week. Must have TEFL qualification and should have experience with the age range 11-18.

Applications to Matthew Twiggs, Director of Studies, at the above address.

DORSET INTERNATIONAL COLLEGE: Cambridge House, 7 Knyveton Road, Bournemouth BH1 (tel 01202-316611; fax 01202-318811; e-mail info@dorsetinternationalcollege.co.uk). A British Council recognised small language school which runs junior and adult courses all year round. Encourages a close relationship between staff and students. Situated in the centre of a seaside town ¹/2 hour from the New Forest, and 1¹/2 hour's train journey from London.

EFL Teachers (1-5) to work 9am-5pm. 2 year's experience of teaching English required.

Activity Leaders (2). 4 hours a day. 2 year's experience required.

Receptionist (1/2) to work 9am-5pm. Min. age 19. GCSEs required.

Staff wanted from July to September. Min. period of work 1 month. Accommodation not available. Overseas applicants welcome.

Applications from 1 June to the Administration Manager at the above address.

EAGLE INTERNATIONAL SCHOOL: Tiami, 55 Elms Avenue, Lilliput, Poole, Dorset BH14 8EE (tel/fax 01202-745175; e-mail eaglesch@aol.com).

Teacher/Leaders (15) needed to work with overseas students in the 11-17 age range. Duties Wages £180 per week. Work available over the Easter and Summer vacations. Duties will involve giving classes in English conversation and supervising students on the activity programme. Periods of work will be EasterPreference given to B.Ed and P.G.C.E. Modern Languages and English/Sport/Drama students.

Applications to J. Rees, Principal.

THE ENGLISH CENTRE SALISBURY: The Duchess of Albany Building, Ox Row, Salisbury, Wiltshire SP1 1EU (tel 01722-412711; fax 01722-414604; e-mail info.ecs@twinschool.co.uk). Small but expanding language school in the centre of Salisbury. Offers English tuition to groups of international students in a friendly work environment.

EFL Teachers (5). £13.33 per hour minimum. To work mornings and some afternoons. Applicants must be TEFL qualified with experience teaching multi-lingual groups.

Social Activity Organisers (2). From £5 per hour. To work afternoons and some weekends. Applicants must have proof of organisational skills. Minimum age 18.

Staff required from June-September. Board and accommodation is not provided. Enthusiasm and energy needed. *Applications* from March to the Principal at the above address.

THE ENGLISH COUNTRY SCHOOL: 18 Riverside, Winchcombe, Cheltenham, Gloucestershire GL54 5JP (tel/fax 01242-604067). A British Council accredited English language summer school in Southern England and Scotland, for children and teenagers providing 'fun, friendship and learning in a healthy, natural environment'.

English Teachers (8) to teach English and assist with sports and crafts. Wages from £300 per week live-in, with time off. Must have EFL qualifications, and/or PGCE/B.Ed.

Sports Organisers (2). Wages from £300 per week live-in, with time off. Must have relevant sports coaching qualifications.

Min. period of work 3 weeks between mid July and mid August. *Applications* from April to the Director. Interview necessary.

HARROW HOUSE INTERNATIONAL COLLEGE: Harrow House Drive, Swanage, Dorset BH19 1PL (tel 01929-424421; fax 01929-427175). An all year round school in a beautiful location with superb facilities, catering for all ages of students from over 45 different countries.

EFL Teachers (20) to teach up to 40 lessons per week, 9am-5pm, June-August; pay rates from £6.50 to £8 per 45 minute lesson. Possibility also of helping with evening activities and one full day excursion every two weeks, both paid extra. No accommodation is available but assistance may be given in finding it. Applicants must have EFL teaching experience, be at least 21 years old and have some knowledge of foreign languages.

Applications to Andrew Kirby, Principal, at the above address.

THE INTERNATIONAL SCHOOL: 1 Mount Radford Crescent, Exeter EX2 4EW (tel 01392-254102; fax 01392-434432; e-mail helen@internationalschool.co.uk). An International School providing English as a foreign language courses all year round, mostly for adults.

EFL Teachers (25). Wages £8.60 per 45 minute lesson; to teach 20-40 lessons per week. Must possess a recognised TEFL certificate and have teaching experience. Accommodation is available for £70 per week. Teachers needed from June to September for a minimum period of 1 week. Applicants with a high fluency in English and a TEFL qualification are welcome.

Applications from March to Helen Mattacott at the above address.

THE LANGUAGE PROJECT: 27 Oakfield Road, Clifton, Bristol BS8 2AT (tel 0117-9090 911; fax 0117-9077 181; e-mail info@languageproject.co.uk). A small school with a focus on innovative teaching techniques and use of the latest materials; also performs a lot of teacher training.

EFL Teachers (3). who can deliver topic-based lessons using authentic materials of their own making. Wages £220 per week, accommodation available for £90 per week. To work 18 hours per week. Min. period of work of 4 weeks. Positions are available from June to August. TEFL at A or B grade plus 2 year's experience of teaching adults required. Foreign applicants welcome.

Applications should be made from May onwards to Dr Jon Wright at the above address. Interview necessary.

MIDLAND SCHOOL LTD: 7 Alverton Hall, 33 Westcliff Road, Bournemouth BH4 8AY (tel 01202-759595; fax 01202-303265).

Teachers (up to 10). Wages £209-£305 per week. Hours approx. 9am-5pm Monday to Friday, including one excursion day a week and one extra-curricular evening. Most weekends off. Must have at least a B.Ed, preferably with TEFL. Should be keen, able to discipline large groups and enjoy team work.

No accommodation provided but free lunches usually available. Min. period of work 2 weeks in either July or August. Contractual problems make it difficult for positions to be offered to overseas applicants. All applicants must be available for interview.

Applications a.s.a.p. to Miss A. Burton, Director, Midland School Ltd.

RICHARD LANGUAGE COLLEGE: 43-45 Wimborne Road, Bournemouth, Dorset BH3 7AB (tel 01202-555932; fax 01202-555874; e-mail acadman@rlc.co.uk; www.rlc.co.uk).

EFL Teachers (20). £240-£258 per week depending on qualifications and experience. Hours 8.30am-4.30pm Monday to Friday. Teaching 6 or 7 lessons of 45 minutes per day to adults of mixed levels and different nationalities, in classes of about 10 students. Must have first degree in foreign languages/English literature and RSA Prep. Certificate in TEFL.

Help can be given in finding accommodation. Min. work period 2 weeks between 1 June and 30 August. Applicants from America, Canada, New Zealand and Australia will be considered.

Applications from 28 February to the Academic Manager, Richard Language College.

SOUTHBOURNE SCHOOL OF ENGLISH: 30 Beaufort Road, Bournemouth BH6 5AL (tel 01202-422300; fax 01202-417108; e-mail details@ southbourneschool.co.uk; www.southbourneschool.co.uk). A family run school, working for 34 years teaching English as a foreign language. British Council accredited and a member of ARELS and STB.

EFL Teachers (20). Wages £9.50 per hour; to work 15-30 hours per week. Must have one of the following qualifications; PGCE, B.ed., Cert Ed., RSA Cert EFL, RSD Diploma EFL, TESOL, Trinity Diploma.

Sports Organisers/Assistants (8). Wages £180-£300. Either residential or to work 30 hours a week. Sports training useful. Minibus driver useful.

Free accommodation on residential courses. Staff required from mid June-end August.
Applications from Easter to the Principal, at the above address.

SUL LANGUAGE SCHOOLS: 7 Woodlands Avenue, Tywardreath, Par, Cornwall PL24 2PL (tel 01726-814227; fax 01726-813135; e-mail claire@sul-schools.com). A well-established business which provides language holiday courses in Cornwall, Devon, Somerset + Midlands and Ireland for foreign teenagers. Courses run for 2-4 weeks from April to September.
EFL Teachers. Wages dependant on experience and qualifications but are usually from £23 per morning of 2^1/2 hours. To work mornings and possibly afternoons, supervising activities. Accommodation is available at some centres. Teachers required from April-August for a minimum period of 2 weeks. Applicants should be TEFL qualified or hold a languages degree or teaching qualification. An interview is usually required.
Applications from January to Claire Frost at the above address.

TORBAY LANGUAGE CENTRE: Conway Road, Paignton, Devon TQ4 5LH (tel 01803-558555; fax 01803-559606; e-mail tlc@lalschool.org). A large school with very good resources. CELTA training centre so there is excellent teacher support and guidance. Maximum class size of ten students. Also runs a small residential centre in North Devon.
EFL Teachers (40). Wages £8.50 per hour; to teach an average of 22^1/2 hours per week. Must be CELTA or equivalent or PGCE with TEFL experience. No accommodation available. Teachers required from last week of June to the third week of August for minimum of 2 weeks.
Applications from 1 March to the Director of Studies at the above address.

Medical

ELITE CARE NURSING AGENCY: 14 Silver Street, Barnstaple, Devon, EX32 8HR (tel 01271-346666; fax 01271-344222; e-mail elitecare@sosi.net).
Qualified Nurses (20) minimum wage £9 per hour. To work in hospitals, nursing homes etc. Must be at least RGN/RMN.
Care Assistants (30) to work in clients' own homes or nursing homes as live-in carers. Wages at a minimum of £4.20 per hour, carers must be at least 18 and have carework experience.
Nursing Auxiliaries (30) to work in district and cottage hospitals for a minimum of £5.17 per hour. Must be experienced carers and at least 18 years old.
Work available around the year. *Applications* to K.M. Harding, Branch Manager at the above address.

EXERCISE INDEPENDENCE: 1 The Green, East Knoyle, Salisbury (tel/fax 01747-830504; e-mail live.aware@virgin.net). A disabled teacher of remedial exercise needs help from a team to establish a project from his own home around exercise, diet and living independently. Some group work and meditation.
Carers/Personal Assistants (2) to run house, look after and being part of an organised team in order to enable an active and disabled person to live a normal and healthy alternative lifestyle.
Wages negotiable, full board and accommodation. To work variable hours. Min. period of work of 6 months. Positions are available from October 2001. Need caring flexible attitude. Fluent English required.

Applications and enquiries should be made as soon as possible to Michael Mitchell at the above address, preferably by e-mail.

THORNBURY NURSING SERVICES: 17 Whiteladies Road, Clifton, Bristol, BS8 1PB (tel 0117-923 8443; fax 0118-973 2546; e-mail recruitment@thornbury-nursing.com).
Registered And Auxilliary Nurses to work nationwide carrying out day and night-shift agency nursing work in NHS and private hospitals and nursing homes. Candidates must have 6 months experience within the last two years of clinical nursing and UKCC Registration for qualified nurses. All aplicants must pass an interview prior to being accepted. Wages are from £15.50 per hour for registered nurses, or from £8 per hour for auxiliary nurses, with holiday pay on top of the basic rates.
To obtain positions *contact* the agency at the above address.

Outdoor

BOLDSCAN LIMITED: Unit 4 Tonedale Business Park, Wellington, Somerset TA21 OAW (tel 01823-665849; fax 01283-665850). A company that manufactures marquees and hires them out to the event industry.
Marquee Erectors (15-20) Work involves the erection of marquees for local events, weddings and shows. Wages £4.00-£4.50 per hour, to work 40-60 hours per week. Applicants must be at least 18 years old. Period of work from April 1st to September 30th for a minimum of 4 weeks. Accommodation not available.
Applicants should *apply* from mid February to Mr P.Cornish at the above address. Interview necessary.

BURNBAKE CAMPSITE: Rempstone, Corfe Castle, Wareham, Dorset BH20 5JJ (tel 01929-480570; e-mail info@burnbake.com; www.burnbake.com). Long established campsite.
Campsite Assistants. to handle enquiries, serve the shop, help with cleaning and rubbish collection and carry out general site maintenance and customer service duties. One required 3 May to 9 September, two needed 12 July to 6 September. Wages of £160 per week with free mobile accommodation. To work 8am-12pm and 5pm-7pm over a 6 day week.
For *applications* or further details, contact Tim Bircham at the above address.

COLIN SIMPSON: Unit 8, Elm Tree Business Park, Sheepway, Portbury, Bristol, BS20 7TF (tel 01275-372237; fax 01275-372728; e-mail enquiries@marquees-simpson.co.uk).
Marquee Erectors (6) required from mid-June until mid-September to erect marquees. The work is paid at £4 per hour and is usually made up of ten hours or more per day over a 5 day week, with some weekend work. Employees must be over 18 and a full driving licence would be helpful, but not essential.
Applications should be made to G. Davies, Operations Manager.

J.F. COLES t/a V.T. COLES: Stephens Farm, Spaxton, Near Bridgwater, Somerset TA5 1BU (tel 01278-671 281; fax 01278-671530).
Pea And Bean Pickers (20). Piece work rates, hours 7am-4pm. Minimum period of work 6 weeks between June and September. Accommodation: own tents required, water and portaloos available. No experience necessary. Overseas applicants welcome. *Applications* from end of May to Mr and Mrs Coles at the above address.

K.S. COLES: Cheston House Farm, Cheston, Wellington, Somerset TA21 9HP (tel 01823-664244; fax 01823-660325; e-mail kscoles@btinternet.com). Situated in one of the most attractive areas of England, K.S. Coles have been trading for over 30 years and now supply several of the major multiples with fresh produce.

Pea Pickers (60 Or More). Period of work approx. mid June to end August. Piece work at £2.50 per 21 lb picked. 5-6am start; 4.30pm finish. Minimum age 18.

Applications to Mrs C.M. Coles, Partner, or Miss S. Coles, at the above address.

THE COURTS: Holt, Trowbridge, Wiltshire BA14 6RR (tel/fax 01225-782340; e-mail on ntrust.org). A twentieth century creation in the style of Hidcote Manor, 7 acres in total, with an arboretum.

Gardener (1). To work with three others maintaining an important National Trust garden. To work variable hours from 1 March to November. Min. period of work one month. Min. age 20. Applicants should be motivated with some experience. Overseas applicants welcome. Free accommodation available.

Apply from 1 March to Mr Troy Smith, Head Gardener, at the above address. Note that it is preferable for candidates to be available for an interview.

CUTLIFFE FARM: Sherford, Taunton, Somerset TA1 3RQ (tel 01823-253808).The farm is within easy walking distance from Taunton town centre, with all the facilities available in a large country town.

Fruit Pickers (30+) to pick strawberries, raspberries, runner beans, plums, etc. Wages at piece work rate plus bonuses. Some accommodation may be available in caravans. Period of work late May to early August. Min. age 18. Overseas applicants welcome, provided they have obtained the necessary work visa.

Applications to A.P. & S.M. Parris at the above address.

M. J. DAVISON: Ploddy House, Newent, Gloucestershire GL18 1JX (tel 01531-820240).

Farm Assistants. Varied range of work to be performed on arable and poultry farm. Wages at Agricultural Wages Board rates or piecework rates. Early starts when required. Min. period of work of 1 month from May to October. Applicants must be over 18 and authorised to work in the UK. Accommodation will be in own tent but washing, cooking and toilet facilities are available.

Applications to M. J. Davison, Owner, at the above address from March onwards.

THE DORSET BLUEBERRY COMPANY: Hampreston, Wimborne, Dorset BH21 7LX (tel 01202-579342; fax 01202-579014; e-mail jobs@dorset-blueberry.co.uk). Britain's primary producers of fresh blueberries for major supermarkets.

Pickers and Packers required. Wages are calculated by kg performance and good workers can earn high wages. Positions availaby from July to September.

Applications only accepted through website at www.dorset-blueberry.co.uk/jobs.

MR J.F.P. DOUGLAS: Avon Valley Farm, Bath Road, Keynsham, Bristol BS31 1TS (tel 0117-986 8837).

Fruit Pickers (around 6) to work from the beginning of June to mid August. National minimum wage. Flexible working hours between 6am and 10pm, 7 days per week. Camping with own equipment only. Min. age 16 years. National Insurance cards will be required on arrival. Some supervisory positions may be available, depending on competence. Non-EU applicants welcome, must apply via Concordia or HOPS for work permit and placement, and not directly to farm.

Applications to Mr J. Douglas at the above address. Please enclose a s.a.e. and tel. no.

GRAND WESTERN HORSEBOAT CO: The Wharf, Canal Hill, Tiverton, Devon EX16 4HX (tel 01884-253345). A family business operating unique horsedrawn barge trips on a delightful canal which provides peace, wildlife and nature.

Crew Member for a horsedrawn barge. Must be fit, polite and of clean appearance and able to work as a team member, with ropes, the barge and heavy horses. National Minimum Wage. Flexible working hours from 30 hours to $5^1/_2$ days per week. Min. period of work is 1 week. Positions are available from May to September. Applicants should be 25+ and hold a driving licence. Accommodation not available.

Applications should be made to Mrs P. Brind from 1 April at the above address.

HAYLES FRUIT FARM LTD: Winchombe, Cheltenham, Glos. GL54 5PB (tel 01242-602123; fax 01242-603320; e-mail jobs@hayles-fruit-farm.co.uk; www.hayles-fruit-farm.co.uk). A very friendly family run mixed fruit farm in a beautiful rural location in the Cotswolds. A subsidised hot meal can be provided every evening for people staying in tents.

Fruit Pickers (10) to work 8am to 4pm, picking apples, pears, plums or nuts. Piecework rates, approx. £20-£35 per day. No experience necessary. Min. period of work 3-5 weeks between August and end of September. Min. age 21 years. No accommodation provided. Campsite available.

Applications from 1 July to Mr Martin Harrall at the above address.

MICHAEL H. KEENE & SON LTD: The Moat, Newent, Gloucestershire GL18 1JG (tel 01531-820363). A family run farming company producing apples for supermarkets, cider apples for the cider industry and blackcurrants for the blackcurrant juice market. Situated in an attractive tourist area within easy reach of shops in Cheltenham and Gloucester.

Apple Pickers (12) required for careful hand-picking, starting 1 September. Payment is by recognised hourly rates. To work from 8am to 4pm. Instruction will be given in how to pick carefully. A campsite with showers, toilets and electric cooker is available, but must bring own tent, cooking utensils, wet-weather clothes and boots. There is some mobile home accommodation: please check for availability. A sitting area with TV also provided. No dogs allowed. Please note that applicants from outside the EEA must have permits to work in the UK.

For *applications* call 01531-820363 or 01531-820503 in early August to confirm starting dates.

J.G. MARQUEES: Nettwood Farm, East Harptree, Bristol, BS40 6DA (tel/fax 01761-221372).

Marquee Erectors (2). Wages from £4.30-£5.50 per hour. To work 8.30am-5.30pm Monday to Friday. Positions are available from mid-June to September. Applicants must be able to drive to get to work.

Applications should be made to Jeremy Griffin, Proprietor, at the above address.

NEWTOWN FARM: Newent, Gloucestershire GL18 1JX (tel 01531-820240). **Assistants (20+)** to plant and cut lettuce. Wages at Agricultural Wages Board rates or piecework. To work 5-6 days a week when required. Early start necessary, often 6am. Accommodation provided on a campsite with shower and toilets; some self-catering accommodation also available at a charge. Period of work May to October: preference given to those who can start in May. All applicants must be over 18 and physically fit. EU/EEA nationals and overseas applicants with Work Permits welcome.

Applications, enclosing s.a.e., to Mr J. Davison at Ploddy House, Newent, Glos. GL18 1JX.

POWNEY BROTHERS: 16 Jockey Lane, Bromham, Chippenham, Wilts SN15 2EZ (tel 01380-850340).
Vegetable Harvester/Planter to work from June to October. £3.80 per hour, variable hours. Accommodation possible. Age 16+.

Applications to D. Powney, Owner.

PENROSE MARQUEES: Trevellas, St Agnes, Cornwall TR5 0XS (tel 01872-552494; fax 01872-554106).
Marquee Erectors (2-3) required between May and September. Wages dependant on experience; hours of work vary so employees must be available 7 days a week.

Applications to Rik Evans.

SHULDHAM SOFT FRUIT GROWERS LTD: East Stoke House, Stoke-sub-Hamdon, Somerset TA14 6UF (tel 01935-822300; fax 01935-824596; e-mail shuldham@aol.com). Set in beautiful countryside in southeast Somerset. Nearby towns for good shopping and nightlife. Excellent transport links. Family farm, small and friendly.
Pickers/General Farm Hands (20) needed from 24 May to 31 August to pick soft fruits including strawberries, blackberries, tayberries, gooseberries, rasberries and redcurrants. To work 6 days a week 5/6 hours per day. Involves early starts (6-6.30am) usually finishing at about midday. Some late afternoon picking. Minimum of £3.60 p.h., up to £6/£7 per hour possible with piecework. No accommodation provided but camping with own gear if necessary at nearby campsites. Applicants should be strong, determined and conscientious.

Applications to Simon Shuldham, Managing Director.

SOUTH PETHERTON FRUITFUL FARM: c/o 4 Estate Cottages, Mapperton, Beaminster, Dorset DT8 3NR (tel 01308 863 201). A long established strawberry/raspberry grower with a high quality protected crop.
Fruit Pickers (6) to pick strawberries and raspberries from late May to August. Wages either £3.50 per hour or at piecework rates. Washing facilities provided.

Applications to Mr Crocker at the above address.

WHITE MOTOR BOATS: 7 Old Station Road, Upwey, Weymouth, Dorset DT3 5NQ (tel/fax 01305-813246; mobile tel 0777-8286892). Tourist passenger boat operators plying between Weymouth and Portland.
Coxswain (1/2). Wages £6 per hour. Boatmasters grade 1 or 2, VHF certificate, sea survival, basic first aid, and fire fighting certificate.
Coxswain's mate (1/2). Wages £4.50 per hour. No qualifications required as training given but boating experience useful.
To work 8 hours for 7 days a week but could be full or part-time. Good customer

skills plus public safety, smart appearance and dress code important. Positions are available from April 1 to October 31. Foreign applicants welcome if English is proficient. No accommodation available.

Applications to Mr Ian Robertson at the above address from February. Interview necessary.

Sport

CHRISTCHURCH BOROUGH COUNCIL: Civic Offices, Bridge Street, Christchurch, Dorset BH23 1AZ (tel 01202-495000; fax 01202-482200; g.foyle@christchurch.gov.uk). Christchurch's beaches are friendly, neighbourhood beaches which have not been commercialised with the lively, cosmopolitan town of Bournemouth close by. Christchurch is a great place to work, rest and play.

Beach Lifeguards (4) needed July-September, to work 10am-6pm Monday to Saturday. £4.75 per hour. NARS Beach Lifeguard preferable, but will accept RLSS Bronze Medallion (with training).

Seasonal Leisure Assistants (4) needed April to September, 9am-5pm Thursday to Monday. £4.75-£6 per hour. Leisure qualifications would be an advantage.

Patrol Boat Crew (4) needed April to September. £5-£6 per hour. Hours vary according to local tides. RYA Powerboat Level 2 and above.

Applications to Gary Foyle, Leisure Operations Supervisor.

GREENBANK SWIMMING POOL: Wilfrid Road, Street, Somerset BA16 0EL (tel 01458-442468). A very busy, privately run open-air swimming pool with over 1,000 bathers during hot periods.

Lifeguards (3) to lifeguard and clean the pool and premises. Wages from £4.30 per hour. To work 35 hours per week on a rota basis. Standby required during busy periods. Min. period of work of May to September. Royal Life Saving Society's National Pool Lifequard Qualification expected. No accommodation available.

Applications should be made from 1 March onwards to Mr D. Mogg, Pool Manager, at the above address. Interview necessary.

J.S. KING RACING STABLE: Elm Cross House, Broad Hinton, Near Swindon, Wiltshire SN4 9PF (tel 01793-731481; e-mail trishking_new.uk). A racing stable training national hunt and flat horses.

Full Time Groom (1-2) Wages £200 per week; to work 6½ days per week. Applicants must have experience of all stable duties and preferably ride well.

Part Time Groom (1-2) Wages £4-£5 per hour; to work for 6 hours at weekends. Applicants need not have riding experience but must have experience of stable duties.

All of the above positions involve mucking out stables, grooming and exercising racehorses. Accommodation is available for no charge. Staff are required from May 1st to October for a minimum period of 2 weeks.

Applications should be sent to Mrs P.M. King at the above address from April onwards.

KNOWLE MANOR & RIDING CENTRE: Timberscombe, Minehead, Somerset TA24 6TZ (tel 01643-841342; fax 01643-841644; e-mail knowlemnr@aol.com; welcome.to/knowle). Knowle Manor is a residential riding holiday centre based in Exmoor National Park. Set in 80 acres of grounds with indoor heated swimming pool, trout lake, croquet and badminton areas.

Riding Instructor to work 5 days a week. Salary £160+ per week. Applicants must have B.H.S.A.I.

Ride Leaders (2) to work approx. 40 hours a week. Salary £144+ per week. Experience with horses essential. Recommended B.H.S. Riding and Road Safety. Mature outlook also needed. Minimum age 18.

Domestic Helpers (3) to clean and to perform waiting duties in hotel. Wages £147 per week. To work approx. 35 hours a week. No experience necessary but applicants must be cheerful.

Minimum period of work for all positions July to end of August or preferably September. Board and accommodation is provided free of charge. Suitably qualified foreign applicants welcome.

Applications from February onwards to Sue Lamacraft at the above address.

MENDIP OUTDOOR PURSUITS: Laurel Farmhouse, Summer Lane, Banwell, Weston-Super-Mare BS29 6LP (tel 01934-820518). A multi-activity mobile centre established in 1987 for clients aged 8 years and above. Training available in safety, education, technical skills and NVQs.

Instructors. £150+ per week. Min. age 21.

All instructors to work 5 days per week. Must hold qualifications in outdoor pursuits. Accommodation is **not** provided. Min. period of work 2 weeks between June and September. Overseas applicants able to communicate well in English welcome. All candidates must be available for interview.

Applications to J. Hayward at the above address.

MILL ON THE BRUE ACTIVITY CENTRE: Trendle Farm, Bruton, Somerset BA10 0BA (tel 01749-812307; fax 01749-812706; e-mail millonthebrue@compuserve.com). An outdoor activity centre (2 hours from London, 1 hour from Bath and Bristol) offering activities such as canoeing, climbing, archery etc.

Domestic Staff. £155-£162 based on 42 hour week. Accommodation and board provided. Min age 17 years. English lessons provided for overseas applicants. Needed January to beginning of December.

Group Leaders. Wages from £142.20 to £162 per week; based on a 46 hour week with deductions made for board and accommodation. Min. age 19. Qualifications such as First Aid and advantage. Staff required from June/July until the end of August. Applicants must attend a 24 hour selection in March and a training week. Overseas applicants welcome though require good level of English. Long term instructors, residential post, employed January-November.

Application forms from Ruth Braithwaite, Mill on the Brue Activity Centre.

WEST-ANSTEY FARM EXMOOR: Dulverton, Somerset TA22 9RY (tel 01398-341354). A working farm and stables adjoining open moorland four miles from Dulverton, the nearest town. Lovely riding county, moorlands, fields and woods.

Riding Assistants (2). Must be able to take out rides and lead beginners when necessary. Hours vary depending on schedule of activities. Min. age 16. Must be fairly light, a good rider and with experience of going on riding holidays or of conducting treks and caring for ponies, horses and people. Sense of fun, helpfulness and a cheerful disposition essential. Must also be willing to help indoors when necessary.

Pocket money plus B & L provided. Applicants must be non-smokers and able to get on with both adults and children. Accommodation only available for females. Work available all year round. Min. work period 8-10 weeks.

Applications with a contact phone number and photograph a.s.a.p. to the Proprietor, West-Anstey Farm Exmoor.

Voluntary Work

Conservation and the Environment

THE MONKEY SANCTUARY: Looe, Cornwall PL13 1NZ (tel 01503-262532; e-mail info@monkeysnctuary.org; www.monkeysanctuary.org).
Volunteers are required to work 40 hours per week in the sanctuary that is home to a colony of Amazonian grey woolly monkeys. Volunteers are essential in allowing the team of keepers to care for the colony. Help is needed in the kiosk, and with cleaning while the sanctuary is open to the public between April and September; during the closed season (October to March) volunteers assist with general maintenance work and cleaning. No qualifications are necessary but workers must have an interest in animal welfare and conservation.
Food and accommodation are provided at a charge of £35 (£25 for students, £15 unwaged) per week. Min. age 18. Overseas applicants with a good standard of English welcome.
Applications, four or five months in advance, should be made to Mike Brown at the above address, enclosing stamped s.a.e. or International Reply Coupon.

ST GEORGE'S ISLAND: (Craft Centre) Looe, Cornwall PL13 2AB (tel 07836-522919).
The privately-owned St George's Island, located one mile off the South Cornish coast, is open to visitors as a non-profitmaking project. Only 1 boat is allowed to bring visitors to the island at half hourly intervals, so that all visitors are met by the owner. Four Volunteers are required for conservation work and to attend to day visitors to the island, i.e. meeting the boats, helping in the craft shop, etc. Working hours vary according to the weather and tides. Self-catering accommodation is available at a cost of 15 a week. Min. period of work one week between Easter and the end of September/early October.
Send *Applications* as soon as possible (please note – s.a.e. or IRC essential for a reply) to R.A. Atkins at the above address.

Heritage

LUNDY COMPANY: Lundy Island, Bristol Channel, North Devon EX39 2LY (tel 0123-431831; fax 01237-431832; e-mail island@lundyisland.co.uk).
Lundy is an island off the North Devon coast owned by the National Trust with 23 letting properties, a pub and a shop.
Volunteer Positions. There are various outdoor positions available involving conservation and farm work and general island duties. The jobs are variable according to the time of year. Volunteers need no experience but must have lots of enthusiasm. Accommodation is provided free of charge and there is a reduced fare on boat trips. Volunteers are required from April to September for a minimum of 1 week.
Applications should be sent to the Warden at the above address from January onwards.

Vacation Traineeships

Law

BURGES SALMON SOLICITORS: Narrow Quay House, Narrow Quay, Bristol BS1 4AH (tel 0117-902 2725; fax 0117-902 4400; e-mail lisa.head@burges-salmon.com; www.burges-salmon.co.uk).
Burges Salmon is a leading regional law firm with a reputation for quality and an ability to attract people and clients normally regarded as the preserve of City firms. Based in Bristol some 75% of the firm's clients are situated outside its South West base and over recent years, Burges Salmon has witnessed an extraordinarily high and sustainable rate of growth. The firm provides national and international clients with a full commercial service through four departments: Company Commercial, Litigation, Property, Tax and Trusts. Specialist areas of the firm include: agribusiness, banking, competition, corporate finance, dispute resolution, e-commerce, environment, human resources, IP and IT, and transport. Full fees are paid for both the CPE and LPC and maintenance grants of £3,500 LPC and £4,000 CPE (£2,000 p.a.).
Places for 2002: 34; Duration: 2 weeks; Remuneration; £150 per week; Closing Date; 22 February 2002, 20-25 training contracts for September 2004.
Applications and queries to Miss Lisa Head, Graduate Recruitment and Development Manager, at the above address.

WILSONS SOLICITORS: Steynings House, Fisherton Street, Salisbury SP2 7RJ (tel 01722-412412; fax 01722-411500; e-mail cd@wilsons-solicitors.co.uk).
Wilsons offers **Summer Placements** for 10-14 students. Applicants should be either Law students or university students considering a career in law. Salary is £60 per week. Placements occur in June-July at Head Office, and last for 2 weeks. No accommodation is provided.
Applications by March to Carole Davidson.

Science, Construction and Engineering

DEVONPORT MANAGEMENT LIMITED: Devonport Royal Dockyard, Devonport, Plymouth P21 4SG (tel 01752-605665; fax 01752-552887; david.penelrick@devonport.co.uk; www.devonport.co.uk)
Traineeships are offered in Production, Projects, Nuclear Safety and Design Areas.
There are available **60 Sixth-form Placements** for 10 weeks, **6 Undergraduate Positions** for 16 weeks during the summer, and there are **6 Sandwich Year Positions (YIA).**
Applicants should be Sixth-formers wishing for a career in Engineering and Undergraduates should be reading Engineering Degrees. Wages are available on request. The traineeships are held in Devonport. No accommodation is provided but help is available for arranging lodgings and finding contacts. Any suitably qualified applicants will be considered but all applicants will need to be cleared with the Ministry of Defence Security. This is not possible for many non-nationals.
Applications should be made to the Training Manager at the above address, preferably by e-mail.

MESSIER-DOWTY LTD: Cheltenham Road East, Gloucester GL2 9QH (tel 01452-712424; fax 01452-713821; e-mail vikki.strong@messier-dowty.org; www.messier-dowty.com).
Messier-Dowty is a world leader in the design, development and manufacture of landing gear systems, with an annual turnover of US$540 million. The company's capability is the supply of fully integrated landing gear systems for a wide range of aircraft including large commercial, regional, business, military and helicopters.
3 or 4 Engineering and Manufacturing based Traineeships are offered which will be over the summer or for a full year. Wages of approx £1,000 per month. Summer positions will be for a period of 12 weeks, the offer of a year in industry is mostly for post A-level students lasting from September to August. Traineeships will be in Gloucester. Some assistance may be provided to find accomodation.
Applications should be made from as soon as possible to Vikki Strong at the above address.

RENISHAN PLC: New Mills, Wotton-Under-Edge, Gloucestershire GL12 8TR (tel 01453-524524; fax 01453-524901; www.renishaw.com).
Summer Engineering Placements (approx. 80) are available within the technical divisions for minimum periods of 6 weeks. Competitive wages. Competence and qualifications in engineering, maths, IT or physics will be of assistance. Opportunities are available for 'A' level, post 'A' level, college, and university students. Positions are available at the New Mills Site (Wotton-Under-Edge) and the Woodchester Site (Nailsworth). Accommodation is not provided although assistance may be given. Foreign applicants welcome, providing they have work permits, if required.
Applications should be made no later than the end of April to Mr Gwyn Jones, Personnel Manager, at the above address.

TYCO ELECTRONICS UK LIMITED: Faraday Road, Dorcan, Swindon, Wiltshire SN3 5HH.
Tyco specialises in the design and development of radiation chemistry techniques for commercial applications and applied technologies for industrial use. It has invested large amounts of research money into the treatment of plastics by high energy electronic beam radiation.
The company offers limited **Vacation Placements** to students reading for degrees in Chemistry, Physics, Electronics, Electronic, Mechanical or Manufacturing Engineering and Materials Technology, although other scientific disciplines may also be appropriate. Experience is useful but not essential. Positions are available between June and October and are based in Swindon.
Applications should be sent by the end of March to Ms Lorraine West, Pertemps Recruitment Partnership, 102 Commercial Road, Swindon, Wiltshire, SW1 5PT.

The South Coast

Prospects for Work.

Hotel and catering jobs should not be too hard to come by along the southern coast as long as you begin your search in good time. In Hastings, for example, many hotels open just for the holiday season and vacancies are generally for unskilled workers. Early enquiries are advisable in view of the likely difficulties in finding accommodation. Holiday camps in the area, such as the Combe Haven Holiday Park or Pontins at Camber Sands, always need seasonal summer staff. For details of work in the Hastings area contact Hastings Jobcentre on 01424-784300.

Eastbourne has roughly ten times as many hotels as Hastings and throughout the season all types of hotel and catering vacancies are available. A large number of seafront kiosks also need staffing throughout the summer. Eastbourne hosts an annual Airborne week that attracts hundreds of thousands of visitors and staff are required to sell programmes, act as stewards and clean up afterwards. Eastbourne Jobcentre (1-3 Langney Road, Eastbourne BN21 3QF; tel 01323-532444) operates a student register throughout the summer and Christmas seasons that endeavours to match students to suitable vacancies. Anyone wanting to look for work in the area can contact Employment Service Direct at Ashdown House Jobcentre on 0845-6060 234; for the price of a local telephone call staff can complete a comprehensive jobsearch of vacancies locally or nationwide.

Holiday camps in West Sussex always need seasonal staff too. Bognor Regis Jobcentre (01243-224200) is the main contact for Butlins, the largest employer in the region. Butlins is just one of the many holiday camps along the South Coast, others include Sussex Beach Holiday Village, Sussex Coast Holiday Village, Church Farm Holiday Village and Pontins Ltd in Combe Sands, near Rye. Most of these provide live-in accommodation as well.

As well as work connected with the tourist industry, southern England is a good area for agricultural work, particularly in the hop fields and orchards of Kent (the 'Garden of England') during September. Around Ramsgate on the south Kentish coast, greenhouses require people to pick tomatoes for much of the summer season. Thanks to technology and new crops, it is possible to find agricultural work at any time of year. Wages are not bad, but be prepared for an early morning start. Seasonal jobs of this kind are advertised in the Ramsgate Jobcentre (tel 01843-258258).

The South Coast is one of the principal areas for English language schools, which require teachers, youth leaders and supervisors. The majority of schools can be found at coastal resorts: Hastings, Bexhill, Eastbourne, Brighton, Hove and Bognor Regis, and in Tunbridge Wells, Thanet and Canterbury inland.

Sporting activities, including the Farnborough Air Show held from 24th-30th July, generate a short-term requirement for staff to help with catering and car parking. In Southampton, exhibiting companies employ canvassers during the weeks running up to the Boat Show at Olympia in London. Southampton Jobcentre can be contacted at 61-64 High Street, Southampton (tel 023-8053 8600) for more information.

Both Jersey and Guernsey have thriving tourist industries, and the fact that Jersey is exempt from VAT, capital gains tax or inheritance tax means that financial services thrive there. However, potential jobseekers should be aware that Jersey retains the right to deport non-UK Nationals; even EEA/EU citizens need a work permit before they can be employed in the Channel Islands.

Business and Industry

CHILSTONE GARDEN ORNAMENTS: Victoria Park, Fordcombe Road, Langton Green, Kent TN3 ORE (tel 01892-740866; fax 01892-740249). Manufacturers of reconstituted stone architectural items and garden ornaments.
Workshop Helpers (20) to help with the mixing, etc. Must be strong and energetic.
Office Assistant to help with general office duties. Typing would be an advantage.
    Wages and hours by arrangement. Interesting and varied work available throughout the year. Applicants must find own accommodation. *Applications* to the Manager at the above address.

ORDNANCE SURVEY: Romsey Road, Maybush, Southampton, Hampshire SO16 4GU (tel 023-8079 2141 fax 023-8079 2572; e-mail service@barkerpersonnel.co.uk; www.barkerpersonnel.co.uk).
Temporary Staff are obtained through *applications* to Barker Personnel Services, 23 Burlington House, Portland Terrace, Southampton SO14 7EN (tel 023-8021 1629).

REGENT LANGUAGE HOLIDAYS: 40-42 Queens Road, Brighton BN1 3XB (tel 01273-718620; fax 01273-718621; e-mail holidays@regent.org.uk; www.regent.org.uk). Regent operates four high quality residential centres in Southern England. They specialise in summer language holidays.
Administrative Assistants (4). £175-£225 per week. Graduate, proven accounting/banking experience/skills. Full board and accommodation provided.
    Applications at any time to Recruitment at the above address.

SATURDAY VENTURE ASSOCIATION: PO Box 9, Chichester, West Sussex PO20 7YD (tel/fax 01243-513464; e-mail SVA2@btinternet.com;)

SVA2@talk.com. A small charity founded to support young disabled people, their siblings and friends. Currently setting up a project to form a nationwide support and club for young disabled people.

Project Work (2) involving research, correspondence and fund raising.

Wages from £5 per hour, free accommodation. To work 15-20 hours weekly. Min. period of work of dependent of exact position. Positions are available from October 2001 to September 2002. A-levels or postgraduates. Mobile if possible. Good English essential.

Applications should be made as soon as possible to the Chairman at the above address. Interview may be required.

SYSTEMSOLID LTD: The Sanderson Centre, 15 Lees Lane, Gosport, Hampshire PO12 3UL (tel 02392-524331; fax 02392-510287; sales@sanderson-centre.com).

Decorator/Handy Person (1) needed from 1 July to 30 September to perform general decorating and other manual duties. Hours from 9am-5pm. Wages on application.

Contact Mr A.C. Smith, Director.

TONY FRESKO ICE CREAM: Warren Farm, White Lane, Ash Green, Aldershot, Hampshire GU12 6HW (tel 01252-315528; fax 01252-334537; e-mail icecream@tonyfresko.freeserve.co.uk). Mobile ice-cream outlet, with a fleet of fifteen vans.

Drivers (25) for mobile ice cream sales at various shows and fetes and on rounds of industrial and housing estates. Wages from £7 to £10 per hour. To work approx. 11am-9pm, 7 days of the week available. Min. period of work of 6 weeks. Positions are available from March to October. Full driving licence required. Foreign applicants with appropriate work permits and acceptable spoken English welcome. No accommodation available.

Applications should be made from February onwards to Mr J Sawyer at the above address. Interview necessary.

Children

DWEEZILS ADVENTURE CENTRE: c/o Asda Stores, Newgate Lane, Fareham, Hants PO14 1TT (tel 01329-221956). Provides a warm, friendly and safe environment for childrens play, parties and various playgroup activity sessions.

Playleader (2) to work flexible hours at a creche open seven days a week from July 24 to September 3. Jobs involves interaction with children from 2 years nine months to nine years, cash handling and minimal paperwork. Some childcare experience necessary. Minimum age 18.

Applications to Michelle Harris, Centre Manager.

3D EDUCATION AND ADVENTURE LTD: Business Support, Osmington Bay, Weymouth, Dorset DT3 6EG (tel 01305-836226; fax 01305-834070; e-mail darren@3d-education.co.uk). 3D is a specialist provider of activity and educational experiences for young people. Owned by Center Parcs, 3D has been operating since 1991 and gone from strength to strength year on year.

Activity Instructors (500) Employed and trained as either multi-activity instructor, field studies instructor, specialist watersports instructor or IT instructor, staff will work with children at specialist holiday centres across the south of England as well as across the UK and Europe with Pontins and Center Parcs.

Field studies instructors must hold or at least be gaining a relevant degree. IT instructors need to have a broad range of IT skills. Any sports coaching awards or national governing body awards are advantageous, if applying for Activity instructor and Watersports instructor postitions, although those with relevant experience will be considered. Training courses are held from late January through to July, so there is plenty of opportunity to develop your skills and qualifications.

Most important is an applicant's enthusiasm, personality and energy, coupled with a true desire to work in the outdoor leisure industry. Excellent accommodation and catering packages are offered with payment and working hours as covered by minimum wage and working time legislation. Minimum period of work 14 weeks.

Applicants should telephone 01305-836226 for a recruitment pack between September and June. Before employment all applicants must complete a residential training programme in the UK.

LEISURE SERVICES: Council Offices, Rushmoor Borough Council, Farnborough Road, Farnborough, Hampshire GU14 7JU (tel 01252-398745).
Playleaders needed every school holiday to help organise a daily programme of activities and events for children aged 5-11. Wages £5 per hour, under review. Accommodation is not available. Hours: 8:30am-5:30pm (with a break for lunch) from Monday to Friday. Period of work every school holiday except Christmas. Min. age 18. Applicants should have experience of working with children and be good organisers. Sports coaching qualifications and arts and crafts skills would be an advantage. 2 day training course provided.
Applications all year round to D.A. Wall at the above address.

VILLAGE CAMPS: Personnel Office, Dept 815, Rue de la Morâche 14, 1260 Nyon, Switzerland (tel +41 22-9909405; fax +41 22-9909494; e-mail personnel@villagecamps.ch; www.villagecamps.com). Village Camps has been organising camps, tours and activity holidays for children for over 25 years. Set up in 1972 to serve the international community in Geneva, it has now developed into an organisation that leads sports, language, activity and leadership camps for children throughout Europe.
Support Staff (Chefs, Kitchen Staff, Bar/Tuck Shop Staff, House Keepers, House Counsellors), Drivers, Counsellors and Activity Specialists in swimming, archery, tennis, outdoor education, soccer, arts and crafts, mountain biking, gymnastics and drama.
Nurses. Qualified RSN or equivalent.
All the above required to work in childrens' spring, summer, autumn and winter camps in the UK and Europe. Experience of working with children and knowledge of a second language is an advantage. Accommodation and board are provided. Accident and liability insurance is provided, along with a generous allowance. All staff must be 21 or over. Minimum period of work 2 weeks. Suitably qualified foreign applicants are welcome. A telephone interview is required.
Go to the above website for more information or contact the above address for an *application pack.*

Holiday Centres and Amusements
ATHERFIELD BAY HOLIDAY CAMP: Chale, Ventnor, Isle of Wight PO38 2JD. Small family owned holiday centre providing holidays for school parties,

families and the over 50s. Situated 8 miles from Ventnor on a cliff top, in 14 acres of grounds, and on own foreshore.
Waiting Staff (8). Basic wage £90 a week, plus tips.
Kitchen Porters (8). Basic weekly wage £90.
Bar Staff (2). Basic wage £90 per week. Overtime available.
Snack Bar Assistants (4), Stillroom Assistants (2). Basic weekly wage £90. All staff to work approx. 36 hours a week. Free B & L. Experience not essential but must have friendly personality. Use of camp facilities when off duty. Min. age girls 16, boys 17. Training given. Employment from 5 May to early October. Min. period of work 12 weeks.
Applications, which must include a s.a.e. for a quick reply, from 15 March to Mrs M. Williamson, Atherfield Bay Holiday Camp.

BRIGHTON SEA LIFE CENTRE: Marine Parade, Brighton, Sussex BN2 1TB (01273-604234; fax 01273-681840).
Catering/Retail/Admission Staff (1-2). Work entails stocking up and pricing goods, including one stock-take, light cleaning, till work, greeting the public and selling the centre's guide book. Wages on application.
Applications to the Personnel Manager at the above address. Interview necessary.

BUCKLEYS YESTERDAY'S WORLD: 89/90 High Street, Battle, East Sussex TN33 0AQ (tel 01424-774269; e-mail info@yesterdaysworld.co.uk; www. yesterdaysworld.co.uk). Tourist attraction incorporating a museum of shops and social history and a gift shop selling nostalgic items. Situated opposite the Abbey Gatehouse at Battle.
Customer Care Assistants (3) wanted to work variable hours including one day at weekends. National minimum wage. Must be smart and reliable with a pleasant personality and the ability to deal well with customers. Min. age 15. To work between Easter and September during Easter/Whitsun/Summer vacations. No accommodation available.
Apply to the Manager at the above address. Note all applicants must be available for interview. Please apply before and not later than May.

HARBOUR PARK LTD: Seafront, Littlehampton, West Sussex BN17 5LL (tel 01903-721200; fax 01903-716663; www.harbourpark.com) A family enertainment centre situated right on the sea front with rides and attractions for all ages including a coffee bar, burger bar and ice cream parlour.
Ride Operators. Minimum age 18 years. To work 5/6 days per week including weekends.
Catering Persons. Minimum age 18 years. To work 5/6 days per week including weekends.
Wage £3.20 per hour plus accomodation. Period of work June-September: must be able to work July and August. Overseas applicants eligible to work in UK welcome.
Applications must be received by end of April.

SAUSMAREZ MANOR: St Martin, Guernsey, Channel Islands GY4 6SG (tel 01481-235571; fax 01481-35572).
Housekeeper to do housework on a regular basis and clean the Manor House which is open to the public. Hours: 3 hours per day at £3 per hour plus free food and lodging. Afternoons and most evenings free. Period of work May to October although it is understood that one person may not be able to work the entire

period. Should ideally have experience of working *en famille*. Sons, nephews and nieces (young twenties) are in and out all the time.

Horticultural/Garden Design Student also welcomed to work with the groundsman in sculpture park/garden for some/all the summer. Wages at £3 per hour plus food and ldoging. Working hours plus or minus 3 hours a day.

Overseas applicants welcome. Interview necessary, but can be conducted by phone. Early application is advised and appreciated because applicants generally either come back the following year or send a friend because they enjoy it so much. *Apply* from January to Peter de Sausmarez at the above address.

SUSSEX BEACH HOLIDAY VILLAGE: Earnley, nr Chichester, West Sussex PO20 7JP (tel 01243-671213). A secluded holiday village by the sea which caters for up to 600 guests. Facilities include outdoor heated pool, tennis courts, crazy golf and supermarket.

Bar Staff (8). To work split shifts. Min. age 18 years. Must have experience and be trustworthy with money.

Counter Assistants (3) And Grounds Person. Experience not essential, training provided.

All staff (22 years and over) receive £4.10 per hour (plus tips for bar and waiting staff). Hours: 39 over 6 days. Min. work period 5 weeks between March and November. Must be adaptable, trustworthy and of smart appearance. Overseas applicants eligible to work in the UK and with good English welcome.

Applications to Mr Allan Chamberlain, Deputy General Manager, Sussex Beach Holiday Village.

VECTIS VENTURES LTD: Blackgang Chine, Vetnor, Isle of Wight PO38 2HN (tel 01983-730330; fax 01983-731267; e-mail vectisventuresltd@ btinternet.com). Blackgang Chine and Robin Hill are 2 visitor attractions on the Isle of Wight with a range of family attractions. Open daily throughout the summer, attractions include a small number of rides and also activity play areas.

General Park Assistants (15) to work on rides, in retail outlets and catering facilities and for gardening and car parking. Also the possibility for drama students to help with the summer show. Wages are £4.10 per hour, to work 5-6 days a week. No accommodation available. Applicants should be aged between 18 and 25. No experience is necessary but applicants should be friendly and outgoing.

Staff are required from April to September/October and must work from July to August a minimum period of 8 weeks. Overseas applicants are welcome but must have good English.

Applications should be sent to Pam Wyeth, Front of House Manager at the above address between January and April. Interview necessary.

Hotels and Catering

ALBION HOTEL: Freshwater Bay, Isle of Wight PO40 9RA (tel 01983-753631/406654).

General Assistants. To work 5½ days a week, with split shifts for breakfast, lunch and dinner. Wages by arrangement. All meals provided free. Applicants should be aged 18-25 years. Some experience desirable. Applicants must be available for the whole season from Easter until the end of October.

Applications from February to the Manager, The Albion Hotel.

THE ANGEL HOTEL: North Street, Midhurst, West Sussex GU29 9DN (tel 01730-812421; fax 01730-815928; e-mail Angel@hshotels.co.uk).
Waiting/Bar Staff (2) needed from June to September for 40 hours p.w. maximum. Wage £90 per week including accommodation. Minimum age is 18 years.
Applications to C. Hansen, General Manager.

BAILIFFSCOURT HOTEL: Climping, Nr. Littlehampton, West Sussex BN17 5RW (tel 01903-723511; fax 01903 723107; e-mail bailifsfscourt@ hshotels.co.uk). Built by Lord Moyne of the Guinness Empire in 1927, situated in 30 acres, 200 yards from the beach. A chapel dating back to the 13th Century is situated in the hotel grounds.
Restaurant Staff (2/3). Wages £4 per hour; to work 8 hours a day. Must be 18 years or older and have silver service experience.
Porters (2). Wages £4 per hour; to work 8 hours a day. Duties include luggage handling, serving morning coffees and afternoon teas and the setting up of conferences. Accommodation is available free of charge, with a £100 key deposit refunded at the end of employment. Period of work from mid May to late September/October. Minimum period of work 3 months.
Applications to Karen Wilson, Training and Personnel Manager, from the beginning of April.

BALMER LAWN HOTEL: Lyndhurst Road, Brockenhurst, Hampshire SO42 7ZB (tel 01590-623116; fax 01590-623864; e-mail BLH@btinternet.com).
Waiting Staff (2-4) to work 40 hours per week, including weekends, serving two meals per day; breakfast 6.30-11.30am, lunch 12.15-3pm, or dinner 6.30-11pm.
Wages on application minus £20 for accommodation. Applicants should be over 20 years old and while previous experience of the hotel industry is an advantage training will be given.
Applications to Mrs Joanne Hamilton, Personnel and Training Manager.

CAREYS MANOR HOTEL: Lyndhurst Road, Brockenhurst, New Forest, Hampshire SO42 7RH (tel 01590-623551; fax 01590-622799; e-mail careysmanor@btinternet.com; www.careysmanor.com). An attractive 3 star hotel in the beautiful countryside of the New Forest with 79 bedrooms, 2 restaurants, and a health and fitness club with 500 members. Employs 120 staff.
Restaurant Staff (3) to work a 50 hour week.
Kitchen Staff (2) to work a 50 hour week.
Wages of £160-£200 per week. Board and lodging is available for £35 per week. Min. period of work 1st July to 15th September. Applicants must be over 16 and have qualifications. Overseas applicants considered.
Applications from April to S.G. Elliott.

COMFORT INN ARUNDEL: Junction A27/A284, Crossbush, Arundel, West Sussex BN17 7QQ (tel 01903-840840; fax 01903-84984; e-mail admin@gb642.u-net.com). The Comfort Inn Arundel is a new 53-bedroomed hotel located near Arundel town centre. It offers spacious en-suite rooms, a restaurant and bar.
Sous Chef (1) Part-time or full-time.
Receptionist (1) to work 5 days a week, 7am-3pm or 3pm-11pm shifts. Wage at least National Minimum Wage.
Waiting Staff (2/3). Part-time and full-time positions available. Wages on

application. Must be at least 16.

No accommodation is available but meals are provided whilst working. Foreign applicants with a good knowledge of English, especially spoken, are welcome. Permanent positions are available.

Applications any time to the Duty Manager at the above address.

CONGRESS HOTEL: 31-41 Carlisle Road, Eastbourne, Sussex BN21 4JS (tel 01323-732118; fax 01323-720016).
Staff required to work 37^1/2 hours over 5^1/2 days per week. £130 per week plus B & L. Min. age 18 years. Period of work March to November. Min. period of work 3 months.
Applications to Sandie Howlett, Director, Congress Hotel.

COPTHORNE HOTEL EFFINGHAM PARK: Copthorne, West Sussex RH10 3EU (tel 01342-711705; fax 01342-716039; e-mail lisa.benham@mill-cop.com). A 4 star hotel situated in 40 acres of parkland with 122 bedrooms, healthclub, tennis courts, a 9 hole golf course and extensive conference and banqueting facilities.
Restaurant Staff, Bar Staff Wages are £173 per week; to work 40 hours per week over 5 days. Whilst experience is preferred it is not essential. References are required.
Conference Waiting & Bar Staff for casual work. Wages £4.10 per hour; hours are as required. Work is available throughout the year. No experience is needed. Accommodation is available at a charge of £33.50 per week. Some items of uniform are provided, as are all meals. There are on and off the job training opportunities. Overseas applicants are welcome to apply only if they have a work permit and subject to a telephone interview.
Applications to the Personnel and Training Manager at the above address at any time.

DUKE OF NORMANDIE HOTEL: Lefebvre Street, St. Peter Port, Guernsey GY1 2PJ (tel 01481-721431; fax 01481-711763; e-mail dukeofnormandie@gtonline.net). 3 crown hotel catering for guests in a friendly, informal, homely way. One minute's walk from the town.
Chambermaids, Plate Service Restaurant Staff And Bar Waiting Staff. Salaries by negotiation. Live-in accommodation provided. Hotel experience essential. Permanent positions available.
Applications any time to the Manager, Duke of Normandie Hotel.

FARRAR'S HOTEL: 3-5 Wilmington Gardens, Eastbourne, East Sussex BN2 4JN (tel 01323-723737; fax 01323-732902).
Room Assistants (2) to work from 8am-2pm. Wages of £3.50 per hour plus tips.
Day Porters (2) to work from 10am-2pm and 5pm-9pm. Wages of £3.50 per hour plus tips.
Restaurant Staff (2) to work from 7-11am and 6-9pm. Wages £3.50-£4 per hour.
Needed to begin work as soon as possible. Minimum age 20. *Applications* to the Manager at the above address.

GRAND HOTEL: Grand Parade, St. Leonards, Hastings, East Sussex TN38 0DD (tel 01424-428510;fax 01424 428510).
General Hotel Workers (2) to clean bedrooms and work in the laundry and kitchen. Wages 3 per hour. Accommodation available for one person only. Period of work June and September. Overseas applicants welcome.

Applications to Mr Peter Mann at the above address.

THE GRAND HOTEL GROUP: The Grand Burshin Hotel, The Harbour, Folkestone, Kent CT20 1TX (tel 01303-854513; fax 01303-854549). The hotel is perfectly positioned over-looking Folkestone Harbour and has a well-earned reputation as one of the UK's great entertainment hotels.
Waiting Staff, Kitchen assistants. Must be aged 16+.
Bar Staff, Housekeeping Staff. Must be aged 18+.
Payment at National Minimum Wage rates. Variable working hours. Min. period of work of 2 months. Positions are available from June to October. Intermediate English required. Accommodation not available.
Applications should be made from May onwards to Jo McKelvie. Interview necessary.

GRANGE MOOR HOTEL: St Michaels Road, Maidstone, Kent, ME16 8BS (tel 01622-677623; fax 01622-678246; e-mail reservations@grangemoor.co.uk). 50 bedroom family run hotel with banquet room seeks staff for office christmas dinners/parties.
Waiting Staff (10), Washers Up (6) to work hours to suit between 1st and 23rd December for lunches and evening meals. Some Christmas Day work available between noon-5pm at double time. Wages £5 per hour, cash paid weekly. Waiting staff required to provide plated service for Christmas dinners, full training will be given, applicants must be over 17, friendly, helpful and polite. No accommodation available.
Applications to Mrs Christine Sedge, at the above address.

GREENHILLS HOTEL AND RESTAURANT: St. Peter's Valley, St. Peter, Jersey JE3 7EL (tel 01534-481042; fax 01534-485322).
Night Porter, Day Porter, Bar Assistant, Waiting Staff (2), Kitchen Staff (2), Receptionist to work a 42 hour, 6 day week. Wages of at least £140 per week live in. Period of work from April to September. Min age 18.
Applications to the Manager at the above address but please note: only apply if available to work from the end of March to 15 October.

HIGHFIELD COUNTRY HOTEL: Route d'Ebenezer, Trinity, Jersey JE3 5DT (tel 01534-862194; fax 01534-865342; e-mail reservations@highfieldjersey.com). Situated 4 miles from St Helier, the hotel is a short distance from beaches on the North Coast.
Second Chef (1). Wages on application. Must be over 20 and hold a 7061/2 qualification.
Dining Room Staff (2). Must have experience and be over 20.
Bar Person (1). Must have experience and be over 20.
Porters (2). Must have experience and be over 20.
Receptionists (2). Should be computer trained. Preferably over 25.
All positions on application ,work 42 hours a week. Live-in accommodation is available. Period of work 23 March to 31 October. Overseas applicants considered. Interview not necessary.
Applications from February to David Lord.

HILTON AVISFORD PARK HOTEL: Walberton, Arundel, West Sussex BN18 0LS (tel 01243 551215). With 139 bedrooms, conference and banqueting for up to 600 and extensive leisure facilities.
Restaurant, Banqueting And Bar Staff required to work in busy food and

beverage departments. Wages from £4 per hour.

Applications to Karen Isted, Personnel & Training Manager, at the above address.

HILTON BASINGSTOKE: Old Common Road, Black Dam, Basingstoke, Hampshire RG21 3PR (tel 01256-460460; fax 01256-840441).
Restaurant Attendants (5) needed immediately for full-time (39 hours per week) or part-time work. Wages are £4.37 per hour.
Kitchen Porters (2) needed immediately to clean pots, dishes and maintain high kitchen standards. Hours of work are 6am-2pm, 2-10pm, 10pm-3am for £5 per hour with accommodation available.
Room Attendants (6) to start in May or June, with wages of £4.50-£5 per hour.
Conference And Banqueting Attendants (3) to work from 7am-3pm or 3-11pm for £5.50 per hour. Work involves setting up rooms for weddings as well as waiting work and assisting guests with luggage.

Applications to Rebecca Gwilliam, Human Resources Manager, at the hotel.

HOTEL L'HORIZON: St Brelade's Bay, Jersey, Channel Islands JE3 8EF (tel 01534-494404; e-mail hotelhorizon.@jerseymail.co.uk; www.hotelhorizon@ jerseymail.co.uk). A 4 star 107 bedroom hotel, located on one of the island's beautiful beaches. Hotel L'Horizon offers a unique work experience for employees who prove themselves to be dedicated, responsible and efficient, with further employment prospects after the seasonal contracts terminate.
Food and Beverage Service Attendants, Room Attendants, Kitchen Porters. To work a 6 day week.
Commis Waiting Staff/Chef de Rangs. To work a 5 day week.

All applicants must be presentable, have excellent customer care skills and have worked within a similar environment before. Uniform and meals on duty and accommodation provided. Overseas applicants who have good English considered.

Applications should be made by application form available together with further information from the above address and website.

LAKE HOTEL: Shore Road, Lower Bonchurch, Ventnor, Isle of Wight PO38 1RF (tel 01983-852613; e-mail richard@lakehotel.co.uk; www.lakehotel.co.uk). A small hotel (20 rooms) in a quiet, peaceful location. Very busy and a high standard of service and cleanliness. Family run. Close to beach.
Chamber Staff (2). To work 39 hours a week. Shifts: 7.30am-12.30pm and 6.30-8.30pm.
Waiting Staff (2). To work 40 hours a week. Shifts as above.

All staff work 6 days for £125 a week, plus free B & L. Some experience required, and applicants should have a sense of humour, be tidy and polite, and be able to work quickly and under pressure. Overseas applicants with good English welcome. Min. period of work $3^1/2$ months between May and end of October. No replies for shorter periods of work.

Applications from January to Mr Wyatt, Lake Hotel.

LONSDALE, SMITH'S, EDEN AND PALM COURT HOTELS: 51-61 Norfolk Road, Cliftonville, Margate, Kent CT9 2HX (tel 01843-221053; fax 01843-299993). A family run group of private hotels. Hotels have indoor heated swimming pools and sports facilities. All rooms are en suite and have telephones, colour TVs and tea and coffee making facilities.
Restaurant Staff/Room Attendants (4). Wages £70 per week including food and

accommodation.

Chefs. Pay on application.

To work 40 hours over 5 days a week (usually on split shifts) with no overtime. Must be over 18. Min. period of work 3 months all year round. Overseas applicants welcomed.

Applications from January to Mrs Ann Smith. Interview not necessary.

LUCCOMBE HALL HOTEL: Luccombe Hall Hotel, Luccombe Road, Shanklin, Isle of Wight PO37 6RL (tel 01983-862719; fax 01983-863082; e-mail reservations@luccombe.co.uk). Luccombe Hall Hotel is on a popular I.O.W. beach with tennis, squash, indoor and outdoor pools, gym, sauna etc.

Kitchen Staff (1-2), Waiting Staff (1-2), Room Attendants (1-2) for the school holidays. Live in or out. Pay £80 per week while training, and £100 per week thereafter (live-in); or £4.25 per hour (live out). Split shifts, 5/6 days per week. Hotel will train if no previous experience: applicants should be cheerful, reliable and sober.

Applications to Jill Roseman, Manager.

THE MASTER BUILDERS HOUSE HOTEL: Buckler's Hard, Nr Beaulieu, Hampshire SO42 7XB (tel 01590-616253; fax 01590-6162978; e-mail res@themasterbuilders.co.uk).

Commis Waiting Staff to work in the 2-rosetter Riverview Restaurant. Serve at breakfast, lunch, afternoon teas, dinner and conference set-up.

Bar Staff in the bar and gallery to serve drinks and pub food.

Chamberstaff servicing guestrooms and evening turndown.

Wages £4.08-£4.32 per hour plus tips. Accommodation may be available; single room (£30pw), shared (£25pw), including 3 meals daily. Positions available from end April/May to end August/September. Applicants need good English; a pleasant outgoing personality; to enjoy countryside; and be good team players in international team.

Applications to Christine Mayley, General Manager, at the above address.

MORVAN FAMILY HOTELS: 57 Rouge Bouillon Street, St Helier, Jersey JE2 3ZB (tel 01534-873006; fax 01534-876424; email morFamho@itl.net). A company in operation for 42 years which runs 5 hotels on the picturesque island of Jersey.

Staff required for various posts ranging from head chefs through to chamber staff. Wages by arrangement; accommodation is available at a cost of £42.50 per week, plus meals. Min. period of work 6 months between March and October.

Overseas applicants considered. Interview not necessary. *Applications* from January to Adrian T. Gordon, Group Personnel Manager

NATIONAL TRUST ENTERPRISES: The Restaurant, Chartwell House, Mapleton Road, Westerham, Kent TN16 1PS (tel 01732-866368).

Catering Assistants (8). Wages on application. Hours negotiable.

Applications at any time to the above address.

OCKENDEN MANOR HOTEL: Ockenden Lane, Cuckfield, Haywards Heath, West Sussex RH17 5LD (tel 01444-416111; fax 01444-415549; e-mail ockenden@hshotels.co.uk; www.hshotels.co.uk).

Commis Waiting Staff to work in the restaurant and bar and at functions. Wages of at least £90 per week plus tips and accommodation; to work split shifts over a 5-day week.

Period of work by arrangement around the year for a minimum of 3 months. Applicants must be aged at least 18 and have restaurant experience; silver service experience desirable.

Applications to Kerry Turnes, Manager, at the above address.

OLD COURT HOUSE HOTEL: Gorey Village, Grouville, Jersey JE3 9FS (tel 01534-854444; fax 01534-853587; e-mail ochhotel@itl.net). A 3 star, 58 bedroom establishment located in the Channel Islands opposite the beach and on a frequent bus route into St. Helier. Lively village location with plenty of amenities.

Silver Service Waiting Staff (6). Wages on application, 42 hours per week over $5^1/2$ days. Previous experience is essential.

Commis Waiting Staff (2). Wages on application. Hours as above. Training will be given.

Hall Porters (2). Wages on application. Hours as above. Bar experience is an asset.

Chambermaids (5). Wages on application, 42 hours over 6 days per week. Previous experience is essential.

Breakfast Chef (1), Chefs De Partie (2). Wages on application, 42 hours over $5^1/2$ days. Experience in a similar position essential.

Min. age 18. Positions available from May to late September/October; min period of work May-September inclusive. Shared accommodation available in twin rooms with private bathrooms for about £40 per week. An interview is not necessary. High standards of work and appearance are expected.

Apply from March/ early April to Mr R.A.D. Smale, Manager or Mr. P. Winch, Restaurant Manager at the above address.

PAYNE AND GUNTER: Goodwood Racecourse, Goodwood, Chichester, West Sussex PO18 0PS (tel 01243-775350; fax 01243-784490). Payne and Gunter are the caterers for Goodwood Racecourse, supplying waiting, bar and catering staff on race days and motor spectacular events.

Waiting Staff, Silver Service Staff, Porters, General Catering Assistants, Table Clearers And Washing Up Staff. Between 400 and 1,000 staff are employed per event on a casual basis. Wages are £4.50-£5.50 per hour. Must be at least 18, no experience necessary. To work on various race days from May to September. Meals are provided on duty and free transport from various pick-up points is provided.

Applications from March/April to the Staffing Manager, at the above address.

PORTELET HOTEL: St Brelade, Jersey, Channel Islands JE3 8AU (tel 01534-741204; fax 01534-746625). A family hotel situated on the coast, catering for 160 guests.

Hall Porters, Commis Barman, Commis Wine Waiting Staff needed. Wages from £162 a week. To work 42 hours per week over 6 days. Min. age 18. Full-board accommodation is available at £49 a week. Period of work May to October; min. 4 months. EEA applicants with a good knowledge of English considered.

Applications from April onwards to Mr Mario Dugini, Manager, at the Portelet Hotel.

THE PRIORY BAY HOTEL: Priory Drive, Seaview, Isle of Wight PO34 5BU (tel 01983-613146; fax 01983-616539; e-mail jane@priorybay.co.uk; www.priorybay.co.uk).

Kitchen Porters, Waiting Staff, Bar Staff, Room Attendants, Chefs: Many

Vacancies. To work the summer seson beginning in May/June. Wages by arrangement plus tips and accommodation provided. To work up to 48 hours per week. All applicants should have experience in the catering or hospitality trade and a working knowledge of English.

Applications should be sent to David Cule, General Manager, at the above address.

HOTEL REX: St Saviours Road, St Helier, Jersey JE2 4GJ (tel 01534-731668; fax 01534-766922; e-mail hotelrex@localdial.com; www.localdial. com/users/hotelrex/). Established 40 years ago, the hotel is 5 minutes from St Helier.
Receptionists (2). Wages £175 per week plus bonus. Must have computer experience.
Day Porter (1). Wages £165 per week plus bonus. Should have some experience.
Waiting Staff (2) And Waitresses (2). Wages £165 per week plus bonus. Must have silver service experience.
Commis Chef (1). Wages £165 per week plus bonus. Must be experienced.
Kitchen Porter(1) Wages £155 per week plus bonus.
All staff work 42 hours a week. Accommodation is available at a cost of £47 per week. Staff share accommodation, with a max. of 2 per room. Uniforms are supplied by the hotel. Min. period of work 6 months between April and October. French and Italians are encouraged to apply.
Applications form 1st March to N. Berenguer, Hotel Manager. Interview necessary.

ROYAL BEACH HOTEL: South Parade, Southsea, Portsmouth, Hants PO4 0RN. A three star, 115 bedroom, seafront hotel commanding stunning views over to the Isle of Wight.
Waiting Staff (3) to serve breakfast, lunch and dinner and functions as required.
Room Attendants (2) to be responsible for cleaning guest bedrooms, bathrooms and corridors.
National minimum wage applies, plus tips. To work 5 days per week in shifts. Min. period of work 12 weeks. Accommodation available plus meals/uniform. Overseas applicants welcome. *Applications* to the Personnel Manager at the above address.

THE ROYAL HOTEL: Belgrave Road, Ventnor, Isle of Wight PO38 1JJ (tel 01983-852186; fax 01983-855395). The only AA 4 star hotel on the Isle of Wight. Pleasant working conditions and friendly staff.
Waiting Staff (4), Chamber Staff (4). £140-£160 per week. To work at least 45 hours per week. Training available. Accommodation provided at no extra cost. Staff required from April to October; min. period of work the three months of July, August and September. Overseas applicants welcome, members of staff from France, Spain and South Africa already employed.
Interview required or trial work period is necessary. *Applications* from March 1st to the Personnel Manager/General Manager at the above address.

ROYAL ESPLANADE HOTEL: Ryde, Isle of Wight PO33 2ED (tel 01983-562549; fax 01983-563918). Owned by Shearings Hotels, the hotel has an 11 month season and is closed in January. It offers various benefits of working for a large company. Hotel is situated on the seafront.
Waiting Staff, Kitchen Porters, Chamber Staff, Bar Staff. From £3.20 per hour plus tips. To work 39 hours per week. Max. age 28 years. All staff work 6

days per week. Free B & L. No experience needed. Full in-house training is given.

Applications enclosing photograph to Mrs C. Davies, General Manager.

SEYMOUR HOTELS OF JERSEY: 1 Wharf Street, St Helier, Jersey JE2 0ZX (tel 01534-875926; fax 01534-780726; email brightfuture@seymourhotels.com; www.seymourhotels.com). The largest hotel group in the Channel Islands, with 4 hotels catering for all aspects of the leisure, business and conference markets.
Receptionists (20). Wages were £189 per week in 2001. Some previous experience is required. Computer skills and languages are an advantage. Must be over 18.
Waiting Staff (35). Wages were £185 per week in 2001. Some positions require specific skills eg. silver service. Must be over 18.
Bar Staff (15). Wages were £184 in 2001. Previous experience needed. Must be over 18.
Commis Chefs, Chefs De Parti, Sous Chefs (20). Wages were £178-£250 in 2001. Applicants must have experience relevant to the level of the position.
Room Attendants (20). Wages were £164 per week in 2001. Some experience would be useful.
Porters (10). Wages were £184 in 2001. Some experience would be useful.

All staff work 42 hours a week over 5/6 days. Accommodation is provided at a cost of £49 per week, including meals and uniforms. Min. period of work 6 months between March/April and end October. Full training is provided where appropriate. There are opportunities for career development and permanent employment.Applicants should be UK/EEC citizens, with a basic level of spoken English.

Applications from February to Mrs S. Armes, Group Personnel and Training Manager. Interview necessary, but may be conducted by telephone.

STOCKS ISLAND HOTEL: Sark, via Guernsey, Channel Islands GY9 0SD (tel 01481-832001; fax 01481-832130; e-mail stocks@sark.net; http://www.stocks-sark.com). Sark is a beautiful and remote rural island 20 miles from France; fishing, farming and eco-tourism provide the main local employment.There are no motor cars and no airport. Visitors come to enjoy a break from the pressures of modern living. Stocks is a traditional old farmhouse and home of the Armorgie family.
Silver Service Waiting Staff for general waiting and some cleaning duties in an award-winning restaurant. Must possess silver-service skills, a pleasant personality and caring attitude.
Kitchen Porter for general kitchen cleaning duties and some vegetable preparation in a high quality kitchen with a brigade of qualified chefs. Must work extremely cleanly, efficiently and quickly. Overseas applicants considered.
Bistro Staff for general waiting and cleaning duties in busy but informal Bistro restaurant. Must be attractive with pleasant personality and very good references. The ability to work quickly, cleanly and efficiently are essential.

Wages £110 per week, tax-free with no deductions. B & L provided. Private medical health cover provided. To work maximum of 60 hours per week over 6 days. Fifteen members of staff required to work from April until October, with two additional workers between June and September. Overseas applicants welcome but must speak the standard of English of a native. Preferred age group 20-35.

Sark is an isolated and unspoilt island. Applicants must be able to adapt to the unique working environment. For further details *contact* Mr Paul Armorgie,

Stocks Island Hotel and Restaurants.

THISTLE BRIGHTON HOTEL: Kings Road, Brighton, BN1 2GS (tel 01273-763237; fax 01273-820692; e-mail hr.brighton@thistle.co.uk).
Waiting Staff (2) required from May onwards to provide food service in the hotel's restaurant, working between 5 and 39 hours a week in shifts (6.30am-3pm, 10am-5.30pm, 3-11.30pm) for £4.18 per hour plus tips.
Bar Person (2) needed from June, to serve in a Mediterranean style cafe-bar. Post offers between 5 and 39 hours a week for £4.18 per hour plus tips. Applicants must be over 18 years of age.
Room Attendants (4) wanted to carry out housekeeping and room cleaning work. Hours of work 9.30am-4.30pm with 8-39 hours of work available per week. Wages are £3.98 per hour plus an incentive package.
Concierge/Hall Porter (2) wanted for front reception, guest liaison and to carry luggage. To work a 39 hour week either 7am-3.30pm or 3-11.30pm, with wages of £4.08 plus tips. At least one applicant must be over 21 for insurance purposes.
Night Guest Services Porter (1-2) for immediate start, to work 39 hours per week 11pm-7.30am. Task include general setting up duties, some food preparation and hotel security. Wages are £4.84 plus tips. At least one applicant must be over 25.

All remuneration schemes include a benefits package. *Applications* or requests for further details should be made to Jason Fox, Human Resources Manager at the above address.

Language Schools

CICERO LANGUAGES INTERNATIONAL: 42 Upper Grosvenor Road, Tunbridge Wells, Kent TN1 2ET (tel 01892-547077; fax 01892-522749; e-mail enrolments@cicero.co.uk; www.cicero.co.uk). A small, friendly and professional language school accredited by the British Council and a member of ARELS. Students are mainly in their 20s and 30s, from over 70 countries.
EFL Teachers (5) to teach students of many nationalities (average age 25). Salary £10-£12 per hour. Hours of work variable. Period of work mid July to end of August, min. period of employment 4 weeks. Accommodation is not available. Applicants must have a degree and TESOL/CTEFLA qualifications. Experience also important. Punctuality and a professional attitude are essential.
Applications from April to the Director of Studies, Cicero Languages International.

CONCORDE INTERNATIONAL SUMMER SCHOOLS LTD: Arnett House, Hawks Lane, Canterbury, Kent CT1 2NU (tel 01227-451035; fax 01227-762760;e-mail info@concorde.ltd.uk; www.concorde.ltd.uk). Concorde International has been organising summer schools for over 25 years in prestigious locations in the south of England. They have a high return rate of students and teachers.
EFL Teachers (approx. 150). To teach in summer schools. Wages £230-£275 a week depending on course. An average working week consists of 15 hours tuition and supervising 20 hours of activities, but weeks vary according to individual programmes. Both residential and non-residential positions are available. Applicants should have the RSA CTEFLA or Trinity College certificate TESOL or equivalent or PGCE in an appropriate subject, and some summer school experience.
Course Directors (approx. 8) to ensure the smooth running of the centre and

liaise with Head Office, the local host family organiser and the group leader. Other duties include holding staff meetings and weekly in-house training sessions, briefing teachers and standing in for them if required. Wages £400 a week. Both residential and non-residential positions are available, depending on the centre. Applicants must hold a RSA Dip. TEFL or Trinity College diploma in TESOL and have a minimum of 5 years' summer school experience.

Assistant Directors Of Study (approx. 8) to ensure the smooth running of the centre, liase with Head Office, oversee the daily routine and give support to staff, in addition to 15 hours' tuition a week. Wages £280 a week. Positions are residential and non-residential. Applicants must hold RSA Dip. TEFL or Trinity College London Diploma and have several years' teaching experience.

Centre Managers (approx. 8) to ensure smooth running of the social programme and take care of the students' health and welfare. Other duties include checking transfer arrangements, liasing with Head Office, and regular staff at the centres. Positions are residential. Wages £300 per week. Applicants should preferably hold a qualification in leisure management although other management qualifications/experience will be considered.

Period of work June, July and August for all positions. *Applications* to the Vacation Course Director at the above address.

EASTBOURNE SCHOOL OF ENGLISH: 8 Trinity Trees, Eastbourne, E.Sussex BN21 3LD (tel 01323-721759; fax 01323-639271; e-mail english@esoe.co.uk). Runs language courses for students aged 16 and over from all around the world. The freetime programme is lively and varied.

Assistant Social Organiser (1). Responsible post suiting someone energetic, enthusiastic and reliable. Some experience with overseas students an advantage. Min. age 20. To work 6 days per week (flexi-time). Required from mid June to mid September. Accommodation not available. Interview necessary.

Applicants should make *applications* with a CV to Graham White, Principal, from early 2002 at the above address.

EMBASSY CES: Lorna House, 103 Lorna Road, Hove, E. Sussex, BN3 3EL (www.embassyces.com tel: 01273 322353; e-mail vacjobsuk@ embassyces.com; fax: 01273 322381). Embassy CES is a division of Study Group International, part of the Daily Mail and General Trust family of companies, and is a world leader in quality international education. Embassy CES organises summer schools for international students, combining English lessons and an activity/excursion programme at schools and universities around the UK.

Activity Leaders to organise a variety of daytime, evening and weekend activities. Experience of working with children or in the leisure or tourism industry is desirable, but full training will be given. All applicants must speak fluent English, have enthusiasm and initiative, and be hardworking.

EFL Teachers to teach and participate in the activity programme. Previous experience is desirable. Full board accommodation is available at residential centres.

Apply from February onwards either online at www.embassyces.com (click on the Summer Jobs in the UK link) or contact the Recruitment Department for an application pack.

EMBASSY CES: Palace Court, White Rock, Hastings, TN34 1JY (tel 01424-720100; fax 01424 720323; e-mail hastings@embassyces.com; www. embassyces.com). All year round language school with large summer centre.

Teachers Of English as a foreign language wanted for July and August to teach adults and children; to also assist with a programme of social activities/excursions. Residential posts available. Cambridge CELTA (formerly CTEFLA) certificate required.

Sports & Social Activity Organisers required during July and August. Graduates and Undergraduates, min age 20. Qualifications in sports coaching, first aid, arts and crafts etc. an advantage. Accommodation available. Work includes running a full activity programme: discos, excursions, sports, local visits etc. Applicants should have common sense and a good sense of fun. Overseas applicants with a sufficient knowledge of English considered.

Applications from January to the above address.

HASTINGS ENGLISH LANGUAGE CENTRE (HELC): St Helens Park Road, Hastings, East Sussex TN34 2JW (tel 01424-437048/441549; e-mail clive@helc.co.uk; www.helc.co.uk). Adult only British Council accredited school.

EFL Teachers (10) £130-£230 for 15-24 hours per week. Degree and CELTA (or equivalent) required. Staff wanted from mid June to October. Min. period of work 4 weeks. Accommodation not available.

Applications from middle of March to Hastings English Language Centre at the above address.

ITS ENGLISH SCHOOL: 43-45 Cambridge Gardens, Hastings TN34 1EN (tel 01424-438025; fax 01424-438050; e-mail itsbest@its-hastings.co.uk). A small, professional, language school situated in the centre of Hastings and accredited by the British Council.

EFL Teachers. All applicants must have Trinity College Cert. TESOL or RSA CELTA: £141 for 15 hours per week, £225.60 for 24 hours per week. Applicants with Trinity College Diploma TESOL or RSA DELTA: 15 hours per week – £162: 30 hours per week – £324. Non residential.

Minimum period of work 3 weeks, between June 20th and September 16th.

Contact Mark Turner, Director of Studies after April 1st at the above address.

KENT SCHOOL OF ENGLISH: 3 Granville Road, Broadstairs, Kent CT10 1QD (tel 01843-874870; fax 01843-860418; e-mail enquiries@kentschool.co.uk). A medium-sized school specialing in short courses for groups from 21 countries; a dynamic, energetic, enthusiastic and friendly place to work.

English Language Teachers (30), Social Activity Assistants (6). £150-£210 per week. To work 30-35 hours per week from Monday to Saturday. Min. period of work of 4 weeks. Positions available mid-June to mid-September. Applicants should be over 18 and teachers require the relevant TESOL or CELTA certificte.

Applications welcome from 1 March to Chris McDermott at the above address.

LTC INTERNATIONAL COLLEGE: Compton Park, Compton Palace Road, Eastbourne, East Sussex BN21 1EH (tel 01323-727755; fax 01323-728279; e-mail learnenglish@ltccollege.demon.co.uk). A private language school running courses for adult students and residential courses for young learners.

Residential Teachers (5). Wages from £205 per week, with free board and lodging. To teach 15 lessons per week, includes evening and some weekend social and residential duties. Minimum of RSA/Cambridge CELTA or Trinity Cert. TESOL required.

Residential Welfare Officers (4). Wages from £165 per week, with free board and lodging. To work 40 hours per week, including evenings and weekends.

Would suit a student. First Aid an advantage.

Staff required from 25th June-2nd September. Overseas applicants for teaching posts must have competence in English to the standard of a native speaker.

Applications from February to Paul Clark, Director of Studies, at the above address.

PASSPORT LANGUAGE SCHOOLS: 37 Park Road, Bromley, Kent BR1 3HJ (tel 020-8466 5925; fax 020-8466 5928; e-mail dos@passport.uk.com). Runs language programmes in different centres from Ormskirk to Worthing for students mainly from Europe and the Far East. Courses take place throughout the year, but summer is the busiest time.
EFL Teachers. Required at various centres throughout Britain to teach international students aged 11-17 and assist with afternoon and evening leisure activities. Min. age 21. Applicants must have RSA/UCLES or Trinity College Certificate TESOL or be state qualified teachers with EFL experience. Training day is held. Approx 15-30 hour, 6 day week for 2-10 weeks between July and August. Salary £160-£300 per week depending on experience and position. Board and accommodation provided in residential schools. Teachers must arrange own travel and insurance.

Applications to the Director of Studies at the above address.

ST. BEDE'S INTERNATIONAL SUMMER SCHOOL: The Dicker, Hailsham, East Sussex BN27 3QH (tel 01323-443818; fax 01323-848188; e-mail summer.school@stbedesschool.org).
EFL Teachers (10) needed from 30 June to 17 August to teach 15 hours per week plus pastoral care and assisting with sports and activities. £250 p.w. plus accommodation. Must hold either CERT TEFL, D. TEFLA or QTS.

Apply to Nigel Heritage, Director.

REGENCY SCHOOL OF ENGLISH: Royal Crescent, Ramsgate, Kent CT11 9PE (tel 01843-591212; fax 01843-850035). A British Council recognised school and a member of ARELS.
Temporary EFL Teachers (15). Guaranteed 14 hours of teaching per week, but up to 28 hours usually available. Must hold at least a Trinity College or RSA Certificate. £10 per hour.
Activity Leaders (3). £100 per week for 20-30 hours' work. Must be sporty and enthusiastic.

Min. period of work 6 weeks between June and September. Overseas applicants with a standard of English as high as that of a native speaker considered. The school has hotel accommodation but this is often full during the summer.

Applications from April to Jocelyn Flaig, Director of Studies, Regency School of English.

REGENT LANGUAGE HOLIDAYS: 40-42 Queens Road, Brighton BN1 3XB (tel 01273-718620; fax 01273-718621; e-mail holidays@regent.org.uk; www.regent.org.uk). Regent operates four high quality residential centres in Southern England. They specialise in summer language holidays.
EFL Teachers (40). Wages from £225-£255 per week for 15 hours tuition and 7 afternoon or evening sessions. Will assist in social programme. RSA/Trinity qualified.
Centre Managers (4). Wages from £375-£425 per week. Graduate, preferably

Masters/RSA/Trinity qualified with appropriate management experience and a proven and successful track record.

Welfare Assistants. (4) Wages from £175-£225 per week. Graduate, preferably social or youth work experience.

Full board and accommodation provided. *Applications* at any time to Recruitment at the above address.

RICHARD LEWIS COMMUNICATIONS: Riversdown House, Warmford, Hants SO32 3LH (tel 01962-771111; fax 01962-771050; e-mail steve.allison@rlcglobal.com; www.crossculture.com). An international company committed to providing training solutions in the areas of language, cross culture and communication skills. The company operates in 5 continents, and offers career opportunities to travel.

English Teachers to work from June to September. Wages from approximately £275 per week depending on experience/qualifications, with food and accommodation provided. To teach from 9am-5pm; will also be expected to attend dinner daily and perform one evening duty such as escorting a trip to a pub or the theatre a week. Applicants should have a university degree, RSA/Trinity TEFL certificate and at least 1 year's teaching experience.

Applications to Steve Allison, Director of Studies, at the above address.

SCANBRIT SCHOOL OF ENGLISH: 22 Church Road, Bournemouth, BH6 4AT (tel 01202-428252; fax 01202-428926; e-mail info@scanbrit.co.uk).

EFL Teachers (10) to teach for 20-30 hours a week from 9am-4pm Mon-Fri over the summer for between £9.10-£10.70 per hour. Applicants should have some teaching experience and a minimum RSA Certificate TEFL qualification.

Sports/Social Organisers (2) to work 30-40 hours per week over the summer, for £6.30 per hour. Previous experience necessary.

Administration Assistant to work 35 hours per week during office hours over the summer. Should have previous experience of using Windows 98, including Word and Excel. Wage £6.50 per hour.

Applications to A. Hardy, Principal.

SCHOOL OF ENGLISH STUDIES FOLKESTONE: 26 Grimston Gardens, Folkestone, Kent CT20 2PX (tel 01303-850007; fax 01303-256544; e-mail info@ses-folkestone.co.uk). Founded in 1957, the School of English Studies Folkestone is a serious, professional and successful language school.

English Tutors (10) Wages £300-£350 per week; to work 35 hours per week. Applicants must have a UK degree and a TEFL qualification.

Sports & Activities Co-Ordinators (4) Wages £250 or more per week; to work 35 hours per week. Applicants must be 21 or over and have some appropriate qualifications.

Both positions available involve working with students of English from overseas. Accommodation is not available. Staff are required from 27 June to 23 August for a minimum period of 4 weeks.

Applicatons to David Foley, Principal at the above address from February onwards.

STAFFORD HOUSE SCHOOL OF ENGLISH: 8/9 Oaten Hill, Canterbury, Kent CT1 3HY (tel 01227-452250; fax 01227-451685; e-mail enquiries@staffordhouse.com). The summer school has mixed nationality classes with a max. of 15 students per class. Ages 12-adult. Emphasis is on productive skills and fluency-based activities.

EFL Teachers (35). Rates of pay on application. Min. period of work 1 week between June and September. TEFL qualifications such as RSA/Trinity Certificate or RSA/Trinity Diploma required. Reliability, energy and enthusiasm are essential.

Applications to either Naomi Cooper or Mike Turner at the above address.

WARNBOROUGH UNIVERSITY: International Offices, 8 Vernon Place, Canterbury CT1 3WH (tel 01227-762107; fax 01227-762108, e-mail admin@warnborough.edu, www.warnborough.edu or warnborough.ac.uk).An international university offering undergraduate and graduate degree programmes by Distance Learning and/or Onsite through affiliated campuses worldwide. Scholarships available to all nationalities.

Mentors, EFL Teachers, Tour Guides, Translators, Activity Organisors sought regularly. Please see website for all openings. Payments vary depending on teaching and on the employment offered.

Apply on line (viceprez@warnborough.edu) or by fax/post to the Vice President for Administration.

Medical

CAREWATCH (EASTBOURNE AND HASTINGS): Unit 14, Swan Business Centre, Hailsham, East Sussex BN27 2BY (tel 01323-849444; fax 01323-849222) Carewatch is a provider of homecare services to the elderly and less able.

Carers (10) Wages £4.10-£5.50 per hour, hours and period of work to suit. Applicants must be 18 or over; no qualifications are needed but applicants must be able to provide 2 references. Applicants from abroad are welcome but must be English speaking. No accommodation available.

Applications should be sent as soon as possible to the Manager at the above address. An interview is necessary.

OPTIONS TRUST STAFF RECRUITMENT: 4 Plantation Way, Whitehill,Bordon, Hampshire GU35 9HD (tel 01420-474261, e-mail optiontrust@pvm.ndo.co.uk).

A non-profit making organisation, set up and run by a number of disabled people who employ staff to enable them to live in homes of their own in the community. **Personal Assistants (10-12).** £90-£200 a week plus free B & L. The work involves personal care, domestic duties and driving. Min. period of work 6 months at any time of year. Min. age 18. Driving licence required but no previous experience is necessary.

Applications to Mrs V. Mason at the above address.

Outdoor

ADRIAN SCRIPPS LTD: Moat Farm, Five Oak Green, Paddock Wood, Tonbridge, Kent TN12 6RR (tel 01892-832406; fax 01892-832721).

Hop Pickers. Approx. £150 a week. Work involves mechanical picking of hops for a period of 4-5 weeks from 1 September.

Piecework Fruit Pickers to pick apples and pears growing on small trees for 4-5 weeks from early September.

Self-catering accommodation provided. Min. age 18.

For more details and *applications* write to Adrian Scripps Ltd. at the above address, enclosing s.a.e, after 1 June. Please note that no bookings are taken before July 1.

AMBERVALE FARM: North Common Lane, Sway, Lymington, Hampshire SO41 8LL. New Forest farm five minutes away from the sea by car.

Live-In Assistant to help with horses and manual work on the farm; tidying, gardening and building. All accommodation, home cooked meals included as well as horse riding and swimming.

Applications enclosing a s.a.e. only to Mrs C.M. Nicholson-Pike at the above address.

S.C. AND J.H. BERRY LTD: Gushmere Court Farm, Selling, Faversham, Kent ME13 9RF(tel 01227-752205/752838). A family run farm in a beautiful area of Kent, which grows a range of crops to sell to supermarkets, wholesalers and brewers.

Apple Pickers/Hop Pickers (15). Wages at standard Agricultural Wages Board Rates. Apple picking mostly paid at piece work rates. To work a standard 39 hours per week, plus up to 16 hours overtime. Work cannot be guaranteed during wet weather. Self-catering accommodation in caravans available for approx. £14 a week: blankets, pillows and separate kitchen, lounge and shower facilities are provided, as well as TV room and various sporting facilities. Applicants should bring their own sleeping bags, towels, etc. as well as wellington boots and waterproof clothing.

Workers are needed for the entire period between 25th August and 28th September. Applicants should be students over 18 years old. EEA applicants considered. Possession of a driving licence would be an advantage.

Applications (with s.a.e. or IRC) should be sent from 1 May to Mr J.P.S. Berry at the above address.

BRAMSHOT HOUSE: Fleet, Hampshire GU13 8RT (tel 01252-617304). A family who need help with their large garden, chickens, ducks, general repairs and maintenance. Would suit anyone wanting a working holiday. 45 minutes by train from London.

Gardeners/Painters/Carpenters (1-2). £20 pocket money per week. Flexible working arrangement averaging 3-5 hours per day. Plenty of free time for sightseeing. Self-contained fully furnished flat provided, also produce from the garden when available and use of bicycle, tennis court and swimming pool. Some skill in painting, gardening or carpentry essential. Overseas applicants welcome.

Applications to Mrs P.A. Duckworth at the above address.

BROGDALE FARM: Brogdale Road, Faversham, Kent ME13 8XZ (tel 01795-535286; fax 01795-531710). Home of the National Fruit Collections and centre for the conservation and evaluation of fruit crops.

Fruit Pickers (4-6). To work from June until the end of October harvesting fruit crops. Min. age 17. Englsh speaking essential; must be eligible to work in the UK. To work a basic 39 hour week. To be paid agricultural wages, board rates. Accommodation available at £15 per week. Min. stay 12-16 weeks.

Applications to the Farm Manager at the above address.

BUTLER BROS. (MARDEN): Cornwells Farm, Marden, Tonbridge, Kent, TN12 9NS (tel 01622-831385; fax 01622-832939; e-mail butlerbros@farmline.com).

Supervisors (2) wanted for May-July.

Tractor Drivers (2) wanted for May-July.

Strawberry Pickers (12) wanted May-July.

Apple Pickers (6) needed in September/October.

Supervisors (2) needed for August/October.

Tractors Drivers (2) needed for August/October.

All positions are paid at above minimum wage rates, with some accommodation available. Employees work a 5 day week plus overtime and some weekend work, previous experience is useful but not essential.

For *applications,* contact J.M. Lutener, Partner, at the above address.

CHANDLER & DUNN LTD: Lower Goldstone, Ash, Canterbury, Kent CT3 2DY (tel 01304-812262; fax 01304-812612; e-mail chandlerdunn@btclick.com). **Fruit Pickers (numbers variable)** for periods between the end of May and the end of September. Daily paid casual fruit picking Monday to Saturday from 8am to 4pm approximately. Most picking is piecework so opportunity for fast pickers to earn more. No accommodation on farm but good campsite very close. Must be aged at least 16 and entitled to work in the UK.

Applications to Anne Helbling, Farm Secretary at the above address.

CHARRINGTON FRUIT FARMS: Old Cryals, Cryals Road, Matfield, Tonbridge, Kent TN12 7HN (tel 01892-72 2372; fax 01892-72 3311). **Fruit Pickers (6-10).** Casual rate paid, flat rate during harvest time. Minimum age 18 years. Usual min. period of work 1 week between end of August and first week of October. No accommodation available so applicants should live locally. Must be healthy and willing to work hard and for long hours when the weather permits. Overseas applicants welcome but must have work permit and visa if coming from non EU countries.

Please *apply* from July to Charrington Fruit Farms at the above address/e-mail.

S.H. CHESSON: Manor Farm, Oldbury, Ightham, Sevenoaks, Kent TN15 9DG (tel 01732-780496; fax 01732-780509; e-mail andrew@manorfarm1. demon.co.uk; www.manorfarm1.demon.co.uk). Situated approx. 64km from London. Approx. 2km from station and shops. **Fruit Pickers (20)** to work 6 days per week picking strawberries (June-Sept) and apples/pears (Sept/Oct). Hours of work vary depending on the nature of the job. Start time 6.30am-8.00am; finish 2-5pm. Day off alternate Sat/Sun. Wages: piecework in region of £125-£175 per week. Minimum work period 4 weeks between 1 June and 10 October. Campsite charges £11.20 per week; kitchen, showers, laundry, tv/video room, canteen, outdoor recreations, outings and entertainment provided. Bring your own tent. Minimum age 18. EU/EEA citizens welcome. Non EU/EEA citizens must apply for necessary work permit through Concordia.

Apply in writing for an application form, from March 1 to Mr A.T. Chesson at the above address. All applicants must enclose a s.a.e. Visit their Website at www.manorfarm1.demon.co.uk.

CLOCK HOUSE FARM LTD: Clock House Farm, Coxheath, Maidstone, Kent ME17 4PG (tel 01622 743955/747198; e-mail Clockhousefarm@farmline.com; www.members.farmline.com/manda/). A Kentish fruit farm situated seven miles south of Maidstone growing strawberries and raspberries. There are also plums, apples and pears to be harvested later in the season. **Soft Fruit Pickers/Packers.** Approx earnings £25-£45 per day (piece work rates for picking). No qualifications required but previous experience helpful. Campsite accommodation with facilities available at £20 per week. Applications accepted from those able to start between mid May and mid June with work being available until October (the suggested minimum period of work being three weeks). Overseas applicants welcome but those from outside the EU must hold a valid work permit.

Applications from 1st January to Mr R.K. Pascall at the above address.

ELPHICKS FARM: Scuffits, Hunton, Maidstone, Kent ME15 ORY (tel 01622-820758; fax 01622-820754). A family owned company supplying top quality fruit to all the national supermarkets.

Apple Pickers (6). Wages £4.00 per hour minimum. To work 8-9 hours per day. Caravan accommodation provided. Min. age 19 years. Period of work end of August to end of September. Overseas applicants must have valid working visas.

Applications (enclosing s.a.e. or IRC) to be sent no earlier than 1 April and no later than 31 May to Mr S.S. Day, Elphicks Farm.

EWELL FARM: Edward Vinson Ltd., Graveney Road, Faversham, Kent ME13 8UP (tel: 01795-539452; fax 01795-539509). A friendly fruit growing company with several farms.

Fruit Pickers to work June to October. Wages at piecework rates; £30-£50 possible depending on ability. No accommodation available. Hours flexible, but typically 7am-3pm; weekend work available but time off as needed without restrictions. Applicants should be at least 16 and reasonably healthy.

Applications to Mr Ben Ashdown, Harvest Manager, at the above address.

S. FERMOR: Oakdene Farm, Sutton Valence, Maidstone, Kent ME17 3LS (tel 01622-843332; fax 01622-843332). Small fruit farm.

Fruit Pickers (5). Paid at piecework rates.

To work Monday-Friday; possibly 7 days per week. Basic accommodation available. Min. period of work 1 week between June and September. Min. age 18.

Applications at any time to Mrs J. Fermor at the above address.

H.E. HALL & SON LTD: Little Pattenden, Marden, Kent TN12 9QL (tel 01622-831376; fax 01622-831654).

Fruit Pickers (10). Paid piecework based on £4.10 per hour. 8am-3pm, Mon-Fri, but flexible hours and days dependent on weather and crop. Basic self-catering accommodation available at no cost. Min. period of work 1 day between mid August and mid October. Min. age 20. No previous experience necessary but it is useful. Male and female staff welcome. Overseas applicants considered if work authorisation is in order and English is spoken.

Applications from June onwards to Peter Hall by telephone.

HILL FARM ORCHARDS: Droxford Road, Swanmore, Hampshire SO32 2PY (tel 01489-878616; email hifol@farmline.com). Pleasantly situated between Portsmouth and Southampton, with shops and pubs nearby. Picking apples and pears for high class outlets.

Apple Pickers (up to 50). Required September to October.

Pay as set by Agricultural Wages Board and piece work rates at the height of the seasons. Hours: 8.00am-4.30pm Monday to Friday, with occasional weekends. Min. fee campsite available. Min. period of work 1 week. Applicants must be eligible to work in the UK.

Applications by post to Mr Paul Roberts, Farm Manager, at the above address.

HUGH LOWE FARMS LTD: Barons Place, Mereworth, Maidstone, Kent ME18 5NF (tel 01622-812721; fax 01622-813489). Farms growing quality

strawberries and raspberries for local markets and supermarkets.
Soft Fruit Pickers (50). Piece work rates. To work 6 days per week. Min. age 18. Campsite with facilities provided: bring own tent, sleeping bag and cooking utensils. Busy but pleasant working conditions. Work available from May to September (May arrivals particularly welcome). EEA nationals welcome.

Write for *application* form, enclosing s.a.e., to the above address.

JERSEY CYCLETOURS: 2 La Hougue Mauger, St. Mary, Jersey, JE3 3AF (tel 01534-482898; fax 01534-484060). The company's bikes (Trek, Giant, Dawes) are the best maintained and equipped hire bikes in Jersey; it needs people who are keen and able to maintain our standards.
CYCLE MECHANIC, DELIVERY DRIVER needed from April to the end of September. Mechanic must have experience in bike building and repair and driver must have a clean driving licence. Wages aae. Working week 30-40 hours per week.
Contact **Daniel Wimberley at the above address.**

LANGDON MANOR FARM: Seasalter Road, Goodnestone, Faversham, Kent ME13 9DA (tel 01795-530035).
Soft Fruit Pickers & Agricultural Workers required to pick and pack all types of soft fruit to a very high standard. Minimum age 18. Pickers will be trained and should be hard working and conscientious. Min. work period of 4 weeks between mid May and October. Pickers especially welcome in June. Hours 6am to 3pm with some work in evenings. Piecework rates paid. Workers will be expected to pick at the required speed.

Accommodation available in mobile homes, cost £21 per week. Facilities include showers, toilets, mess room, kitchen, bus to shops. Group outings, discos and barbecues organised. English lessons given 2 nights per week. Easy access to London (by train 50 minutes). Early booking advised; notification of acceptance March. Overseas applicants welcome but those from outside the EEA must hold a valid work permit.

Applications to the above address enclosing a s.a.e. or IRC to ensure a reply.

LAUREL TREE FRUIT FARM: Boar's Head, East Sussex TN6 3HD (tel 01892-661637 or 01892-654011; mobile 0468-980308; fax 01892-663417).
Pickers (20) for top fruit picking (apple and pear). Wages £3.60 per hour, to work 6 hours per day. Period of work depends on harvest, but probably 20 days between 25th August and 30th September (approx). No accommodation available, but limited camping is permitted. Overseas applicants with valid working visas welcome. No interview necessary.

Applications from 20th August onwards to Robert Booker (mobile phone 0468-980308) or evenings at the above number.

F.W. MANSFIELD & SON: Nickle Farm, Chartham, Canterbury, Kent CT4 7PL (tel 01227-731441; fax 01227-731795).
Fruit Pickers And Packers (50-100) to pick and pack apples, pears, strawberries, plums, cherries and pumpkins. National minimum wage or piecework rate; to work variable hours a week, plus overtime - as they wish. Accommodation in caravans for £25 per week with communal kitchen and washing facilities. Cash daily during harvest. Workers needed from May-November, must be aged at least 18, fit and hard working.

Applications to the Farms Manager at the above address.

C.E. MURCH LTD: Amery Court Farm, Chapel Lane, Blean, Canterbury, Kent CT2 9HF (tel 01227-471774; fax 0207-6812014; e-mail cemurch@aol.com).
Fruit/Asparagus Pickers (8). Wages at piecework rates, equivalent to around £5 per hour; to work 6-8 hours per day. Accommodation in shared caravans is available at a cost of £20 per week. Workers required for a minimum of 2 weeks. Work is available from May 1st to mid July, then from September 5th to October 5th. Foreign applicants with a good understanding of English and a valid work permit are welcome; please do not apply unless you have a valid work permit.
  Applications from April to Charles Atkins.

A.R NEAVES & SONS: Little Sharsted Farm, Doddington, Near Sittingbourne, Kent ME9 OJT (tel 01795-886263; fax 01795-886470). A friendly family run business which has been running for sixty years and supplies fruit to the supermarkets.
Strawberry Pickers (20) for casual work. Wages on a piecework basis, to work 8 hours a day Monday to Saturday. Applicants must be over 18; no experience is necessary. Pickers are required from June 1st to July or August for a minimum of 6 weeks, however as there are other fruits (cherries, plums, apples) there could be up to 3 months work available.
  Overseas applicants with a valid work permit are welcome. Accommodation is available at a charge of £15 per week. *Applications* should be sent to Sarah Neaves/Martin Harman from the beginning of May onwards at the above address.

NEWMAFRUIT FARMS LTD: Howfield Farm, Howfield Lane, Chartham, near Canterbury, Kent CT4 7HQ (tel 01227-738221; fax 01227-738086; e-mail Enquiries@Newmafruit.co.uk). A fairly large organisation, with a personal supervisor for all the students; a new accommodation area has just been built.
Fruit Pickers/Packers. Wages national minimum wage or piecework rate. Accommodation available at £20 per week. Workers required from 6th June to 30th September. Overseas applicants are recruited through Concordia (see Work Permits and Special schemes section).
  Applications from March to Mr Melvyn Newman at the above address.

R.H. NIGHTINGALE & PARTNER: Gibbet Oak Farm, Appledore Road, Tenterden, Kent TN30 7DH (tel 01580-763492; fax 01580-763938). Ideally situated only 2 miles from town with all amenities, campsite and mobile homes with usual facilities.
Strawberry Pickers to work from May to July.
Apple Thinners to work from June to July.
Apple/Pear Pickers (up to 15) to work from 25 August to 30 September.
  To work 5-9 hours per day, depending on ripening of crops. Payment at piecework rates. Applicants should be fit, willing and able; age not important. Overseas applicants welcome, but those from outside the EU must hold a valid work permit.
  Applications to P.J. Nightingale at the above address.

PERRYHILL ORCHARD: Bolebroke Lodge, Edenbridge Road, Hartfield, East Sussex TN7 4JJ (tel 01892-770595).
Fruit Pickers (8-10). To work 4-8 hours per day picking mainly apples and top fruit. Wages £20-£45 per day. Must be aged at least 18 and have plenty of common sense. Work available during August, September and October.
  Please *apply* to Mr J. Smith at the above address.

F.G. PIERCE & SONS LTD: Orchard Place Farm, Comp Road, Borough Green, near Sevenoaks, Kent TN15 8QX (tel 01732-883169; fax 01732-885559; e-mail f.g.pierce@farming.co.uk). Orchard Place Farm is a large strawberry farm situated in the heart of the Kentish countryside, only 30 miles from London.
Soft Fruit Pickers (50) required from end of May to September. Payment at piecework rates.
Fruit Packers (20) required from June to September. Hourly rate of pay as set by Agricultural Wages Board.
No qualifications required. To work approximately 7 hours a day, 6 days a week. Camping available (must bring own tent). Facilities include showers, toilets, games/tv room, kitchen and lounge area. Weekly transport to shops. Group outings and barbecues organised. Easy access to London (40 minutes by train).
Overseas applicants welcome, but those outside the EEA must hold a valid work permit. *Applications* can be sent at any time to Caroline Pierce, at the above address.

REDSELL GROUP: Nash Court, Boughton, Faversham, Kent ME13 9SR (tel 01227-751224 or 07889-308731; e-mail patgoode@redsell.com; www.redsell.com).
Hop And Fruit Pickers (30-40) needed to work on 200 acres of hops and 300 acres of top fruit for about four weeks from around 25th August. Basic accommodation provided free of charge. Workers must provide own bedding and cooking utensils. Hops are picked on an hourly rate based on a 52-hour week; fruit is paid at piecework rates. *Contact* Pat Goode.

SOUTHERN MARQUEES: 22 Peters Road, Locksheath, Southampton, Hamps SO31 6EQ (tel 01489-575372; e-mail sales@southernmarquees.co.uk). Excellent reputation for marquee hire, particularly for weddings, corporate events and parties. In operation 11 years.
Marquee Erectors (4). Wages £5 per hour. To work 30 hours per week plus overtime. Min. period of work of 4 months. Positions are available from end of April to the end of September. Need to be aged over 21 and have a minimum of 7 feet of reach, a strong back and loads of stamina; job involves heavy lifting. Clean driving licence. No accommodation available.
Applications should be made from end of March onwards to Hugh and Mandy Reigate at the above address. Interview necessary.

SPELMONDEN ESTATE CO. LTD: Spelmonden Farm, Goudhurst, Kent TN17 1HE. Situated on the A262 between Lamberhurst and Goudhurst. Nearest train stations are Paddock Wood or Marden on the line from Ashford to Charing Cross
Hop, Apple, Pear, Plum And Cobnut Pickers. August 14th to early October for 45 hours or more per week. Pay between £147 and £198 (depending on exemption from tax). Piecework for apple picking is per bin. Self catering accommodation in 2/3/4 bedrooms plus TV room, showers etc. Cost £10 per week. Applicants must be authorised to work in the UK.
Applications in writing only from May 1st (enclosing s.a.e.) to the Managing Director at the above address.

SUNRISE FRUITS: The Street, Stourmouth, nr. Canterbury, Kent CT3 1HY (tel 01227-721977; fax 01227-728633).
Strawberry/Raspberry Pickers to work from June to October. Also some general farm work. To work approximately 40 hours per week; good piecework

rates paid. Accommodation is available at a small charge, a £5 booking fee is returnable after the first working week. Minimum period of work 4 weeks. No experience or qualifications needed but applicants should be self-motivated.

Early *application* is recommended to the above address.

TILMANSTONE SALADS: Wigmore Lane, Eythorne, Near Dover CT15 4ND (tel 01304-382061/833061; fax 01304-382443). A part of Geest foods, Tilmanstone salads prepares and packs salad and deli products.

Production Operatives (100) To prepare and pack salad products. Wages £5.05 per hour; to work alternate 6 and 4 day weeks for 8 hours a day. No experience is required. Applicants must be at least 21 years old.

Staff are required from March to September for a minimum period of 1 month. Overseas applicants are welcome but must have a valid work permit and understand enough English to comply with health and safety and food safety training.

Applications should be sent to Corinna Redsull at the above address from February onwards.

VIBERT MARQUEES: Manor Farm, Rue du Manoir, St Ouen, Jersey, JE3 2LF (tel 01534-482970; fax 01534-482905; e-mail vibmarq@localdial.com). Long established, family-run business with 6 full-time and 20 seasonal workers.

Marquee Erectors (10). Wages from £6 per hour. To work from 8am to finish, varied hours including overtime and weekends, approx. 50 hours per week. Period of work runs May-September; min. period of work of July to September. Applicants must be 17+ and hard working. Foreign applicants who speak good English are welcome. No accommodation available. Working shirts are provided free; shorts are recommended.

Applications should be made from January onwards to Gary Vibert at the above address.

WAKELEY BROTHERS (RAINHAM, KENT) LTD: The Oasts, Spade Lane, Hartlip, Sittingbourne, Kent ME9 7TT (tel 01634-386304; fax 01634-386305).

Fruit Pickers required. Period of work from July-September. Wages based on Standard Agricultural Rate. Applicants must be hard working. Accommodation (hot showers, TV room, etc.) provided on a self catering basis at £20 per week. Foreign applicants with work permits and acceptable spoken English welcome.

Applications to Mrs G Wakeley, at the above address.

R.J. WALKER: Little Postern, Postern Lane, Tonbridge TN11 0QU (tel 01732-353290).

Apple Pickers (5) to work for three weeks during September. Piecework rates. Min. age 18. No accommodation available.

Applications by mid-August to Mr Walker at the above address.

L. WHEELER & SONS (EAST PECKHAM) LTD: Bullen Farm, East Peckham, Tonbridge, Kent TN12 5LX (tel 01622-871225; fax 01622-872952). A hop farm within an hour's journey of London. Local facilities such as shops and pubs are available.

Apple Pickers (20). 6 hour day, 5¹/₂ days a week.

Hop Pickers (20). 8-9 hour day, 5¹/₂ days a week.

Approx. £4.10 per hour with the possibility of bonuses. Minimum period of work 5 weeks between 20 August and 30 September. Accommodation available with just a charge for electricity. Overseas applicants authorised to work in the

UK welcome.
Applications from June to the Manager at the above address.

L. WHEELER & SONS (YALDING) LTD: Bockingfold, Marden, Tonbridge, Kent TN12 9PH (tel 01892-730224/07808200404; fax 01892-722532). Farm is in mid Kent, near Paddock Wood railway station.
Fruit Pickers required for apple picking. Wages paid at piece rate per bin filled, hours flexible with low cost accommodation available. Work available from September 1st approx. for 3 weeks to a month. Applicants must be fit.
Applications to M.J. Wheeler, Director, at the above address.

M.J.M. & G.A. WYANT AND SON: The Packhouse, New Place Farm, Ickham, Canterbury, Kent CT3 1RA (tel 01227-728538; fax 01227-721110). A family run horticultural business growing and packing vegetables for major supermarkets to a very high standard.
Vegetable Harvest Workers (50), Vegetable Packhouse Staff (12). Wages at piecework rates, some hourly work at £5 per hour. To work 40 hours per week plus overtime. Must have energy, dexterity, self-motivation, common-sense and the ability to follow instructions. Accommodation is not available. Staff required for a minimum of 1 month between Mid-July and Early-October. Overseas applicants with excellent English are considered.
Applications from 1st June to Geraldine Wyant at the above address.

WORKING WONDERS: Wapsbourne Manor Farm, Sheffield Park, Uckfield, East Sussex TN22 3QT (tel01825-723414; fax 01285-722451; e-mail recruitment@wowo.co.uk) A specialised working holiday company.
Seasonal Agricultural Work; also some light industrial and service industry work. Wages are minimum of £3.75 per hour. There is plenty of opportunity for weekend and overtime work. The sometimes demanding work requires flexibility, motivation and plenty of spirit. Applicants should be self disciplined with good social skills and a valid working visa.
   Inexpensive accommodation available in a caravan park in the Sussex countryise, one hour south of London.
Applications to Working Wonders at the above address.

Sport

ALBOURNE EQUESTRIAN CENTERE: Henfield Road, Albourne, West Sussex BN6 9OE (tel 01273-832989; fax 01273-833392). An approved British riding school and livery yard, also Council approved. Regularly hold affiliated and unaffiliated shows and clinics.
Working Pupils (2-3) training for BHS exams. Work will consist of general yard work, riding tuition and the opportunity to compete at shows and events.Wages depending on experience; to work $5^1/2$ days a week from 8am to 5.30pm. Applicants must be 16 and over. Accommodation is available at a charge of £30 per week. Students of all nationalities are considered, some experience with horses is prefered.
   Staff are required at any time for a minimum of 3 months. *Applications* should be sent to Megan Hughes at the above address. References required.

ARUN DISTRICT COUNCIL: Arun Civic Centre, Maltravers Road, Littlehampton (tel 01903-737662; fax 01903-713059). Local authority employer.
Beach Lifeguards (6-8). Wages of £4.50 per hour. Hours to be discussed. Min.

period of work of a season. Positions are available from May to September. Boat handling, powerboat driving, PWC and beach life guard training are all advantageous. Minimum age 16. No accommodation available.

Applications should be made from January onwards to Barry Welch, Foreshore Officer, at the above address. Interview necessary.

CALSHOT ACTIVITIES CENTRE: Calshot Spit, Fawley, Hampshire SO45 1BR (tel 023-8089 2077; fax 023-8089 1267; email calshot.ac@hants.gov.uk; www.hants.gov.uk/calshot). One of the biggest outdoor adventure centres in Britain, overlooking Southampton Water and the Solent, Calshot is perfectly located. It provides lessons, courses, short breaks and holidays in a wide range of water and land-based activities.

Activity Instructors (10) to work February to October. Wages £212 per week. Applicants must be over 21 and have experience and qualifications in dinghy sailing, canoeing, windsurfing, etc. Experience in skiing or climbing or other outdoor activities an advantage. Applications from September for following year.

Visiting Instructors to work all year round for single sessions, days, weekends. Must be fully qualified applicants over 18. Activities include dinghy sailing, canoeing, windsurfing, powerboating, rock climbing, skiing, and snowboarding.

Summer Helpers to assist with activities and pastoral care of youngsters aged 10-16. To work July/August. Applicants must be over 18.

High levels of training and staff development are undertaken. Staff accommodation normally available. Good opportunities exist for internal promotion.

Kitchen Assistants to work June to August on casual cover, £5 per hour.

Gatekeeper to work 5 weeks July to August, £5 per hour

Applications to Calshot Activities Centre at the above address.

THE GUIDE ASSOCIATION: Foxlease, Lyndhurst, Hants SO43 7DE (tel 023-8028 2638; fax; 023-8028 2561; e-mail Foxlease@guides.org.uk). A centre owned by the Guide Association and used by schools, guides and scouts throughout the summer months. Residential and camping; canoeing, archery, climbing and swimming pool all on site.

Activity Instuctors (4). Wages £4.50 per hour; to work 40 hours per week or more if desired. Accommodation is available at a charge of £30 per week. Staff required between April and September; minimum stay is July and August. Applicants must be 18 or over and have at least two of the following: BCU (canoeing), GNAS (archery), Single Pitch Supervisor (climbing), National Pool Lifeguard. Suitably qualified foreign applicants are considered.

Applications from November to Hilary Chittock at the above address.

HILSEA LIDO: c/o Victoria Swimming Centre, Anglesea Road, Portsmouth PO1 3DL (tel 023-9282 3822; fax 023-9287 1781).

Casual Lifeguards (20) required for the open-air Hilsea Lido between 26 May and 14 September. Wages are £4.50 per hour. To work from 11am-7pm daily with overtime as required, although the work is dependant on the weather. Applicants must be over 16 and have a National Pool Lifeguarding Qualification.

Applications in writing to A.D. Baker, Manager, at the Victoria Swimming Centre.

MEDINA VALLEY CENTRE: Dodnor Lane, Newport, Isle of Wight PO30 5TE (tel 01983-522195; fax 01983-825962; e-mail info@medinavalleycentre.org.uk). An outdoor education and activity centre providing fieldwork courses for schools

in Biology and Geography, Key Stage 2 to A-level. Also provides RYA sail training for adults and children.
Seasonal Temporary RYA Dinghy Sailing Instructors needed from the end of July to August. Must have RYA dinghy sailing instructor qualifications.
Applications to Peter Savory.

REGENT LANGUAGE HOLIDAYS: 40-42 Queens Road, Brighton BN1 3XB (tel 01273-718620; fax 01273-718621; e-mail holidays@regent.org.uk; www.regent.org.uk). Regent operates four high quality residential centres in Southern England. They specialise in summer language holidays.
Social Directors(4). £275-£325 per week. PGCE sports qualified. Full board and accommodation provided.
Applications at any time to Recruitment at the above address.

SHEPWAY DISTRICT COUNCIL: c/o Hythe Swimming Pool, South Road, Hythe, Kent CT21 6AR (tel 01303-269177).
Beach Lifeguards (4). to perform patrol services including litter picking and normal lifeguard duties on Folkestone Beach. Wages £4.50 per hour. To work 8 hours per day. Usual period of work is 8 weeks. Positions are available from July to early September. Should be aged 18+, beach lifeguard qualifications required, English essential. People living locally can be given training at Hythe Pool. Overseas applicants welcome with appropriate qualifications and if they can arrange their own accommodation.
Applications should be made from 1 March onwards to Paul Cannon or Graham Newing and include a CV

TRAVEL CLASS LTD: 14 Queensway, New Milton, Hampshire BH25 5NN (tel 08705-133773; fax 08705-133774; e-mail paul@travelclass.co.uk). Trading as Junior Choice Adventures, operates activity adventure holidays in six residential centres in Cornwall, Devon, the Isle of Wight and Kent. School groups during term time.
Activity Instructors, Watersports Instructors. Wages on application. To work as an activity instructor instructing a complete range of outdoor activities. No formal qualifications needed as free 2-3 week training course provided. Nationally recognised qualification in archery, fencing, shooting, first aid, climbing, abseiling plus in-house training in other activities. Must be over 18, hard working, sense of humour and have enthusiasm to instruct children.
Senior Instructors And Centre Managers. Wages on application. Must have experience, and for watersports relevant qualifications. Experience of leadership and management needed for Centre Managers role.
75 positions available from March to late July/September. Accommodation, food, uniform are all provided at a charge of £50 per week. All nationalities welcome but must have a good command of English.
Post or e-mail for application details to Paul Jackson at the above address.

Voluntary Work

Conservation and the Environment
CELIA HAMMOND ANIMAL TRUST: High Street, Wadhurst, East Sussex TN5 6AG (tel 01892-783820; fax 01892-784882; http://web.ukonline.

co.uk/chat).

A animal rescue and re-homing service and sanctuary that also offers low cost neutering and vaccination clinics.

Volunteer Rescue Workers (4), Volunteer Administrative Staff (4). Hours are negotiable.

Veterinary Nurses (4), Veterinary Surgeons (4), Veterinary Receptionists (2). Wages and hours are negotiable. A love of animals and an interest in animal welfare are essential. Accommodation is available at a cost to be negotiated. Staff are required all year round. An interview is required.

Applications to Miss Roma Brawn at the above address.

Festivals and Special Events

BROADSTAIRS FOLK WEEK: Pierremont Hall, Broadstairs, Kent CT10 1JH (tel 01843-604080; fax 01843-866048; e-mail info@folk_week.demon.co.uk; www.broadstairsfolkweek.com).

The Broadstairs Folk Week Trust, a registered charity, organises events throughout the year and an annual festival. 2002 will be the festival's 37th year. The whole town and its promenade, jetty, bandstand, taverns, halls, churches and streets becomes the venue for international music, song and dance.

Volunteers (120+) are needed as door stewards, information and shop staff, PA and sound technicians, drivers, campsite stewards and collectors. Volunteers are also needed to handle publicity and liaise with international personnel. Posts are unpaid, but staff receive a season ticket for access to all events. Free camping is available. Volunteers work 4 hours a day. Minimum period of work 3 days between 9th and 16th August. Overseas applicants with good English are considered.

Applications from March to Jane de Rose. Interview is not necessary

Heritage

HAMMERWOOD PARK: Hammerwood, near East Grinstead, Sussex RH19 3QE (tel 01342-850594; fax 01342-850864).

A Grade I listed building built in 1792, open to the public and providing exclusive, limited accommodation. The restoration of the house and garden is a family project; the estate was derelict in 1982.

Voluntary Staff (2+) required to help in all aspects of running a historic house and garden. To work 3-4 days per week. No wages are paid but full board and accommodation are provided. Applicants must have the ability to deal with the public and be able to carry out tasks as they arise, even the mundane. Staff required from Easter to the end of September for a minimum period of 1 month. Suitable foreign applicants with a good level of English are welcome. An interview is desirable.

Applications from January to David Pinnegar at the above address.

MID HANTS RAILWAY (WATERCRESS LINE): Railway Station, Alresford, Hampshire SO24 9JG (tel 01962-733810; fax 01962-735448; e-mail watercressline@compuserve.com; www.watercressline.co.uk)

A preserved steam railway running trains between Alresford and Alton.

Volunteers Needed: work available, both full-time and part-time. Tourism students are particularly encouraged to apply, and there is the possibility of work for engineering students.

Staff are required from May to September for a minimum of 2 months.

Applications should be sent to Mr R. Gordon at the above address from the beginning of February.

Vacation Traineeships

Science, Construction and Engineering

GIFFORD AND PARTNERS: Carlton House, Ringwood Road, Woodlands, Southampton SO40 7HT (tel 023-8081 7500; fax 023-8081 7600; e-mail mail.soten@gifford-consulting.co.uk).

Gifford and Partners is a firm of consulting engineers particularly interested in the design of building and highway structures and in marine works worldwide. Each summer the firm takes on up to **Six Students** to work in its Head Office and in the regional office in Chester. Student engineers work within a design team in a multidisciplinary consultants design office. Disciplines include civil, structural, building services, environmental and geotechnical engineering; also land surveyors and archaeologists.

Traineeships last for up to three months and are open to students reading Civil or Structural Engineering at university. Suitably qualified applicants from abroad are welcome. The salary in 2001 was £160 a week.

Interested candidates should *contact* Mr Bruce Cozens, Personnel Manager, by 1 March.

ROKE MANOR RESEARCH: Roke Manor, Romsey, Hampshire SO51 0ZN (tel 01794-833185; fax 01794-833451; e-mail jobs@roke.co.uk; www.roke.co.uk).

Roke Manor Research offer **20 Vacation Traineeship Placements** in its Romsey office. Applicants should be computer literate undergraduates studying Electronics, Software, Maths or Physics. Placements are available in Electronics design and Software design for research and development in communications software and sensors. Students' salary starts from £1000 per month and placements last 8 weeks. Help can be given to find accommodation. Security clearance is required for those working on sensor research and development.

Applications from February to Hayley Duke-Glover at the above address.

Travel and Tourism

HOTEL HOUGUE DU POMMIER: Castel, Guernsey, Channel Islands (tel 01481-256531; fax 01481-256260; e-mail hotel@houguedupommier.guernsey.net; www. hotelhouguedupommier).

An attractive farmhouse style hotel on the west coast of Guernsey. Busy in summer with visitors from UK, France, Germany and Switzerland.

Hotel Hougue du Pommier does not offer formal traineeships, but certain positions are open to **Students Of Catering** hoping to develop their skills and gain valuable work experience. The positions are mainly in the restaurant.

B & L is provided free of charge. Applicants are not required to attend an interview. Further details about jobs available and *applications* from Mr Steven Bone, General Manager, at the above address.

East Anglia

Prospects for Work.

East Anglia is not one of the most promising areas in which to look for temporary summer employment. However, Norfolk and Cambridgeshire are major agricultural areas and fruit picking, packing and processing work provide comparatively good prospects. King's Lynn, Wisbech and East Dereham (near Norwich) are the principal centres.

In and around King's Lynn the *Lynn News* carries general job advertisements. Factory work is the main source of summer employment in the town, as local food factories employ temporary production operators between June and September. The Jobcentre in King's Lynn keeps a register of people looking for temporary seasonal work, though you are still advised to check in person on a regular basis. Priority is given to the local unemployed or students whose permanent home is King's Lynn. A lot of this work is governed by the weather, and is therefore irregular. King's Lynn Jobcentre can be contacted at Lovell House, St Nicholas Street, King's Lynn PE30 1LR (01553-734900). The *Eastern Daily Press*, which is circulated throughout Norfolk and in northern Suffolk, also lists general job vacancies.

Temporary tourism and holiday-related jobs are most easily found in Hunstanton, Cromer, Lowestoft and above all Great Yarmouth which, after Blackpool, is Britain's major entertainment resort. You can contact Great Yarmouth Jobcentre at Copperfield House, The Conge, Great Yarmouth NR30 1EJ; tel 01493-633300. Lowestoft Jobcentre (The Marina, Lowestoft, NR32 1HL; tel 01502-403200) has seasonal vacancies for local holiday camps from around February each year, particularly in catering and retail. Hunstanton has a number of large hotels which consistently require staff, particularly in the summer season. While some live-in accommodation is provided by employers in Hunstanton, this is harder to come by in King's Lynn and Wisbech (where rented lodgings are also in short supply). Wisbech Jobcentre (tel 01945-675821) has general job adverts in the *Fenland Citizen*, which comes out every Wednesday, and the *Wisbech Standard*, which comes out every Friday. Temporary factory work for local large employers and lots of seasonal picking/packing work is available as well as many vacancies requiring skilled workers that cannot be filled.

In Ipswich it is worth visiting the JobShop at Westgate House, 5 Museum Street which is solely dedicated to job vacancies. The *Evening Star* has a pull-out jobs section every Wednesday which services not only Ipswich, but the surrounding areas.

As a major tourist attraction and language school centre, a number of associated jobs can be found in Cambridge. The town's Jobcentre (Henry Giles House, 73-79 Chesterton Road, Cambridge CB4 3BG, tel 01223-545000) usually has summer opportunities for catering staff and jobs teaching English as a foreign language. There is also agricultural work available in the area picking soft fruits and later in the year, picking potatoes. A major local agricultural contractor uses the Earl of Derby pub car park on Hills Road as a pick-up point in the early morning for those wanting work. The contractor also offers agricultural work on a camping basis in many parts of England. The *Cambridge Evening News* newspaper advertises job vacancies on Wednesdays and Fridays.

Felixstowe, on the Suffolk coast, is usually a good source of temporary work, particularly catering and retail together with a few jobs in leisure. Felixstowe Jobcentre is at 29-31 Hamilton Road, Felixstowe, Suffolk IP11 7AZ; tel 01394-623300. Ipswich Borough Council and Suffolk County Council usually need to recruit temporary staff over the summer too.

Business and Industry

GRAND UK HOLIDAYS: The Old Bakery, Queens Road, Norwich, Norfolk, NR1 3PL (tel 01603-886751; fax 01603-886702). Britain's largest coach tour operators catering exclusively for the over 55s in over 140 resorts and destinations throughout the UK.

Couriers (25). £160 net per week plus optional excursion and tips. To work on eight-day coach tours. Applicants must be friendly and have an outgoing personality and the ability to relate to those aged over fifty-five. Accommodation and food provided. Staff needed from April to October.

Applications to the above address.

Children

EXPERIENCE UK LTD: 48 Fitzalan Road, London N3 3PE (tel 020-8922 9739; fax 020-8343 0625; e-mail xuk@xkeys.co.uk; www.campsforkids.co.uk). Residential camps in East Anglia for children aged 6-17 years.

Childrens Leaders, Cooks, Kitchen Assistants, Cleaners. Qualifications or experience in first aid, life saving, arts/crafts, sports, or teaching are helpful.

Competitive wages. Free board. Applications from teachers or student teachers preferred.

More details and *application* forms available on the above website.

IPSWICH BOROUGH COUNCIL: Civic Centre, Civic Drive, Ipswich IP1 2EE (tel 01473-433514; fax 01473-433636; e-mail jane.hennell@ipswichgov.uk).
Playworkers (12) Wages £3.63 per hour.
Playsupervisors (3) Sportscheme Leaders (3) Daycamp Leaders (2) Wages £4.63 per hour; to work Monday to Friday. Applicants must be aged 18+ and have experience of working with children.
Pitch And Putt Attendants (2) Wages £4.60 per hour; to work from mid June to the end of August. Applicants must be aged 18+ and have cash handling experience.

Staff are required to work for a minimum of 4 weeks during the summer holiday period.

Applicants should apply to the Leisure Services (01473-435000) at the above address from early March.

KIDS KLUB: The Lodge, The Hall, Great Finborough, Stowmarket, Suffolk IP14 3EF (tel 01449-742700; fax 01449-742701; e-mail info@kidsklub.co.uk).
Activity Supervisors (30). Salary at least £100 per week. Min. age 18.
Activity Instructors (15). Salary at least £125 per week. Must have National Governing Body awards. Min. age 18.
Matrons (4). Salary at least £125 per week. Must have first aid or nursing qualifications. Min. age 21.
General Assistants (4). Salary at least £75 per week. Min. age 16.

All positions are for 6 days per week. Staff are required from March 1st or July 1st to August 31st. Min. period of work 4 weeks. Accommodation is available at no extra charge.

Applicants from overseas welcome; a phone or personal interview is required. *Applications* from January to Ian Lewis at the above address.

Holiday Centres and Amusements

ADVENTURE ISLAND: Western Esplanade, Southend-on-Sea, Essex, SS1 1EE (tel 01702-468023; fax 01702-601044).
Ride Operators, Catering Staff, Cashiers (50-60) required for the summer, wages and hours by arrangement, staff must be over 18.
Applications to the Personnel Department, at the above address.

BANHAM ZOO: The Grove, Banham, Norfolk NR16 2HE (tel 01953-887771; carlw@banhamzoo.co.uk; www.banhamzoo.co.uk). Situated between Attleborough and Diss on the B1113 Norwich to Bury St Edmunds Road. One of the largest and most exciting wildlife attractions in the country with over 1,000 animals, many of which are critically endangered.
Catering Staff & Retail Assistants required from Easter to September. Wages on application.

For *applications* or enquiries write to Mrs Gill Germany at the above address: applicants considered will be invited for interview. Please note: no accommodation available.

CAMP BEAUMONT DAY CAMPS LTD: Beaumont Lodge, Overstrand Hall, Overstrand, Norfolk. NR27 0JJ (tel 01263-579666; fax 01263-576312; e-mail jobs@campbeaumont.com). Vacancies are currently available for all camps, which run for six weeks during July and August.

Group Leaders (250) (minimum age 18 years) These posts require previous leadership experience with young people and/or a well developed interest in sports, music, drama, arts and crafts or any recreational pursuits as the job entails looking after and instructing groups of children.

Activity Instructors (minimum age 21 years). The role is similar to that of a Group Leader, but with responsibility for planning and instructing a particular activity or group of activities. Applicants must either hold the appropriate recognised qualification and/or be highly experienced in that particular activity.

Nursery Leaders (minimum age 18 years) must have NNEB/BTEC or equivalent qualification or trainee Nursery Nurses. They need to have proven communication skills in relation to children and the ability to create structured activity sessions that allow incidental learning to take place.

Camp Nurse/First Aider must be a Registered nurse and/or first aid qualified (Red Cross or St John's Ambulance 'First Aid at Work' qualification).

Camp Director/Assistant Camp Director Need relevant management experience, activity camp knowledge, leadership flair, co-ordination and planning ability is essential, and the ability to communicate at various levels – with children, parents, overseas teachers (residential camps) and staff, and to take overall responsibility for the running of camp, including areas such as: programming, personnel management, customer care, diplomacy, transport, financial control and health and safety.

For further details and *applications* regarding any of these posts, camp locations and salary information, please contact Jayne Gosling, Recruitment Co-Ordinator.

COLCHESTER ZOO LTD: Maldon Road, Colchester, Essex CO3 5SL (tel 01206-331292; fax 01206-331392; e-mail colchester.zoo@btinternet.com). The zoo has gained a reputation as one of the most modern and forward-thinking zoos in the UK.

Retail Staff (12), Catering Staff (12), Site Cleaners (4), Face Painters (3), Gardeners (2). No accommodation available.

To request an application form for *applications* please send a s.a.e. to Colchester Zoo. Note all applicants must be available for interview.

IMPERIAL WAR MUSEUM: Duxford, Cambs CB2 4QR (tel 01223-499300; fax 01223-837267). Duxford was a former RAF fighter airfield during the Battle of Britain and is steeped in history. Today Duxford is Europe's premier aviation museum and visitor attraction.

Museum Assistants (6-9) to invigilate within the museum, assist visitors, monitor exhibitions and carry out cleaning duties. Wages £9,695 per annum, pro rata, to work 40$^{1}/_{2}$ hours a week. Must be 17 or over, hold a driving licence and be eligible to work in the UK. Period of work from March to October. Foreign applications welcome providing a good understanding of the English language is possessed.

Applications before March to the Personnel Office at the above address. An interview is required.

PLEASURE AND LEISURE CORPORATION plc: Pleasure Beach, South Beach Parade, Great Yarmouth, Norfolk NR30 3EH (tel 01493-844585; fax 01493-853483; e-mail GYPBeach@aol.com or Nigelthurs@aol.com). Leisure and amusement park with over 25 rides and other attractions over 9 acres.

Ride Operators (50). At least National Minimum Wage. Full uniform and staff concessions on rides and food outlets provided. Working hours variable according to the time of the season. Min. period of work of 4 weeks. Positions are available from March to September. Must be aged 18+ and with good spoken English. No previous experience necessary as training provided. Accommodation not available.

Applications should be made from March onwards to Nigel Thurston, Personnel Manager. Interview necessary.

Hotels and Catering

ALEXANDERS INTERNATIONAL SCHOOL: Bawdsey Manor, Bawdsey, Woodbridge, Suffolk IP12 3AZ (tel 01394-411633; fax 01394-411357; e-mail english@alexandersint.demon.co.uk). An international summer school for 11-18 year olds from all over the world. English Language tuition plus specialist sports courses.

Domestic Assistants (6) And Estate Workers (6) Wages commensurate with experience; to work 40 hours a week including weekends. Must be 21 or over. Period of work from 18th June-28th August. Minimum period of work 2 weeks. Free accommodation is available.

Applications to the Administration Office from March to the above address.

ARUNDEL HOUSE HOTEL: Chesterton Road, Cambridge CB4 3AN (tel 01223-367701; fax 01223-367721; e-mail info@arundelhousehotels.co.uk; www.arundelhousehotels.co.uk). A 2 Star private hotel in the centre of Cambridge with 103 bedrooms, á la carte restaurant, bar and conservatory.

Waiting/Bar Staff (5). Wages £4.45 per hour; to work 39 hours per five day week. Overtime paid at single time. No accommodation is available. Staff required at Easter and from June-October for a minimum period of 8 weeks. Applicants should be 18 or over, experience is not essential.

Applications in writing to Mrs Diana Duggen at the above address.

BRIDGE HOTEL: Clayhythe, Near Waterbeach, Cambridge CB5 9HQ (tel 01223-860252; fax 01223-440448).

Bar Staff (2) wanted for June, July and August. Wages £4.50 per hour. Applicants must be over 18.

To *apply* contact Maggie Manson, Owner, at the above address.

THE BRUDENELL HOTEL (REGAL): The Parade, Aldeburgh, Suffolk, IP15 5BU (tel 01728-452071; fax 01728-454082; e-mail info@brudenellhotels.co.uk, www.brudenellhotels.co.uk). Regal is a new company that owns 100 hotels. The Brudenell Hotel is one of the smaller ones with 47 bedrooms, and is very old and right on the sea front.

Waiting Staff (4). To work approx. 40 hours a week. Must be over 18.

Bar Person (1). To work approx 40 hours a week. Experience necessary. Must be over 18.

Supervisors (2). To work approx. 40 hours a week. Must be over 20 and have at least 1 year's waiting experience.

Housekeeping Person (1). To work 20-30 hours a week. Must be over 16.

National minimum wage. A wide variety of work is available, mainly on shifts. Staff will be trained in-house to wine taste, stock-take etc. Staff can learn about other departments other than their own if they wish. Accommodation is available for a deduction of 50p of the hourly wage. Min. period of work 2 months between 1st June and 30th September. Suitably qualified overseas applicants considered. Interview necessary, at least over the telephone.

Applications to the Restaurant and Bar Manager.

GREAT ADVENTURES: Grafham Water Centre, Perry, Huntingdon, Cambridgeshire PE28 OBX (tel 01480-810521; fax 01480-812739; e-mail grafham. water@education.cambridgeshire.gov.uk; www.grafham-water-centre.co.uk).
Catering Assistants (3) to work May-July. To work 8 hours per day; wages of £180 per week plus food and accommodation. Applicants need a basic food hygiene certificate. Domestic assistants also required.
    Applications to Wyn Austin, Manager, at the above address.

HAVEN PASSENGER CRUISES LTD: Unit 36, Dry Drayton Industrial Estate, Cambridge CB3 8AT (tel 01954-212564; fax 01954-212567; e-mail info@georgina.co.uk). The Georgina is a passenger cruiser on the river Cam.
Crew (5 or 6) for the riverboat Georgina to work between May and September; to carry out bar work, serve food and for general crewing tasks (tying/untying ropes, opening/closing locks on river). Full training given. Wages of £4.25 per hour plus tips. Applicants must be at least 18 and proficient in English.
    Applications to Nick Bennett, Operations Manager.

HILTON NORWICH HOTEL: Cromer Road, Norwich, Norfolk NR6 6JA (tel 01603-410544; fax 01603-487701; e-mail personnel.manager@norwich. stakis.co.uk). Close to Norwich International Airport, the hotel has 121 rooms, two busy restaurants and large function rooms.
Bar Hosts, Banqueting Hosts, Waiting Staff (20-30 in total). Wages £4.10 per hour. To work part-time or full-time shifts – must be flexible. Min. period of work of 20 weeks. Positions are available all year. Minimum age 18. Overseas applicants welcome.
    Applications should be made to Karen Lawrence, Personnel Manager, as soon as possible. Interview necessary.

KENTWELL HALL: Long Melford, Sudbury, Suffolk CO10 9BA (tel 01787-310207; fax 01787-379318). A redbrick Tudor mansion in rural Suffolk offering re-creations of Tudor domestic life. Staff on the 20th century side ensure smooth running of event for the public.
Retail And Catering Staff (10) to serve in a temporary shop/restaurant in a marquee during 16th century re-creations; duties also include marshalling school parties. Wages by arrangement; must make own arrangements for accommodation. Minimum age 16; applicants need a pleasant manner and to be fit as they will be on their feet all day. Period of work 4 weeks from 20th June-16th July.
    Applications should be sent to Nicola Carr, Administrator, at the above address.

THE LODGE HOTEL: Old Hunstanton Road, Hunstanton, Norfolk PE36 6HX (tel 01485-532896; fax 01485-535007). A Grade II listed Hotel close to a beach with 22 ensuite bedrooms; popular with bird watchers and golfers.
Waiter And Bar Person. Required for 20-40 hours per week from early July to late September. Salary £4-£4.20 per hour, depending on age and experience. Must have some relevant experience. Min. period of work 6 weeks; accommodation can be provided. Overseas applicants welcome.
    Applications should be made as soon as possible to Mr A.G. Best, Proprietor, at the above address.

MARLBOROUGH HOTEL: Sea Road, Felixstowe, Suffolk IP11 2BJ (tel 01394-285621; fax 01394-670724).

Housekeeper/Waiting Staff (2) needed from May to October inclusive. £80 per week plus tips, food and accommodation. To work 5 days in 7, a maximum of 50 hours per week.
Commis Chef (1) same dates and work conditions as above.
Receptionist (1) same dates and pay as above. To work 5 days in 7, shift work 7am-3pm or 3-11.30pm.
   Minimum age for all staff is 18 years and must speak English.
   Applications to Sharon Petley, General Manager at the above address.

OASIS LEISURE CENTRE: King's Lynn & West Norfolk Borough Council, Central Promenade, Hunstanton, Norfolk PE36 5BD (tel 01485-534227; fax 01485-534227). A seafront leisure centre comprising pools, slides, roller skating, café, squash and tennis courts.
Catering Assistants (6). Experience of fast food service required, plus basic food hygiene certificate. Wages National Minimum Wage. To work up to 47 hours, 6 days per week. Period of work April to October. Accommodation is not available.
   Applications from February onwards to Nick Rafferty, Senior Duty Officer, at the above address. Applicants should be available for interview.

PALMS HOTEL: Southend Arterial Road, Hornchurch, Essex RM11 3UJ (tel 01708-346789; fax 01708-341719).
Room Attendants (6), Restaurant/Conference Waiting Staff (6), Bar Staff (6) needed from June to the first week of September. Pay £4.19 per hour. Silver service required for waiting staff in conference and banqueting. Training provided for all jobs. Minimum age is 18.
   Apply to Tad Duthart, General Manager.

STOKE BY NAYLAND CLUB AND HOTEL: Keepers Lane, Leavenheath, Colchester, Essex CO6 4PZ (tel 01206-262836; fax 01206-263356). A Golf Club and 30 bedroomed hotel situated in the beautiful Dedham Vale.
Bar and Waiting Staff, Kitchen Porters, Chamberpersons, and Cleaners needed especially for weekend work. Accommodation is available in caravans or in shared houses. Wages and period of work by arrangement.
   Applications to the Personnel Manager at the above address.

TOPSAIL CHARTERS LTD: Cooks Yard, The Hythe, Maldon, Essex CM9 5HN (tel 01621-857567; fax 01621-840567; e-mail info@top-sail.co.uk). Based in Maldon but also working in London and Ipswich. Private functions and public trips on historic sailing barges. A small company, very customer-orientated, with a great team of staff on board.
Bar Worker, Host/ess, Catering Assistants (3) for work on Thames sailing barges. Must be flexible and combine galley and bar work. Wages approx. £6 per hour. Must be flexible about hours, up to 50 per week. Positions are available from April to September. Some bar/catering experience preferable. No accommodation provided.
   Applications to Stephanie Valentine from Easter onwards. Interview necessary.

Language Schools

ALEXANDERS INTERNATIONAL SCHOOL: Bawdsey Manor, Bawdsey, Woodbridge, Suffolk IP12 3AZ (tel 01394-411633; fax 01394-411357; e-mail english@alexandersint.demon.co.uk). An international summer school for 11-18 year olds from all over the world. English Language tuition plus specialist sports courses.

Residential Sports Assistants (24). Wages £200-£245 per week; to work 48 hours per week over 6 days, including weekends. Applicants must be undergraduate sports teachers or qualified professional coaches and 21 years or older.

EFL Teachers (24). Wages approx. £350 per week; to work 6 days a week including a Saturday or Sunday. Must be RSA certified TEFL or better and 23 years or over. Period of work from 18th June-28th August. Minimum period of work 2 weeks. Free accommodation is available.

Applications to the Administration Office, from March to the above address.

ASPECT ILA: 75 Barton Road, Cambridge (tel 01223-357702; fax 01223-311939; e-mail enquiries@aspectworld.com). Long-established year-round english language school with large junior summer school.

Teachers (30), Social Organiser, Director of Studies, Centre Manager. Wages from £250 to £340 according to position. Work is full-time. Min. period of work is two weeks. Positions are available from July to mid-August. CELTA is required for all teachers, DELTA for the centre manager, and sports coaching experience is preferable for the social organiser. Accommodation is available for £50 per week.

Applications should be made to Jane Bloomfield from March onwards. A telephone interview will be required.

BELL YOUNG LEARNERS: Lancaster House, South Road, Saffron Walden, Essex CB11 3DP (tel 01799-581880; fax 01799-516690; e-mail staff.yl@bell-centres.com). The Bell Educational Trust runs residential courses for overseas students aged 8-17 during the summer period at seven independent UK schools. All the positions below are residential with full board and lodging and 24 hours leave per week.

Sports & Social Staff (several) June to August. From £40 per day.

Course Assistants (several) From £20 per day. Non-teaching.

Course Directors July to August. From £65 per day. Must have degree and teaching qualifications.

Directors Out Of Course Activities From £50 per day. Degree in sports sciences/drama/tourism and managerial experience.

House Supervisors From £40 per day. Degree and preferably a teaching qualification. Acts a bit like a house warden, responsible for the welfare of all students.

Director Of Studies From £50 per day. Degree and RSA/Cambridge Dip. TEFLA or equivalent experience of teaching EFL to young learners.

EFL Teachers From £40 per day. Degree, TEFL qualification and teaching qualification preferred.

Nurses (3) to run morning and evening surgery and helping with pastoral and welfare matters. From £45 per day.

Team Leaders (5) From £45 per day. Graduate or equivalent and teaching qualification.

Activity Leaders (5) From £33 per day. Preferably a graduate and have special skills to offer, e.g. trampolining coach.

Activity Assistants (10) preferably an undergraduate. Age 20 years plus and responsible for children. Wages of £25 per day plus full board and accommodation.

Full job descriptions of all the above can be obtained from Bell Young Learners. *Applications* to Sue Nellis, Recruitment Secretary.

BRIAR SCHOOL OF ENGLISH: 8 Gunton Cliff, Lowestoft, Suffolk NR32 4PE (tel 01502-573781; fax 01502-589150; e-mail briareducation@fsbdial.co.uk). Runs holiday language courses for foreign language learners on the Suffolk coast. In business since 1960.

Teachers Of English. From £8 per hour. To work up to 6 hours daily. TEFL qualifications or experience preferable. Applicants must possess either a degree or a teacher's certificate.

Sports Instructors. From £6 per hour. To work up to 6 hours per day. Must hold at least an L.T.A. Part 1 certificate.

Successful applicants for both jobs can earn extra pay by leading excursions on Saturdays to Norwich, Cambridge, London and other local places of interest. Min. period of work 3 weeks between end of June and end of August. Accommodation is not available. Teaching

Applications should be sent to Ms H. Sterne and Sports Instructor applications to Mr N. J. Doe, at the above address.

CAMBRIDGE ACADEMY OF ENGLISH: 65 High Street, Girton, Cambridge CB3 0QD (tel 01223-277230; fax 01223-277606; e-mail sheila@caeco.demon.co.uk). Situated in the leafy suburb of Girton, the Academy runs non-residential courses for teenagers and young adults, and residential courses for the 10-13 age group.

EFL Teachers to teach English to teenagers. Required for 3 week courses between June 24 and August 23; wages of approx. £800 per course. The job involves 21-24 hours teaching a week. Must have RSA TEFL/Trinity College certificate or equivalent and experience.

Applications to S. Levy at the above address.

THE EAST SUSSEX SCHOOL OF ENGLISH: 92 Portland Road, Hove, BN3 5DN (tel 01273-736404; fax 01273-770672; e-mail esse@mistral.co.uk).

EFL Teachers (5) required for July and August, working hours negotiable. Wages according to qualifications and experience. Applicants must have at least PGCE, CELTA or DELTA qualifications.

Applications to Tony Gill, Principal, at the above address.

CAMBRIDGE CENTRE FOR LANGUAGES: Sawston Hall, Church Lane, Sawston, Cambridgeshire CB2 4JR (tel 01223-835099; fax 01223-837424; e-mail ar70@dial.pipex.com).

EFL Teachers (6+), Activities Organisers (3), Social And Welfare Officers (1-2) required July-August to staff residential summer camps for children aged 10-17. Wages £250 per week with free accommodation.

For details and *applications* contact John F. Sullivan at the above address.

EFL INTERNATIONAL LANGUAGE SCHOOLS: 221 Hills Road, Cambridge CB2 2RW (tel 01223-240020; fax 01223-412474; e-mail pippa.cusimano@ef.com).

Activities/Accommodation Assistant (1) needed from end of June to beginning of September. Work involves providing support to the accommodation officer in the mornings, filing, faxing, meeting students and telephone work with host families and overseas offices. Afternoons are spent working in the activities office booking events, hotels etc. acting as a guide on trips and supervising sports events. Wages about £165 per week. To work Monday to Friday 8.30am to 5.15pm but with occasional evenings instead of afternoons. Weekend work may be available at extra rate of pay. Accommodation could be made available in exchange for some supervision in the residence.

Must be aged 18+ and a good communicator, interested in sport and computer literate.

Applications to Pippa Cusimano, School Director.

INTERNATIONAL LANGUAGE ACADEMY CAMBRIDGE: 12-13 Regent Terrace, Cambridge CB2 1AA (tel 01223-353019; fax 01223-464730; e-mail pippa-sutcliffe@ilacambridge.com). Recognised by the British Council, a language school which runs summer courses for 14-18 year olds and adults.
Teachers (10-15). Wages range between £235 and £255 per week depending on experience; to teach 20 lessons and social programme activities. Applicants must be UCLES, RSA, CELTA or Trinity qualified.
Activity Instructors (2). Wages are £180 per week; to work 40 hours per week. Sports coaching qualifications are useful. Staff are required from 27th June-30th August for a minimum period of 2 weeks. Overseas applications welcome but an interview is required.

Applications from 1st March to Pippa Sutcliffe at the above address.

NEW SCHOOL OF ENGLISH: 52 Bateman Street, Cambridge CB2 1LR (tel 01223-358089; fax 01223-315276; e-mail newschool@dial.pipex.com).
EFL Teachers (4/5) to work from July to August. 21 contact hours per week and one extra-curricular duty is required per fortnight. Pay for RSA CELTA qualified teachers is £12 per hour or £15 per hour for those with RSA DELTA (diploma). Minimum qualification RSA CELTA.

Applications to Elizabeth Cane, Director of Studies, at the above address.

STUDIO SCHOOL OF ENGLISH: 6 Salisbury Villas, Station Road, Cambridge CB1 2JF (tel 01223-369701; fax 01223-314944; e-mail richard. mountford@studiocambridge.co.uk; www.studiocambridge.co.uk). The oldest of the permanently-established Cambridge language schools, and a founder member of the ARELS organisation
EFL Teachers for young people's courses (age 10-15 and 14-17). Applicants should have CTEFLA, CELTA, TESOL and/ or EFL experience.
Activity Organisers for young people's courses (ages as above). Applicants should have interests/abilities in sport, art, music or drama, and need stamina, initiative and enthusiasm.
Course Directors And Assistant Course Directors (ages as above). Applicants should have good organisational and managerial skills. Some EFL or summer camp experience preferred.

Residential and non-residential posts available, mainly between July and August but also at other times of the year; only those who speak English as if it were their first language need apply. *Applications* to Richard Mountford at the above address.

Outdoor

BOXFORD (SUFFOLK) FARMS LTD: Hill Farm, Boxford, Sudbury, Suffolk CO10 5NY. (tel 01787-210348; fax 01787-211106). A family owned company supplying fruit to major supermarkets. Situated in beautiful countryside within an hour's train journey from London.
Fruit Pickers And Fruit Packers required to work on farms and packhouse

situated on the Suffolk/Essex border. The work involves the picking and packing of soft and top fruit (strawberries, raspberries, apples etc). The season is from June to July for soft fruit and the middle of August to the end of October for apples. Hours of work and wages are variable subject to the crop and weather. Self catering caravan accommodation is available and the camp has toilets, showers, laundry facilities and TV. Workers must be over 18 years old with a liking for outside work and with valid working visas and work permits. Transport will pick up in Colchester between 2pm and 3pm but it is essential that the farm is contacted 24 hours before arrival.

Applications to the Personnel Manager at the above address.

C & I MARQUEES: Cornsland, Hall Lane (north of A1277), Upminster, Essex RM14 1TX (tel 01708-343484; fax 01708-344745). A family run business that manufactures and hires marquees throughout the South East.
Marquee Erectors (5). Wages £4.00 per hour; to work 7am-5pm Monday to Friday. No accommodation is available. Staff required for a minimum of 4 weeks between 1st June and 15th September. Must be 16 or over; no experience necessary, just commitment and fitness. Foreign applicants with good spoken English are welcome.

Applications from April to Julian Saich at the above address.

FIVEWAYS FRUIT FARM: Fiveways, Stanway, Colchester, Essex CO3 5LR (tel 01206-330244; fax 01206-330828; e-mail fiveways.fruit.farm@ farming.co.uk). A medium sized farm run by two brothers growing mainly strawberries, cherries and apples. Situated in a rural oasis on the outskirts of Colchester with shops close by.
Fruit Pickers (17-22). Strawberry picking from May-September; apple picking from August but principally from September to October; orchard work and many semi-skilled jobs in propagation tunnels and French tunnels etc.; packing fruit for supermarkets. Wages at piece work rates, approx. £100-£200+ per 5-7 day week. Hours flexible, start at 6am with hourly work also available. No overtime.

Minimum period of work 4 weeks. Meadow next to farm available for camping. Caravans on site with all facilities, including showers, cooking facilities and television. Charge £19 per week. Supermarket, post office, off-licence and launderette within a 5 minutes walk from the farm. Overseas students aged over 18 welcome.

Applications from the beginning of the year to Alistair Mead, c/o Fiveways Fruit Farm.

FRIDAYBRIDGE INTERNATIONAL FARM CAMP: March Road, Fridaybridge, Wisbech, Cambridgeshire PE14 0LR (tel 01945-860255; fax 01945-861088).
General Agricultural Workers to harvest strawberries, apples, broccoli, potatoes and salads and to help with many other jobs. To normally work 5-6 days per week, but this cannot be guaranted. Bed, breakfast and evening meal provided at a reasonable weekly charge, payable in advance.

Club, disco, swimming pool, tennis courts, basketball, volleyball, day trips, free English lessons (conversational) and many other facilities provided. Vacancies available all year round. Min. period of work 3 weeks. Staff vacancies also available for drivers, bar work, shop staff, kitchen asistants, administrative staff and English teachers. EU students aged 16-30 welcome.

Send s.a.e./IRC for brochure (*Applications* on official forms only) to Bookings, Fridaybridge International Camp.

G'S MARKETING LTD: Hostel, Barway, Ely, Cambridgeshire CB7 5TZ (tel 01353-727314; fax 01353-727255).
Production Operatives required from October to the end of April to trim, pack and label salad and vegetable crops plus some farming positions. Must be fit and willing to work. Wages at piecework rates (average £180 per week). Evening meal and accommodation provided on site. Minimum age 18.
Applications to Sharon Gudgeon, Hostel Recruitment Officer, at the above address.

HADLEY MARQUEES LTD: Unit 9, Minton Enterprise Park, Oaks Drive, Newmarket, Suffolk, CB87YY; e-mail lowri.allpress@virgin.net). A friendly company where good work is rewarded highly.
Marquee Erectors (4-6) Wages £6 per hour; to work 10 hours a day Monday to Saturday, no overtime paid. No accommodation available. Applicants must be prepared to work flexible hours, weekends and occasional long hours. It is important to be physically fit as the job involves lifting heavy materials. Staff are required from the end of April to September/October. Overseas applicants are welcome.
Applications should be sent to Lowri Allpress at the above address from February onwards. Interview necessary.

HIGHFIELD TIFFANY MARQUEES: Klondyke Farm, Broads Road, Burwell, Cambridge CB5 OBQ (tel/fax 01638-743860; e-mail the info@thehighfieldsgroup.co.uk; www.thehighfieldsgroup.co.uk).
Marquee Hire Labourers (up to 4) to assist with marquee hire from June to August. Long hours available subject to workload. Wages from £4 p.h. Accommodation can be arranged at a cost to be advised. Must be physically fit.
Contact Gary Chapman, Proprietor.

INTERNATIONAL FARM CAMP: Hall Road, Tiptree, Essex CO5 0QS (tel 01621-815496; e-mail ifc@tiptree.com).
Fruit Pickers. Pay at piecework rates (according to amount of fruit picked). Hours 8am-4pm Monday to Friday; some weekend work. Full B & L provided for approx. £57 a week. Age: 10-25 years. Min. work period 2 weeks between early June and mid-July.
Overseas applicants welcome, but places for non-EEA nationals are open only to full-time students who have not completed their studies. *Applications* to be sent as early as possible to the above address: s.a.e. (or IRC if writing from abroad) essential for reply.

ISLEHAM FRESH PRODUCE LTD: Whitehall Farm, Temple Road, Isleham, Ely, Cambs CB7 5RF (tel 01638-780087; fax 01638-780056; e-mail mail@ifpltd.co.uk).
Graders And Pickers wanted for the grading and packing of fresh produce. Wages are negotiable; to work 8am to 4pm with the possibility of overtime. Applicants must be over 18. Staff are required from September to February for a minimum period of 6 months. Overseas applicants are welcome.
Applications should be sent to Alan Bailey at the above address from August onwards.

A.E. MARSHALL FARMS: Old Shields Farm, Ardleigh, Colchester, Essex CO7 7NE (tel 01206-230251; fax 01206-231825).
Fruit Pickers (20-40) to work from the end of May to July. Wages by arrangement, paid out weekly. To work from 8am-4pm, 6 days per week. Min.

age 18 years. Camping and dormitory accommodation available for around 15 people, own equipment is required.

Applications should be sent to Gail Marshall at the above address.

M & B MARQUEES: Hawk Cove, Battles Bridge, Essex SS11 7RL (tel 01268-562622; fax 01268-574228; e-mail sales@mb-marquees). Family-run business, established 25 years ago.

Marquee Erectors (up to 10). Wages negotiable. Positions are available from May to September. Applicants should be 21+, driving licence an advantage. No Accommodation available. Foreign applicants welcome.

Applications should be made from April onwards to Mr S Moxey at the above address.

MAYFAIR MARQUEES: 3 Horizon Works, Dereham Road, New Costessey, Norwich NR5 OSE (tel 01603-747200; fax 01603-749100; e-mail mayfair.marquees@zoo.co.uk). A small marquee, furniture and tableware hire business covering Norfolk, Suffolk and Cambridgeshire.

Marquee Erectors (5) Wages £4.40 starting rate; to work 40 hours per week but also overtime paid at $1^1/2$ times the starting rate. Applicants should be at least 5'11 and 19 years old or over. Staff are required from mid May to the end of September. Overseas applicants are welcome. No accommodation available.

Applications should be sent to Andrew Cocker at the above address from January onwards. Interview necessary.

OUTBACK INTERNATIONAL LTD: Jark House, Beechhurst, 8 Commercial Road, Dereham, Norfolk NR19 1AE (tel 01362-691608; fax 01362-691593). Recruitment agency that require staff all year round for farm and production work in and around the Norfolk and Suffolk area.

Production Staff to pick, pack, cut, sort, label and box fruits, vegetables, meats, poultry, toys, dairy products, flowers and much more. Wages from £4 to £6 per hour plus overtime and holiday pay. Farm work paid at piecework rates. Self-catering accommodation is available for £57.50 per week, including free transport to and from work. Catered accommodation is available between £82.50 per week, including 3 meals, laundry, wake-ups, tel/fax and transport to and from work.

Min. period of work 4 weeks at any time of year. Main farm season is May-October. Applicants must be 18-35 years old. Overseas applicants with EU/EEA passport or work authorisation, and good English are considered. Interview not necessary. *Applications* with I.D. at least 2-3 weeks before arrival date to Natalie Aston or Irene Abru (Spanish and Portuguese).

R. & J.M. PLACE LTD: Church Farm, Tunstead, Norwich NR12 8RQ. Large soft fruit growers in the centre of the Broadland National Park.

Fruit Picking, weather permitting, details on application. Accommodation available for approx. £42 per week, including breakfast, in purpose-built dormitory blocks. Tents and caravans are not permitted. Must be in good health. No previous experience necessary. Social activities in camp include tennis, volleyball, badminton, basketball, football, pool and many other activities. Open between end of February and November. Overseas applicants welcome.

Applications with s.a.e. to the Administrator, R. & J.M. Place Ltd.

H.R. PHILPOT & SON LTD: Barleylands Farm, Barleylands Road, Billericay, Essex CM11 2UD (tel 01268-532253; 01268-290222; e-mail barleyfarm@aol.com). Established arable farmers with farms in Essex and Suffolk.

Tractor Drivers (10) Hard physical work during pea vining and general harvest. Must be adaptable to take on any job when asked. Wages £5 per hour; to work from the end of June until the end of September. Applicants need a valid driving licence.

Staff are required to work for 3 months. Accommodation is available for £10 per week and a deposit which is returned at the end of employment. Overseas applicants are considered but must have a valid work permit for the UK and be able to understand and speak English.

Applications should be sent to Robert Willy at the above address from February onwards.

C & A SANDERSON: Bramley House, Cox's Lane, Wisbech, Cambridgeshire PE13 4TD (tel 01945-583023). A small family run farm, which is situated just 1 mile from town, growing fruit for processing and wholesale markets.
Strawberry Pickers (8-10). Piecework rates. To work Monday to Friday and sometimes Sunday mornings. Pickers must be willing to work hard, with early start common. Free campsite, washroom with hot and cold water and toilet. Period of work approx. 3-4 weeks, commencing late June. Overseas applicants welcome.

Applications to Mr A. Sanderson, Bramley House.

STOKE FARM: Battisford, Stowmarket, Suffolk IP14 2NA (tel 01449-774944; fax 01449-616045; e-mail davidupson@talk21.com). A family run fruit farm.
Fruit Pickers (5+) To pick apples and pears. Wages as set by the Agricultural Wage Board; to work 6 or more hours a day. Applicants must be over 18 and should state whether they have had previous experience.
Staff are required from September until the end of picking for a minimum period of 1 week. Please note that no accommodation is available.

Applications should be sent to David Upson at the above address from July onwards.

WALLINGS NURSERY: 38 Harwich Road, Lawford, Manningtree, Essex CO11 2LS (tel 01206-230163; fax 01206-230863). A modern glasshouse nursery growing strawberries.
Stawberry Pickers (10). To pick strawberries in modern glasshouses. Wages £4.50-£6.50 per hour, piece rates apply. To work 6-8 hours a day. Accommodation is available at a cost of £20 per week. Workers required for a minimum of 2 months between 1st April and 30th May. Applicants must be 20 or over; foreign applicants with appropriate permits if non-EU nationals, welcome.

Applications between January and March to Christopher Batchelor at the above address.

PAUL WILLIAMSON LTD: Church Farm, Bradfield Combust, Bury St Edmunds, Suffolk IP30 OLW (tel 01284-386333; fax 01284-386155).
Horticultural Staff (10) wanted from mid May to mid October mainly for work picking strawberries, raspberries, apples and pears. Wages at Agricultural Wages Board rates. To work mainly from 8am to 4pm Monday-Friday with some Saturday work. Applicants should be aged over 18. Space available for tents (own equipment required) with showers, toilets and kitchen and washing facilities available.

Applications to Mr P.R. Williamson, Director, at the above address.

Sport

BRADWELL ENVIRONMENTAL & OUTDOOR CENTRE: Bradwell Waterside, nr Southminster, Essex CM0 7QY (tel 01621-776256; fax 01621-

776378: e-mail adventure@bradwell.freeserve.co.uk). A local authority-run high quality multi-activity residential centre for young people and adults. Based on the edge of the River Blackwater in Essex, it is an excellent site for all water and land based activities.

Sailing (4) Canoeing (2) and Archery Instructors. Wages negotiable. To include B & L. To work approx. 8 hours per day. RYA Instructors Certificate essential or BCU/GNAS. Min. work period 4 months between April and October inclusive.

Applications in January/March to the Principal, Bradwell O.E Centre.

OASIS LEISURE CENTRE: King's Lynn & West Norfolk Borough Council, Central Promenade, Hunstanton, Norfolk PE36 5BD (tel 01485-534227; fax 01485-534227). A seafront leisure centre comprising pools, slides, roller skating, café, squash and tennis courts.

Pool Attendants (12-14). National Pool Lifeguard Quaification essential, experience of leisure industry an advantage. Wages £3.83 per hour. To work up to 47 hours/6 days per week. Period of work February to October. Accommodation is not available. Applicants should be available for interview.

Applications from February onwards to the Duty Manager, at the above address.

Voluntary Work

Archaeology

SEDGEFORD HISTORICAL AND ARCHAEOLOGICAL RESEARCH PROJECT: A long-term investigation of an English parish concentrating at present on Iron Age, Saxon and medieval periods.

Archaeological & Historical Fieldworkers (75) wanted from mid July to late August. Subsistence charge of approx. £80 per week. Hours 8.30am-5pm, 6 days a week with Saturdays off. It is recommended that students come for a minimum of two weeks. No professional qualifications needed.

Request for *application* form with SAE to Mrs Chris Kelly at Moonstones, 8 Rose Court, Sedgeford, Norfolk PE36 5LR (www.sharp.org.uk).

Festivals and Special Events

HESSE STUDENT SCHEME: Hesse Student Scheme, Aldeburgh Productions, Snape Maltings Concert Hall, Snape, Saxmundham, Suffolk IP17 1S(P tel 01728 687100; fax 01728 687120; e-mail admin@aldeburghfestivals.org).

Aldeburgh Productions has grown out of the Aldeburgh Festival founded in 1948 by Benjamin Britten, Peter Pears and Eric Crozier. Inspired by this legacy, Aldeburgh Productions today ensures that the Suffolk Coast remains a world-renowned meeting place for artists, students, academics and audiences.

Volunteers to assist in the varied duties involved in the day-to-day running of the Aldeburgh Festival of Music and the Arts 7-23 June. Duties can include programme selling, page turning, invigilating exhibitions, assisting with stage moves and bus conducting on the coaches that run from Aldeburgh to all concert venues. In addition, students are also expected to devise, rehearse and perform in a concert of their own – one of the free events publicised in the Aldeburgh Festival booking brochure. In exchange, two groups of 12 students are awarded a grant which covers tickets to all Festival events together with bed and breakfast accommodation in Aldeburgh for each half of the Festival.

Applications are welcomed from anyone between the ages of 18 and 25 (on 1 June) irrespective of current course or occupation. Applications from overseas are particularly welcomed. A willingness to help, no matter how mundane the task, together with a passion for music are essential.

For further details and an *application* form contact Clare Lovell, General Administrator. The closing date for applications is 30 April.

Heritage

KENTWELL HALL: Long Melford, Sudbury, Suffolk CO10 9BA (tel 01787-310207; fax 01787-379318).

A privately owned Tudor mansion, situated in park and farmland, approximately 1.5 miles from the historic town of Long Melford, famous for its annual recreation of Tudor life which takes place for 3 weeks during June and July, and in which up to 1,500 schoolchildren visit on weekdays and the public at weekends.

Volunteer Tudors (700) needed for historical re-creations. Duties consist of demonstrating 16th century life and activities to visiting schoolchildren and the public. The re-creations run for 7 days a week for 4 weeks; most volunteers stay one or two weeks during June/July. Take 16th century skills or learn them there. All ages and Nationalities welcome. Applications to Mary Fitzgerald at the above address.

All meals, evening entertainment and space on campsite provided for volunteers only. Applicants can be of any age; and interest in the 16th century would be helpful. For these positions *Applications* must be made in January or February. *Applications* should be sent to Nicola Carr at the above address.

Physically/Mentally Disabled

BREAK: Montague Lodge, 1 Montague Road, Sheringham, Norfolk, NR26 8LN (tel 01263-822161; e-mail Glenys.G@break-charity.org; www.break-charity.org). Registered charity no. 286650.

Break has opportunities for **Volunteers** at two centres on the Norfolk coast providing holidays and respite care for children and adults with physical and/or learning disabilities or other special needs. Volunteers are needed to help with guests' care, join in a programme of activities and carry out housekeeping tasks.

BREAK provides weekly out of pocket expenses, plus free B & L and travel expenses within the UK. To work 40 hours a week on a rota for a min. period of work 6 weeks. Placements of up to 12 months are avialable. Overseas applicants welcome but must be able to understand and speak English to a reasonable standard.

Applications to Mrs G. Gray at the above address.

Vacation Traineeships

Law

MILLS AND REEVE: Francis House, 3-7 Rodwell Street, Norwich NR2 4TJ (tel 01603-693346; fax 01603-693248; e-mail graduate.recruitment@mills-reeve.com; www.mills-reeve.com).

Mills and Reeve are a leading law firm based in Norwich, Cambridge and

Birmingham who offer a full range of corporate, commercial, property, litigation, and private client services to a mix of regional businesses and national household names.

Mills and Reeve offer a **Formal 2 Week Placement Scheme** at each of their offices. Students gain experience in four main departments, attend seminars and take part in extra curricular events. There are 25-30 placements throughout June or July; preference is given to penultimate year law students, final year law students and all those who have already graduated and are interested in a legal career. Wages are £110 per week. Overseas applicants are welcome but must have a valid work permit.

Applications should be sent to Stephen Trowbridge, Graduate Recruitment at the above address before 1 March 2002.

Media and Marketing

BRITTEN-PEARS SCHOOL FOR ADVANCED MUSICAL STUDIES: Snape Maltings Concert Hall, Snape, Saxmundham, Suffolk IP17 1SP (tel: 01728 687100; fax 01728 687120; email: admin@aldeburghfestivals.org). Aldeburgh Productions has grown out of the Aldeburgh Festival founded in 1948 by Benjamin Britten, Peter Pears and Eric Crozier. Inspired by this legacy Aldeburgh Productions today ensures that the Suffolk Coast remains a world-renowned meeting place for artists, students, academics and audiences.

Intern. An opportunity launched in 2000 for one or two students/recent graduates to work on a voluntary basis in the Britten-Pears School for Advanced Musical Studies to support a small permanent team during the height of the season. Ideally, one intern to be appointed for the months of June and July and a second for the months of August and September. An invaluable opportunity to gain an insight into the workings of an internationally renowned arts organisation and to gain a grounding in arts administration which will be useful in furthering a career in this field. This position would suit an enthusiastic, energetic, level headed individual who would like to learn more about the running of a busy, unusual arts organisation. Previous office experience is not as essential as the willingness and ability to learn and to adapt. Duties will include driving the School car or minibus (if over 21), assisting with keeping files and databases in good order and providing clerical support to the School staff. Excellent secretarial and organisational skills together with a sound knowledge of English and its written and spoken use essential; knowledge of classical music desirable. Accommodation in Aldeburgh and a per diem to cover all meals will be provided.

For further details please *contact* Clare Lovell, General Administrator.

Science, Construction and Engineering

GARDLINE SURVEYS: Admiralty Road, Great Yarmouth, Norfolk, NR30 3NG (tel 01493-850723; fax 01493-852106).

The largest independent survey company which operates a fleet of 6 fully equipped vessels. The vessels operate worldwide, covering Europe, the Far East and West Africa.

Gardline Surveys is involved in hydrographic and marine geophysical surveys. The company offers a variable number of **Placements** in several different fields, including Seismic/Hydrographic survey work for surveyors, geophysicists and electronic engineers; there will also be some office work. The company recruits a maximum of two trainees for each area.

Vacancies are open to students on relevant degree courses, with a preference for those in their second or third year of study. Overseas applicants are welcome.

Trainees are based in Great Yarmouth from where they will be sent to work on survey. Shared accommodation is sometimes available. The salary for 2001 was £7,250 p.a. pro rata, plus 26 per day field allowance.

Applicants should *contact* Dr K.P. Games, Geophysical Director, at the above address, preferably in the New Year.

HARLOW CHEMICAL COMPANY LTD: Central Road, Templefields, Harlow, Essex CM20 2BH (tel 01279-436211; fax 01279-444025).
Manufacturers of polyvinyl alcohol and the market leader in stabilisers for the PVC industry. Also suppliers of water based dispersions to the paint and adhesive industries.

Harlow Chemical Company Ltd offers **Vacation Traineeships** to two students each summer. These are to work within Research & Development or Technical Service Laboratories. The placements last for 6-8 weeks and are open to university undergraduates reading for a degree in Chemistry or related subject. Accommodation is not provided.

Applications should be made in April or May to the Personnel Manager, at the above address.

MARCONI PLC: The Resourcing Centre, Cambridge Business Park, Cowley Road, Cambridge CB4 0WZ (e-mail matthew.baggs@marconi.com). Marconi is one of the largest communications and information management businesses in the world. They operate in more than 100 countries, employ 49,000 people and are established partners to a vast range of customers, from governments to internet companies, major telcos to world's top corporations. Typical products: public and corporate ATM optical networks; global e-logistics solutions; digital image scanning and transmission equipment; Internet security systems; bandwidth, data and knowledge services; hand-held infrared sensors; Public Access Mobile Radio infrastructure.
Vacation Training Opportunities exist in the major divisions of Networks, Enterprise and Wireless. Those interested can find out further information from their careers advisor or any of the major professional engineering institutions.

Applicants can write to the above address for an information pack on current opportunities within the group.

RAYTHEON SYSTEMS LTD: The Pinnacles, Harlow, Essex CM19 5BB(tel 01279-426862; fax 01279-407286; e-mail clare.lane@raytheon.co.uk).
Raytheon Systems Ltd is a world leader in the design and delivery of high technology products and systems for both the defence and commercial sectors. Already employing 2,000 people across the UK, we see the new millennium providing the challenge of significant growth as we continue to bring the best and most innovative technical solutions to our UK and overseas customers.

Each year Raytheon Systems offers **3-4 Opportunities** for students to work in hardware support and electronic engineering. On-the-job training will be provided. Applicants should preferably be students who have successfully completed one year of their university course.

Placements last all summer with the possibility of follow-on work at Christmas and Easter. Placements are located at Harlow. The company can help in finding accommodation, but would prefer applicants to live locally.

Applications by February to Claire Lane.

The Midlands

Prospects for Work.

The Midlands region includes a number of large industrial towns, the most notable of which is Birmingham. Temporary jobs in these centres tend to involve warehouse and factory work or the retail trade; the main glut of vacancies arises from September onwards for the run up to Christmas. In addition, the larger local authorities, such as Birmingham and Coventry, take people on as playleaders and recreation assistants (Birmingham Jobcentre: Centennial House, 100 Broad Street, Birmingham B15 1AU). Some car dealers require people to deliver cars around the country.

Tourism in the Midlands is concentrated in Warwick and Stratford-upon-Avon, the Cotswolds and Herefordshire. In this last county, the town of Ledbury has been a good source of work in the past (but not for fruit picking as farmers tend to employ foreign students) although this now varies from year to year; rented accommodation is scarce there. Ledbury Jobcentre is at Crown Buildings, Bye Street, Ledbury, Herefordshire HR8 2AB. Hereford is likely to be a better base, with the *Hereford Times* (Thursday) and the *Hereford Admag* (Wednesday) both displaying local job vacancies; alternatively, contact the Hereford Jobcentre at Bath Street, Hereford HR1 2LG. In Staffordshire, Alton Towers Leisure Park takes on temporary ride attendants, shop staff and so on.

Fruit and hop picking jobs are available in the Vale of Evesham, Herefordshire and Lincolnshire, but in general the Midlands is an area where 'pick your own' farms are popular. Spalding and Boston in Lincolnshire are centres for agricultural packing. In Lincoln itself, most temporary jobs are in the retail or hotel trade. There is now a very strong retail trade in Lincoln with the Tritton Road area attracting several large new employers, the most recent being Debenhams. There are good opportunities for employment at the Lincolnshire Show, a two day event that is held yearly in mid June, job vacancies are advertised from April. To apply for work either visit the Lincoln Jobcentre (280 High Street, Lincoln LN2 1LL) or call 01522-342061/342065 in May or early June. The *Lincolnshire Echo* is the best local newspaper for job vacancies.

Oxford is a popular centre for language schools and there are opportunities not only for EFL teachers but also for sports instructors and social organisers. These and other jobs may be advertised in the *Oxford Times* (out on Friday) and the *Oxford Mail* (daily). Alternatively, for up-to-the-minute information on both jobs and accommodation look out for the coloured spreadsheet *Daily Information* (daily in term time, weekly during vacations) on noticeboards, in shop windows etc. There is, of course, competition for any summer jobs from those students at the city's two universities who choose to stay in Oxford for the summer.

The industrial heartlands of the Midlands provide plentiful opportunities for Vacation Traineeships, particularly in the field of science and engineering.

Business and Industry

ADVANCED ALCHEMY LTD: St Edburgs Hall, Priory Road, Bicester, OX26 6BL (tel 01869-3637036; fax 01869-363710; e-mail info@advanced-alchemy.com).
Teleresearchers wanted to work for at least 15 hours per week by this business research company. Researchers are required with English or any of the European languages to conduct interviews by telephone, either working within UK (9am-12.30pm, 1.30-5.30pm) or continental (8am-noon, 1-4.30pm) business hours. Rates of pay are between £5.50 and £6.50 per hour.
Ideally candidates should have previous experience of teleworking, using MS Access databases and experience of the IT, printing or telecomms industries, but training will be given.
For *applications* and information contact Marlies Vanneuville, HR Officer.

CATHEDRAL SECRETARIAL AGENCY: 2nd floor, Akrill House, 25 Clasketgate, Lincoln, LN2 1JJ (tel 01522-530955; fax 01522-530721; e-mail jean@cathedralsecretarial.co.uk).
Temporary Secretaries, Temporary Office Staff. Pay above minimum wage, applicants should have keyboard skills and experience is an advantage.
Legal Secretaries required at good rates of pay.
Applications to Mrs J. Albans, Proprietor, at the above address.

DISCOVER TRAVEL AND TOURS: Pierpoint Street, Worcester, WR1 1YD (tel 01905-613746; fax 01905-613747). Discover Travel and Tours is the UK's largest supplier of accommodation and services to the international travel trade in Europe.

Temporary Reservation Assistants (3-5) to take reservations, make bookings and load details onto computer. Wages from £4.40 per hour. To work 37 hours per five day week with possible overtime. Minimum period of work of three months. Positions are available between March and September. Applicants must be computer literate. Knowledge of German, Spanish and English required. No accommodation available.

Applications available from January/February to the above address.

FARMSHOP.NET: Swan Lodge, Station Road, Upper Broughton, Melton Mowbray, Leics. LE14 3BH (tel 0800-169 7009; e-mail ian.jalland@ farmline.com; www.farmshop.net). Internet home delivery company. Young, energetic company.

Boxpackers (1-2) Wages at National Minimum Wage rate; to work variable hours. Possibility of accommodation.

Applications to Ian Jalland, preferably by e-mail.

PORTABLE FLOORMAKERS LTD: Redhill Marina, Ratcliffe on Soar, Nottingham NG11 0EB (tel 01509-673753; fax 01509-674749; e-mail sales@portablefloormakers.co.uk).

Labourers (4) needed from May to September to work on a production line packing, loading and assembling floor panels. Wages a minimum of £4 per hour possibly rising to £6 per hour, plus piecework.

Applications to the above address.

PALETHORPES: Maer Lane, Market Drayton, Shropshire TF9 3AW (tel 01630-692394; fax 01630-658785; e-mail marie.toth@palenthorpes.co.uk).

Operatives (100) to work on a factory line producing hot pies. Wages from £4.40 per hour plus a shift allowance. A 24 hour operation, all shifts available. Min. period of work of 1 week. Positions are available from July onwards; placements also available for periods of 3 weeks over Christmas. No qualifications although food hygiene or first aid would be useful. Minimum age 16. No accommodation available.

Applications should be made to Helen Allsopp at the above address.

RUTLAND WATER CYCLING LTD: Whitwell Cycle Centre, Rutland Water, Nr Oakham, Rutland LE15 8BL (tel 01780-460705; fax 01780-460792; e-mail info@ rutlandwater.co.uk). Most successful commercial cycle hire operator in the UK.

Retail Staff (4). Wages from £4 per hour. To work 3 to 5 days a week. Positions are available from Easter to September. Fluent English essential. Minimum age 17. Must be fit, healthy and able to use a computerised till. Foreign applicants with work permits and very good spoken English welcome. No accommodation available.

Applications should be made from January onwards to Paul Archer at the above address. Interview required.

K.H. TAYLOR LTD: The Freezing Station, Sheffield Road, Blyth, Worksop, Notts (tel 01909-590000; fax 01909-590001).

Inspection and Quality Control Personnel, Packers, Stackers (Approx. 50). Wages £4.34 per hour. To work 8 hours per day in shifts 6am-2pm, 2-10pm or 10pm-6am, Monday to Friday, with some weekend work available. No experience or qualifications needed. Must have own transport. Interview not necessary.

Applications (quoting telephone number) from the beginning of June to K.H. Taylor Ltd at the above address.

Children

ACTIVE TRAINING AND EDUCATION TRUST: Kildare, Manby Road, Malvern, Worcs. WR14 3BD (tel 01684-562400; fax 01684-562716; e-mail enquiries@ te.org.uk). A charitable trust running residential 'super-weeks' in holiday periods for children from a variety of schools, areas and backgrounds.
Monitors (20) to look after children on residential holidays. To work for 7-10 days at various times in July and August. Staff receive pocket money only. Applicants must be over 17 and must be able to attend a 7-day residential training course in the Easter vacation.
Minimum period of work is 1 week. Board and accommodation are provided at no charge. Overseas applicants are welcome to apply but must speak good enough English to follow the course and take responsibility for children. A suppporting letter is required from someone who has known the applicant well for at least 5 years.
Applications should be sent to Chris Green, Director at the above address.

LEICESTER CHILDREN'S HOLIDAY CENTRE: Mablethorpe, Quebec Road, Mablethorpe, Lincolnshire LN12 1QX (tel/fax 01507-472444). A charity that provides free holidays for children from the inner city of Leicester, based on the East Coast of England. For anyone interested in working with children this is a fairly unique opportunity which offers hands on experience leading to an excellent grounding for a future career.
Activity Leaders (12). Kitchen/Dining Room Staff (4). Wages paid at National Minimum Wage, based on a 48 hour week.
Cook/Chef. National min. wage is paid, based on a 48 hour week. To work a 6-day week. A deduction is made for food and accommodation.
Activity Leaders required to organise, instruct and supervise an outdoor activities programme for children aged 7-12 years. Energy, enthusiasm and a good sense of humour essential.
Staff needed from beginning of May to end of August. Min. age 18.
Write for an *application* form (enclosing s.a.e.) from December to H. Eagle-Lanzetta at the above address.

CITY LEISURE: Oxford City Council, Third Floor, St Aldate's Chambers, Oxford OX1 1DS (tel 01865-252181; fax 01865-252783; e-mail tstevens@ oxford.gov.uk). City leisure manage 9 sports and leisure centres for Oxford City Council - including swimming pools, an ice rink, sports halls, etc.
Playscheme Assistants/Leaders (12+). Wages from £5.20 per hour for assistants and £7.30 per hour for leaders. To work Monday to Friday 10am-3pm. Min. period of work of 6 weeks. Positions are available from May to August. 16+, desirable to hold a Community Sports Leaders Award. Spoken English required. Accommodation not available.
Applications should be made from March onwards to Tim Stevens. Interview necessary.

PGL TRAVEL: Alton Court, Penyard Lane (874), Ross-on-Wye, Herefordshire HR9 5GL (tel 01989-767833; www.pgl.co.uk/personnel). Over 300 staff needed to assist in the running of activity centres in Shropshire, Oxford and the Wye Valley. Europe's largest provider of adventure holidays for children has offered outstanding training and work opportunities to seasonal staff for over 40 years.
Qualified Instructors in canoeing, sailing, windsurfing, pony trekking, hill walking, fencing, archery, judo, rifle shooting, fishing, motorsports, arts and

crafts, drama, English language and many other activities. Min. age 18.

Group Leaders to take care of small groups of children and ensure that they get the most out of their holiday. Previous experience of working with children necessary. Min. age 18.

All staff receive £50-85 per week plus free B & L. Vacancies available for short or long periods between February and October. Overseas applicants eligible to work in the UK welcome.

Requests for application forms to the Personnel Department at the above address.

Holiday Centres and Amusements

THE ABBEY COLLEGE: Wells Road, Malvern Wells, Worcs WR14 4JF (tel 01684-892300; fax 01684-892757; e-mail abbey@cix.co.uk; www.abbey-college.co.uk). A beautiful residential campus with students from over 30 nations.
Activities Staff/Sports Staff. £130-£150 for 6 days work a week. Min. age 18.
Welfare And Admin. Staff (3). £130 per week for 6 days work.

Sports qualifications and experience of summer schools preferred. Accommodation, meals and laundry facilities provided for all staff, plus free use of all sports and leisure activities and excursions. Work available from mid June to end of August. Overseas applicants welcome to work 3 weeks and get 1 week's free English classes and accommodation free of charge, worth £410.

Applications from February to the Personnel Department at the above address.

ALTON TOWERS: Alton, Staffordshire, ST10 4DB (tel 01538-704039; fax 01538-703007; e-mail jane.alexander@alton-towers.com). Part of the Tussauds group, Alton Towers is a large and nationally known rides and theme park. Culture of teamwork and high level of customer service. Up to 1200 seasonal positions are available.
Rides and Shows: Operators, Ride Assistants, Services Assistants, Hosts
Retail: Food and Beverage, Games, Shops, Ride Photos.
Front of House: Admissions, Call handling and Guest Services.
Security, Medical and Traffic: Security Officers, Nurses, Traffic assistants.
Finance: Strongroom team members.
Hotel: Housekeeping, Restaurant and Bar, Conference and Events, Chefs and Kitchen Teams, Reception, Leisure.
Wages at national minimum rate and above depending on position. To work 2,3,4,5 or 7 days per week including weekends and bank holidays. Positions are available from March to October. No specific qualifications or experience are required as training is given. Minimum age 16. Foreign applicants with work permits welcome. Help with finding accommodation can be given.

Applications should be made from February onwards to the HR Department or the Employment Service at the above address. Interview necessary which may be by telephone.

BJ's LEISURE LTD: Sea Lane, Ingoldmells, Skegness, Lincolnshire PE25 1NU (tel 01754-874212; fax 01754-871805; e-mail bjsleisure@barclays.net). Amusement arcades, combining ten pin bowling, go-karts, family showbar and diners.
Bar Staff, Catering Staff, Play Area Staff, Floor Walkers, Cleaners, Bowling Receptionist. Wages and hours on application. Min. period of work of 26 weeks. Positions are available from March to October. No accommodation available.

Applications should be made from February onwards to Mrs Barbara Thompson at the above address. Interview required.

BUTLINS SKYLINE: Roman Bank, Skegness, Lincolnshire PE25 1NJ (tel 01754-761502).
Staff to work in residential/retail catering, leisure and sports, technical services, retail shops/supermarkets, housekeeping, security, finance/administration/bookings, as lifeguards, in retail bars, environmental and gardens, entertainments and funfair, guest services and nursery. Competitive rates of pay and benefits. Accommodation available to those who live 25 miles away or more. Staff needed around the year; fixed term contracts available. Minimum age 18. All applicants will be required to have a personal interview prior to any offer of employment.
   Applications to above address marked for the attention of Recruitment. Interview required.

DRAYTON MANOR PARK LTD: near Tamworth, Staffordshire B78 3TW (tel 01827-287979; fax 01827-288916). A family owned and run theme park which celebrated its 50th birthday in 2000, and is one of the top 5 theme parks in the UK.
Seasonal Caterers (130), Seasonal Ride Operators (130), Ticketing Staff (30), Retail Staff (60). Wages by arrangement; hours negotiable. No accommodation is available. Period of work from the end of March to the end of October. No experience necessary as full training is given. Applicants must be 16 or over.
   Applications from December to Tim Sadler at the above address.

DUDLEY & WEST MIDLANDS ZOOLOGICAL SOCIETY LTD: 2 The Broadway, Dudley, West Midlands DY1 4QB (tel 01384-215314; fax 01384-456048; e-mail Marketing@dudleyzoo.org.uk).
Part-Time Casual Workers (20-30) needed between 1st April and 5th September to work between 9.45am-3.30/5.15pm 3-5 days per week, including some weekends. Work involved includes staffing retail kiosks, face-painting, a chairlift and a bouncy castle. Applicants should be at least 16.
   Applications should be sent to the Operations Manager, at the above address.

FANTASY ISLAND: Blue Anchor Leisure Ltd., Sea Lane, Ingoldmells, Skegness, Lincolnshire PE25 1RH (tel 01754-874668; fax 01754-874146). Fantasy Island is the largest indoor theme park in Britain, with a large funfair.
Maintenance Staff (20+). Wage negotiable. To work 6 days a week.
Ride Operators (100+), Cleaners (20+), Security (20+), Arcade Floorwalkers (20+), Cashiers (12+) required for seasonal work. Wage from £3.50 at 18 or £4.10 at 21 per hour to work a six day week. No accommodation is available. Period of work from 1st March-31st October. Full training is provided and foreign applicants who speak English are welcome.
   Applications from January to Andy Reavley or Jo Epps with two named photos.

HATTON COUNTRY WORLD: Hatton Country World, Hatton House, Warwick CV35 7LD (tel 01926-843411; fax 01926-842023; www.hattonworld.com). Hatton Country World comprises some 35 shops selling rural crafts, antiques, specialist foods etc. in Victorian-style buildings in the Warwickshire countryside. Within Country World there are also children's rides and a farm park.
Retail Assistants, Farm Park Guides, Restaurant Staff (several of each) for the summer holidays and other bank holiday periods. Hours are from 10am-5pm on a rota basis which includes weekends and bank holidays. Wages on application. Must have own transport to rural location.
   Applications to the Personnel Department at the above address.

THE OXFORD STORY: 6 Broad Street, Oxford OX1 3AJ (tel 01865-790055; fax 01865-791716).
Outdoor Marketing Staff (2) to work from June to September. Wages negotiable; to work flexible hours 3-4 days per week. Applicants should be aged at least 18 with good communication skills and outgoing personalities, be capable of approaching people and prepared to wear costumes if necessary.
Applications to Lucy Jones, Marketing Manager, at the above address.

Hotels and Catering

ABBEY COLLEGE: Wells Road, Malvern Wells, Worcs., WR14 4JF (tel 01684-892300; fax 01684-892757; e-mail abbey@cix.co.uk; web site www.abbey-college.co.uk).
Catering And Cleaning Staff (5) required to work 40 hours per week. Salary £100 per week. Relevant experience an advantage. Accommodation, meals and laundry facilities provided for all staff, and free use of all sports and leisure activities and excursions. Work available from mid June to the end of August. Overseas students are welcomed, to work 3 weeks and get 1 weeks free English classes and accommodation, worth £410.
Applications from March to the Personnel Department at the above address.

THE BANBURY HOUSE HOTEL: Oxford Road, Banbury, Oxon OX16 9AH (tel 01295-259361; fax 01295-270954; e-mail banburyhouse@compuserve.com; www banbury-house.co.uk). A three star 63 bedroomed hotel in the heart of Oxfordshire. An extensive menu is offered and the hotel has an enviable reputation in catering for company dinners, weddings and conferences.
Waiting Staff (4) to serve food and beverages to customers and be responsible for hygiene and general preparation. Areas of work include bar (must be over 18), restaurant, and function rooms.
Room Attendants/Cleaners (2-3) to service the guest bedrooms and public areas to a high standard; daytime hours.
Commis Chef (2) to assist in the preparation of food for all outlets and maintain a clean, safe and hygienic environment
. Various shifts and hours available. Min. rate of pay £4.25 per hour live-out or £75 per week including accommodation and utilities. Meals provided.
Applications to Debbie Churchman at the above address.

THE BRANT HOTEL: The Brantings, Groby, Leicester LE6 0DU (tel 01162-872703; fax 01162-321255). A traditional country inn set in a rural position, yet only minutes away from the city centre. Comprises a comprehensive bar and restaurant which is open 7 days a week.
Bar Staff (3), Restaurant Staff (3) for full or part-time work June-September. Wages by arrangement. Minimum age 18. Foreign applicants with work permits and acceptable spoken English welcome.
Applications to Karen Pollard at the above address.

CROWNE PLAZA HOTEL: Central Square, Birmingham B1 1HH (tel 0121-224 5020; fax 0121-224 5113).
Food And Beverage Assistants (5) to help clear tables and serve guests' meals. Wage £4.00 per hour. To work up to 40 hours a week.
Housekeeping Assistants (10). Duties include cleaning guests' rooms and public areas. Wage £4.10 per hour. To work up to 40 hours a week.
Staff are required from 1st of June to 31st September. No accommodation is

available. An interview is required.
Applications from 1st May to the Human Resources Manager.

DE VERE CARDEN PARK HOTEL: Chester, Cheshire CH3 9DQ (tel **01829-731000 or 01829-731586; fax 01829-731032; e-mail debbie.corbett@ devere-hotels.com).**
Waiting Staff, Room Assistants, Bar Assistants, General Assistants (20) required to work 39 hours per week, either full-time or on various part-time shifts. Wages currently under review.
Applications to the Personnel and Training at the above address.

DONNINGTON PARK FARMHOUSE HOTEL: Melbourne Road, Isley Walton, Nr Derby DE74 2RN (tel 01332-862409; fax 01332-862364; e-mail info@parkfarmhouse.co.uk). A small family run hotel with friendly young staff (mostly in their mid 20s). The hotel has 15 bedrooms, a function barn and a caravan park. Located next to Donington Park Motor Racing Circuit.
General Assistant (1-2) to work mainly split shifts in all areas: bar, breakfast serving, evening waiting, washing up, room cleaning, etc. Wages £4.50 per hour. To work 41 hours over 5 days a week. Subsidised accommodation is provided. Min. period of work 4 months between March and October.
    Previous relevant experience preferred but not essential. Overseas applicants with good spoken English will be considered. Interview preferred, unless distance makes this difficult.
Applications from February to John or Linda Shields.

ETTINGTON PARK: Alderminster, Stratford upon Avon, Warwickshire CV37 8BU (tel 01789-450123). A Grade 1 Listed Neo-Gothic 4 star hotel, with a 2AA Rosette restaurant. It has 48 luxurious bedrooms and suites and conference facilities for up to 100 guests.
Waiting Staff (2), Housekeeping Assistants (5). Wages £4.09 per hour; to work 40 hours per week, 5 days out of 7. Period of work April to October. Applicants must have previous experience of work in a similar establishment.
Applications to Jane Dobson, H.R Administrator, at the above address.

GROVE HOUSE: Bromesberrow Heath, near Ledbury, Herefordshire HR8 1PE (tel 01531-650584; e-mail rossgrovehouse@amserve.net). This large country house is set only 3 miles outside Ledbury and has a tennis court and next door swimming pool for use of students who are treated as part of the family. The Malvern Hills are within walking or biking distance.
General Assistants (1/2) to work in a guest house, providing general maintenance both in and out of doors, gardening etc. Wages £35 per week including free B & L and outings on day off. Applicants should be physically strong. Work available all year round for any length of time. Riding occasionally available.
Applications with CV and photo, to Mrs E. M. Ross at the above address.

THE HOLT HOTEL: Oxford Road, Near Steeple Aston, Oxfordshire OX25 5QQ (tel 01869-340259; fax 01869-340865; e-mail info@hothotel-oxford.co.uk). Fifteenth-century coaching inn with 86 bedrooms, 9 conference suites and an AA Rosette restaurant.
Kitchen Porters required for busy kitchen, minimum 40 hours a week with overtime available. Basic £200 a week. Accommodation available at £35 a week all in.
Chamber Staff also required to service bedroom and keep hotel public areas clean; minimum 40 hour week. £175 a week basic with accommodation available

at £35 a week all in.

All nationalitities welcome. These positions and others are available all year round; minimum stay 8 weeks. For details *contact* Andrew Timms, Manager, at the above address.

HOTHORPE HALL CHRISTIAN CONFERENCE CENTRE: Theddingworth, Leicestershire, LE17 6QX (tel 01858 880257; e-mail sheila@ hothorpe.co.uk; web site www.hothorpe.co.uk). 18th century manor house surrounded by beautiful countryside catering for up to 150 residents and with 50 full and part-time staff.

Team Assistants (3 or 4) are required throughout the year. Duties include serving meals to guests, washing up, and servicing guest bedrooms. Salary (approx. £100 per week) plus full B & L provided. To work approx. 36 hours/6 days a week. Min. age 18. Minimum period of work 3 months. Overseas applicants from EU countries only, or with valid working visas, who can speak and understand English well. All applicants should be committed Christians.

Applications form and further information from Mrs Sheila Dunning, Director, Hothorpe Hall.

HOW CAPLE GRANGE HOTEL: How Caple, Herefordshire HR1 4TF (tel 01989-740208/740668; fax 01989-740301). Set in a rural location approx. 3 miles from the M50 motorway. Business is mainly party bookings and function trade.

Chef/Cook (1-2). Approx. £120-£150 per week plus free B & L. To work approx. 40 hours per week. Min. age 18. No experience necessary but must be willing to work within other aspects of hotel work. Own transport absolutely essential. Staff needed between Easter to October and Christmas period.

Applications to the Proprietor, How Caple Grange Hotel. Please telephone to check for vacancy availability.

THE JERSEY ARMS HOTEL: Middleton Stoney, Oxon OX6 8SE (tel 01869-343234; fax 01869-343565; e-mail jerseyarms@blestwestern.co.uk; www.jerseyarms.co.uk). A privately owned and managed high-class country inn with 20 bedrooms.

Housekeeping Assistant (1). Wages £500 per month. To work 45 hours over 5 days a week. Accommodation and meals provided for £24.00 per week. Uniform is provided. Min. period of work 1 month at any time of year. Min. age 18.

Applications to Mrs Livingston at the above address.

MARRIOTT FOREST OF ARDEN HOTEL and COUNTRY CLUB: Maxstoke Lane, Meriden, Warwickshire CV7 7HR (tel 01676-526101; fax 01676-521025; e-mail denise-waite@marriotthotels.co.uk).

Bar Staff (4) to provide bar and table service, applicants must be at least 18.

Waiting Staff (8) for food and beverage service, minimum age 16.

Commis Chefs (4) for food preparation and cooking, would suit a catering college student.

Welcome Host for general portering and concierge work with some buggy or valet driving. Applicants must have a full clean licence.

Night Porter to carry out general porter, concierge and room service work, must be over 18.

Room Attendants (2) needed to clean and service guest rooms. Staff must be at least 16 years old.

Golf Starter/Marshalls (2) personnel with a sound knowledge of golf wanted to marshall courses.

Golf Retail Assistants (2) for work in a golf shop and for booking tee times.
Golf Concierge (2) to act as receptionist and take tee bookings.

Staff are required for all positions between May-September, although posts can be from July-September to fit in with school/college holidays. Wages are £4.24 per hour for all posts except for Commis Chef and Night Porter (£4.55) and Golf Retail (£4.65); bar and waiting staff may also get tips. Some accommodation is a available at a cost of £50 per week deducted from wages. Hours of work can vary between 20-40 per week, with overtime possible, staff get 2 days off in every 7. All golf posts require a sound knowledge of golf.

Applications should be made to Denise J. Waite, HR Manager, at the above address.

THE NATIONAL TRUST: Belton House, Grantham, Lincolnshire NG32 2LS (tel 01476-566116; fax 01476-579071).
Catering Assistants to work in a busy assisted service restaurant. To work Wednesday to Sunday, including bank holiday Mondays. Staff needed from end of July-end of September. Experience of working with the public desirable. No accommodation available.

Applications from February/March to Hazel Hook, Assistant to the Property Manager, at the above address

NOW 'n ZEN: Lower Wilcroft, Bartestree, Hereford HR1 4BE (tel 01432-850220; fax 0870-7051420; e-mail jobs@nowandzen.co.uk). Now 'n Zen is one of the most popular caterers at music festivals. Working from marquees and selling great world foods, this is an efficient, happy and people-friendly organisation.
Catering Assistants needed to help in busy vegetarian world food stalls, working at summer music festivals. Duties include vegetable preparation, serving, light cooking, cleaning, packing etc. Pay of approx. £3.75 p.h. Tent accommodation and food provided.

Applicants must be able to work happily in a team, have lots of stamina, be lively, conscientious, adaptable, good humoured and like music and the festival scene.

Applications to Ron Zahl, Proprietor.

OXFORD THAMES FOUR PILLARS HOTEL: Henley Road, Sandford-on-Thames, Oxford OX4 4GX (tel 01865-334444; fax 01865-334400; e-mail Thames@four-pillars.co.uk; www.four-Pillars.co.uk). A four star hotel. Banqueting in 3 different suites at any one time for up to 300 and up to 4 bars open. Weddings every weekend. Very food and beverage orientated.
Casual Bar Staff (3) with bar experience.
Casual Waiting Staff (3) with silver-service experience.

Wages for both positions 4 per hour. Working hours are varied. No accommodation is available. Min. period of work 4 months between June and September. Applicants must be over 18. Overseas applicants entitled to work in the UK considered. Interview necessary.

Applications from spring to Celia Lewis, Deputy General Manager.

PARADISO RISTORANTE ITALIANO: Drummond Road, Skegness, Lincs PE25 3EB (tel 01754-767866; e-mail helen@lanzetta.freeserve.co.uk).
Waiting Staff, Kitchen Staff required throughout the year, mainly May to October. Wages and hours to be arranged. Some accommodation is available. Minimum period of employment 3 months. Must be 18 years or over and have a good level of English. Outgoing personality and desire to work hard essential.

Applications at any time to Gerardo Lanzetta, at the above address.

PEN-Y-DYFFRYN COUNTRY HOTEL: Rhydycroesau, Nr Oswestry, Shropshire SY10 7DT (tel 01691-653700; fax 01691 650066; www.peny.co.uk). A small family run hotel located 5 minutes from Oswestry.
General Hotel Worker (1), General Kitchen Assistant (1). Wages £4 per hour with accommodation provided. To work 4/5 days a week. Min. period of work 6 weeks between May and October. Overseas applicants considered.
Applications at any time to Miles Hunter. Interview necessary.

QUALITY HOTEL WARWICK: Chesford Bridge, Kenilworth, Warwickshire CV8 2LN (tel 01926-858331; fax 01926-858153).
Housekeeping/Restaurant Staff (2-3). To work 5 days out of 7; salary £4.25 per hour. Accommodation is available at £22 per week. Staff are required all year round and no experience is necessary. Minimum period of work 10 weeks.
Applications to the Manager at the above address at any time.

PRINCESS RIVER CRUISES: c/o The Park Yacht Inn, Trent Lane South Colwick, Nottingham NG2 4DS (tel 0115-9100 400; e-mail endtrent@aol.com). Nottingham's largest and most luxurious river cruiser. Day and evening cruises on the river Trent, specialising in corporate entertainment.
Saloon Staff (4) to perform general bar and waiting work. Work is very service orientated. Wages £4 per hour. To work 37½ hours per week. Min. period of work of 3 months. Positions are available from April to October. Applicants should be 21+ with previous experience preferred but not essential. No accommodation available.
Applications should be made from March onwards to Stuart, Ian or Suzanne at the above address. Interview necessary.

THE RANDOLPH HOTEL: Beaumont Street, Oxford OX1 2LN (tel 01865-247481; fax 01865-791678; www.heritage-hotels.com). Oxford's premier hotel.
Housekeeping/Catering Assistants needed to work at The Randolph in Oxford, The Eastgate hotel in Oxford, The Bear Hotel in Woodstock and The Upper Reaches in Abingdon. Wages on application 39 hours over five days per week. No accommodation available. To work from June to September; min. period of work eight weeks. Overseas applicants with good English welcome. Minimum age 18.
Apply from April to Phil Westwood, Human Resources Manager, at the above address.

ROWTON HALL COUNTRY HOUSE HOTEL AND HEALTH CLUB: Whitchurch Road, Rowton, Chester CH3 6AD (tel 01244-335262; fax 01244-335464). Set in eight acres of award winning grounds, Rowton Hall is renowned for fine food and wine and its wedding and conference facilities.
Waiting Staff required to work a five-day week. Wages £4.50 per hour. Staff are required from April-October. Accommodation is available at a cost of £50 per week.
Applications with a CV at any time to Linda Formstone at the above address.

SHILLINGFORD BRIDGE HOTEL: Shillingford Hill, Wallingford, Oxfordshire OX10 8LZ (tel 01865-858567; fax 01865-858636).
Hotel Work of all types, full-time. Varying rates of pay. Limited accommodation. Min. period of work 3 months. *Applications* to the Duty Manager at the above address.

STOURPORT STEAMER CO: 99 Areley Common, Areley Kings, Stourport-on-Severn, Worcs DY13 0NL (tel 01299-871177; fax 01299-824646; e-mail sales@Riverboathire.co.uk). Passenger boat operator, trips long and short, day and evening. Party groups.

Bar and Catering Staff(6). Wages from £4.80 per hour. To work various hours, mainly evenings and part-time. Min. period of work of 8 weeks. Positions are available from June to September. Excellent English essential as loud music can make it difficult to hear. Must be capable of team work and of keeping work and public areas clean and clear of glasses and plates.

Applications should be made from Easter onwards to Mrs Sue May.

STRATFORD MOAT HOUSE: Bridgefoot, Stratford-Upon-Avon, Warwickshire CV36 4SA (tel 01789-279988; fax 01789-298589). 250 bedroom hotel in town centre location. Busy, friendly environment. Part of Queen's Moat House Hotels.

Waiting and Bar Staff (4-6). Wages £4.15 per hour. Some accommodation available at £125 per month. To work varied hours. Min. period of work of 3 months. Positions are available from June to early October. Good English essential. Minimum age 18. Training provided but applicants need customer service skills.

Applications should be made from as soon as possible to Heidi Morris, Recruitment Manager. Interview necessary.

VILLAGE LEISURE HOTEL: Centre Park, Warrington, Cheshire, WA1 1QA (tel 01925-240000; fax 01925-445240; e-mail jackie.kiley@village-hotels.com).

Room Assistants (2) to work 20-25 hours per week, including some weekends, from 9am-2pm. Period of work May to September with wages of £3.90 per hour.

Bar Staff (2) to work at least 20 hours per week between May and September, wages £3.90-£4.05 per hour. Must be over 18 and have their own transport.

For more details *contact* Jackie Kiley, Personnel and Training Manager at the above address.

WELCOMBE HOTEL AND GOLF COURSE: Warwick Road, Stratford-Upon-Avon, Warwickshire CV37 0NR (tel 01789-295252 ext. 633/634; fax 01789-413809; e-mail personnel@welcombe.co.uk; www.welcombe.co.uk). Four star hotel in country setting near Stratford-Upon-Avon.

Room Attendants (2). £10,000 p.a. pro rata.

Hall Porter (1). £9,000 p.a. pro rata.

Linen Porter (1). £8,500 p.a. pro rata.

Commis Waiting Staff (2). £8,500 p.a. pro rata.

Receptionists (1/2). £9,000 p.a. pro rata.

Accommodation is available for £35 per week. Min. period of work of 6 months. Positions are available from 1 June onwards. Must speak at least conversational English. Minimum age 21. Foreign applicants welcome.

Applications should be made from April onwards to the Personnel Office at the above address. Interview necessary, by telephone at least.

WESTWOOD COUNTRY HOTEL: Hinksey Hill Top, Oxford OX1 5BG (tel 01865-735408; fax 01865-736536; e-mail reservation@westwoodhotel.co.uk; www.westwoodhotel.co.uk). Situated in lovely woodland settings just 2^1/2 miles from Oxford city centre, the hotel is recently refurbished and offers high quality food and accommodation.

General Assistants (2). Min. £120 per week plus B & L. To work approx. 45 hours per 5^1/2 day week. Hours by arrangement with flexible day off. Min. age 18. Tidy appearance required. Min. period of work 3 months between May and October. Overseas applicants welcome.

Applications to Mr Tony Healy, Proprietor, at the above address.

WESTON PARK ENTERPRISES LTD: Weston Park, Weston-under-Lizard, Shifral, Shropshire TF11 8LE (tel 01952-852104; fax 01952 850430; e-mail howard@western-park.com) A large stately home offering a very high standard of cuisine and service.

Waiting Staff. Job includes an element of cleaning and moving furniture. There is also some basic food preparation involved. National minimum wage; to work for breakfast, lunch or dinner - variable hours. Applicants must be aged 16 or older, and be well presented. No accommodation is available. Staff are for breakfast, lunch or dinner - variable hours. Staff are required all year round. Applications from overseas are welcome if they have the appropriate permits for work.

Applications should be sent to the Operations Manager at the above address as soon as possible. Interview may be necesary.

THE WILD DUCK: Ewen, Cirencester, Glos GL7 6BY (tel 01285-770310; fax 01285-770924; e-mail wduckinn@aol.com).

Waiting/Bar And General Assistants (2). To work 5 days per week at the national minimum wage. Staff required from June to October; minimum period of work 6 weeks. Accommodation not available. Minimum age 18. Interview is necessary.

Apply from May onwards to Tina Mussell at the above address.

WORCESTER STEAMER CO: Severn Street, Worcester, WR1 2NF (tel 01905-354991; fax 01905-673541; e-mail wscjb@aol.com).

Bar Staff/Crew Members (10) to perform mostly general bar duties. Wages from £4 per hour plus bonus scheme. To work mostly evenings and weekends. Positions are available from Easter to October. Good English essential. Minimum age 18+. No accommodation available.

Applications should be made as soon as possible to V. Hooper at the above address. Interview required.

Language Schools

THE ABBEY COLLEGE: Wells Road, Malvern Wells, Worcs WR14 4JF (tel 01684-892300; fax 01684-892757; e-mail abbey@cix.co.uk; www.abbey.college. co.uk). A beautiful residential campus with students from over 30 nations.

TEFL Teachers (15). £230-£310 per week. Must hold at least an RSA/Trinity Prep. Certificate and have at least one year's experience. Previous summer school experience preferred. Accommodation, meals and laundry facilities provided. Work available from mid June to the end of August. All year positions also available. Min. period of employment 4 weeks. Free use of all sports and leisure activities and excursions open to all employees.

Applications from March to Personnel Department at the above address. Interview necessary.

ASPECT ILA OXFORD: 108 Banbury Road, Oxford OX2 6JU (tel 01865-515808; fax 01865-310068). A language school in North Oxford with a young and lively atmosphere.

Teaching Staff (10-15). Minimum age 21. Teaching general English to mixed nationality groups aged 16+. CELTA or equivalent required.

Social Assistants (1-2). Minimum age 18. To assist the social organiser with arranging and promoting social events and sporting activities.

Accommodation Assistant. Minimum age 18; must have access to a car. To assist the accommodation officer, mainly by recruiting and inspecting new host families.

Administration Assistant. Minimum age 18. To undertake general administrative duties; computer literacy an advantage.

All jobs are on a full-time basis with wages to be arranged. Some accommodation may be available in student residences; this is free if 'warden' responsibilities are undertaken. Staff are required from May/June until the end of August, and an interview is necessary. Overseas students with valid working visas are welcome.

Applications from March/April to the School Manager at the above address.

CONCORD COLLEGE: Acton Burnell Hall, Acton Burnell, Shrewsbury, Shropshire SY5 7PF (tel 01694-731631; fax 01694-731219; e-mail summercourse@ concordcollegeuk.com; www.concordcollegeuk.com). An independent international school. Fully residential with excellent facilities on campus.

Residential Summer Course EFL Tutors (10-15) Applicants must hold as a minimum the RSA Certificate in TEFL.

Summer Course Sports Tutor (2-4) Applicants must have the appropriate coaching qualifiations.

For both positions working hours are variable and the salary is dependant on qualifications and experience. Accommodation is provided at no charge. Staff are required from the start of July to August 25th for a minimum period of 3 weeks.

Applications and enquiries should be sent to John Leighton, Director of Summer Courses at the above address as soon as possible.

EF LANGUAGE TRAVEL: Cherwell House, 3rd Floor, 1 London Place, Oxford OX4 1BD (tel 01865-200720; fax 01865-243196; www.ef.com).

EFL Teachers, Leaders, Actvity Coordinators needed to teach teenage overseas students and organise leisure activities between June and the end of August. Teachers are paid £18+ per half day session (or £26+ if with a TEFL qualification); leaders are paid £198 per week. Applicants should be university students aged at least 19. Good knowledge of Oxford and London required.

Applications to Petros Panayiotou, Manager, at the above address.

ENGLISH LANGUAGE & CULTURAL ORGANISATION: Lowlands, Chorleywood Road, Rickmansworth, Hertfordshire WD3 4ES (tel 01923-776731; fax 01923-774678; e-mail efl@elco.co.uk).

TEFL Teachers (20) for July/August. Must have CELTA or equivalent degree and preferably a minimum of two years experience.

Applications to Noelle Caremore, Head Office Co-Ordinator, at the above address.

GLENFIELD ENGLISH COURSES: Glenfield, Boars Hill, Oxford (tel 01865-735370; fax 01865-730246). An extremely friendly residential school offering itensive EFL together with a range of sports, excursions and social activities to overseas students aged 10-18.

English Teachers (2-3) live-in, to teach students on residential courses. Salary subject to contract but roughly £275 per week with all meals and own study bedroom provided. Periods of work: usually July only or July/August. Minimum age 21, maximum age 25. Sporting ability, particularly in tennis or sailing and some TEFL experience useful but applicants must speak English perfectly, that is, as well as a native speaker.

General Domestic Assistant to help with cooking, housework etc. Minimum age 20. Overseas applicants especially welcome. Knowledge of English is not essential. Live-in, with meals and own study bedroom provided. Salary subject to contract but roughly £90 per week. To work from 20th June for either 5 or 9 weeks. Applicants must be legally entitled to work in the UK.

Applications for all types of post to Mr or Mrs Horwood at the above address. Applicants must be available for interview in May. In exceptional cases interviews may be arranged in Paris or Madrid and candidates preferring this option should say so.

OXFORD ENGLISH CENTRE: 66 Banbury Road, Oxford, OX2 6PR (tel 01865-516162; fax 01865-310910; e-mail office@oxfordenglish.co.uk).
EFL Teachers (5-10) to work 20 hours per week in July and August. Wages by arrangement based on qualifications, applicants should have at least a first degree and RSA Prep. certificate.
Activities Helpers (4) to work full or part-time between June and September. Applicants should be at least 19, job suits students on vacation.
Cafe Staff (2) to work from 8am-3pm in July and August, wages of £5 per hour. Training given but applicants should be clean, quick and with good presentation skills.
Applications to Graham Simpson, Principal.

OXFORD HOUSE SCHOOL OF ENGLISH: 67 High Street, Wheatley, Oxford OX33 1XT (tel 01865-874786; fax 01865-873351; e-mail oxford.house@dial.pipex.com; www.oxford-house.co.uk). Small, personal school near Oxford, catering for mixed nationality students (individuals and small groups only). A friendly working environment.
Admin/Secretarial/Social Organiser (1) from May to September. Approx. £150 per week. 3 hour day; flexible but mainly 3 hours per morning Monday to Friday, plus two hours evenings. Minimum age 20. Qualifications: knowledge of languages, first aid, secretarial and office skills.
English Teachers (1-2) from July to the end of August or September. Wages: approx. £276 per week. 23 hours of class contact per week plus occasional supervisory/social duties. Min. RSA Certificate, TEFL or equivalent plus relevant experience.
Applications a.s.a.p. to Mr R.I.C. Vernede, Principal, Oxford House School of English.

SEVERNVALE ACADEMY: 25 Claremont Hill, Shrewsbury, Shropshire SY1 1RD (tel 01743-232505; fax 01743-272637; e-mail enquiry@severnvale.co.uk). A small school running English courses for foreign students, both adults and juniors.
EFL Teachers (5-10). £250 a week. Board and accommodation available for £84 per week. To teach Monday to Friday daytime. Degree and TEFL qualification (e.g. RSA/UCLES/TESOL certificate) and experience necessary. Spoken English to the standard of a native required. Min. period of work of 4 weeks. Period of work 1 July to 20 August.
Applications from Easter onwards to Mr J.W.T. Rogers, Principal, Severnvale Academy. Interview required.

ST CLARE'S OXFORD: 139 Banbury Road, Oxford OX2 7AL (tel 01865-552031; fax 01865-310002; e-mail shortcourses@stclares.ac.uk; www.stclare.ac.uk). An educational charity which operates a range of courses for students from around the world throughout the year and has residential premises in North Oxford.
EFL Teachers (20). To teach 15-26 hours per week. From £16 per hour. Must have Dip. TEFLA.

Activity Staff (20). £195 per 40 hour week. Min. age 20 years. Experience of organising activities and sport essential.

Accommodation available free to those who chose to undertake pastoral activities. Min. period of work 3 weeks between June and September. All applicants must be available for interview.

Applications from March to the Director of Short Courses at the above address.

SUL LANGUAGE SCHOOLS: 7 Woodlands Avenue, Tywardreath, Par, Cornwall PL24 2PL (tel 01726-814227; fax 01726-813135; e-mail claire@sul-schools.com). A well-established business which provides language holiday courses in Cornwall, Devon, Somerset + Midlands and Ireland for foreign teenagers. Courses run for 2-4 weeks from April to September.

EFL Teachers. Wages dependant on experience and qualifications but are usually from £23 per morning of 2¹/₂ hours. To work mornings and possibly afternoons, supervising activities. Accommodation is available at some centres. Teachers required from April-August for a minimum period of 2 weeks. Applicants should be TEFL qualified or hold a languages degree or teaching qualification. An interview is usually required.

Applications from January to Claire Frost at the above address.

Medical

BELVADERE CARE LTD: Suite B-1, 56 Teville Road, Worthing, West Sussex BN11 2LX (tel 01903-537499; fax 01903-521654).

Care Assistants required for agency work in nursing and rest homes and to work with people with learning/physical disabilities. Wages are between £5.10-£6 per hour. Applicants must be over 18.

Applications to Celia Madgwick, Director, at the above address.

BNA: 12 Clarendon Place, Leamington Spa CV32 5QR (tel 01926-883653; fax 01926-886652; e-mail bna@bna.uk.com). A nursing agency supplying regular staff to various sectors including private patients, nursing homes, residential homes and NHS hospitals.

Auxiliary Nurses And Care Assistants to work with private patients and in nursing and residential homes. Wages £5.13-£11.63 per hour. Job may involve working at night and weekends. Applicants must be aged 18+; no experience is necessary as training will be given. Vacancies are ongoing and there is no minimum period of work. Overseas applicants are welcome.

Applications should be sent to Sara Higgins, Manager, at the above address. Two references are needed.

NIGHTINGALES CARE: 343 Blackburn Road, Darwen BB3 0AB (tel 01254-771574). An agency accredited to the social services.

Community Carers (20) for caring and cleaning in the homes of clients in the local community. Wages £3.80 per hour to work 8am to 10pm. Applicants should hold NVQ1,2 or have 2 years experience in the care sector and must be mobile. Minimum age is 18 years old. Staff are required for a minimum of 1 month.

Applications should be sent to Linda or Sue at the above address.

OXFORD AUNTS CARE AND NURSING AGENCY: 3 Cornmarket Street, Oxford OX1 3EX (tel 01865-791016/7; fax 01865-242606). Providing live-in help to enable elderly and disabled people to remain in their own homes.

Temporary Positions for nurses and carers for the elderly and disabled. Experience and good references essential. Overseas applicants must have a good standard of English and be eligible to work.

For *applications*, everyone must be able to attend an interview and provide three references.

Outdoor

AI MARQUEES: 25 Castlecroft Road, Finchfield, Wolverhampton, West Midlands WV3 8BS (tel 01902-765353; fax 01902-765353).
Marquee Erectors (3+) needed from May to September to erect marquees, load and unload, set up furniture, carpet interiors, clean etc. Hours flexible, sometimes long. Wages £4.50 p.h. Must be fit and willing to work hard.
Applications to the Proprietor at the above address.

ALFRESCO MARQUEES: Unit 31, Barnwell Workshops, Barnwell, Peterborough, Lincolnshire PE8 5PL (tel 01832-273500; fax 01832-275064; e-mail alfrescomarquees@aol.com).
Marquee Erectors (7). Wages on application. To work 5 or 6 days per week, plenty of overtime available. Positions are available from June to September. An HGV or 7.5 tonne lorry driver an advantage but not necessary. Minimum age 18.
Applications should be made at any time to Kate Maltby at the above address.

AMBERLEY MARQUEES: Units 4-6, Oaks Way Industrial Estate, Station Road, Earl Shilton, Leicestershire LE9 7EX (tel/fax 01455-841445; e-mail marquees@amberley.fsbusiness.co.uk).
Marquee Erectors (3). Wages £5 per hour plus time and a quarter overtime. Work is 8 hours a day starting at 8am Monday to Friday with possibility of weekend work and evenings as overtime. Desired period of work from May to October. Applicants should hold a clean driving licence, and being over 25 is preferable but not essential. No Accommodation available.
Applications should be made from February onwards to Stewart Brices at the above address. Interview and CV necessary.

C. DE ANGELIS & SON: 333 London Road, Wyberton, Boston, Lincs. PE21 7AU (tel/fax 01205-722891; e-mail P.DeAngelis_@excite.co.uk). A medium size family run farm, growing fruit and vegetables for the processing industry.
Soft Fruit Pickers (100) required from 23 June for about 3 weeks.
Plum Pickers (50) required from 20 August for about 3 weeks. Includes ladder work.
Apple Pickers (50) required from 7 September for about 4 weeks. Includes ladder work.
To work variable hours from Monday to Friday. Camping available on site.
Applications to the above address.

BADSEY FIELDS NRS LTD: Badsey Fields Lane, Badsey, Evesham, Worcestershire WR11 5EX (tel 01386-830944; fax 01386-833668).
General Horticultural Workers (10+) to work from June onwards. Wages at Agricultural Wages Board rates. To work a 40 hour week or as arranged.
Applications to P. Campagna, Director, at the above address.

T. W. & H. R. BRIGDEN LTD: Pullens Farm, Ridgeway Cross, Near Malvern, Worcestershire WR13 5JN (tel 01886-880232; fax 01886-880814).

Field Supervisors (4) required to work with foreign students, picking strawberries and raspberries. Wages paid at hourly rates for approx. 8 hours a day, 6 days per week (weather permitting). Must have fluent English and a full clean driving licence. Accommodation is available. Min. age 21.

Accommodation Manager to supervise foreign student workforce. Period of work from early June to mid/end August, staying for full period of time if possible. Accommodation available. Must have full clean driving licence; min. age 21. Applicants must speak fluent English and possess a work permit.

Applications at any time to Mrs Brigden at the above address. Interview necessary.

BRIAR POOL FARM: Cledford Lane, Middlewich, Cheshire CW10 OJS (tel 01606-737670; fax 01270-528241; e-mail Rachel@riwilliamson.freeserve.co.uk) **Seasonal Marquee Erectors** to put up and dismantle tents during season May to October; there is a possibility of starting work in June, July, August or September according to applicants' availability. Pay at a minimum of from £4 p.h. but is related to performance at erecting and dismantling. Must be able, fit and strong. Driving licence an advantage.

Apply to Andrew Willis or Rachel Williamson.

S.H.M. BROOMFIELD & SON: Elmbridge Fruit Farm, Addis Lane, Cutnall Green, Droitwich, Worcs WR9 0ND (tel 01299-851592; fax 01905-621633). A well-situated, thriving fruit farm dedicated to growing premium fruit (Best Midland Orchard winners 1996-2000).

Fruit Pickers (20) to work from June 10th to October 20th. Piecework rates of pay (£4.10-£7.50 per hour according to working speed). To work 5 to 6 days per week. No experience or qualifications are necessary as full training is given on site. Min. age 17; min. period of work varies depending on the season. Limited accommodation is available for £1.50 per night. Camping, toilet and washing facilities free.

Applications from May 25 to Colin Broomfield, Partner, at the above address.

H.J. AND S.J. FORTNAM: Puckmoor, Fosbury Fruit Farm, Putley, Ledbury, Herefordshire HR8 2QR (tel 01531-670613). A farm growing apples, pears and plums. Beautiful countryside but near to amenities.

Fruit Pickers (10). Wages according to Agricultural Wages Board rates. To work 1 September to October. Previous picking experience useful. Campsite available with showers and toilets.

Overseas applicants entitled to work in the UK considered. Interview not necessary. *Applications* from June to Mrs F. Fortnam.

C. FRANCIS: Paddock House, Bear lane, Pinchbeck, Spalding, Lincolnshire PE11 3XA (tel 01775-723953; e-mail cecilfrancis@aol.com). A small family company in the fens close to Peterborough. All strawberries are grown in large polytunnels and on a table top system, so pickers stay dry and do not need to bend down.

Soft Fruit Pickers(20). To work approx. 8 hours a day, 5 days per week. Staff needed from 1 June to 1 October. Min. period of work 4 weeks. Accommodation provided for weekly charge of £30 (hostel). Showers, cooking and sporting facilities included. Min. age 18. Overseas applicants with work permits welcome.

Applications from 1 April to the Office Manager at the above address.

C.M. & G.W. GOACHER LTD: Green Acres, Wood Lane, N. Whatley, Retford, Notts. DN22 9NG (tel 01427-880341; fax 01427-880341)

Fruit Pickers/Packers to work from mid June to mid July.Wages at Agricultural Wages Board stipulated rate. To work from 8am-3pm, with some extra work available; some weekend work possible. Limited accommodation may be possible with sufficient notice, but these jobs will mainly be of interest to locally based applicants. Applicants must be fit and have common sense.

Applications to Mrs Judith Goacher, Company Secretary, at the above address, giving background info. and reference contacts.

HARGREAVES PLANTS LTD: Lowgate, Gedney Dyke, Spalding, Lincs PE12 0BL (tel 01406-366300; fax 01406-366321; e-mail sales@hargreavesplants. co.uk; www.hargreavesplants.co.uk).
Plant Nursery Workers. A wide range of work is available from April-September, at both good piecework rates and hourly pay. Mobile home accommodation is available situated on a campsite which is noted for its friendly atmosphere. Student and foreign applicants are particularly welcome.

Applications by both post and e-mail are welcomed.

HAYGROVE FRUIT: Redbank, Ledbury, Herefordshire HR8 2JL (tel 01531-633659; fax 01531-635969; e-mail fruit@haygrove.co.uk).
Fruit Pickers mainly for strawberries.
Supervisors And Drivers must be experienced.
6 day week. April-October. Mobile home accommodation available from £3 per day. Daily paid casual workers for picking, paid piecework rates. Negotiable hourly rate for drivers and supervisors. Weekend day trips and English tuition available. Some knowledge of English needed. You must arrange own travel and insurance and bring a sleeping bag and appropriate clothes.

Write to the above address for more information from February. Non EEA nationals must arrange work permits before applying. Cannot arrange work permits for you.

MR & MRS JOHN LEWIS: Yearsett Court Farm, Linley Green, Whitbourne, Worcestershire WR6 5RQ (tel 01886-884782; fax 01886-884351). Located 25 miles south of Birmingham, the farm provides fruit for major supermarket and wholesalers.
Strawberry Pickers (20-25). Paid by weight picked. To work 6am-1pm, 6 days a week.
Packhouse Staff (5). To work approx 8 hours per day, 6 days a week.
Accommodation is available in self-catering caravans at a cost of £10 per week. Workers required from 1 June to 15 July for periods from one day or up to 6 weeks as desired. No experience necessary as training is given. Must be over 18 and fit. Students must produce student cards and university documents.

Applications from February to Mrs J. Lewis at the above address.

LITTLE PETERSTOW ORCHARDS: Peterstow, Near Ross on Wye, Herefordshire HR9 6LG (tel/fax 01989-730270).
Fruit Pickers (4) needed from June 6th-July 16th and September 10th-October 5th. Payment at hourly rates of at least £3.75 per hour or at piecework rates with which an average picker will earn £3.75 per hour but £6.00 per hour is possible. To work approximately 6 hours per day, 6 days per week weather permitting. Showers, cooking, tv, clothes washing, table tennis etc. provided in a separate block on a caravan/camp site.

Applicants must be aged at least 18. *Applications* to Richard J. Wheeler, Owner/Partner, at the above address.

MAN OF ROSS LTD: Glewstone, Ross-on-Wye, Herefordshire HR9 6AU (tel 01989-562853; fax 01989-563877). Situated in the Wye Valley, the farm supplies mainly to supermarkets.
Fruit Harvesters (30) to pick strawberries, cherries, plums, apples and pears. Piecework rates. Hours according to crop needs, approx. 6-8 hours a day, 5-6 days a week. Min. age 18 years. Min. period of work 1 month between June and September (July is a quiet month). Accommodation available on campsite for £10 per week. Overseas applicants welcome, provided they have the necessary work permits.
   Applications from January to Karen Jackson at the above address.

MANOR FARM: Church Lane, Chilcote, Near Swadlincote, Derby DE12 8DL
Strawberry Pickers required to pick late May onwards. Wages are available on a piece rate system. Working hours starting 6.30/7.00am preferred. Campsite available at a weekly charge, washing machines, showers and toilets on site. Note that no cooking facilities are available: workers must provide their own. Min. period of work one day. Non EU applicants must have work permits. Applicants must be serious workers, no time wasters.
   Applications to the above address f.a.o. Mrs Nicola Busby. Must apply in writing with a s.a.e. or IRC or no reply will be sent.

THE MARQUEE COMPANY: 1 Eldon Way, Crick Motorway Industrial Estate, Crick, Northants NN6 7SL (tel 01788-822922 or 07784-263072; fax 01788-823333; e-mail sk@the-marquee-company.com).
Marquee Erectors for a well-established and fast growing company supplying modern aluminium frame structures. Work involves installing marquees and associated equipment at stately homes, sports grounds, corporate venues, race tracks in the Midlands and throughout the UK from May to October inclusive. Overseas applicants from Australia, New Zealand and South Africa especially welcome.
   Pay at £4 p.h. minimum. Overnight allowance of £50 per night when working away from base. Must be prepared to find own accommodation near Northampton, Rugby or Leicester. Applicants have to be physically fit and able to work long hours with enthusiasm and able to learn quickly.
   Contact Glen Cartwright, Installations Manager.

PENNOXSTONE COURT: Kings Caple, Hereford HR1 4TX (tel 01432-840289). A busy fruit farm with a multi-national atmosphere situated in a beautiful part of England.
Strawberry Pickers (35) from mid-May to end September.
Raspberry Pickers (10) for month of July.
   Wages on average £25-£35 per day, based on piecework rates. To work 6 days per week. Accommodation is limited. Some caravan accommodation may be available, though plenty of camping accommodation is available with full facilities. Trips arranged to places of interest on days off. Applicants should be able to fit in with cheerful, friendly atmosphere. Min. age 18. Overseas applicants welcome.
   Applications for all pickers to be submitted, between April and first week in July and enclosing s.a.e. or IRC, to Mr N. J. Cockburn at the above address.

SIDDINGTON FARM: Leadington, Ledbury, Herefordshire HR8 2LN (tel 01531-632664; fax 01531-632232).
Strawberry Pickers (30). Piecework rates. Hours: 7am-2pm, Sunday to Friday inclusive. Campsite provided for those bringing their own camping and cooking equipment. Kitchen, TV room, toilets and showers are provided. No fruit picking experience necessary. Friendly working atmosphere. Period of work from first

week in June for approx. 8 weeks. Overseas applicants eligible to work in the UK welcome.

Applications to Mrs Houlbrooke at the above address.

STANLEY & PICKFORD: Rectory Farm, Stanton St John, Oxford OX33 1HF (tel 01865-351214; mobile 07976-302404; fax 01865-351679; e-mail s.and.p@farmline.com; www.rectoryfarmpyo.co.uk). Runs a pick-your-own, and are suppliers of potatoes, strawberries, raspberries and other fruits.

Fruit Pickers (30) to pick mainly strawberries and raspberries approx. June 5-approx. August 5th. Wages at piece work rates. If the weather is suitable there is picking every day; hours of work are informal, but pickers can expect to work in the mornings and part of the afternoon. Accommodation is available on the farm in mobile homes and caravans with cooking facilities, communal room, showers etc. Previous experience would be an advantage. The farm employs field trainers to help staff pick correctly and efficiently.

Contact Mr R.O. Stanley, Partner, at the above address for a full information pack giving information on the work available, rates of pay, accommodation, training, accommodation etc.

SNOWDEN'S MARQUEES: 2nd Drove Eastern Industry, Fengate, Peterborough, PE1 5XA (tel 01733-294613/4; fax 01733-345672; e-mail owen@snowdens.co.uk). Snowdens Marquees are part of the Owen Brown Group. They are a leading marquee hirer in the show and hospitality market.

MARQUEE ERECTORS (50). Wages from £300 approx per week. To work an average of ten hour days, six days per week. Wage according to hours worked. Minimum period of work of four months. Work available from April 1st to October 31st. Minimum age 18. Applicants must be fit, and prepared to work long and unsociable hours. Employees will be visiting some major events such as Ascot, Epsom, British Grand Prix, Newmarket and Goodwood. No accommodation available. Foreign applicants with work permits and acceptable spoken English welcome

Applications **should be made from March 1st 2002 to Owen Brown or Paul Smith at the above address. Interview required; by telephone if necessary.**

STOCKS FARM: Suckley, Worcestershire WR6 5EH (tel 01886-884202; fax 01886-884110). The farm is situated in an area of outstanding natural beauty within reach of Worcester, Hereford and Malvern. It supplies supermarkets with fruit and breweries with hops.

Harvest Workers for harvesting hops by machine and fruit picking. Wages at usual agricultural rates. Self catering accommodation available. Work available from June to October. Applicants should like working in the countryside.

Applications to Mr R. M. Capper, Stocks Farm, at the above address.

WITHERS FARM: Wellington Heath, Ledbury, Herefordshire HR8 1NF (tel/fax 01531-635504; e-mail Withers.fruit.farm@farmline.co.uk)

Casual Farm Workers (10) for various jobs including driving, supervising and picking. Wages either £4 per hour or piecework; to work 6 days per week. Accommodation available. Min. period of work 4 weeks between 1st March and 31st October.

Applications from January to G. Leeds at the above address.

WITHERS FRUIT FARM: Wellington Heath, Ledbury, Herefordshire HR8 1NF (tel/fax01531-635504). A large soft fruit farm and apple grower in a beautiful setting with a large accommodation block.

Strawberry Pickers (10) Wages per hour or piecework rates; to work 6 days per week. Picking in the mornings and weeding, planting and irrigation in the afternoons.

Supervisors (4) Wages £4.50 per hour; to work 6 days per week. Must be strong and be able to use own initiative.

Accommodation is available in shared caravans at a charge of £20 per week. Minimum period of work 1 month between June and September. Overseas applicants with work permits welcome.

Applications from 1 May to Mr Mark Pritchett at the above address.

Sport

AVALON TREKKING: 40 Waverley Gardens, Etching Hill, Rugeley, Staffordshire WS15 2YE (tel/fax 01889-575646). Operating throughout the UK aiding groups of waalkers along long distance foot paths.

Walking Guides/Drivers. Wages £80-£100 per week plus free board and accommodation. To work a 6 day week. Staff required from April to November; minimum period of work 1 week. Applicants must be over 25 years old with experience of walking/guiding, and able to drive a minibus.

Applications from February to the above address.

CITY LEISURE: Oxford City Council, Third Floor, St Aldate's Chambers, Oxford OX1 1DS (tel 01865-252181; fax 01865-252783; e-mail TSTEVENS@ OXFORD.GOV.UK). City leisure manage 9 sports and leisure centres for Oxford City Council including swimming pools, an ice rink, sports halls, etc.

Lifeguards/General Recreation Assistants (20+). Wages from £5.14 per hour, with enhancements for shifts, night and weekend work. To work various hours. Min. period of work of 6 weeks. Positions are available from May to August. 16+, desirable to hold a lifesaving qualification. Spoken English required. Accommodation not available.

Applications should be made from March onwards to Tim Stevens. Interview necessary.

NORTHFIELD FARM: Flash, nr Buxton, Derbyshire SK17 0SW (tel 01298-22543; fax 01298-27849; e-mail northfield@btinternet.com). BHS approved riding centre and working farm, situated in a small village. There is a post office and a pub 100 yards away. 30 horses are used, including an Andalusian stallion at stud, a few breeding mares and young stock.

Trek Leaders (2). Approx. minimum pay £90-£100 per week plus free B & L. To work 8am-5pm, $5^1/2$ days per week. Work available from April to September/October; min. work period July-August, preferably June also. Applicants must be competent riders, good with people and preferably car drivers; Riding and Road Safety Test and First Aid qualification also preferred. Must also be prepared to help out on the farm when needed.

All applicants should be available for interview. *Applications* between March and May only (no applications before March) to Mrs E. Andrews, Northfield Farm, at the above address.

NORTH KESTEVEN SPORTS CENTRE: Moor Lane, North Hykeham, Lincoln LN6 9AX (tel 01522-883311; fax 01522-883355).

Part-Time Lifeguards required during all vacations. Must have RLSS Pool Lifeguard (NPLQ), with spinal qualifications. Previous experience preferred.

Approx. £4.39 per hour, with uniform provided. To work variable hours between 6.45am and 11pm including bank holidays. Application forms available from the centre.

PEAK DISTRICT HANG GLIDING CENTRE: York House, Ladderedge, Leek, North Staffordshire ST13 7AQ (tel 07000-426445; e-mail Mike@HANG-GLIDE.co.uk).
Hang Gliding Instructor(S) (1/2) to work from July to September. Wages £80 per day. Hours by arrangement. Must be experienced.
Telesales Assistant/Secretary. Wages and period of work by arrangement. Must have a good telephone manner.
Applications to Mike Orr at the above address.

WATERWORLD: Festival Way, Festival Park, Etruria, Stoke-on-Trent, ST1 5PU (tel 01782-205747; fax 01782-201815; www.waterworld.co.uk).
Lifeguards required for holiday periods. Wages dependant on age. Applicants must be over 16 and hold RLSS National Pool Lifeguard qualification.
For details please *contact* the David Fleet, Personnel Manager at the above address.

WOODLANDS STABLES: Woodlands Lane, Market Rasen, Lincolnshire LN8 5RE (tel 07971-940087). Stables with 25 horses in training for flat and jump races.
Stable Hands (2) to ride and take care of horses and for general stable work. Wages from £125-£200 per week depending on experience, accommodation provided at £10 per week. To work 7am-4pm with 3 hours for lunch. Min. period of work of 3 months. Positions are available all year. Applicants should preferably weigh under 10 stone, not smoke, ride well and live in. Foreign applicants welcome.
Applications should be made as soon as possible to Mr M. Chapman at the above address. Interview necessary.

WOODSIDE FARM: Hopwas Hill, nr Tamworth, Staffordshire, B78 3AR (tel 01827-62901; fax 01827-68361).
Stable Girls/Boys required to muck out and bed down race horses, working from 7.30am-5.30pm with ¹/₂ hour for breakfast and 1¹/₂-2 hour lunch breaks. No age limit but applicants should have a pleasant attitude and if capable of riding race horses weigh under 9 stone 7 pounds (60 kilos).
Farm Workers and Stud Workers for stud work with thoroughbred horses. Work involves tractor driving, tending sheep, mucking out mares and foals, bringing in and putting out young stock. Hours of work 8am-5pm with ¹/₂ hour breakfast and 1 hour lunch breaks. Applicants must have a pleasant attitude, a basic knowledge of horses (or at least no fear of them) and be responsible with vehicles.
Wages for all positions at national minimum wage level plus help with finding accommodation. Work available at any time of year.
For *applications* contact Joy McMahon at the above address.

Voluntary Work

Children
BIRMINGHAM PHAB CAMPS: c/o M.S. Wallis, 2 Lenchs Green, Edgbaston, Birmingham B5 7PX (tel 0121-440 5727).

Established in 1967, PHAB Camps is a charity run by volunteers, so administrative costs consume less than 1% of funds. 100 children take part each summer.

Volunteers (17+) to take groups of disabled children, or mixed groups of disabled and able-bodied children, aged 8-17 for one-week holidays between end of July and end of August. No pocket money, but board and lodging provided; volunteers will need to get to Birmingham to meet the coach. Must be able to work, play with, care for, and entertain the children; many children need feeding and changing, but the holidays are fun. (Volunteers who are male, qualified nurses or able to drive mini-buses especially welcome). More information available at www.bhamphabcamps.org.uk.

Applications to Maxine Wallis, Chairman, at the above address.

B.Y.V. ASSOCIATION LTD: 4th Floor, Smithfield House, Digbeth, Birmingham B5 6BS (tel/fax 0121-622 2888).
Volunteers act as key-workers with 2 or 3 children during the week. Children are from disadvantaged backgrounds and greatly benefit from the positive contact.
Volunteers (120 per year) needed to accompany children on week-long summer breaks, either residential or camping, in Wales and the Midlands. No qualifications are necessary as training is available, but an interest and experience of work with children and young people is advantageous. All volunteers are police-checked. No wages are given, but all expenses on the camp are met. Camps take place in the school summer holidays; approx. 21 July to 24 August. Commitment is required 24 hours a day for the length of the camp. Birmingham and Midlands based volunteers are particularly encouraged to apply.

Applications from January to the BYV Volunteer Co-ordinator at the above address.

Conservation and the Environment

EAST MIDLANDS NATIONAL TRUST: Stableyard, Clumber Park, Worksop, Nottinghamshire S80 3BE (tel 01909-486411; fax 01909-486377).
Founded in 1895, the National Trust is the largest conservation charity in Europe, caring for historic houses, industrial monuments, coastlines and open countryside, in order to enable public access.
Opportunities exist for **Volunteers** to perform a variety of indoor and outdoor tasks. Hours of work vary, depending on the project available. Min. period of work 4 weeks. Min. age 18 years. No remuneration or accommodation is provided and access to personal transport is usually essential. Volunteers receive travel expenses and other benefits, such as free entry to National Trust properties.
Enquiries and *applications* to the above address.

ROYAL SOCIETY FOR THE PROTECTION OF BIRDS: The Lodge, Sandy, Bedfordshire SG19 2DL (tel 01767-680551; fax 01767 692365; e-mail volunteers@rspb.org.uk; www.rspb.org.uk/vacancies).
Volunteer Opportunities available locally working on nature reserves, undertaking practical management work, working with visitors, office tasks and helping with survey work. There are local and youth groups who require help and assistance, and a wide variety of opportunities for volunteers with specialist skills to put their expertise and experience to good use.
Residential Opportunities on RSPB Residential Voluntary Wardening Scheme; accommodation is provided (min. stay 1 week, max. 1 month, Saturday to Saturday only) on one of 32 nature reserves across the UK. 16+. Tasks are many and varied, including practical management and survey work and helping in

visitor centres. Overseas applicants with good spoken English welcome.

For further details, visit the website or contact the Volunteers Unit at the above address. For information on Wardening scheme send a self-addressed label with two first class stamps or an international reply coupon.

Festivals and Special Events

BIRMINGHAM INTERNATIONAL FILM AND TELEVISION FESTIVAL: 9 Margaret Street, Birmingham B3 3BS (tel 0121-212 0777; fax 0121-212 0666).

The Birmingham Film and TV Festival is one of the UK's leading moving image festivals. It screens the best of international cinema and has developed specialisms in TV drama and South Asian cinema.

Volunteer Festival Assistant, Technical Assistant, Press And Marketing Assistants And Runner (3/4). All positions are unpaid, although reasonable travel expenses will be met. To work initially 3-5 days per week, then 6-7 days per week during the Festival build-up, and the Festival itself. No accommodation available. Applicants should be studying or have studied a media orientated degree, or have some experience in film and TV. The posts involve long hours, so applicants should be enthusiastic and not afraid of working hard. However, the work is very rewarding, provides the opportunity to work and learn at the same time and gain good contacts for the future. Suggested min. period of work 2 months between July and September. An interview is necessary.

Applications from May/June to Ms Yen Yau, Deputy Director.

CHELTENHAM FESTIVAL OF LITERATURE: Town Hall, Imperial Square, Cheltenham GL50 1QA (tel 01242-263494; fax 01242-256457; e-mail sarahsm@cheltenham.gov.uk).

The Cheltenham Festival of Literature will be in its 52nd year in 2002 and is the largest and most popular of its kind in Europe. There is a wide range of events including talks and lectures, poetry readings, novelists in conversation, creative writing workshops, exhibitions, discussions and a literary festival for children.

Festival Volunteers (25) to look after both the authors and the audience as well as helping with the setting up of events, front of house duties, looking after the office and assisting the sound crew. To work for 10 days from 12-21 October; the hours at the festival are fairly long, the festival day runs from 10.00am- midnight. Applicants should be graduates over 20, who have an interest in literature, arts administration or events management.

Volunteers are given free accommodation, food and drink. Free entry to all events is also provided. Overseas applicants are welcome but must have a very high standard of spoken and written English.

Applications should be sent to Sarah Smyth, Festival Director from June onwards to the above address.

Heritage

BERRINGTON HALL: Near Leominster, Herefordshire HR6 0DW (tel 01568 615721; e-mail berrington@smtp.ntrust.org.uk; http://www.ntrustsevern.org.uk). A National Trust Property. Provides the opportunity to mix with people from all walks of life with a common interest in conservation.

Car Park Attendant (1). To work Bank Holidays.

Garden Help, Office Assistant, Shop Help and Events Co-Ordinator.

Volunteer Room Stewards (11) required every day from April to October.

These are volunteer posts which are available all year round. Min. age 18 years. No accommodation is available but travel costs are provided (up to 40 miles round trip). Volunteers who offer 50 hours of work receive a volunteer card entitling them to free entry to National Trust Properties in the UK and 10% discount in the shops. Overseas applicants welcome.

Apply a.s.a.p. to the House Steward at the above address. Interview required.

IRONBRIDGE GORGE MUSEUM TRUST: The Wharfage, Ironbridge, Telford, Shropshire TF8 7AW (tel 01952-583003; fax 01952-588016).
A World Heritage site. **Volunteers** required for demonstrations of exhibits, site maintenance, street animation and wardrobe. Min. age 18. Must have good communication skills, be reliable and self motivated, and have excellent spoken English. Volunteers required from April to October; the Trust is open Monday-Sunday 9.45am-5.15pm. Min. period of work 2 weeks.

Some historical background is a plus, although training, costume, equipment and supervision are provided. Workers are given a luncheon voucher for a full days volunteering, plus free entry to other I.G.M.T. sites. Museum insurance covers all volunteers. No accommodation available. Overseas applicants welcome providing their English is of a good standard.

An interview is not essential although it would help both parties to visit prior to placement. Other opportunities to volunteer are available at the Museum's other sites in the valley.

Applications year round to Lisa Wood, Blists Hill Victorian Town, at the above address.

LUDLOW MUSEUM: 47 Old Street, Ludlow, Shropshire SY8 1NW (tel 01584-873852; fax 01854-872019).
The museum covers the geology and history of the area around Ludlow. It is a small place attracting mainly tourists visiting this beautiful region of Britain.
Voluntary Museum Workers (2-3) needed from June to August. To work either 9am-5pm Monday-Friday or part-time at least three days a week. Applicants should be interested in museums and need good spoken and written English.

Those interested in making *applications* should contact Ms K.J. Andrew, County Curator of Natural History, at Ludlow Museum Office.

MUSEUM OF CANNOCK CHASE: Cannock Chase Council, Valley Road, Hednesford, Cannock, Staffordshire WS12 5TD (tel 01543-877666; fax 01543-428272; e-mail museum@cannockchasedc.gov.uk)
A small yet busy museum on an ex-colliery site telling the history of coal mining and domestic life in the local area.
Volunteer Museum Attendants are required to work variable hours 2-3 days per week including weekends. These positions are intended to offer unpaid work experience but there is the possibility of some paid hours if work becomes available. A variety of tasks will be involved including reception work, working with school and adult groups, tourist information, greeting the public and working in the museum stores and library. Applicants should be 18 or more with a good basic education and preferably with some knowledge or interest in museums or history. Must have an interest in working with children, experience of public speaking, a good telephone manner, be willing to work with the public and be of smart appearance. Staff are required from May/June to August. Overseas applicants are welcome but must have a good standard of English.

Applications should be sent to Miss Lee Smith at the above address no later than April.

WIRKSWORTH HERITAGE CENTRE: Crown Yard, Wirksworth, Derbyshire DE4 4ET (tel 01629-825225; e-mail heritage@crownyard. fsnet.co.uk). The 'Wirksworth Story' in a former silk mill offers a mock lead mine, information about local customs and social history. Family-friendly.
General Museum Assistant. Must be able to communicate confidently with the public and pro-active and enthusiastic and able to help with all aspects of running a small museum. Working hours to be arranged. Min. period of work of 1 month. Positions are available all year. No accommodation available.
Applications should be made from March to Mrs M. Vaughan at the above address. Interview necessary.

Physically/Mentally Disabled

LIFESTYLES INDEPENDENT LIVING PARTNERSHIP: Worcestershire Lifestyles: Woodside Lodge, Lark Hill Road, Worcester WR5 2EF (tel 01905-350686; fax 01905-350684; e-mail worcslifestyle@care4free.net). An independent charity established in 1991 to enable disabled people to exercise freedom of choice, extend their horizons, and make decisions about the lifestyle they wish to pursue.
Volunteer Workers are needed to enable people with a disability to lead as normal a life as possible in their own home. Duties can include intimate personal care, cooking, housework, shopping and sharing leisure interests. Full-time work in shifts can include weekends and sleeping over. Volunteers receive free accommodation in the counties of Herefordshire and Worcestershire, plus an allowance of £58.88 per week. Accommodation is shared with other volunteers, and all heating and lighting bills are paid by the social services.
Volunteer workers are required at all times of year. The normal minimum commitment expected is four months, but it may be possible to arrange placements during college vacations. Volunteers should be aged at least 18 and be honest, trustworthy, reliable and caring.
Applications should be sent to the Volunteer Recruiter at the above address.

Vacation Traineeships

Accountancy and Insurance

NEWBY CASTLEMAN: West Walk Building, 110 Regent Road, Leicester LE1 7LT (tel 0116-254 9262; fax 0116-247 0021).
Chartered accountancy practice with 11 partners and 130 employees providing total financial service to small and medium sized enterprises.
The company offers **Vacancies For 2 Students** to experience working in a chartered accountant's practice. The work will involve assisting in accounts preparation and audit. Students at any level are invited to apply. Salary of £80 per week
Placements last for 8 weeks in the summer and are located in Leicester. No accommodation is provided.
Applications by 3rd March to M.D. Castleman, Partner.

Business and Management

THE BOOTS COMPANY: Graduate Recruitment Department, D31 Building, Nottingham NG2 3AA (tel 0115-959 4571; www.bootscareers.com).

An international organisation operating in retail, manufacturing and the marketing of leading consumer brands.

The Boots Company offers undergraduate students opportunities available in a variety of areas including marketing, logistics, retail management, finance, personnel, engineering, telecommunications, manufacturing and technical, and information systems. Placements last for 8 weeks over the summer vacation and take place at the Head Office in Nottingham. Accommodation is provided.

Applications should be made via www.bootscareers.com.

The Law

WRAGGE & CO: 55 Colmore Row, Birmingham B3 2AS (tel freephone 0800 0969610;; fax 0121-214 1099; e-mail gradmail@wragge.com; www.wragge.com). Wragge & Co is a leading law firm providing a full range of quality legal services to clients in commerce, finance and industry. Wragge & Co enjoys a national reputation in areas such as corporate, dispute resolution, insurance litigation, property, employment, tax, information technology, EU/Competition, transport and utilities, project finance and banking. Wragge has also built 'Top five' reputations in selected niche areas such as construction, intellectual property and pensions.

Wragge & Co offers **20 one week placements during Easter and 48 two week placements during the Summer**. These places are offered to second and third year students studying both law and non-law subjects. The work involves drafting, research, meeting clients, visits to court and analysing contracts. students receive £160 per 5-day week

Apply by application form or on-line by 31 January 2002.

Media

VACATION WORK PUBLICATIONS: 9 Park End Street, Oxford OX1 1HJ (tel 01865-241978; fax 01865-790885; www.vacationwork.co.uk).

Since its establishment in 1967 Vacation Work has become widely recognised as a leading publisher of employment directories and travel guides for young people. It currently features over forty titles in its catalogue including *Summer Jobs in Britain, Work Your Way Around the World* and *Travellers' Survival Kit Australia and New Zealand.*

In 2002 the company will be looking for one or two people to work in an **Editorial Capacity** during the summer vacation. The work will involve assisting the editorial staff in the process of revising and up-dating the company's books. Duties are likely to include general secretarial and clerical work, organising mailings to featured organisations and editorial research and re-writing.

All candidates should be proficient at operating a word processor, and should be able to demonstrate an interest in or knowledge of the publishing business. Some writing or editorial experience is preferred. Applicants must be capable of working on their own initiative without direct supervision, although help and guidance will be given where necessary. They must be entitled to work in the UK and speak English as well as if it were their first language. The pay will be around £180 per week. Please note that no direct assistance can be given with finding accommodation.

Applications should be sent to Mr Charles James at the above address around Easter in order to arrange an interview.

Science, Construction and Engineering

ALSTOM POWER. Technology Centre, Cambridge Road, Whetstone, Leicester LE8 6LH (tel 0116-2845601; fax 0116-2845461).

The Whetstone site has been involved in gas turbines since Sir Frank Whittle worked there in the 1940s. The company aim to follow his innovative example by developing the leading edge technologies of the future. The Technical Centre is part of the newly formed world leader in power generation, the Alstom Power Group. At Whetstone they specialise in engineering design, research and development.

Each year they offer approximately **Four Vacation Placements** for people studying the wide scope of engineering and related technical subjects at university. Students will work on specialised engineering projects and develop a wide variety of skills. The placements usually last for between 10 and 12 weeks over the summer, with occasional vacancies during Christmas and Easter. Pay is commensurate with the candidate's age and qualifications.

Applications should arrive before April and be addressed to Ms Hilary Watkins, HR Officer, at the above address or by e-mail to Hilary.Watkins@power.alstom.com

CONOCO LTD: Humber Refinery, South Killingholme, Immingham, North Lincs. DN40 3DW (tel 01469-571571; fax 01469-555141).
Comoco Ltd. have positions for **3 Vacation Trainees** to work in their Chemical Engineering Department during the summer. Applicants should be university students in their penultimate year. The work involves trouble-shooting, de-bottlenecking, assisting with the day-to-day running of the plant to optimise throughput. Students receive £925 per month and help is given in finding accommodation.

Applications to R. Reed during November at the above address.

GIFFORD AND PARTNERS: Carlton House, Ringwood Road, Woodlands, Southampton SO40 7HT (tel 023-8081 7500; fax 023-8081 7600).
Gifford and Partners is a firm of consulting engineers particularly interested in the design of building and highway structures and in marine works worldwide. Each summer the firm takes on **Students** to work in its regional office in Chester. For further details see their entry in *The South* chapter.

QINETIQ: Knowledge and Information Systems Division (Mal) Recruitment Centre, D307, St Andrews Road, Malvern, Worcestershire WR14 3PS (tel 01684-895642; fax 01684-894318).
Multi-disciplined teams are engaged in a broad spectrum of research, providing the principle focus for space research, satellite/land communications, imagery exploitations, parallel computing, software engineering, and command and control systems.

The Knowledge and Information Systems Division (Malvern) offers up to **20 Placements** for students over the summer vacation as well as placements for those undertaking sandwich course industrial placements. Trainees are employed on Research Science and technology-based projects at various locations throughout the UK.

The placements are open to undergraduates on Science or Engineering courses and last between 10 and 51 weeks. Competitive salaries offered.

Application forms are available at the above address. Early *applications* are recommended.

SIEMENS COMMUNICATIONS LTD: Siemens Communications Ltd, Technology Drive, Beeston, Nottingham, NG9 1LA (Tel 0115-9434925; Fax 0115-943 3078; e-mail opsjobs@siemenscomms.co.uk; siemenscomms.co.uk)
Siemens Communications Limited are a world class solutions provider employing 2,600 people and improving the business of their 40,000 customers.

They currently have opportunities within various functions of the business for undergraduates seeking placement experience at the site in Nottingham.

One 3-month and one 12-month **Trainee Hardware Engineer** are needed for the Engineering Development Centre; the circuit design team wishes to appoint placement students with expertise in all aspects of digital design including microprocessor, memory and programmable logic design. One 3-month and one 12-month **Trainee Test Development Engineer** is needed for the Engineering Development Centre; Siemens are looking for enthusiastic undergraduates studying a technology related course such as software or electronic engineering. Three 3-month and three 12-month **Trainee Software Engineers** are needed for the Engineering Development Centre; the Applications Development Group is a software group producing applications associated with the core communications infrastructure. One 3-month and one 12-month **Trainee Manufacturing Engineers** are needed for the Manufacturing Facility: the manufacturing technical support team are skilled engineers providing a comprehensive support service to manufacturing, including provision of a Maintenance Team, Test Development Team and the Manufacturing Engineering Team.

For further details or to *apply*, please write enclosing your CV and stating which placement you are interested in to Miss Karen Gaynor, Personnel Officer at the above address.

PSA PEUGEOT CITROEN: Ryton Manufacturing Division, Ryton-on-Dunsmore, Coventry CV8 3D2 (tel 02476-886000; fax 02476-886064). Car manufacturer.
Vacation Trainees (300) to help fix components to the vehicles on the production line. Wages from £1,600 per month. A small number will be taken from the end of May and the greatest intake will be from middle June with a decrease in August. Work is located at the Ryton Manufacturing Plant, Ryton-on-Dunsmore, Coventry.

Experience of a production environment would be advantageous but not essential. Transport would be required as no public transport to the plant. Experience of shift work would be advantageous. All who apply would need to be aware that this would be a very busy production environment. Please call for more information. Minimum age 18 years old, should be in full-time education.

Apply to Tracy Higgins, Personnel Assistant, for an application form on 02476-886199.

The North

Prospects for Work.

While job vacancies in the tourist trade are scattered throughout the northern region, they are most abundant in the larger coastal resorts, the Yorkshire Dales and the Lake District.

The main resorts along the east coast are Bridlington, Filey, Whitby and Scarborough, Britain's fifth most popular seaside destination. Scarborough and Filey have a large number of seasonal vacancies, comparatively few of which have live-in accommodation. Further north lie South Shields, Whitley Bay and Berwick. Berwick has two large holiday centres run by British Holidays employing seasonal staff from April-October with some live-in work available. As well as hotels and restaurants, amusement arcades are another source of employment, particularly in Bridlington. Live-in jobs are comparatively rare. South of Scarborough along the coast are four major holiday centres run by Haven Leisure Ltd; Primrose Valley, Blue Dolphin, Cayton Bay and Reighton Sands. Job Centres advertise vacancies and seasonal vacancies appear in the Scarborough Evening News six days a week (Thursday is the main day). Anyone interested in a seasonal position should contact either Scarborough Job Centre or the Personnel Department on 01442-230300 at Haven Leisure Ltd's Head Office in Hemel Hempstead. It is best to apply in January.

The principal tourist centre of the west coast is Blackpool, which has many vacancies for its many hotels, amusement arcades and fun parks. In addition Blackpool has an especially long season, remaining busy until the end of the illuminations in November. The *Blackpool Evening Gazette* offers a mailing service on request and has a special 'Jobs Night' edition every Thursday. Few jobs offer live-in accommodation and accommodation can be difficult to find during the summer months.

Morecambe, Fleetwood, Southport, Thornton, Cleveleys and Lytham St Anne's, also in Lancashire, are popular tourist haunts too. Hexham in Northumberland has opened a new golf course recently. It is also worth contacting the local golf clubs directly.

There are lots of seasonal jobs in Northumberland at Haggerston Castle Holiday Park in Berwick and in hotel and catering in the area from Amble to Berwick; Alnwick Jobcentre has a student register that matches people to seasonal vacancies.

In the main tourist centres in the Lake District – Windermere, Bowness-on-Windermere, Ambleside and Grasmere – jobs are available in holiday camps as well as hotels. Unfortunately, unless you are lucky renting a room in the Lake District it is likely to cost more than your weekly wage, so unless you are offered live-in accommodation or are willing to camp, the chances of saving much money are minimal. Hotels in the Lake District start advertising for staff about three weeks before Easter; wherever possible they will take on the same staff for the summer season too.

York and Harrogate are both on the tourist trail, and there is therefore a demand for extra hotel staff and shop staff. Your best chance of getting a job is to apply well in advance of the end of the student term. The York Races may offer opportunities for two or three days' work. Similarly a wide range of short-term work is usually available in July during the Great Yorkshire Show, 13th-15th, in Harrogate: jobs are advertised in the Jobcentre about a month beforehand. Three miles north of Ripon, the Lightwater Valley Theme Park takes on large numbers of seasonal staff which are also advertised in the Harrogate Jobcentre. In this area consult the *Yorkshire Evening Post* or *York Evening Press* for job advertisements.

Factory work provides a source of seasonal work in the North, with large factories recruiting extra people to work over the summer, mainly from June until September. They include Nestlé Rowntree and Terry Suchard in York and KP foods in Cleveland. Other factories to approach, either direct or through the local Jobcentre, are: Ben Shaws in Pontefract; Crystal Drinks Ltd in Featherstone; Unique Images in Bradford; and Glaxo Operations, Kerry Foods Ltd and Mono Containers in Durham. In the Durham area agencies such as Manpower usually recruit for this type of work.

The North has experienced rapid growth in call centre operations, predominately at Doxford Park in Sunderland. Companies such as London Electricity, One2One, Axiom, Littlewoods Home Shopping, Barclays and Subscription Services Ltd have relocated to this site. Other call centre operations throughout the region include Transco and BT call centre at North Tyneside, Abbey National at Stockton and Orange Telecommunications at Darlington. These operations are known to employ students on a temporary basis. There is usually a 3-4 week training period and most applicants need good keyboard skills and experience in customer care. Local job centres should be contacted for details.

Various local authorities, such as Gateshead, South Tyneside and Sunderland, may have work on playschemes or may need holiday cover in their many clerical departments. Newcastle and other large towns are the best places to try for retail jobs. The tourist trade in the Newcastle area is currently booming and it is a good place to look for work in the hotel and catering industry. Other places recommended for general summer work are Alnwick, Bamburgh, Corbridge, Haydon Bridge, Hexham, Seahouses, Barnet Castle, Durham and Redcar.

City Councils and Local Authorities are worth contacting to find out about significant forthcoming events which may need extra staffing.

Business and Industry

ADAM EAGLE ASSOCIATES: 6 Front House, Hagg Bank, Wylam, Northumberland NE41 8JT (tel 01661-853090; e-mail eagle@wylam75.freeserve. co.uk). A fundraising company which specialises in working with Wildlife Trusts.
Membership Officers (45) to work throughout Manchester, Teeside, Cheshire, Durham and Northumberland/Newcastle. Officers needed to represent the local Wildlife Trust, promoting it to the general public of the area. Some house-calling, distributing booklets to people who express an interest in wildlife conservation. Strictly no selling or persuasion, full training given.

Work is part-time for 2-3 hours each weekday evening, starting at 5.45pm. Wages £4.00 per hour plus commission, average pay £120 per week. Must be aged 23 or over, presentable, mature manner and ideally have experience of dealing with the general public. Staff required between March and October for a minimum of 8 weeks.

Information pack and information on *applications* from Adam Eagle at the above address.

FRASER EAGLE LTD: The Globe Centre, St. James Square, Accrington, Lancs. BB5 ORE (tel 01254-357732; fax 01254-879461; e-mail melissa@frasereagle.co.uk). A rapidly expanding group of companies with diverse interests in all aspects of passenger carriage travel and management.
Co-Ordinators needed all the time, all year round to assist with co-ordination of coaches/minibuses at rail stations and other major venues. £5 p.h. plus allowances. Applicants need a good geographical knowledge of the UK and excellent customer service skills and pro-active personality. Minimum age is 18 years.

Applications to Melissa Greenwood, Support Officer, at the above address.

CONTRACT DATA RESEARCH LTD/CDR GROUP: Eccles House, Eccles Lane, Hope, Hope Valley S33 6RW (tel 01433-621282; fax 01433-621292; e-mail tony@cdrgroup.co.uk). A small company based in the heart of the Peak District, currently employing 14 staff. Hard work in a friendly and relaxed atmosphere.
Data Processors (2-4). Wages £4.10 per hour; to work $37^1/2$ per week. The job involves transferring information from paper records/plans to a computer database. No accommodation is available. Staff are required for a minimum of 2 months between June and October. Overseas applicants with a good understanding of English and the necessary qualifications are welcome. Please note that an interview is required.

Applications from May to Tony Witham at the above address.

SUNNYHURST NURSERIES LTD: Blackgate Lane, Tarleton, Preston, Lancs PR4 6UT (tel 01772-812266; fax 01772-816420). Salad and vegetable plant suppliers to commercial growers.

Pallet Stackers (2). Wages from £4.50 per hour. To work up to 40 hours per five day week. Minimum period of work one month. Positions are available from April to July. Applicants should have fork-lift truck driver's certificate. Fork-lift driving is necessary to assist the manual aspects of the work. Minimum age 21. No accommodation available. Foreign applicants with work permits and acceptable spoken English welcome.

Applications should be made from February to K. Marshall at the above address. Interview required.

Children

ACORN ADVENTURES: Acorn House, 22 Worcester Street, Stourbridge DY8 1AN. Multi-activity centres in the Lake District and North Wales. Acorn adventure are the leading provider of outdoor adventure camps for schools, youth groups and families, operating 9 activity centres in France, Italy, Spain and the UK.
Instructors. Must hold at least Instructor status with e.g. BCU or RYA, or have passed SPSA or MLTB assessment. Other nationally recognised coaching awards may be considered.
Assistant Instructors. Must be registered as training for the above award(s).
Support Staff. Maintenance and/or catering. No experience necessary.
Fully Qualified Nurse.
Please note that all staff must be available from April/May to September: full period only.

For further information or for *applications*, please contact the Recruitment Department for a full information pack on 01384-446057 or fax 01384-378866 or e-mail topstaff@acornadventure.co.uk.

CHERUB NURSERIES & PRE-SCHOOLS LTD: Cherub Childcare Centre, Lindsey Place, Arcon Drive, Anlaby Rd, Hull (tel 01482-509598; fax 01482-576650). A well established company of 3 children's day nurseries in the Hull Area that has been in practice for 20 years.
Nursery Nurses (2), Nursery Assistants (2). To care for children 6 weeks to 8 years old, providing a high standard of care; a clean and hygienic nursery with safety is always the main priority. Basic wages. To work a maximum of 40 hours per week. Min. period of work of 4 weeks. Positions are available from June to September. Should be 18+ and NNEB B-tec qualified. Foreign applicants welcome. No Accommodation available.

Applications should be made from as soon as possible to Paula Walton at the above address. Interview necessary.

CITY LEISURE: Civic Centre, Chorley Road, Swinton, Salford M27 5BB (tel 0161-7284070; 0161-7284101). City Leisure is a DSO of the City of Salford; it manages 11 facilities in Salford which provide playschemes throughout the summer holidays.
Temporary Playscheme Workers (25) to provide quality care for children during the pay and play schemes. Wages £6.40 per hour; to work Monday to Friday, 10-30 hours per week during the school holidays. Applicants must be over 18. Experience of working with children is desirable as is a sporting background.

Staff are required from 22 July to 30 August for a minimum period of 6 weeks. Overseas applicant are welcome but must be able to attend an interview in May/June.

Applications should be sent to Dawn Williams at the above address from May onwards. Interview necessary.

KIDS AT HEART: Low Moor Lane, Lingerfield, Knaresborough, N Yorks, HG5 9JN (tel 01423-862192; 01423-860371; e-mail info@kidsatheart.co.uk)
Play Worker needed for the school holidays on a full or part-time basis to assist in preparation of activities and play programmes. Experience with children necessary.
Nursery Nurse/Assistant for June to September as holiday cover. Must have relevant experience.
Wages according to experience.
Applications to Diane Pearson, Manager, at the above address.

NST ADVENTURE: Recruitment, Chiltern House, Bristol Avenue, Blackpool FY2 0FA (tel 01253-530311; fax 01253-356955; e-mail info@nstjobs.co.uk; www.nstjobs.co.uk). An Outdoor Activity and ICT residential centre for children aged 9-13. NST Adventure is a division of NST Travel Group, Europe's leading educational tour operator.
Activity/Ict Instructors (20) To instruct a range of outdoor activities and ICT and to assist with the evening entertainment programme. While qualifications are valued they are not essential as full training will be given prior to working with guests.
Catering Assistants (5) to assist the Catering Manager and be involved in all aspects of kitchen work. No previous experience required.
Maintenance/Cleaning Assistants (4) To assist the Maintenance manager. No previous experience required, but an interest in DIY useful.
Staff requied from January through to November. All positions are residential. Minimum period of work 2 months. Average working week 42 hours over 6 days. Wages in line with NMW.
For more information and an application form please contact the above address.

YMCA NATIONAL CENTRE: Lakeside, Ulverston, Cumbria LA12 8BD (tel 015395-31758; fax 015395-30015). The camp is set in 400 acres of woodland on the shores of Lake Windermere in the Lake District National Park, and is one of the largest camps in Europe.
Day Camp Leaders (30). £15 a week during training, £25 thereafter plus travel expenses within Great Britain and free B & L. To work $5^1/2$ days a week, 9am-5pm. Min. age 18 years. Some experience of outdoor activities is advantageous and an interest in working with children necessary. The work involves leading groups of children aged 8-13 years in a wide range of activities, from environmental awareness to rock climbing. Min. period of work 8 weeks between early July and the end of August.
Application forms available from October to Easter from Day Camp Director YMCA National Centre.

Holiday Centres and Amusements

ALLEN (PARKFOOT) LTD: Howtown Road, Pooley Bridge, Penrith, Cumbria CA10 2NA (tel 017684-86309; e-mail park.foot@talk21.com; www.parkfootullswater.co.uk). Family run caravan and camping park by Lake Ullswater, the second largest lake in the Lake District. Set in magnificent scenery and perfect for outdoor activities; close to Penrith for shopping.
Bar Staff working hours 6pm to midnight. Min. age 18 years.
Kitchen Assistants (4) to help the head cook prepare meals, clear tables, operate the dishwasher and work the till. Hours 8am-2pm and 6-11pm.
Cook/Chef to prepare cooked breakfasts, lunches and evening meals. Hours 8am-2pm and 6-11pm.

Adventure Supervisor (1) to run a children's action club from the Park. Activities include archery, tennis, baseball, volleyball, football, arts (raft making and crafts) and pool tournaments. Hours 9am-5pm Monday to Friday during school holidays.

Nanny/Mothers Helps (2) each to look after two school age children and help with household duties. Live-in position. Must be able to drive.

Secretary/Receptionist (1) required from May-September. Must enjoy meeting people and have a pleasant telephone manner. To work alternative early/evening shifts and shared weekends.

Wages negotiable according to experience. Accommodation can be arranged in shared staff caravans. Period of work Easter, May Bank Holidays and from June to mid-September.

Applications from Easter, enclosing colour photo, details of work experience and dates of availability, to Mrs B. Mowbray or Mrs F. Bell, Parkfoot Caravan Park.

FARSYDE STUD & RIDING CENTRE: Robin Hood's Bay, Whitby, North Yorkshire YO22 4UG (tel 01947-880249; fax 01947-880877; e-mail farsydestud@talk21.com). A family run stud farm with five holiday cottages. The centre is set in 70 acres of grassland in the North York Moors National Park, and a short walk from the beach.

General Assistant for support duties. £3 per hour for min. of 20 hours per week. Accommodation in house, cottage or caravan provided for £40 per week. Applicants must be competent riders, willing, self-motivated, cheerful, non-smokers, adaptable, able to relate well to children and adults, and also enjoy country life. Min. period of work 6 weeks between May/June and September/October. Overseas applicants eligible to work in the UK and with basic English welcome.

Applications to Mrs A. Green, Owner/Manager, Farsyde Stud & Riding Centre.

LIGHTWATER VALLEY ATTRACTIONS LTD: North Stanley, Ripon, North Yorkshire, HG4 3HT.

Catering/Retail/Games/Attractions Assistants needed between 26 May and 3rd September, for weekends in September and October and between 20-28 October. Hours of work are on a 7 day rota working between 9.45am and 5-6pm, with wages according to age: 16-17 £3, 18-20 £3.35, 21+ £3.90 per hour. All posts require applicants to be at least 16 years old.

Applications should be made in writing to Chris Steed, Training Manager.

MOTHER SHIPTON'S CAVE & THE PETRIFYING WELL: Prophecy House, High Bridge, Knaresborough, N. Yorks HG5 8DD (tel 01423-864600; fax 01423-868888; e-mail MotherShipton@compuserve.com).

Park Assistants for a tourist attraction from mid-June to the end of September inclusive and weekends throughout the year. Variable rates of pay depending on age. $8^1/2$ hours per day, up to 5 days a week. Minimum age is 16 years.

Apply to Adrian Sayers.

OASIS LAKELAND FOREST VILLAGE: Temple Sowerby, Penrith, Cumbria CA10 2DW (tel 01768-893004; fax 01768-893001; e-mail angela. richardson@bourne-leisure.co.uk). Set in the beautiful Lake District, Oasis is one of the UK's premier leisure resorts. Their aim is to provide unforgettable holidays with the highest standards of service and friendliness in a superb setting.

Catering Staff. Wages £4.02 per hour; to work 40 hours per week. Previous experience not essential.

Lifeguards. Wages £5.68 per hour; to work 40 hours per week. Must have NPLQ or equivalent qualification.

Lakeside Instructors/Assistants. Wages start £4.02 per hour; to work 40 hours per week.

Staff are required for a minimum of 3 months between June and September. Permanent positions are available.

Applications to be sent to the above address.

PLEASURELAND LTD: Pleasureland Amusement Park, Marine Drive, Southport PR8 1RX (tel 01704-532717; fax 01704-537936; e-mail mail@pleasurelandltd.freeserve.co.uk). An approved Investor in People and Positive Against Disability employer.

Ride Operators (60). Min. age 18.

Cleaners For Grounds (4). Minimum age 17 years.

Toilet Cleaners (5). Min. age 17 years.

Car Park Attendants (6). Min. age 18 years.

Catering Assistants (40). Min. age 17 years.

Arcade Cashiers (6), Arcade Attendants (12). Min. age 18.

Supervisors and Team Leaders

Wages start at the National Minimum Wage and go up according to age and experience. National Vocational Qualification (level II) offered in Mechanical Ride Operations and customer service, with others pending. All staff to work 5 or 6 days per week. No experience necessary unless otherwise stated as full training will be provided. Minimum period of work one day between March and April. No accommodation available but local B & Bs cost approx. £15 per night. Overseas applicants with a good standard of English considered. Applicants should be able to attend an interview.

Applications between March and August to the Staff Services Department, Pleasureland Amusement Park.

RIPLEY CARAVAN PARK: Ripley, Harrogate, North Yorkshire HG3 3AU (tel 01423-770050).

Assistant Wardens (2) for general duties, including gardening, and cleaning shower block and swimming pool. Positions suitable for a mature couple. Wages specified on application. Period of work Easter to end of October. Accommodation not provided, but can bring own tent/caravan.

Applicants must be able to attend an interview. *Applications* from early 2002 to Mr P. House, at the above address.

WENSLEYDALE CREAMERY VISITOR CENTRE: Gayle Lane, Hawes, North Yorkshire DL8 3RN (tel 01969-667664; fax 01969-667638).

Visitor Centre Staff (up to 6) needed from May-November to work in the five departments of the Visitor Centre. From £3.60/£3.80 per hour depending on age; 30-35 hours per week, five days a week. Age 18+. No accommodation available but help may be given in finding it.

Apply to Daniel Bradley, Catering Manager.

Hotels and Catering

THE BLUE BELL HOTEL: Market Square, Belford, Northumberland NE70 7NE (tel 01668-213543; fax 01668-213787; e-mail bluebel@globalnet.co.uk). A family run hotel with the youngest team of staff in a Three Star Hotel anywhere

in Northumberland.
Receptionists (2) for telephone/reception duties from 8am-4pm or 4-11pm, 5 days per week. Wage by arrangement with variable tips. Should ideally be aged 21.
Waiting Staff (2) to work from 7.30am-3pm or 6.30-11pm. Wages by arrangement plus good tips. Minimum age 18.
    Accommodation provided. Period of work from April to November. Applicants for either position need commitment and dedication.
    Applications to Paul Shirley, Partner, at the above address.

BRACKENRIGG INN: Watermillock, Penrith, CA11 0LP (tel 01768-486206; e-mail eqnuiries@brackenrigginn.co.uk; www.brackenrigginn.co.uk). Rural lakeside hotel 5 miles from the nearest town.
General Assistants. Wages and hours by arrangement with 2 days off per week. Period of work from June to September. Min. age 18 years. Applicants must enjoy the countryside and be prepared to work very hard. Training is provided so experience is not necessary. Overseas applicants welcome.
    Applications to the Manager at the above address.

BRATHAY HALL TRUST: Ambleside, Cumbria LA22 0HP. A residential training centre situated on the north west shore of Lake Windermere.
Domestic Assistants needed for general domestic work such as washing-up, cleaning rooms, assisting chefs, bar work. Good pay and conditions, single room accommodation available if necessary. Applicants must be prepared to work hard, up to 40 hours a week with 2 days off per week. Min. age 18. Staff needed all year round, min. period of work 3 months. Applicants must be prepared to attend an informal interview.
    Applications, in writing, to the Housekeeper at the above address.

BURNSIDE HOTEL: Kendal Road, Bowness on Windermere, Cumbria LA23 3EP (fax 015394-43824; e-mail john@burnsidehotel.com).
Restaurant Staff (1/2) to help out in busy restaurant. Five-day week, 40-45 hours a week, 2 days off. Wages £160 p.w.
    Applications to Mr Whalley, Assistant Manager.

CHADWICK HOTEL: South Promenade, Lytham St. Annes, Lancashire FY8 1NP (tel 01253-720061; fax 01253-714455; e-mail sales@thechadwickhotel.com).
Restaurant Personnel (2). Wages £150-£170 per week depending on age and experience. To work 45 hours per week. Min. period of work 8 weeks at any time of year. No accommodation is available. Overseas applicants are considered. Interview preferable but not necessary.
    Applications to Mr. Corbett at any time.

COPTHORNE HOTEL MANCHESTER: Clippers Quay, Salford Quays, Manchester M5 2XP (tel 0161-873 7321; fax 0161-873 7318; e-mail karen.humphreys@mill-cop.com). 166 bedroomed hotel just outside Manchester boasting event facilities for 150, 2 restaurants, bars and a leisure club. Good transport to the city centre.
Room attendants (2). Wages £4.40 per hour. 16+. Physically strong with a good eye for detail.
Bar staff (2). Wages of £4.80 per hour. 18+. Experience in cash sales an advantage. To work $37^1/2$ hours over 5 days including weekends and evenings (bar staff). Min. period of work of 4 months. Positions are available from June to October. Foreign applicants welcome. No Accommodation available.

Applications should be made from May onwards to Karen Humphreys at the above address. Interview necessary.

DERWENTWATER HOTEL: Portinscale, Keswick CA12 5RE (tel 017687-72538; fax 017687-71002). Diament Ltd. is an I.I.P. Company which won the International Environmental Award 1995 and Excellence for People award; nominated employer of the year in May 2000. The hotel has 46 bedrooms/19 self-catering apartments and stands on the lake shore. Guests return to share the friendliness and enjoy the beautiful surroundings.
WAITING STAFF (2). From £118 per week. 5 days, 40 hours. Experience not essential.
BAR PERSON (1). From £118 per week. 5 days, 40 hours. Experience essential.
CHAMBERPERSON (1). From £118 per week. 5 days, 40 hours. Experience not essential.
Staff required for a minimum of 4 months between May and October. Accommodation available. Min. age 18. Overseas applicants with the ability to speak and understand English welcome. *Applications* **from mid April to the Personnel Department at the above address, enclosing a stamped addressed envelope.**

THE FAMOUS SCHOONER HOTEL: Northumberland Street, Alnmouth, Northumberland NE66 2RS (tel 01665-830216; fax 01665-830287). The famous Schooner Hotel, a listed 17th Century Coach Inn is 100 yards from the beach and a golf course.
General Assistants. Wages negotiable. There is a high tipping potential. To work 40-45 hours per week. Live-in accommodation available. Min. work period 4 weeks between mid-June and mid-September. Overseas applicants with good English welcome.
Applications a.s.a.p. to the Manager, the Schooner Hotel.

GEORGE WASHINGTON HOTEL: Stone Cellar Road, High Usworth, Washington, District 12, Tyne and Wear NE37 1PH (tel 0191-4029988; fax 0191-4151166). The hotel has 103 bedrooms, a restaurant and conference facilities for up to 200, a leisure club and an 18 hole golf course.
Restaurant Waiting Staff, Bar Staff. Wage negotiable. Min. age 18. Previous experience required. To work hours as required. No accommodation available. Staff needed from July to December. Min. period of work 8 weeks
Applications from May to Amanda Peacock at the above address. Applicants must be available for interview.

GLENRIDDING HOTEL: Glenridding, Penrith, Cumbria CA11 0PB (tel 017684-82228; fax 017684-82555; e-mail lynn@glenridding hotel.demon.co.uk). Lake District hotel. Suited to outdoor types. Surrounded by fells and Lakes.
Food & Beverage Staff (2). 18-25 year olds required for general hotel work over a 40 hour week on a six to eight month contract. Period of work between March-September or April-October. Wages by arrangement with accommodation provided and a share of tips, plus a bonus of £65 per month worked on completion of contract.
Candidates should *contact* John Dawes, Senior Manager, at the above address.

M.B.& J. GOODWIN LTD: Low Skirlington Caravan Park, Skipsea, nr Driffield, Humberside YO25 8SY (tel 01262-468213/468466; fax 01262-468105). **Bar Staff (2), Receptionist (1), Kitchen Staff (2), Entertainer (1)** to work on a holiday caravan site. Wages £180 per week. Normal hours, approx. 45 per week, including weekends and evenings. Free accommodation provided in a caravan. Period of work from June to September. Overseas applicants welcome.

Applications to M. B. & J. Goodwin Ltd.

GRASMERE HOTEL: Grasmere, nr Ambleside, Cumbria LA22 9TA (tel/fax 01539-435277; www.grasmerehotel.co.uk). A very busy 12-bedroom, award winning country house hotel.
Assistant Cook (1). £150 a week.
General Assistant (1). £150 a week. Duties include waiting, bar work, housekeeping, reception, office work and some kitchen work.

All staff work 40 hours, 5 days a week. Live-in accommodation available for women only: own room with TV provided. Min. age 21. Preferably college trained or at least 1 year's experience. Min. period of work 6 months, February to December. Overseas applicants with good knowledge of English welcome.

Applications to Mr P. Riley, Proprietor, at the Grasmere Hotel.

HOLIDAY INN CARLISLE: Parkhouse Road, Carlisle, Cumbria CA3 OHR (tel 0870-4009 018; fax 01228-543178).
Waiting Staff (6); must have previous experience of restaurant work and contact with customers.
Bar Staff (4); must have previous experience of bar work.
Porters (2) for part-time work; must have previous experience of contact with customers.
Chamber Staff (4); previous experience an advantage but enthusiasm is even more important.
Grill Chef; must be qualified.

Rates of pay from £3.60-£4.75 per hour depending on age and experience. Limited accommodation available. Period of work June-August and October.

Applications to Robert Crews, General Manager, at the above address.

HOLMHEAD FARM GUESTHOUSE: Hadrian's Wall, Greenhead via Brampton, Near Carlisle CA8 7HY (tel 016977-47402). A bed and breakfast offering evening dinner parties situated on the Hadrian's Wall path with beautiful rural surroundings; positions therefore not suitable for socialites. Only 4 bedrooms to service and a clientele from all over the world, especially America.
General Assistants (1) required to help run a guest house. Wages £80 a week including B & L within a friendly home environment. Own mobile home with all facilities. To work up to 9 hours per day, 5 days a week with extra days off wherever possible. Duties include helping prepare and serve meals, washing up and cleaning rooms. Period of work Easter to 1 November. Min. period of work June to end of August. Min. age 18. No experience required. Overseas applicants with spoken English and the correct documentation welcome (owner speaks Norwegian). Candidates should be available for interview, though if this is difficult references may suffice.

Applications from January to P. Staff, Proprietor, at the above address.

LADY ANNE MIDDLETON'S HOTEL: Skeldergate, York (tel 01904-611570; fax 01904-613043). Independent 52 bedroom hotel located in the city centre, with own health and fitness club, conference and event rooms. Primarily catering for the leisure and small conference trade.
Waiting Staff (2), Chamberpersons (2). Up to £4.30 per hour. To work 39 hours per week. Min. period of work 3 months at any time of year. Accommodation is **not** available. Min. age 21. Overseas applicants welcome.

Applications at any time to Mr M. Harrison at the above address. All applicants should be able to supply a current CV

LEEMING HOUSE HOTEL: Watermillock, Ullswater, nr Penrith, Cumbria CA11 0JJ (tel 017684-86622; fax 017684-86443; www.Heritage-Hotels.com). Beautiful country house hotel set in own grounds with access onto the lake. Very good staff accommodation available within grounds.
Waiting Staff (4). Experience needed.
Bar Staff/Porters (2). Previous bar work experience required.
Chamber Staff (4).
Salary for all staff from £136.50 a week. To work 5 days a week with consecutive days off. Accommodation provided (some shared) plus all meals. Ages: 18-35 years. Overseas applicants eligible to work in the UK and with good English welcome. Min. period of work for 6 months.
Applications to the Personnel Manager, Leeming House Hotel.

LINDEN HALL HOTEL: Longhorsley, Morpeth, Northumberland NE65 8XF (tel 01670-500000; fax 01670-500001; www.lindenhall.co.uk).
Restaurant and Bar Staff/Silver Service Staff (10) required by this hotel for summer or weekend work. Staff will carry out general food and beverage service in two restaurants, bars and banqueting suites. Hours of work are flexible, up to 8 hours per shift, days and evenings. In return wages are £3.87 per hour plus tips and accommodation may be available. Candidates should be between 18-30 years old, have basic food and beverage experience and a smart, clean appearance.
Applications should be made to the above address.

LINDETH FELL HOTEL: Bowness-on-Windermere, Cumbria LA23 3JP (tel 015394-43286; e-mail kennedy@Lindethfell.co.uk; www.Lindethfell.co.uk). A country house hotel set in magnificent grounds on the hills above Lake Windermere, offering good views and excellent cooking in a friendly atmosphere.
General Assistants (3). £160 a week plus free B & L. To work 40 hours a week. Duties include helping in the dining room, bedrooms and kitchen. Work available all year. Applicants must be available for interview. Overseas applicants in early 20s and with good English welcome.
Applications from 1 January to P. A. Kennedy, Owner, at the above address.

MALLYAN SPOUT HOTEL: Goathland, near Whitby, Yorkshire (tel 01947-896486; e-mail mallyan@ukgateway.net). Hotel with predominantly young staff, in beautiful quiet countryside.
Waiting Staff (2), Kitchen/Still Room Assistants (2), Chamber Staff. £100 a week plus free B & L. To work 40 hours/5 days per week. Intelligent workers preferred. Work available all year for a minimum of 4-6 months, do not apply for less than 4 months. Overseas applicants considered. *Applications* with s.a.e. to Mrs Heslop, Mallyan Spout Hotel.

MOTEL LEEMING LTD: Bedale, North Yorkshire DL8 1DT (tel 01677-423611; fax 01677-424507). Part of Leeming Service Area (A1/A684 Intersection).
General Assistants (2). To work 5 days a week. Must be hotel or catering students.
Kitchen Assistants (3). Split and straight shifts over 5 days. Must be catering students.
Receptionist.
Senior Waiting Staff (2). Wages plus tips. Split shifts, 5 days a week. Must be hotel or catering student with experience of silver service.

Other Waiting Staff (3). Wages plus tips. To work 5 days a week.

Bar Staff (1). Split shifts, 5 days a week. Must have previous bar and cash handling experience.

Shop Assistants (2). Straight shifts, 5 or 6 days a week.

Cafe Assistants (6). Straight and split shifts over 5 days.

Cafe Assistants-Night Shift (2). Straight shifts, 5 nights a week.

Wages to be arranged. B & L available. Min. age 18. Min. period of work 8 weeks between June and October. *Applications* from April to Mr C. A. Les, Motel Leeming Ltd.

NEWCASTLE HOLIDAY INN: Great North Road, Seaton Burn, Newcastle-upon-Tyne NE13 6BP (tel 0191-2019988; fax 0191-2368091). The hotel is situated on the outskirts of Newcastle, just off the A1/A19.

Casual Room Attendents (10). To work approx. 20 hours a week.

Casual Events Waiting Staff (20), Bar Staff (5). To work approx. 20-25 hours a week.

Wages by arrangement. No accommodation is available. Minimum period of work 2 months between June and September. Applicants must be over 16 and have a good general education. Overseas applicants considered. Staff must be flexible and prepared to work shifts and late shifts. An interview is necessary.

Applications from May to Personnel and Training Co-ordinator.

THE OLD KING'S HEAD HOTEL: Church Street, Broughton-in-Furness, Cumbria LA20 6HJ (tel/fax 01229-716293; e-mail garyokh@aol.com). A small family run hotel in a beautiful area of the country, remote from city life and with minimal public transport. Has 6 bedrooms and a busy restaurant serving an average of 100 meals per day in the busy season.

Bar Person (1), Waiting Staff (2), General Assistant (Kitchen/Laundry) (1). Wages from £4.10 per hour. All staff work flexible hours, either part-time or full-time, including evenings and weekends. Staff must work bank holidays. Must be over 18, capable, honest and reliable. Wages are dependant on experience and aptitude. Training available. Accommodation is available at a cost of approx. £30 per week. Employees are expected to work and assist in other areas as necessary, rather than observe strict job demarcation.

Min. period of work 2 months between Easter and October. Overseas applicants with understandable spoken English are considered. Only those shortlisted will be contacted.

Applications from 1 March to Gary or Jackie McClure.

PATTERDALE HOTEL: Patterdale, Lake Ullswater, near Penrith, Cumbria CA11 0NW (tel 017684-82231; fax 017684-82440). A friendly family run, busy 57 bedroom Lake District hotel in beautiful surroundings.

General Assistants. Wages by arrangement.

Experience not necessary unless applying for Chef's position. Min. age 17. Free B & L provided. Opportunities for walking, climbing, etc. Min. period of work 6 months from March to December. Overseas applicants with good English welcome.

Applications from early 2002 to Choice House, 107 Dickson Road, Blackpool FY1 2ET, tel 01253-754211.

PREMIER HOTEL: 66 Esplanade, Scarborough, North Yorkshire (tel 01723-501062).

General Assistants, Room Attendants, Commis-Chef required. Accommodation and all meals provided plus £50 per week plus gratuities. 8 weeks min.(not July and August only), must be able to work May and June, or June and July, or August and September, but applicants who can work for longer will be given preference. Overseas applicants very welcome. *Applications* for working in April, May and June or September and October are especially welcome.

Please make *applications* stating which post you wish to be considered for and giving details of any experience (not essential), to Mr and Mrs M. Simons at the above address.

QUEEN'S HOTEL: Main Street, Keswick, Cumbria CA12 5JF (tel 017687-73333). A 35-bedroom hotel in the heart of the Lake District.
Chamber Staff (1), Waiting Staff (1), Bar Staff (2). £120 a week plus free B & L. To work 40 hours a week. No qualifications or experience necessary. Period of work between July and August. Overseas applicants with good English welcome.
Applications a.s.a.p. to Mr Peter Williams, Proprietor, The Queen's Hotel. Due to numbers only successful applicants will receive a reply.

SHARROW BAY HOTEL: Lake Ullswater, Penrith, Cumbria CA10 2LZ (tel 017684-86301/86483; fax 017684-86349; e-mail enquiries@sharrowbay.com). Luxury hotel and Michelin starred restaurant set in a tranquil postion on the edge of Lake Ullswater.
Stillroom Assistants. Approx. £165 a week.
General Assistants. Min. £165 a week. To work in bedrooms.
All staff to work 50 hours/5 days a week. Free B & L provided. Age: 17-30 years. Must have domestic interests and lots of common sense, and should enjoy living in the country and working as part of a team of perfectionists. Preferred period of work 9 months from early March to end of November. References required.
Applications from January to the Manager, Sharrow Bay Hotel.

ST LEONARD'S FARM PARK: Chapel Lane, Esholt, Bradford BD17 7RB (tel/fax 01274-598795). A family farm open to the public.
Snack Bar Assistant (2). Food handling/preparation an advantage but training is given.
General Farm Workers (2). Experience of working with animals is an advantage.
Shop Assistants (2). Experience is not needed as training is given.
Catering assistants (2). Important to like children.
For all positions wages are dependent on age and experience; to work weekends and school holidays a maximum of 6 hours per day, 3 days per week. Staff are required from April to September. Overseas applicants are welcome. No accommodation available.
Applications should be sent to Denise Wainhouse at the above address from March onwards.

THE VENTURE CENTRE: Lewaigue Farm, Maughold, Isle of Man IM7 1AW (tel 01624-814240; fax 01624-815615; www.adventure-centre.co.uk). Adventure training centre giving introductory instruction in outdoor activities to children aged 9-15 years.
Catering and Domestic Staff. Qualified or experienced cooks to cook, prepare and serve. Also to run the kitchen for groups of residential children (up to 60). Positions available from March to September.
Applications before March to Mr S. Read, Director, the Venture Centre.

WILD BOAR HOTEL: Crook, Near Windermere, Cumbria LA23 3NF (tel 015394-45225; fax 015394-42498; e-mail wildboar@elh.co.uk). A small friendly hotel with a large proportion of live-in staff, surrounded by beautiful countryside.

General Assistant to work in any area of the hotel, but mainly the restaurant, waiting, bar, portering or housekeeping (which involves serving teas/coffees, cleaning the lounges, setting and serving function rooms and other duties). Wage between £499 and £576 per month live-in (no deductions made from the figure for live-in).

Work is live-in in own bedroom with communal facilities, all food, with five days work out of seven. Period of work from May to the end of September/early October. The job involves dealing directly with guests so pleasant and outgoing personalities are essential. Common sense is more desirable than previous experience. The hotel is in the country on a road without public transport so applicants need either own transport or a liking of rural surroundings.

Applications to Jon Bennett, Deputy Manager, or Kieth Everson, Duty Manager, at the above address.

WILLIAMSON PARK: Lancaster LA1 1UX (tel 01524-33318; fax 01524-848338; e-mail office@williamspark.com).
Cafe Assistants (4). National minimum wage. two to work evening intervals during outdoor play, shifts of 2-4 hours, 6 days per week and two for Sunday work (other days may be available) in busy cafe. Evening assistants must be aged 18+ and available in July. Daytime assistants from June to September and aged 16+.

Applications to E. Charlton, General Manager.

YORK MARRIOT: Tadcaster Road, York YO24 1QQ (tel 01904-701000; fax 01904-702308). An IPP accredited hotel that has recently won awards for 5 Star employment practices. It is set in idyllic surroundings, overlooking the racecourse with friendly and cheerful staff.
Food and Beverage Associates (5). to serve food and drink Min. age 17 (18 for bar work). Bar and customer care experience essential. Must have good communication skills, smart presentation and be flexible. Expected to provide own black and whites. For waiting work need silver service experience and own black and whites.
Chamber Staff (2). Must have previous relevant experience. Uniform provided.

All staff work 30-40 hours per week. Wages are £4 per hour. No accommodation provided. Min. period of work 12 weeks throughout the year. Overseas applicants welcome provided they have a good grasp of the English language.

Applications should consist of a CV and covering letter advising availability from March to Jill Jenkins, Personnel and Training Manager, at the above address. All applicants must be available for interview.

Language Schools

CENTRE FOR LANGUAGE STUDY: Leeds Metropolitan University, Beckett Park Campus, Leeds LS6 3QS (tel 0113-283 7440; fax 0113-274 5966; e-mail cls@lmu.ac.uk; www.yorkshirenet.co.uk/mills). English language and activity holiday summer school for foreign students set in beautiful parklands north of Leeds.
English Teachers for 3 weeks between July and August. Salary on application. Applicants must have a degree and at least two years of English teaching experience. No accommodation available.

Apply from 1 April to David Killik at the above address. Note interview is required.

MANCHESTER ACADEMY OF ENGLISH: St Margaret's Chambers, 5 Newton Street, Manchester M1 1HL (tel 0161-237-5619; fax 0161-237-9016; e-mail english@manacad.co.uk). The Academy is an English language school for international students, fully accredited by the British Council and a member of ARELS. The Manchester Academy of English is based in Manchester City Centre, but also runs courses in North and South Manchester.

EFL Teachers (15). Wages from £260 per week. To work Monday to Friday 9am-5pm. Minimum period of work of 4 weeks. Positions are available between July and August. Applicants should have a degree and an RSA or Trinity Certificate or Diploma. No accommodation available.

Applications should be made from February/March onwards to Sandra Kaufman at the above address. Interview required; can be by telephone if necessary.

Medical

APEX NURSING & CARE SERVICES: Emery House, 195 Fog Lane, Didsbury, Manchester, M20 6FT (tel 0161-443 2091; fax 0161-443 4178).

R.G.N. Qualified Nurses, Support Workers, Care Assistants (as many as possible) to work in hospitals, nursing homes, people's own homes, support work, working with those with learning disabilities and mental health problems. Wages and possibility of accommodation to be discussed at interview. Required for all vacations and during term-time. Must have experience in the care field. Training may be possible for suitable applicants. Age 18+

Applications to Front of House at the above address.

KINETIC NURSING SERVICES: Unit 3, Clare Court, Rawmarsh Road, Rotherham S60 1RU (tel 01709-839395; fax 01709-838331; www.kinetic-plc.co.uk).

Carers. Wages £5-£7 per hour; to work hours to suit. Applicants must have experience in caring and be over 18.

Nurses (all grades). Wages £11-£13 per hour; to work hours to suit.

The work offered is usually in nursing homes or hospitals in Rotherham, Sheffield, Doncaster, Chesterfield and Barnsley. Travel expenses are paid. Staff are required all year round. Must speak perfect English.

Applicants should *apply* as soon as possible to J. Clark at the above address. Interview necessary.

Outdoor

KINGFISHER MARQUEES LTD: College Lane, Bunbury, Nr Tarporley, Cheshire CW6 9PF (tel 01829-260550; fax 01829-261865; e-mail sales@kingfishermarquees.co.uk). Kingfisher Marquees provides a professional quality marquee hire service to corporate and private clients.

Marquee Erectors (6) Required for the erection and dismantling of clear-span marquees and all associated furniture and equipment (lighting, heating, audio equipment). Wages from £4.50 per hour; to work up to 10 hours a day Monday to Friday. Applicants should be at least 17 years old; a clean driving licence would be useful. Staff are required from April to October for a minimum period of one month. No accommodation available.

Applications should be sent to Mr J. Steele at the above address from February onwards.

NORTHERN MARQUEES: Unit 5, Steps Lane Industrial Estate, Honley, Huddersfield HD7 2RA (01484-664958; fax 01484-666307).

Marquee Erectors (3) needed from June to September. Wages on application. Minimum age 18.

Contact Andrew Tinker, Owner, at the above address.

E. OLDROYD AND SONS LTD: Ashfield House, Main Street, Carlton, Wakefield, Yorkshire WF3 3RW (tel 0113-282 2245; fax 0113-282 8775). Four generations of experience with fruit and vegetables: high media profile for rhubarb. **Vegetable Harvesters (10)** to work with mobile packing units. Wages at agricultural wage rates. To work part or full-time, up to 8 hours per day; a 39 hour week. Min. period of work of 1 month. Positions are available from January to March and May to September. Minimum age 19. No previous experience necessary as training will be given. No accommodation available. Foreign applicants welcome.

Applications enclosing a cv should be made from March onwards to Mrs J. Oldroyd Hulme at the above address. Interview possibly required.

MILL NURSERIES LTD: Ottringham Road, Keyingham, Hull, East Yorkshire (tel 01964-623664; fax 01964-622986). This very modern tomato nursery uses intensive farming methods.
Glasshouse Tomato Pickers (20). Agriculturally based work, picking glasshouse grown tomatoes. Wages of £4.00-£4.50 per hour, accommodation provided for £30 per week. To work Mondays to Saturdays, (40-50 hours per week). Minimum period of work is two months between March and November. No previous experience necessary.

Applications should be made from the beginning of February to Mr D.E. Lang at the above address. No interview required. Foreign applicants with appropriate visa welcome.

PANAMA SPORTS HORSES: The Stables Cottage, Gisburn Park, Gisburn, Lancashire BB7 4HU (tel/fax 01200-445687; e-mail work@panamasporthorses.co.uk).
Yard Staff (2) to work all summer looking after horses, assisting at shows and carrying out general yard work. Wages are negotiable depending on age and experience, accommodation available.

For further details and for *applications*, contact Ailsa Richardson at the above address.

WILLIAM LEITH & CO: Pier Road, Berwick upon Tweed, Northumberland TD15 1JB (tel 01289-307264; fax 01289-330517).
Marquee Erectors (10). Wages £400-£500 per week; to work 7 days a week, very long hours. Applicants must be over 18; driving licence an advantage.

Applications to the above address.

Sport

ALSTON TRAINING & ADVENTURE CENTRE: Alston, Cumbria CA9 3DD (tel 01434-381886; fax 01434-382725).
Assistant Outdoor Activity Instructors. Free B & L provided and free training given. Should have current driving licence. MLC or canoe qualification useful. Domestic staff also required.

For further details and *applications* contact Mr Dave Simpson, Head of Centre, at the above address.

GRASMERE SPORTS COMMITTEE LTD: Slack Cottage, High Wray, Ambleside, Cumbria LA22 OJQ (tel 015394-32127; e-mail lanes@highwray.fsnet.co.uk) Grasmere Lakeland Sports and Show is the premier

Lakeland traditional event with over 1,000 years of history celebrated in one day.
Stewards (10) Gatemen (10) Wages £20 for the day; to work either from 9am to 1pm or 9am to 3pm. Applicants must be aged 18 or over. Overseas applicants are welcome. Staff are required on Sunday 25 August 2002 to work for a minimum of 4 hours. There is camping available on the field for no charge.

Applications should be sent to Dr C. Lane, Show Director at the above address.

MOUNTAIN VENTURES LTD: 200 Mather Avenue, Liverpool L18 7HD (tel 0151-729 0809; fax 0151-729 0810; e-mail jean.padarn@lineone.net).
Summer Assistants to work for a mountain activity holiday centre from June.
Assistant Instructors (4) also usually needed April-May.

Pocket money of £30 per week plus food, accommodation in a cottage, tent or caravan and some outdoor training opportunities. To work 40 hours per week. No special qualifications are essential, but qualified people are also needed.

Applications to Ms Jean Kewley, Director, at the above address.

KILNSEY PARK AND TROUT FARM: Kilnsey, Near Skipton, North Yorks BD23 5HS (tel 01756-752150 (days) and 01756-752320 (evenings); fax 01756-752224).
General Assistant to work in the fish farm, with tourist visitors, in the children's fishery etc. To work a five day week from 9am-5.30pm or later. Must like the public, including children, be able to handle fish, adaptable, have a friendly attitude and be happy to muck in.
Pony Trekking Leader to work a 5-6 day week in July and August. Should be a good experienced rider able to cope with and organise school groups.

Wages for above positions depend on age and experience; no tips. Accommodation available. *Applications* to Mrs Vanessa Roberts, Partner/Manager at the above address.

NORTH HUMBERSIDE RIDING CENTRE: Easington, Nr Hull HU12 OUA (tel 01964-650250) A riding centre situated close to the sea.
Kitchen Help (1) Wages £50 per week.
Stable Staff (1) Wages £30 per week.

To work 8 hours per day 6 days a week. Applicants should be aged 16+. Both positions involve general help with the running of riding holidays for adults and children aged 9-16. Overseas applicants are welcome. Full board and accommodation are provided free of charge.

Applications should be sent to Toni Biglin at the above address from January onwards.

NORTH YORK MOORS ADVENTURE CENTRE: Park House, Ingleby Cross, near Osmotherley, Northallerton, North Yorkshire DL6 3PE (tel 01609-882571). Private outdoor centre, established for 20 years, set in a National Park, catering for small groups of up to 24 people.
Instructors (2) to instruct in rock climbing, canoeing, caving, orienteering and mountain biking. Also to help with day-to-day running of the activity centre, e.g. equipment repairs and building work.

Wages and hours by arrangement. B & L available. Period of work March to end of September. English-speaking overseas applicants welcome. All candidates must be able to attend an interview.

Applications with s.a.e. from 1 February to Mr Ewen Bennett, North York Moors Adventure Centre.

NORTHUMBRIA HORSE HOLIDAYS: East Castle, Annfield Plain, Stanley, Co. Durham DH9 8PH (tel 01207-230555/235354). A horse-riding centre that offers fully catered holidays for riders of all abilities.

Post Trail Leaders (2). From £164 a week. Outgoing, pleasant personality needed plus good horse-riding skills and knowledge.

Riding Instructors (2). From £200 a week. Must have British Horse Society Instructors Certificate, or equivalent foreign qualifications.

Hotel Staff (2) to cook, clean, and do waiting and bar work. Wages from £164 a week. Must be able to work to a high standard.

B & L available. Period of work Easter to end of October. Min. work period 2 months. Overseas applicants with necessary qualifications, documentation and experience will be considered.

Applications a.s.a.p. to the above address.

THE OUTDOOR TRUST: Windy Gyle, Belford, Northumberland NE70 7QE (tel/fax 01668-213289; e-mail trust@outdoor.demon.co.uk). Registered charity 1052677. Runs outdoor adventure and development courses for all ages and abilities catering for groups and individuals.

Senior Training Instructors (5). Remuneration dependent on one or more of the following NGB awards: BCU, RYA, MLTB, First Aid etc.

Trainee And Voluntary Instructors (10). Receive full board and training. Proficiency in at least one of the traditional outdoor pursuits.

Long hours, 6 days a week. Work is demanding but very rewarding. Min. period of work 2 months but longer term preferable. Discount on outdoor equipment possible.

Applications to recruiting at the above address.

RAMBLERS HOLIDAYS LTD: Hassness, Buttermere, Cockermouth, Cumbria, CA13 9XA (tel 017687-70227). Walking centre situated on shore of Buttermere lake. Offer a 1 week walking holiday. Up to 22 guests, normally aged 40+.

General Assistant (2) needed immediately. To work 5¹/2 days a week, split shifts. Wages to be negotiated. Applicants should have a pleasant personality and be able to work to a high standard.

Contact Ann Spalding, Manageress, for *applications* for these places.

MRS G.S. REES: Cross Farm Racing, Sollom, Tartleton, Preston, Lancs. PR4 6HR (tel 01772-812780; fax 01772-812799).

Stable Staff (2) for racing stables. 40 hours p.w. Monday to Friday and Saturdays until 1pm, plus one weekend in three to be worked. Wages of £150 p.w. plus overtime when going to race meetings. Must have experience with horses and be a good rider. Weight should be under 9st 7lbs.

Applications to Mrs G.S. Rees at the above address.

RIPON OUTDOOR SKILLS CENTRE: 12 Littlethorpe Park, Ripon HG4 1UQ (tel/fax 01748-833614). Runs day courses and adventure holidays. Activities include abseiling, canoeing, rock climbing, mountain walking, caving, windsurfing and mountain biking.

Instructors (2), Chief Instructor (1). £350 per week. Hours specified on application. Must have relevant qualifications, including AALA, BCU, MIC, MLC, LRC, LCL, RYA, SPSA, First Aid and Life Saving. Accommodation is not provided. All applicants must be available for interview.

Applications to Mr J. M. Bull at the above address.

ROOKIN HOUSE EQUESTRIAN & ACTIVITY CENTRE: Troutbeck, Penrith, Cumbria CA11 0SS (tel 017684-83561; fax017684-83276; e-mail deborah@rookinhouse.co.uk) Situated on a hill farm Rookin Housse is a multi activity centre offering quad biking, go-karting, archery as well as an equestrian centre with 38 horses offering trekking, hacking and lessons.

Trek Leaders (2) Wages from £150 per week, to work 40 hours per week. Applicants must be 18 or over, hold Riding and Road Safety qualifications and be able to ride well.

Activity Instructor Wages from £150 per week, to work 40 hours per week. Applicants must be 18 or over and preferably hold GNAS for Archery Leader Award, First Aid Certificate and ATV Qualification. In house training can be provided if applicant does not hold the above.

For both positions work will involve taking clients on activities and the maintenance of equipment and surroundings. There is also a self catering unit which will require cleaning.

Accommodation is available at a charge of £20 per week. Overseas applicants are welcome but must have a work permit and speak good English. Staff are required from June to September and must work July and August.

Applications should be sent to Deborah Hogg at the above address from March.

THE VENTURE CENTRE: Lewaigue Farm, Maughold, Isle of Man IM7 1AW (tel 01624-814240; fax 01624-815615; www.3legs.net/vc). Adventure training centre giving introductory instruction in outdoor activities to adults and children aged 9-90.

Instructors (3). Wage according to experience. Hours dependent on groups under instruction: 7-day week at times. Free B & L. Min. age 18 years. Essential training given to suitable candidates. At least one NGB Award helpful. Min. period of work 1 month between March and August.

Applications before March to Mr S. Read, Director, The Venture Centre.

Voluntary Work

Archaeology

ARBEIA ROMAN FORT: Tyne & Wear Museums Service, Baring Street, South Shields, Tyne & Wear NE33 2BB (tel 0191-454 4093; fax 0191-427 6862; e-mail liz.elliott@tyne-wear-museums.org.uk).

Part of the Tyne and Wear Museums service and within easy reach of Newcastle by metro. South Shields has good parks and beaches and is an ideal base from which to visit nearby cities or countryside.

Volunteers (10 per week) to excavate the site, record and process finds, draw the site and take photographs. To work from 8.45am-4.45pm, Monday-Friday. Volunteers are responsible for their own travel, board and other costs. Needed from June to 30 September. Min age 16; disabled people may find access to the site difficult.

Applications to Elizabeth Elliott, Office Manager, at the above address.

Heritage

LAKELAND ARTS TRUST: Abbot Hall Art Gallery, Kendal, Cumbria LA9 5AL (tel 01539-722464; fax 01539-722494).

An independent charity which runs a prize-winning art gallery and museums of social history, archaeology, and natural history.

Volunteer Curatorial Assistants, Reception Staff, Event Helpers and Coffee Shop Staff are required to work in Kendal Museum, Abbot Hall Art Gallery and the Museum of Lakeland Life and Industry. To work during July, August and September; there may be vacancies at other times. The work would suit both undergraduates and postgraduates hoping to gain museum experience.

The gallery also requires graduate or postgraduate students for **unpaid museum and gallery work experience**. To work 9.30am-5.30pm if using free lodging, part-time hours if living out. Free accommodation only available for 2 staff, but staff must pay for gas, electricity and personal phone calls. Interview if possible. Overseas students welcome, but working English is required.

Applications at any time to Cherrie Trelogan at the above address.

LOSANG DRAGPA BUDDHIST CENTRE: Dobroyd Castle, Pexwood Road, Todmorden, West Yorks OL14 7JJ (tel 01706-812247; fax 01706-818901; e-mail info@losangdragpa.com; www.losangdragpa.com).

Losang Dragpa Centre is a Buddhist College and retreat centre based at Dobroyd Castle in the heart of the Pennines. **Volunteers** are required to help restore the building to its former beauty. Working holidays for a period of at least one week are offered most of the year; free food, accommodation and teachings are provided in exchange for 35 hours work a week.

Volunteers are able to experience life in a Buddhist community, attend teachings and meditations and enjoy beautiful surroundings. Those with specialised skills (plumbers, electricians, decorators, joiners, gardeners, plasterers etc.) welcome but skills are not essential as work can be found for any willing hands. Minimum age 18. Applicants of all nationalities welcome.

Contact the receptionist by telephone between 2-4pm daily for more details.

TOM LEONARD MINING MUSEUM: Deepdale, Skinningrove, Saltburn, Cleveland TS13 4AP (tel 01287-642877; fax 01287-642970; e-mail visits@ironstonemuseum.co.uk).

The Tom Leonard Mining Museum preserves and interprets the ironstone mining heritage of Cleveland and North Yorkshire. This is a unique, award-winning, small, independent museum is run by volunteers on a day-to-day basis.

Museum Guides (6+), Visitor Receptionists (2+), Collection Care (2+). Expenses only are paid; no accommodation provided. Museum is open Mondays to Saturdays. Minimum period of work is four hours per week. Positions are available from July to October. Applicants should be interested in local history and heritage. Minimum age 16.

Applications can be made all year round to the Museum Manager at the above address. Interview preferred.

WORDSWORTH TRUST: Town End, Grasmere, Cumbria LA22 9SH (tel 015394-35544; fax 015394-35748; www.wordsworth.org.uk).

A registered charity (no. 1066184) in the heart of the Lake District. An internationally renowned literary centre with a unique collection, which offers accredited museum training.

Volunteer Museum Assistants (10) needed around the year to guide visitors around Dove Cottage, the home of William Wordsworth, help in the shop and assist in the museum with tasks including providing reception and information services, cataloguing the collection and security. To work a 37^1/2 hour, 5 day week on a 7 day rota; accommodation is available. Applicants must be aged 18 and

over. New Deal placements are available for those who are eligible.
Applications to Catherine Kay, Personnel Officer at the above address.

Social and Community Schemes

L'ARCHE: 10 Briggate Silsden, Keighley, West Yorkshire BD20 9JT (tel 01535-656186; fax 01535-656 426; e-mail info@larche.org.uk).
Seeks to reveal the particular gifts of people with learning disabilities who belong at the very heart of their communities, and who call others to share their lives. There are L'Arche communities in Kent, Inverness, Liverpool, Lambeth, Bognor, Brecon, Edinburgh and Preston where people with and without learning disabilities share life in ordinary houses.
Volunteer Assistants aged 18-65 required to share life and work with people with learning disabilities in an ecumenical Christian-based community. Volunteers receive upwards of £25 per week and free B & L. Staff required all year round for a minimum of three months. After completing the application form candidates are invited to visit the community and interviews are held. Overseas applicants in possession of the necessary work visas are welcome.
Applications by Easter to the above address.

GREAT GEORGES COMMUNITY CULTURAL PROJECT: The Blackie, Great George Street, Liverpool L1 5EW (tel 0151-709 5109; minicom/fax 0151-709 4822; staff@theblackie.org.uk).
Opportunities for anyone over 18 to try alternative education and the arts together with some sport, recreation and welfare in an inner-city context: including youth work, crafts and games; regular workshops with local youngsters; staging exhibitions and events; and projects from cookery to contemporary and African dance, from photography to fashion. Share cooking, cleaning, administration and some rebuilding work. Endless opportunities to learn and unlearn, to teach and to create. Wonderfully long hours. Stamina, a sense of humour and a sleeping bag required. Accommodation provided. Volunteers are expected to stay for at least 4 weeks and to contribute towards food costs. Volunteers are welcome throughout the year and particularly over the summer, winter and spring holiday periods. The Blackie has recently passed its 30th anniversary.
For further *information write* to the Duty Office at the above address.

MADHYAMAKA BUDDHIST CENTRE: Kilnwick Percy Hall, Kilnwick Percy, York YO42 1UF (tel 01759-304832; fax 01759-305962; e-mail info@madhyamaka.org; www.madhyamaka.org).
A large residential Buddhist college situated in a beautiful 40 acre historic estate. The centre offers a range of meditation classes and retreats suitable for all.
Volunteers (usually no more than 5 at any one time) for a variety of jobs including gardening, cleaning, cooking, painting, building and making repairs. Three vegetarian meals a day and dormitory accommodation are provided in return for work; free access is granted to a range of Buddhist meditation classes for those who are interested.
Volunteers may stay for periods of up to one week every three months; they are expected to work for 35 hours a week, or 5 hours per day if staying for a shorter period. No particular qualifications or experience are required but applicants aged over 18 are preferred. Volunteers are asked to bring their own sleeping bag and work clothes.
Applications should be sent to Working Holidays at the above address.

MANJUSHRI MAHAYANA BUDDHIST CENTRE: Conishead Priory, Ulverston, Cumbria LA12 9QQ (tel 01229-584029; fax 01229-580080; e-mail manjushri@manjushri.org.uk).

A residential Buddhist community with over 100 residents, founded in 1977 to provide a peaceful and inspiring environment where people can learn about the Buddhist way of life and practice meditation.

Volunteers needed for various duties including building, kitchen/garden help, and general household work/cleaning. Must have a good sense of humour and a willingness to work. Free board and accommodation are provided in return for work. Volunteers are also welcome to join in with centre activities such as meditation classes and courses.

Volunteers required to work 35 hours per week, Monday to Friday. Staff are needed from May to August, with a min. 1 week work period. Min. age 18. Overseas applicants with a reasonable standard of English welcome. There is no smoking or drinking alcohol on the site.

Apply year round to Fiona Hind at the above address.

Vacation Traineeships

Accountancy and Insurance

COULSONS: P.O. Box 17, 2 Belgrave Crescent, Scarborough, North Yorkshire YO11 1UD (tel 01723-364141; fax 01723-376010).

Coulsons, a firm of chartered accountants, takes on **Trainees** to work in its Scarborough office, mainly during the summer vacation. Candidates would normally be UK undergraduates intending to pursue chartered accountancy as a career. Vacation work would be offered only to students giving an undertaking to take up a training contract with Coulsons on the completion of their academic studies. Local candidates are at an advantage as accommodation is difficult to find.

For further details contact Mr P. B. Hodgson, Student Training Officer in April, at the above address. Please note that only those short-listed will be contacted.

LISHMAN SIDWELL CAMPBELL & PRICE: Administration Office, Eva Lett House, 1 South Crescent, Ripon HG4 1SN (tel 01765-608956; fax 01765-690296; e-mail j.emptage@lscp.com; www.lscp.com).

A firm of Chartered Certified Accountants established in 1938 with 16 offices stretching from Sheffield to Middlesborough. Specialists in dealing with the self-employed, sole traders, partnerships and small business units.

Lishman Sidwell Campbell & Price offers **Vacation Traineeships** to students throughout the year, although the majority of placements are held over the summer vacation. The positions may be in any of the firm's offices.

Students at any stage in their education will be considered, as long as they are seriously contemplating accountancy as a career. Suitably qualified applicants from abroad will also be considered. The salary is fixed according to their age.

Applications should be made as early as possible to the Vacation Training Officer at the above address.

Science, Construction and Engineering

BAE SYSTEMS (MARINE): Waterside House, Barrow, Cumbria, LA14 1AF (tel 01229-875833; fax 01229-875092).

Offers opportunities to approx. 20 students to undertake various projects witin the Operations, Technical, Projects and Service departments. Applicants should be university students studying Electrical Engineering, Mechanical Engineering, Naval Architecture, Engineering with Management, Business or Manufacturing systems. Salary depends on year of study.

Placements occur in June-September in Glasgow or Barrow. No accommodation is provided. Overseas applicants are considered, but security clearance may be a problem.

Applications by March/April to Stephen Grafton.

FILTRONIC COMPONENTS LTD: Airedale House, Royal London Industrial Estate, Acorn Park, Charlestown, Shipley, West Yorks BD17 7SW (tel 01274-531602; fax 01274-531539).

Filtronic Components Ltd is an expanding company dealing in the research, development and manufacture of RF and microwave filters and sub-systems. It offers occasional **Summer Vacation Placements** in electronic design and development.

Those interested should *contact* Lynne Punt, Personnel Officer, at the above address.

RELIANCE GEAR COMPANY LTD: Rowley Mills, Penistone Road, Lepton, Huddersfield HD8 OLE (tel 01484-601000; fax 01484-601001).

Reliance Gear is a design and manufacturing company which specialises in the production of precision gears and general assemblies for use in servo-mechanisms and control applications. The company serves clients in the defence, aerospace, robotic and medical engineering industries.

The company usually offers **Work Experience** over the summer to two or three students who are about to enter their final year of study. Candidates should be motivated and keen to explore the engineering sector as a potential career field. Training is offered through general experience gained in a number of the company's departments, including business sales, marketing, engineering, design, production control and quality control.

Wages are commensurate with the candidate's age, experience, qualifications and the job offered. Overseas applicants will be considered.

Applications, in early January and February, to A D Durie, Design Manager, at the above address.

TEXTRON POWER TRANSMISSION: Park Gear Works, Lockwood, Huddersfield, West Yorkshire HD4 5DD (tel 01484-465500; fax 01484-465512; e-mail hr@davidbrown.textron.com; www.textronPT.com).

Textron Power Transmission is a manufacturing company, operating worldwide in the production of high quality gears and gear units. It has occasional **Summer Vacancies** for students, who will be employed in such areas as Manufacturing Engineering, Production Control, Manufacturing and General Site Services.

Applicants should be studying Mechanical Engineering and have an interest in engineering manufacturing processes and/or gearing. Suitably qualified overseas applicants will be considered. The salary is about £150 per week and no assistance with accommodation is given.

Applications should be made to Central Personnel Training Services, at the above address.

Scotland

Prospects for Work.
The tourist industry in Scotland remains buoyant, particularly in the Highlands, Perthshire and the Islands, and has received huge boosts during the hot spells of recent summers. Since many hotels are in isolated areas, a considerable number of staff have to be recruited from outside. However, you will almost certainly be expected to work for the entire season, and should have the temperament to suit living in a remote place. The Jobcentre in Fort William is a good source for this type of work, as is the Jobcentre in Perth. The majority of hotels in rural Perthshire offer live-in accommodation, and frequently employ students over the summer. The Jobcentre in Inverness advertises vacancies as far afield as Ullapool, Gairloch and Lochcarron on the West coast and Aviemore, Kingussie and Grantown-on-Spey to the South as well as in the town itself. Due to the high level of local unemployment in less remote parts the only vacancies that remain are usually for skilled or experienced staff. While in many areas employers routinely offer accommodation, Inverness is however an exception and few live-in jobs are available there.

Fruit picking jobs are particularly abundant in Perth and Tayside. The season usually lasts from the end of June until mid-September. In addition to the vacancies listed here, fruit-picking jobs are also advertised in the Jobcentre in Blairgowrie, but not in the Jobcentre in Perth which does however list other vacancies.

Edinburgh attracts a considerable number of tourists each year, particularly during the Festival in late August. As a result there is a wide range of jobs available, particularly in hotels. With the introduction of a Scottish Parliament the need for hotel and catering staff in Edinburgh has increased further. If you speak a foreign language you could land yourself a job as a guide, and the District Council engages extra assistants and experienced gardeners to maintain the city gardens and flowers. There are always plenty of vacancies displayed in the Edinburgh Jobcentre. Note that accommodation is rarely provided with a job in Edinburgh, and can be difficult to find.

In the winter season, those seeking employment could try the skiing resorts of Aviemore, Aonach Mor and Glencoe Ski Centre.

Business and Industry

DUNDEE INDUSTRIAL HERITAGE LTD: Verdant Works, West Henderson's Wynd, Dundee DD1 5BT (tel 01382-225282; fax 01382-221612; e-mail admin@dundeeheritage.sol.co.uk)
Retail Staff And Guides (6) Wages £4.10 per hour; to work flexible and variable hours over a 7 day period. Would be an advantage if applicants had previous retail experience and another language(s). Staff are required from June onwards.
Applications should be sent to Rachel Dye at the above address.

THE EDINBURGH SMOKED SALMON CO. LTD: 1 Strathview, Dingwall Business Park, Dingwall, Ross-shire IV15 9XD (tel 01349-860600; fax 01349-860606).
Processing Workers (80) required throughout the summer. Attractive rates of pay, plus attendance and production bonuses. Previous experience may attract a higher rate of pay. Assistance can be given in locating accommodation in Dingwall or Inverness, 12 miles from Dingwall. No qualifications are required.
Applications to the Personnel Officer at the above address.

GUIDE FRIDAY: 133-135 Canongate, Edinburgh EH8 8BP (tel 0131-556 2244; fax 0131-557 4083). Guide Friday operates open-top bus tours of Edinburgh.
Ticket Sellers (5). to work outdoors. Minimum wage plus commission. To work 40 hours over 5 days per week. Min. period of work of 2 months. Positions are available from March to October. Cash sales experience and good customer care skills are an advantage. Foreign applicants welcome. No accommodation available.
Applications should be made from January onwards to Elaine Green at the above address. Interview preferable.

THE STEWARTRY MUSEUM: St Mary Street, Kirkudbright DG6 4AQ (tel/fax 01557-331643; e-mail DavidD@dumgal.gov.uk). Run by the Department for Community Resources of Dumfries and Galloway Council.
Museum Attendants (2) to assist permanent staff in the high season, working predominantly in the cafeteria at the Tolbooth Art Centre in Kircudbright. Wages approx. £4 per hour. To work 15-18 hours per week. No accommodation is available. Min. period of work 13 weeks between mid June and mid September.
Applicants should be over 18 and experience would be useful. Interview necessary. *Applications* by May 1st to Dr David F. Devereux.

Children

PGL TRAVEL: Alton Court, Penyard Lane (874), Ross-on-Wye, Herefordshire HR9 5GL (tel 01989-767833; www.pgl.co.uk/personnel). Over 50 staff needed to assist in the running of children's activity centres in Perthshire. Europe's largest provider of adventure holidays for children has offered outstanding training and work opportunities to seasonal staff for over 40 years.

Qualified Instructors in canoeing, sailing, windsurfing, pony trekking, hill walking, fencing, archery, judo, rifle shooting, fishing, motorsports, English language and many other activities. Min. age 18.

Group Leaders to care for small groups of children and ensure that they get the most out of their holiday. Previous experience of working with children necessary. Min. age 18.

Pocket money from £50-85 per week plus free B & L. Vacancies available for short or long periods between February and October. Overseas applicants eligible to work in the UK welcome.

Requests for application forms to the Personnel Department at the above address.

MRS M.E. THOMSON: Thomas Thomson (Blairgowrie), Bramblebank, Rattray, Blairgowrie PH10 7HY (tel 01250-872062; fax 01250-872266; e-mail mel@thomsonbramblebank.freeserve.uk).

Mother's Help to look after 3 children and a house, cooking etc., on a fruit farm from May/June-late August. Wages plus board, lodging and the use of a car; to work 6 days per week. Should be aged at least 22, a non-smoker and competent licensed drivers and have references; the job could suit a couple as other farm work is available for the partner. See Thomas Thomson entry under *Outdoor* section.

Applications to Mrs Melanie Thomson at the above address.

Holiday Centres and Amusements

ARDMAIR POINT CARAVAN SITE/BOAT CENTRE: Ardmair Point, Ullapool, Ross-shire (tel 01854-612054; fax 01854-612757). Situated in a scenic area 3 miles north of the fishing village of Ullapool on a beach headland facing the Summer Isles

Caravan Site Assistants (2). Duties include reception/shop work, cleaning and grass-cutting. A large proportion of the work is out of doors and involves some tractor driving.

Boat Centre Assistant (1) for boat handling. Duties include renting out small boats and equipment, assisting with repair of fibreglass boats, and the servicing and repair of outboard engines.

Easter Work. Two people required for general pre-season work.

Wage £4.75 per hour plus an end of season bonus. To work 40 hours/6 days per week, with shifts covering 8am-8pm. Accommodation available. Min. age 18 years. All jobs best suited to people interested in water sports and/or outdoor pursuits. Overseas applicants with fluent English welcome.

For further details and *applications* form send s.a.e. to the above address.

BEAUMAINE GAOL AND COURT MUSEUM: c/o Council Offices, Leisure Heritage Department, Llangefri, Anglesey LL77 7TW (tel 01248-4244444; fax 01248-750282). The gaol and court at Beaumaine is a specialist crime and punishment museum with a strong educational role.

Seasonal Museum Attendants (5) Duties include front of house work, reception, sales and customer care as well as operational maintenance and cleaning, care of

the museum and guiding tourists around the museum. Wages £4.40 per hour; to work 30 hours per week from 10.15am-5.15pm on a 7 day rota. Applicants must be Welsh speaking and available to work full-time from April 1st to September 30th.
Applications from early February to the above address. Interview necessary.

SCOTLAND CULROSS PALACE: National Trust for Scotland, Culross, Dunferwiline, Scotland,KY12 8JH (tel; 01383-880359; fax 01383-882675; e-mail cwhite@nts.org.uk). Culross Palace is a property owned by the National Trust for Scotland. It is a 17th century house and is open to the public and not a hotel.
Guides, Tearoom Assistants (5) Wages in line with the national minimum wage; to work for 20+ hours. Min. period of work 3 months from April to September. Applicants must be over 18; experience is preferred but not necessary. Would especially suit students of Tourism, History, Architecture or Catering. Overseas applicants with fluent English are welcome to apply. No accomodation available
Applications should be sent to Claire White from January onwards at the above address. Applications before March

WILLIAM GRANT & SONS: The Glenfiddich Distillery, Dufftown, Banffshire, Scotland AB55 4DH (tel 01340-820373; fax 01340-822083; e-mail david.mair@wgrant.com). Staff conduct tours of Glenfiddich Distillery in an educational but informal way. The distillery is fully operational and this type of work may particularly suit people interested in Scottish Culture or those keen on improving their foreign language skills.
Tour Guides to conduct members of the public on tours of the distillery. £173 for 32¹/2 hours per five-day week. No accommodation available but local B & B costs approx. £60-£70 per week including evening meal. Self catering accommodation can usually be found at £50-£60 per week. Min. age 18 years. Min. period of work end of June to end of August. Must be fluent in at least one foreign European language.
Experience with the general public desirable but not essential. Job requires a bright, cheery and very outgoing personality. Only applicants with fluent English considered. All applicants must be able to attend an interview at the distillery. Interviews are held before or during the Easter Vacation period.
Applications between January and March to Mr D.C. Mair at the above address in writing or by e-mail.

LADY MACPHERSON: 27 Archery Close, London W2 2BE (tel/fax 020-7262 8487).
Holiday Helpers required in holidays for a Scottish Highland home with children and animals. House is at 1,000 ft altitude and near the river Spey. Tennis court. Some indoor work and painting, general help on farm and in house. Pest control/poisons licence and chainsaw licence helpful. B & L provided, wages negotiable. Ample time for touring e.g. Loch Ness, weather rarely very warm. Two character references required.
Applications to the above address.

PRESTHAVEN SANDS HOLIDAY PARK: Shore Road, Gronant, Prestatyn, Flintshire, LL19 9TT (tel 01745-856471; fax 01745-855635). Part of the Bourne Leisure Group; an attractive all-action family holiday park near Prestiatyn and Rhyl.
Lifeguards, Pool Attendants, Bar Staff, Chefs, Receptionists, Retail Staff, Security Officers, Cleaners, Waiting Staff (250 in all): 48 types of employment offered from late April until late October. 39 hours of work a week including Public Holidays, daily hours vary according to job. Wages in line with minimum

wage legislation, with increments according to age and experience.

Except for lifeguards no qualifications are necessary, as training will be given. No live in accommodation is available, therefore applicants must secure accommodation within the local area before applying.

Applications should be sent to Trevor Lewis, Administrator, Haven Leisure Ltd, at the above address.

TUMMEL VALLEY HOLIDAY PARK: Tummel Bridge, By Pitlochry, Perthshire PH16 5SA (tel 01882-634311; fax 01882-634302).
General Assistants (2). From £3.80 per hour plus tips. Accommodation provided, for which about £19.50 per week is deducted from wages. To work 6 days per week, variable hours as required, average 48. Period of work March to October; minimum 10-12 weeks. Min. age 18. No experience needed. Overseas applicants with fluent spoken English considered.

Applications to the General Manager, Tummel Valley Holiday Park.

Hotels and Catering

ABERNETHY TRUST: Ardeonaig, by Killin, Perthshire FK21 8SY (tel 01567-820523; fax 01567-820955; e-mail AT@ardeonaig.org; www.ardeonaig.org). A residential outdoor centre.
Housekeeping Staff (2), Catering Staff (2), General Estate Workers (2) to work 5¹/₂ days a week as part of a residential Christian staff team. Wages £20 per week plus board and lodging. Staff required from June to September; minimum period of work 4 weeks. Minimum age 18. Christian commitment essential.

Applications from January to Philip Simpson, Centre Director, at the above address.

ATHOLL ARMS HOTEL: Bridgehead, Dunkeld, Perthshire PH8 0AQ (tel/fax 01350-727219). A 14-bedroomed hotel catering mainly for fishing parties and tourists, overlooking the River Tay in a conservation village.
Kitchen Porters. No experience required.
Staff (3). Some waiting, bar and kitchen experience.
Required to work 5¹/₂ days per week. Wages £4.20 per hour, accommodation available. Minimum age 21. Applications from foreign nationals permitted to work in the UK who speak English to a conversational level welcomed. Period of work April to October. Min. period of work 6 months.

Applications from January to Mr Cameron at the above address, interview necessary.

AVIEMORE HIGHLANDS HOTEL: Aviemore Mountain Resort, Inverness-shire PH22 1PJ (tel 01479-810771; fax 01479-811473; e-mail sales@aviehighlands.demon.co.uk). Situated in an all year round resort known for its superb environment and offering some of the best skiing in Scotland.
Receptionists, Bar, Waiting, Housekeping And Kitchen Staff. Temporary live-in positions offered all year round. Weekly paid, MROP.

To *apply* send c.v to the above address.

BALMORAL HOTEL: 1 Princes Street, Edinburgh EH2 2EQ (tel 0131-622 8891; fax 0131-558 1766; e-mail sforrest@thebalmoralhotel.com). A 5 star hotel in and elegant Edwardian property in the centre of Edinburgh owned by Rocco Forte Hotels.
Bar/Waiting Staff (6), Room Attendants (6). Wages for all positions from

£4.10-£4.50 per hour for a 39 hour week. To work 5-7 days per week. No accommodation is available. Applicants should be 18+ and have at least 6 months experience. Min. period of work 4 months between April and October. Overseas applicants with good English and work permit considered. Interview necessary.

Applications from March onwards to Susan Forrest at the above address.

CALEDONIAN THISTLE HOTEL: 10-14 Union Terrace, Aberdeen, Scotland AB10 1WE (tel 01224-640233; fax 01224-641627). Part of the Thistle Hotel chain, the 77 bedroom Caledonian is situated in the heart of Aberdeen city centre. **Food Service Staff (2)** for the cafe/bar or dining room. Wage £3.38 per hour (board and lodging included). To work split shifts for a 39 hour week. Min. period of work 3 months from April to October.

Staff should be at least 18 years old, and experience is preferred. Suitably qualified overseas applicants are welcome. *Applications* to Mary Martin from January onwards.

THE CEILIDH PLACE: West Argyll Street, Ullapool, Ross & Cromarty, Scotland IV26 2TY (tel 01854-612103). A complex of buildings including a small hotel with 13 rooms, a bunk house, bar, coffee room, restaurant, bookshop, gallery and venue for music and drama.
Cooks (3) with natural skill and enthusiasm.
Housestaff (2). Must be fit.
Waiting Staff to serve breakfast and dinner.
Coffee Shop Assistants (6). Serving food and drink and clearing tables.
Bar Staff (2). Serving/stocking drinks and assisting with food service.

Wages paid monthly (less board and lodging allowance). Work available between May and October, min. period 3 months: no shorter period considered. Overseas applicants eligible to work in the UK and with necessary documentation welcome.

For further information and an *applications* form write to the General Manager at the above address.

CLACHAIG INN: Glencoe, Argyll PH49 4HX (tel 01855-811252; fax 01855-811679; e-mail jobs@glencoescotland.com; www.glencoescotland.com; www.glencoe-scotland.co.uk). A busy, vibrant country inn set in the heart of Glencoe. Popular year-round with hillwalkers, climbers, mountain bikers, skiers and travellers. Specialists in real ale (award winning) with a significant food trade. A unique experience for customers and staff alike.
General Assistants (15) required throughout the year to help in all aspects of the business; bar work (serving both drinks and food), waiting on tables and helping out in the kitchen, housekeeping, renting and maintaining mountain bikes, and various odd jobs.

Previous experience is helpful, but a friendly outgoing personality and enthusiasm are more important. You must be clean and presentable, able to communicate well, and be able to work well as part of a team. Accommodation and all meals may be provided. The minimum period of work is at least 3 months. Positions are available year round; those able to work over the New Year and Easter have priority when it comes to the summer months.

Applications (with a covering letter and detailed CV) should be sent to Guy Daynes at the above address approximately one month before you are available for work.

CLIFTON HOUSE HOTEL: Nairn, Nairnshire (tel 01667-453119; e-mail macintyre@clifton-hotel.co.uk). A small hotel with a high ratio of staff to guests.

A quiet location on the coast.

Waiting Staff, House And Kitchen Assistants (6-7). Wages and hours by arrangement. B & L provided, charge to be discussed. Experience preferable but not necessary. Common sense and versatility essential. Min. work period 4 weeks between March and October. Overseas applicants who speak French or English welcome.

Applications in writing or by e-mail to Mr J. Gordon Macintyre, Proprietor, Clifton House.

CRAIGARD HOUSE HOTEL: Boat of Garten, Inverness-shire (tel 01479-831 206). Deluxe country house hotel.

Chamber Staff/Waiting Staff (3). Wages on application. Experience an advantage but not essential as training will be given. Min. age 18 years. Required to work until end of October. B & L provided for the right applicants. Overseas applicants with excellent English welcome. $5^1/_2$ days per week. Those with a good personality, willing to work hard and enjoy life in the Highlands please should make *applications* Mrs J. Cunningham at the above address.

CRAW'S NEST HOTEL: Bankwell Road, Anstruther, Fife KY10 3DA (tel 01333-310691; fax 01333-312216). A family run hotel situated to the East of Fife, 9 miles south of St Andrews. It has 50 guest bedrooms, a large function suite, dining room and 2 bars.

Kitchen Hands (2). £195 per week plus end of season bonus. No experience necessary.

Waiting Staff (3). £195 per week. Some silver service experience would be useful, though is not essential.

All staff to work 5 days per week. Accommodation available and meals provided on duty. Min. period of work 3-4 months between May and September.

Applications with photograph and s.a.e. to Mr A. Bowman at the above address.

CRIEFF HYDRO LTD: Ferntower Rd, Crieff, Perthshire PH7 3LQ (tel 01764-651612; fax 01764-653087; e-mail personnel@crieffhydro.freeserve.co.uk). Crieff Hydro is a hotel and leisure resort set in 900 acres of central Perthshire countryside, approximately 20 miles north of Stirling. 216 rooms.

Food and Drink Service Assistants (20). Wages rise from £3.70 to £4.00 per hour on completion of trial period. To work approx. 39 hours per week – overtime available. Min. period of work is 6 months. Positions are available all year. Applicants should be 18+ and have a good level of spoken English; previous hospitality experience preferred. Overseas applicants welcome subject to valid work permits/visas and other travel documents. Accommodation and meals available for £28.50 per week; this does not include insurance or supplies (towels etc.).

Applications should be made to Andrew Leaver or Kelly Fergusson at the above address. An interview is required – by phone if necessary.

CRINAN HOTEL: Crinan, nr Lochgilphead, Argyll PA31 8SR (tel 01546-830261; fax 01546-830292; www.crinanhotel.com). Fishing village and sailing centre in a beautiful location.

Waiting Staff (8), Bar Staff (6), Coffee Shop Staff (4), Room Attendants (10), Receptionists (3). Wages by arrangement; accommodation available. Experience helpful but not essential.

Applications from January to N.A. Ryan, Managing Director, at the above address, enclosing a recent full length photograph.

THE CRINAN HOTEL - SCOTLAND
Crinan, by Lochgilphead, Argyll PA31 8SR
Fishing village and sailing centre in a beautiful location.

Waiting Staff   **Bar Staff**   **Receptionists**
Coffee Shop Staff   **Room Attendants**

Wages by arrangement plus tips, food and accommodation.
Period of work at least 10 weeks between April and October.

Send applications to or telephone
Mr N.A. Ryan, Managing Director, The Crinan Hotel, Argyll, Scotland PA31 8SR.
Tel: 01546-830261 · Fax 01546-830292 · www.crinanhotel.com

CROIT ANNA HOTEL: Fort William, Inverness-shire PH33 6RR (tel 01397-702268; fax 01397-704099; e-mail croitanna@compuserver.com; www.croitanna.co.uk). A 3 star family owned hotel, situated in the most scenic part of the Scottish Highlands.
Housekeeping Staff (2), Waiting Staff (2) Wages £4 per hour; to work 36-40 hours per week. Previous experience is helpful. Accommodation is available at a charge of £2.85 per day, deducted from pay. Staff required for a minimum of 3 months between 1st April and 15th November.
Applications from March to Paul Morgan at the above address.

THE CROWNE PLAZA HOTEL EDINBURGH: 80 High Street, The Royal Mile, Edinburgh EH1 1TH (tel 0131-473 6514; fax 0131-557 9798; e-mail Humanresources@AllianceUK.com). A busy 4 star deluxe city centre hotel situated halfway between a castle and a palace, aiming to provide first class service for an international clientele.
Waiting Staff (5). Applicants must be over 18.
Chambermaids (5). Applicants must be over 16.
Wages for all positions £4.20 per hour plus 10p end of season bonus. No experience necessary. No accommodation is available. Min. period of work is 3 months. Interview necessary (but could be conducted by telephone). Overseas applicants with valid work permits considered.
Applications from March to Human Resources Department.

DALMUNZIE HOUSE HOTEL: Glenshee, Perthshire PH10 7QG (tel 01250-885 224; e-mail dalmunzie@aol.com). Country house hotel on 6,000-acre estate in a remote mountain situation.
General Hotel Staff (6). Wages and hours by arrangement according to type of job. To work 5 days a week. B & L provided. Min. age 18 years. Period of work January to late October. Overseas applicants with good English welcome. Must be able to work the whole of September and for a minimum period of 2 months in total.
Applications to Simon and Alexandra Winton, Proprietors, Dalmunzie House Hotel. Only an application enclosing s.a.e. will receive a reply.

DUNDONNELL HOTEL: Little Loch Broom, Near Ullapool, Ross-shire (tel 01854-633234; fax 01854-633366; e-mail selbie@dundonnell.hotel.co.uk; www.dundonnellhotel.com). Busy family-run 24 bedroomed hotel just south of Ullapool in an area of outstanding mountain scenery. Location is remote but beautiful, and has no discos or shops. The following staff are needed to work in the 3 star quality establishment.

ASSISTANT CHEF/COOK (WITH EXPERIENCE), COMMIS CHEF/COOK, DINING ROOM STAFF (3), ONE TO TAKE CHARGE, GENERAL ASSISTANTS (3) FOR KITCHEN AND STILLROOM, BAR STAFF (2), CHAMBER STAFF (2), PETROL STATION ATTENDANT.

From £150 per 5^1/2 day week, with higher rates for skilled and senior personnel. Free B & L in excellent accommodation (own room). Uniform provided. Min. period of work 12 weeks but longer period preferred. Most posts from Easter to October, with some from mid-May to end of September.

Applications with s.a.e. and photograph, including details of any previous work experience and dates of availability, to Mr and Mrs S.W. Florence, Dundonnell Hotel.

DUISDALE HOTEL: Sleat, Isle of Skye IV43 8QW (tel 01471-833202; e-mail marie@duisdalehotel.demon.co.uk; www.duisdale.com). A country house hotel set in 35 acres of gardens and woodland.
Kitchen Assistant (1). Some cooking experience preferred.
General Assistants (2). Mainly chambermaiding and waiting; some barwork and reception work.

Wages by arrangement. Free B & L provided. Min. age 20. Previous experience preferred. Min. period of work 2 months between April and October. Overseas applicants with fluent English accepted. Staff have each afternoon free as they do not open for lunch.

Applications to Mrs Campbell, Duisdale Hotel.

EDINBURGH CITY TRAVEL INN: 1 Morrison Link, Edinburgh EH3 8DN (tel 0131-656 4344; fax 0131-228 9836). 'Travel Inn' is one of the the biggest and best budget hotel brands in the UK.
Room Attendants (10). To work for 5 days and approx. 40 hours per week.
Food and Beverage Waiting Staff (10). Full and part-time work available. Some experience is preferable.

Wages negotiable, board and accommodation available. Min. period of work of 3 months. Positions are available from July to September. Foreign applicants are welcome but good English must be spoken and bank account and a National Insurance number required.

Applications should be made from June onwards to Elaine Salton at the above address. Interview necessary.

HILTON EDINBURGH GROSVENOR HOTEL: Grosvenor Street, Edinburgh EH12 5EF (tel 0131-226 6001; fax 0131-220 2387; e-mail personnel.manager@edinburgh.stakis.co.uk).
Room Assistants (10) to work 8:30-4:30 for 39 hours a week.
Breakfast Servers (6) to work 6-11:30am for 5 days a week.
Banqueting Hosts (15-20) to work approx.15 hours a week.
Wage for all positions minimum of £4.40 per hour. Training will be given.

Leisure Club Staff (2). Wages £3.45-£3.65 per hour; to work 39 hours per week. Applicants must be 18 or over, those who have pool lifeguard and first aid certificate are preferred.

Housekeeping Staff (2). Wages £3.35-£3.65 per hour; to work at least 16 hours a week. Applicants must be at 16 or over. Period of work from May to September. Minimum period of work 2 months.

Applications from April to the Personnel and Training Manager at the above address.

FREEDOM OF THE GLEN HOTELS: Creag Dhu House, Onich, Near Fort William, Invernesshire, Scotland PH33 4RT (tel 01855-821582; fax 01855-821463; e-mail jobs@freedomglen.co.uk). Three distinctive hotels all in superb Lochside locations offering quality Highland hospitality. Staff can enjoy leisure facilites as well as living and working in the Scottish Highlands.

Service Staff (45), Porters (5), Housekeeper (25), General Assistants (14), Receptionists (11) Wages are £120-£160 per week. All positions are live in, if required (£45 per week full board and lodging) and generally comprise 45 hours per week with a mixture of straight and split shifts. Min. period of work of 3 months. Positions are available from April to October. Previous experience useful, but not essential. Foreign applicants with work permits and acceptable spoken English welcome.

Applications should be made from mid February onwards to Ruth Sime at the above address or completed on-line using www.highlandjobs.com.

GEORGE INTERCONTINENTAL EDINBURGH: 19-21 George Street, Edinburgh EH2 2PB (tel 0131-225-125; fax 0131-226-5644; e-mail sandra – mackinnon@interconti.com). This 195 bedroom hotel is a 4 star de luxe establishment in the city centre. There is a fine dining room, a carvery restaurant, a clan bar and banqueting facilities.

Hall Porter (1). Applicants must possess a driving licence.

Customer Service Agents (3) for the restaurant.

Customer Service Agents (5) for banqueting operations.

For all positions: wages from £9,387 p.a. pro rata, working 40 hours per 5 day week (less considered for banquet work). Minimum age 18; minimum period of work is six months; positions are available between March/April and November/December. Limited accomodation is available (£70 all-inclusive single room, £55 to share). Applicants should be interested in Personnel, enjoy working in a busy and friendly environment, and be able to provide a highly professional service. Foreign applicants with work permits and an ability to understand and speak English are welcome.

Applications should be made from February/March onwards to Sandra MacKinnon or Catherine MacFarlane at the above address. Interview required.

GRAND ISLAND HOTEL: Bride Road, Ramsey, Isle of Man IM8 3UN (tel 01624-812455; fax 01624-815291). A beautiful Georgian hotel overlooking the Ramsey Bay, offering 2 restaurants, bars and leisure facilities.

Day/Night Porters (2), Chef De Partie/Commis Chefs (3), Chambermaids (3), Food/Beverage Staff (4), Receptionist, Trainee Managers (2).

To work 40 hours per week. Details of wages, accommodation etc. on application. Live-in staff accommodation as part of the package at £20 a week. To work from April onwards. All applicants must be college trained.

Applications should be sent to The Deputy/Operations Manager, at the above address.

THE GROG AND GRUEL: Traditional Alehouse and Restaurant, 66 High Street, Fort William PH33 6AE (tel 01397-705078; e-mail jobs@grogandgruel. co.uk; www.grogandgruel.co.uk). A traditional Alehouse situated in the town centre serving a selection of real ales and malt whiskies, with a family restaurant on the upper level, offering home-cooked dishes. Run by brothers Guy and Edward Daynes whose approach to business is informal and friendly – a blend of fun and hard work.

General Assistants (5) to help in bar and restaurant, and possibly in the kitchen. To work a 5 day week (occasionally 6 days) of typically 40 hours. Min. period of work 3 months.

Accommodation cannot be provided, but is available locally. Staff should be at least 18 years old, but enthusiasm and a friendly, outgoing personality are more important than experience.

For further details, or an *application form,* contact the General Manager at the above address.

HILTON EDINBURGH AIRPORT HOTEL: Edinburgh International Airport, Edinburgh EH28 8LL (tel 0131-519 4400; fax 0131-519 4422; e-mail Personnel.manager@edinairport.stakis.co.uk). Recently built 150 bedroom hotel and leisure club within the boundaries of Edinburgh airport, popular with both tourists and business travellers.

Room Assistants (4), Bistro Hosts (Breakfast and Bar) (8). Wage for both positions £4.34 per hour. All staff to work 5 days out of 7 to make up 39 hours. No accommodation is available but meals on duty are provided. Min. period of work 3 months between March and December.

Experience is preferred, although training can be given. Applicants must be over 18. Overseas applicants with a working knowledge of English considered. Interview necessary.

Applications any time to the Personnel Department.

HILTON EDINBURGH GROSVENOR HOTEL: Grosvenor Street, Edinburgh EH12 5EF (tel 0131-226 6001; fax 0131-220 2387; e-mail personnel.manager@edinburgh.stakis.co.uk).

Room Assistants (10) to work 8:30-4:30 for 39 hours a week.

Breakfast Servers (6) to work 6-11:30am for 5 days a week.

Banqueting Hosts (15-20) to work approx.15 hours a week.

Wage for all positions minimum of £4.40 per hour. Training will be given. *Applications* to the above address.

HILTON PLC: Coylumbridge Hotel, Coylumbridge, Aviemore, Inverness-shire PH22 1QN (tel 01479-813076; fax 01479-811706; e-mail hr-coylumbridge@hilton.co.uk). Hilton Aviemore operates 3 hotels and a family entertainment facility in the heart of the Scottish Highlands, whose attractions include golf, watersports and horse riding.

Kitchen, Restaurant Waiting, Bar, & Housekeeping Staff required. To work 39 hours over a 5-day week. Salary £4.01 per hour. Min. age 18. Experience preferred. Overseas applicants with basic English (communication level) welcome. Staff required from June to October. Min. period of work 12 weeks. Accommodation paid for out of wages at a rate of 70p per hour for 39 hours work.

Applications from April/May to the Personnel Department at the above address.

HOLIDAY INN EDINBURGH: Corstorphine Road, Edinburgh EG12 6UA (tel 0870-400 9026; fax 0131-334 9237). Edinburgh's largest hotel with 303 bedroom, various restaurants, bars and leisure facilities.

Waiting Staff (10), Housekeeping Assistants (15), Kitchen Porters (2). Wages of £4.10 per hour for a 40 hour week completed over shifts; uniforms and meals when on duty also provided. Min. period of work of 6 months. Positions are available from April to October. Full training provided. Minimum age 16. No previous experience necessary. Foreign applicants with work permits and acceptable spoken English welcome. No accommodation available.

Applications should be made from March onwards to the Operations Manager at the above address. Interview required by phone if necessary.

HUNTING TOWER HOTEL: Crieff Road, Perth PH1 3JT (tel 01738-583771; fax 01738-583777; e-mail michwlee@aol.com).

Staff for food and beverage service including breakfasts, lunches, dinners, weddings and functions. Wages by arrangement depending on experience plus tips; to live in or out. To work 5 days out of seven including weekends; period of work by arrangement. Applicants with experience of working in a four star country house hotel preferred.

Applications to Michael Lee at the above address.

INVERSNAID PHOTOGRAPHY CENTRE: Inversnaid Lodge, by Aberfoyle, Stirling FK8 3TU (tel 01877-386254; e-mail linda@inversnaidphoto.com; www.inversnaidphoto.com). A residential photography workshop centre which hosts tutors of international repute in areas such as landscape, wildlife, and documentary. Situated on the shores of Loch Lomond, in an area of outstanding natural beauty 1¹/2 hours from Glasgow.

Domestic Helper (1) for general cleaning duties and helping in the centre. Wages £125 per week with free B & L provided. To work 40 hours a week. Min. age 20 and non-smoker. Cleaning and waiting experience preferable. Overseas applicants with good English will be considered. Min. period of work 6 months between April and October. Would prefer applicants to attend an interview.

Applications from February to Ms Linda Middleton at the above address.

LEDGOWAN LODGE HOTEL: Achnasheen, Wester Ross, Highlands of Scotland IV22 2EJ (tel 01445-720252; e-mail info@ledgowanlodge.co.uk; www.ledgowanlodge.co.uk). In an excellent hill walking area attracting clientele from all over the world.

Cocktail Bar, House, Pantry, Kitchen And Waiting Staff. Average gross wage £200 per working 6-day week, depending on age and experience. To work approx. 50 hours a week with 1 day off. Accommodation available in own room. Min. period of work 12 weeks between Easter and October. Overseas applicants with fluent English considered.

Send *Applications* a.s.a.p., enclosing photograph, age and references if possible, to Mr G.T. Millard, Ledgowan Lodge Hotel.

LOCH NESS LODGE HOTEL: Drumnadrochit, Inverness-shire IV63 6TU (tel 01456-450342; fax 01456-450429; e-mail donald@lochness-centre.com or info@ Lochness-hotel.com). Highland lodge which dates back to 1740, near Loch Ness.

All positions in a hotel (50). Wages by arrangement with accommodation provided. Period of work from May to October. Applicants should be aged between 17 and 50; previous experience not necessary.

Applications to Mrs Mary MacIntash, Manager, at the above address.

LOMOND WALKING HOLIDAYS: 34C James St, Riverside, Stirling, Scotland FK8 1UG (tel/fax 01786-447752; e-mail paul@milligan.force9.co.uk). A family-operated company offering a full range of guided walking holidays throughout Scotland.

Holiday Assistants; duties will include driving, shopping and meal preparation. Wages are £200 per week plus meals and accommodation. To work 5-6 hours per day, 7 days a week. Min. period of work is 1 week. Positions are available from April to October. Applicants need to be over 24, have a full, clean driving licence, previous experience of driving vans, and the ability to cook for small groups in hostels.

Applications should be made to Paul Milligan at the above address from November onwards.

MSL LEISURE: Beachcomber, The Promenade, Leven, Fife KY8 4HY (tel 01333-426820; fax 01333-429700; e-mail mmj@msl-leisure.co.uk). Leisure company incorporating amusements, childrens fun park and various food outlets.

Café Assistants (3) to cook, clean and possibly organise children's birthday parties. Wages by arrangement. To work 9.30am-9pm in 4/5 hour shifts. Min. period of work of 2 months. Positions are available from June to September. No accommodation available.

Applications should be made from March onwards to Mr Morris at the above address. Interview necessary.

McTAVISH'S KITCHENS (OBAN) LTD: McTavish's Kitchens, 8 Argyll Square, Oban PA34 4BA or McTavish's Kitchen, High Street, Fort William PH33 6AD (e-mail oban@mctavishs.com or fatwilliam@mctavishs.com). Restaurants in the beautiful West Highland towns of Oban and Fort William.

Food Service, Self-Service Assistants, Kitchen Assistants, Cooks, Drinks Service And Cleaners. There are a number of vacancies, particularly for students, between April and October and also late availability mid-August to end of September. Rate of pay not less than the legal minimum. Accommodation available. EU Nationals or evidence of permission to work in the UK.

Applications in writing with photograph and s.a.e., to the above address.

MONESS HOUSE HOTEL AND COUNTRY CLUB: Crieff Road, Aberfeldy, Perthshire PH15 2DY (tel 01887-820446; fax 01887-820062). A private company offering holiday accommodation in a 12 bedroom hotel and 88 self catering cottages situated in 35 acres of grounds overlooking the picturesque town of Aberfeldy in the heart of Scotland.

Bistro Staff (2), Restaurant Staff (2). Wages from £4.25 per hour live-in. Must be over 18 with food service experience. Bistro staff must have wine service experience.

All staff to work 39 hours a week. Min. period of work 10 weeks between April and October. Overseas applicants with good working English considered. Interview not necessary.

Applications from Feb/Mar to the General Manager.

MORTON HOTELS LTD: The Royal Golf Hotel, Dornoch, Sutherland, IV25 3LG, Scotland (tel 01862-810283; fax 01862-810923).

Breakfast Chef (1-2) to work from 6am-2.30pm; duties consist of preparing breakfasts and lunches and for general kitchen preparation.

Commis chefs (1/2) to help kitchen with breakfasts, lunches and dinners. Wages (+22 years old) £4.10 per hours, (18-21) £3.45 per hour, with live in accommodation available for £20 per week. Period of work May-November.

Applications to Nicola Sharp, Personnel Manager.

NEWTON LODGE: Kylesku, Sutherland IV27 4HW (tel 01971-502070; e-mail newtonlge@aol.com; www.smoothHound.co.uk/hotels/newton). A small hotel in the remote North West Highlands. Ideal place to save money for the summer.
General Assistant required for duties as required including dining room, kitchen help, bedroom work and general cleaning. Wage £120 per 6 day week, including room with shower and meals. Period of work mid May to mid September. Must have previous hotel experience. Non-smoker only.
Applications with photo and reference to Mrs Brauer.

PRIORY HOTELS LTD: The Square, Beauly, Invernessshire IV4 7BX (tel 01463-782309; fax 01463-782531; e-mail reservations@priory.hotel.com; www.priory.hotel.com). Small company operating hotels and restaurants in Invernessshire.
Kitchen Assistants (4), Front Of House Staff/General Assistants (6) required to work in busy hotels in Beauly and Dalwhinnie. Hours: 40 per week. From £120, plus free B & L. Smart appearance, good interpersonal skills and bags of common sense essential. Min. period of work 3 months but six month contract preferred. Good fun with a bustling team of people. Overseas applicants with valid work permit welcome.
Applications any time to Mr S.A. Hutton, Director, at the above address.

QUALITY HOTEL CENTRAL: 99 Gordon Street, Glasgow G1 3SF (tel 0141-221 9680; fax 0141-226 3948; e-mail admin@gb627.u-net.com). A 222-bedroom Victorian railway hotel.
Waiting Staff (1) to work in hotel restaurant. Hours: 7am-10.30am, 11am-2.30pm and 5.30pm-10.30pm.
Housekeeper/Room Attendant (1). Working hours 8am-3pm and 5-8pm.
All staff receive £4.10 per hour if over 22 years and £3.50 if under. Accommodation available for £22.75 per week. Period of work June to December.
Applications to Paul Catford, Regional Personnel Manager, at the above address.

RAASAY OUTDOOR CENTRE: Isle of Raasay, By Kyle, Ross-shire, Scotland IV40 8PB (tel 01478-660266; fax 01478-660200; e-mail info@raasayoutdoorcentre.co.uk). An outdoor centre located on a remote and peaceful Hebridean Island. Sailing, windsurfing, kayaking and climbing offered to clients.
Kitchen Manager (1). Must have at least 6 years cooking and organisational experience. Wages negotiable depending on experience.
Preparation Cooks (2). Must have general cooking experience. Wages negotiable depending on experience.
Kitchen Assistants (2). To perform kitchen preparation and washing up duties. Must be motivated. Wages negotiable depending on experience.
Cafe/Bar/Shop Assistants (3). Must have experience and be organised and motivated. Wages negotiable depending on experience.
Housekeeper (1). Must have organisational and cleaning experience. Wages negotiable depending on experience.
Childminder (1). Must have experience of looking after a three year old. Wages negotiable depending on experience.
Office Person (1). Must have worked in an office and have good computer skills, enjoy working with people and be organised.
All positions are for 44 hours work per week between March and October. Min. period of work 1 month. Board, accommodation and activities provided.
Overseas applicants must speak good English. Interview is necessary.
Applications from March to Freya Rowe at the above address.

ROSEDALE HOTEL: Portree, Isle of Skye IV51 9DB (tel 01478-613131; fax 01478-612531). A family-run hotel located on the harbourside in Portree, the administrative and commercial capital of the island and the adjoining mainland.
Receptionist/Duty Manager (1). Min. age 24. Must be educated to at least A level standard and be well presented, articulate and mature. Hotel background and training essential.
Second Chef (1). City and Guilds 706/1 and 706/2 required, plus two years' post-qualification experience. To assist AA rosette chef and be able to take charge in his absence preparing quality food with imagination and style.
General Assistants (6). To work a mixed rota in many departments but mainly restaurant and bar, with some housekeeping. Aged 21+. Should be well presented, articulate and interested in working with people. Hotel experience an advantage.
Wages specified on application. All staff work approx. 40-45 hours per week. Min. period of work early May to mid October. Priority given to those able to work the full or greater part of the season. An end of season share of gratuities is made upon completion of contract period. Non-smoking applicants only.
Write for an *application form* from mid-February to Mrs Rouse, Manager, at the above address.

THE ROYAL HOUSEHOLD: Buckingham Palace, London SW1A 1AA (tel 020-7930 4832; fax 020-7360 7125).
Assistants for general cleaning/laundry duties of staff accommodation/bedding, and the occasional cleaning of more isolated buildings used for barbecues, at Balmoral Castle. Must be able to work from mid July to mid October inclusive. Not suitable for students returning to college in September. Wages on application; accommodation is provided, as are meals during court visits. To work up to 35 hours per week on a rota. Applicants should be aged between 18 and 50; no previous experience is necessary as training is given. All staff to be security screened before employment; this can take up to 2 months if candidates are from overseas.
Applications, by April at the latest, to Miss Heather Colebrook, Chief Housekeeper, at the above address.

ROYAL ZOOLOGICAL SOCIETY OF SCOTLAND: Edinburgh Zoo Members House, 134 Corstorphine Road, Edinburgh EH12 6TS (tel 0131-334 5001; fax 0131-334 7462). Edinburgh Zoo is Scotland's second most popular tourist attraction, with over half a million visitors a year viewing the world-famous animal collection.
General Catering Assistants (40) for work involving cash handling, customer service and general duties in a busy bistro style restaurant within the zoo. Wages £4 per hour.
Waiting Assistants to work in the highly rated members' restaurant and lounge. Wages of £4 per hour plus tips.
These wages may change depending on the timescale for implementation of minimum wage legislation. To work around 4-8 hours overtime a week at $1^1/2$ times the usual rate. Experience of previous similar work preferred but not essential as full training is provided. To work from 10am-6pm, 5 days a week. Period of work from May to October.
Applications to E Gray, Commercial Services Manager, at the above address.

RUFFLETS COUNTRY HOUSE HOTEL: Strathkinness Low Road, St. Andrews KY16 9TX (tel 01334-472594; fax 01334-478703; e-mail john@rufflets.co.uk; rufflets.co.uk). A privately owned 22 bedroom upmarket hotel which holds two AA rosettes for food quality; young and friendly staff.

Housekeeping Assistant (1), Restaurant Assistant (1), Lounge Service Assistant (1). Wages range from £3.75 (under 21 years) to £4.25 per hour. All staff to work hours as required, 5 days out of 7. Accommodation is available at £3.50 per day. Min. period of work 6 months between 1st April and 30th November.

Experience is not essential, but all applicants must be over 18 years old. European and Australian applicants fluent in English considered. Interview not always necessary.

Applications from January to John Angus.

SCOTLAND'S HOTEL: Bonnethill Road, Pitlochry, Perthshire, Scotland PH16 5BT (tel 01796-472292; fax 01796-473284; stay@scotlands.co.uk). A 75 bedroom hotel with conference facilities, a leisure club, and an Italian restaurant, situated in an excellent location, just two hours away from Edinburgh, Glasgow, Aberdeen and Inverness.

Bar Assistant. £150 per week. Min. age 18 years. Split and straight shifts.
Waiting Staff (2). £150 per week. Silver service training or experience preferred. Split shifts.
House Staff (2). £150 per week. Cleaning or housekeeping experience preferred. Split and straight shifts.

All staff to work 8 hours per day, 5 days per week with no overtime. Single bedroom accommodation available. Free meals on and off duty. Health and Leisure club restricted membership for all staff. Uniform provided and training will be given. Min. period of work 2 months between April and October. Overseas applicants with a good knowledge of English welcome. Where possible it is preferred that applicants are available for interview.

Applications from March to the Personnel Manager at the above address.

STONEFIELD CASTLE GROUP: Stonefield Castle Group, Castlehill, Howwood, Renfrewshire PA9 1DB (tel 0150-570 4000; fax 0150-5703000). Stonefield Castle Group is a collection of hotels and other leisure businesses all located in the West of Scotland.

Waiting Staff. Full-time and part-time positions are available. To work at least 16 hours per week. Applicants should be at least 16 years old.
Leisure Club Staff. To work 40 hours per week. Applicants must be 18 or over, those who have pool lifeguard and first aid certificate are preferred.
Housekeeping Staff. To work at least 16 hours a week. Applicants must be at least 16 or over.

Period of work from May to September. Minimum period of work 2 months. Wages £3.50-£5.00 per hour.

Applications from April to the Personnel and Training Manager at the above address.

SWALLOW HOTEL: 517 Paisley Road West, Glasgow GS1 1RW (tel 0141-427 3146; fax 0141-4190 1602). 3 star, 117 bedroomed hotel near the city centre with leisure facilities, priding itself on excellent customer care and service.

Restaurant Waiting Staff (10), House assistants (4). Wages from £4.10 per hour, various hours. Min. period of work of 2 months. Positions are available from May to August. Experience an advantage. Minimum age 16. No accommodation available.

Applications should be made from March onwards to Angela Bennett at the above address. Interview necessary.

SUMMER ISLES HOTEL: Achiltibuie by Ullapool, Ross-shire IV26 2YG (tel 01854-622282). A remote but renowned hotel offering excellent food and service in a relaxed informal setting. Located on the west coast of Scotland and set in magnificent scenery.

General Assistants for waiting, bar, housekeeping and kitchen.

Wages min. £152 for 50 hours/6 days per week. Free B & L provided. Experience preferred but training given. Applicants should be available for whole season, starting April/May. The jobs are suited to professional motivated people prepared to work hard and make the most of their free time by enjoying outdoor activities.

Applications, with s.a.e. and photograph, to Mr Mark Irvine, Summer Isles Hotel.

THAINSTONE HOUSE HOTEL: Inverurie, Aberdeenshire AB51 5NT (tel 01467-621643; fax 01467-625084; e-mail thainstone.macdonald-hotel.co.uk). A four star country house hotel and leisure club, committed to training employees to a high level.

Waiting Staff (4), Bartenders (2), Housemaids (2). Wages by arrangement. All positions to work a 39 hour week. Min. period of work 3 months Between May and the end of September.

Board and accommodation is available for a 10p deduction from the hourly wage. There are no deductions for meal breaks, and staff may use the hotel leisure facilities. Experience is preferable, but training will be given. References are required.

Applications from April onwards to the Personnel Manager.

M.F. WELLS (HOTELS) LTD.: Gartocharn, Dumbartonshire G83 8RW (tel 01389-713713; fax 01389-713721; e-mail liz.nicols@lochsandglens.com; www.lochandglens.com). A family run hotel and tour group with 5 hotels and its own fleet of coaches.

Kitchen Assistant, Dining Room Staff, Housekeeping Staff & Bar Staff to work 40 hours a week. Wages from £580, accommodation available. Minimum period of work 12 weeks at any time of year; dates of work negotiable.

Applications at any time to Mrs E. Nicols at the above address.

WOODLEA HOTEL: Moniaive, Dumfries-shire DG3 4EN (tel 01848-200209). **General Assistants (2).** £4.20 per hour live-out, for employees over 21 years. Tips in addition. To work variable hours. B & L available for females only. Expected to help in all aspects of hotel including serving in the bar, toilet cleaning and kitchen and dining room work. Staff free to use swimming pool and other sports facilities when not in use by guests. Work available from Easter to end of October. Min. work period 3 months, preferably to the end of September.

Applications enclosing s.a.e., 2 references, personal details, a recent photograph and dates of availability, to Mr M.R. McIver at the above address.

THE WESTIN TURNBERRY RESORT: Turnberry Hotel, Maidens Road, Turnberry, Ayrshire KA26 9LT (tel 01655-331000; fax 01655-331879). A 5 star, luxury golf resort with 132 guest bedrooms and 89 golf lodge rooms over 800 acres on the coast of Scotland. The Resort is part of Starwood Hotels and Resorts Inc, the world's leading upscale hotel company.

Commis Chef. Wages £718 per month.

Chef De Partie. Wages £1,008 per month.

Food and Beverage Waiting Assistant. Wages £718 per month.

Room Attendant. Wages £707 per month.

Guest Service Agent – Front Desk. Wages £786 per month.

Guest Service Agent – Concierge. Wages £697 per month.

Beauty Therapists. Wages £810 per month.

Golf Retail Assistants. Wages £699 per month.

Greenkeepers. Wages £661 per month.

Pool and Gymn Attendant. £810 per month.

Accommodation is provided at a charge of £230 per month inclusive of resort transport and meals. All staff work 39 hours per week with opportunities for overtime. Staff are required between April and June and finish in September or October. Applicants must be eligible to work in the European Union.

Applications should be made in writing to Hamish Peterson, Human Resources Manager at the above address or via e-mail to deborah.allen@westin.com.

Language Schools

EDINBURGH SCHOOL OF ENGLISH: 271 Canongate, The Royal Mile, Edinburgh EH8 8BQ (tel 0131-557 9200; fax 0131-557 9192; e-mail english@edinburghschool.ac.uk). Founded in 1969, ESE is a year round school. Courses are directed by permanent staff, and have the back up of a permanent organisation. Arranges English language summer courses for school children (9-17 years) in Edinburgh and Strathallan.

Activity Leaders to be responsible for the smooth running of the afternoon, evening and weekend leisure programme. The job involves taking students on various cultural visits and organising and supervising sports. One leader is employed for every 10 students. Some leaders are required to live and supervise in halls of residence in addition to the above. Hours by arrangement. B & L available for a few applicants only. Courses are run between mid-June and early September, and also during April. Min. period of work 3 weeks.

Applicants should be aged over 21, with a sound knowledge of one of the above locations. They should be enthusiastic and energetic, have good organisational abilities, get on well with teenagers and be interested in sports and cultural visits. Fluent English speakers only.

Applications to The Principal at the above address.

SCOT-ED COURSES: 6 Blinkbonny Gardens, Edinburgh EH4 3HG (tel 0131-332 1060; fax 0131-623 2154; e-mail scot-ed@cableinet.co.uk). An accredited language school that specialises in summer courses.

EFL Teachers (15) to teach in the summer school. Wages £180 per week, accommodation included. Three hours of teaching per day plus activities, applicants must be CELTA qualified graduates. Foreign applicants eligible to work in the UK welcome. Period of work 20 June-31 August. Minimum period of employment 2 weeks.

Applications from 1 May to John Young at the above address.

Outdoor

BALMORAL ESTATES: Estates Office, Balmoral, Ballater, Aberdeenshire AB35 5TB (tel 013397-42334; fax 013397-42271; www.balmoralestate.co.uk).

Grouse Beaters (6) to work from mid August to the end of September. Beaters receive £18.50 per day plus accommodation, dinner, bed, breakfast and packed lunch in exchange for working 8am-5pm. Applicants must be healthy and fit enough for a day's walking in the Scottish hills.

Applications to P.J. Ord at the above address.

A.P. BARRIE & CO: Colbeggie Farm, Coupar Angus, Perthshire, Scotland PH13 9HA (tel 01828-628666; fax 01828-627878; e-mail apbarrie@sol.co.uk). A specialist producer of soft fruit. Friendly atmosphere with many nationalities.

Fruit Pickers, Packers And Supervisors. Training will be provided. A large

---

A.P. BARRIE
REQUIRE
FRUIT PICKERS & PACKERS
Peak Season 20th June – 20th August

Tel.: 01828-628666

---

amount of picking is done under protection from rain, so full days in good crops are assured. Good piecework rates are offered for those willing to work hard. Must be willing to work long hours when required, but usually 8 hours a day for 5-6 days a week. Period of work April-October. All applicants must be on the farm by 10th July.

Accommodation either in caravans or bring your own tent. Hot showers, kitchen, dining room, recreational areas, games room and laundry area are provided. Entertainment such as Scottish dancing, discos, barbeques and football matches are arranged for the weekends. Bicycles can be borrowed to get to the nearest town, 1¹/2 miles away. Applicants from outside the EU are welcome if they have valid work permits; the farm regrets that it cannot help obtain these.

Applications in writing to Mr Barrie or by e-mail, see above.

MR S. CAMPBELL: Cairntradlin, Kinellar, Aberdeenshire AB21 0SA (tel 01224-790056; fax 01224-791581). A farm growing strawberries and raspberries for supermarkets and a local pick-your-own, situated 7 miles from Aberdeen. **Strawberry/Raspberry Pickers (15).** Piece work rates paid daily. Picking as and when required, weather and crop conditions permitting; days off as arranged. Social evenings, e.g. barbecues and Scottish nights, arranged for student workers. Self-catering accommodation (7) provided in portacabins, with male and female dormitories, kitchen, toilets and showers. Camping area also available for those with equipment. Applicants must bring eating utensils, warm sleeping bags and warm clothing. Period of work 5 July until the end of August. Overseas applicants welcome.

Applications to Mr S. Campbell at the above address. Enclose a stamped addressed envelope to ensure a reply.

HAROLD CORRIGALL: Leadketty Farm, Dunning, Perthshire PH2 0QP (tel 01764-684532; fax 01764-684146; e-mail harold@leadketty.freeserve.co.uk). A small farm with 20 acres of strawberries (9 under tunnels) and 3 acres of raspberries. **Fruit Pickers (10).** Wages approx. £35-£55 per day; to work 7am-4pm per day, 6 days a week. Accommodation is available at a charge of £20 per week. Staff required for a minimum of 4 weeks between June and late August. Applicants must be 18 or over. The farm takes many European students with appropriate permits or authorisation.

Applications from February to Harold Corrigall at the above address.

D.& B. GRANT: Wester Essendy, Blairgowrie, Perthshire PH10 6RA (tel 01250-884389; e-mail cmgrant99@yahoo.com).

Fruit Pickers (50) to pick strawberries and raspberries. Help also required to process fruit for freezing. To work 6 days a week. Rates and shifts to be negotiated. Caravan accommodation provided free of charge. Period of work from July 10 to August 31.

Applications to Colin M. Grant at the above address via e-mail or post with sae.

W. HENDERSON: Seggat, Auchterless, Turriff, Aberdeenshire AB53 8DL (tel 01888-511223; fax 01888-511434). Situated in the heart of the castle and distillery county of Aberdeenshire.
Strawberry Pickers/Packers. Piece work rates: around £20 per day but dependent on size of crop and weather. To work 7 hours per day, 6 days per week, but must be prepared to work variable hours. Self-catering accommodation available, for which there is a charge of £10 per week, but must bring own sleeping bag and eating utensils. Situated 1 mile from main road, with regular bus service between Aberdeen and Inverness. Period of work early July to mid August, min. 4 weeks.

Applications from 30 January onwards to Mr W. Henderson, at the above address.

LOWES FRUIT FARM: Campend Farm, Dalkeith EH22 1RS (tel 0131-220-0416; fax 0131-220- 0417; e-mail sharon@caledoniantrust.com) A busy seasonal fruit farm with a farm shop.
Fruit Pickers (10) Wages piece rate, to work from 8am-4pm.
Shop Staff (3) Wages piece rate, to work from 10am-6pm.
Staff are required from end of June to the end of August for a min. period of 6 weeks. Applicants must be over 18. Basic acommodation is available for £10 per week.

Applications should be made to Sharon at the above address from April.

PURVIS MARQUEES: 50 Lindsay Road, Edinburgh EH6 6NW (tel 0131-554 1331; fax 0131-553 7655; e-mail neil@hibs20.freeserve.co.uk).
Marquee Erectors wanted to work over the summer for around £4 per hour dependant on skills. The work involves erecting and dismantling marquees throughout the UK often working a 7 day week. Applicants should be quick to learn, impervious to the weather and have a sense of humour.

Applications to the above address.

L.M. PORTER: East Seaton, Arbroath, Angus, Scotland DD11 5SD (tel 01241-879989; fax 01241-871220; e-mail susanlmporter@netscapeonline.co.uk). East Seaton is situated on the clifftops by Arbroath where conditions are ideal for growing fruit for Marks and Spencer, Tescos, Sainsburys, Safeway and Asda.
Strawberry/Raspberry Pack House Staff/Pickers (20) for soft fruit picking, in July and August. Piece rate. Hours can vary with the weather conditions but otherwise average 8 hours a day. Youth hostel type accommodation and camp site facilities available. Applicants must be fit as work is hard but well rewarded.

Applications to Deborah Porter, Partner, at the above address.

THOMAS THOMSON (BLAIRGOWRIE) LTD: Bramblebank Works, Blairgowrie, Perthshire PH10 7HY (tel 01250-872266; fax 01250-876092; e-mail thomson@brambank.freeserve.co.uk). The family owned farms are 1km from Blairgowrie in beautiful Perthshire. Produces quality fruit (most with rain protection) for supermarkets. Discos and Scottish dances arranged after work.

STRAWBERRY/RASPBERRY PICKERS (100). Piecework rates, approx. £25-£60 per day. To work 6/7 days a week. No experience required. Min. period of work 6 weeks between 10 June and 20 September. Accommodation available in caravans for £17.50 per week. Overseas applicants welcome, but must have valid work permit, e.g. through Concordia, if outside EU or not studying in UK.

Applications should be made from 1 January to Mrs Melanie Thomson at the above address.

Sport

CAIRNWELL MOUNTAIN SPORTS: Gulabin Lodge, Spittal of Glenshee, Blairgowrie PH10 7QE (tel 0870-4430253; fax 0870-4430254; e-mail cairnwell.h@virgin.net; www.cairnwellmountainsports.co.uk). A multi activity centre and hostel for 30-40 persons. In winter activities include ski school, snow board school and nordic skiing; in summer climbing, walking, hang gliding and adventures activities.

Ski Instructors(2) Wages £200 per week; to work 6 days per week. Must have a national qualification. Required from January 5th to March 10th for a minimum of 5-10 weeks.

Activity Instructors (2) Wages £200 per week; to work 6 days per week. Applicants must have a national qualification. Required from April 16th to June 16th for a minimum of 4 weeks.

Lodge Worker(1) Wages £160 per week. No experience necessary. Required from December to May 30th.

Overseas *Applications* are welcome for the posts of lodge worker and ski instructor.Accommodation is available at a cost of £50 per week.

Applications should be sent to Gustav Fischnaller at the above address as soon as possible. Interview and references are necessary.

CALEDONIAN DISCOVERY LTD: The Slipway, Corpach, Fort William PH33 7NN (tel 01397-772167; fax 01397-772765; e-mail Fingal@sol.co.uk; www.fingal-cruising.co.uk). Organises activity holidays based on a barge cruising the Caledonian Canal/Loch Ness. The 12 guests take part in various outdoor activities at numerous stops along the way. Activities include sailing, canoeing, windsurfing, walking, and biking, with other specialist weeks available. The work is hard, but varied and great fun.

Mate/Instructor (1). £145-£220 per week net of living expenses and depending on experience. Experience and preferably qualifications in open canoeing and mountain walking required (windsurfing and sailing an advantage).

Bosun (1). £90 per week net of living expenses. Main duties: maintenance of boat, driving of safety boat, helping on deck. Training provided. Personal experience of outdoor sports an advantage. Must be keen to learn, with practical nature.

Cook (1) to prepare food for 18 people. £145-£200 per week net of living expenses. Must have experience in good cooking.

Assistant Cook (1 each week, part-time) To work their passage: no wage paid.

All full-time staff to work 6½ days a week and all crew live on board the barge. To work from mid April to mid October. Staff must be available for the whole season to qualify for a bonus with the exception of the assistant cook whose minimum period is one week. A two day recruitment event will be held in February or March.

Applications from December to Martin Balcombe at the above address.

GALLOWAY SAILING CENTRE: Shirmers Bridge, Loch Ken, Castle Douglas DG7 3NQ, South West Scotland (tel 01644-420626; e-mail gsc@lochken.co.uk). A family owned centre in a glorious setting, which aims to give its visitors an enjoyable yet educational time in a safe and friendly atmosphere.

Instructors: Dinghy (10), Windsurfers (5), Canoes (5). Courses start at 10am and finish 5pm. Must be RYA qualified or have a similar level of competence. Overseas applicants with equivalent qualifications welcome.

Cook/General Help (2). No special qualifications needed but experience an advantage.

Chalet Girl (1). Must enjoy working with children.

Wages negotiable, hours variable. Applicants should be versatile, good with people and prepared to accept responsibility. Knowledge of DIY an advantage. Free B & L provided. Period of work from May to September, or peak season only.

Applications to Mr R. Hermon, Principal, at the above address.

GLENCOE OUTDOOR CENTRE: Glencoe, Argyll PA39 4HS (tel 01855-811350). A residential holiday and outdoor activity training centre situated in the north west Highlands amongst the spectacular scenery of Glencoe.

Domestic Assistants/Assistant Instuctor (4). from £135 per week. To work 8 hours per day, 5 days per week: 3 out of 4 weeks domestic work (split shifts, afternoons free) and 1 out of 4 weeks assisting the team of instructors. Plenty of opportunity to take part in activities during free time. Min. period of work 2 months between January and end of July. Min. age 18. Applicants should be committed Christians willing to work hard as part of a Christian team.

Applications a.s.a.p. to Debbie Williams, Director, at the above address.

HILTON PLC: Hilton Coylumbridge Hotel, Coylumbridge, Aviemore, Invernessshire PH22 1QN (tel 01479-813076; fax 01479-811706; e-mail hr-coylumbridge@hilton.com). An excellent new accommodation facility with a good local benefits package.

Leisure Staff. National minimum wage for 39 hours work a week. Must have Lifeguard certificate and First Aid. Possible split shifts over a 5-day week. Min. age 18. Staff required from June to October. Min. period of work 12 weeks. Overseas applicants with basic English (communication level) welcome. Shared accommodation in staff hostel with basic facilities available for £27.30 per week. See Hilton plc for further jobs at the same hotel in the *Hotel and Catering* section.

Applications from April/May to the Personnel Department at the above address.

LATHERON PONY CENTRE: Upper Latheron Farm, Latheron, Caithness KW5 6DT (tel 015934-224).

Staff to work with show ponies and youngstock. £30-£50 pocket money a week depending upon experience. Free B & L. Work available from April to September, no min. period. Some experience required.

Applications to Mrs Camilla Sinclair, Owner, Latheron Pony Centre.

LOCH INSH WATERSPORTS & SKIING CENTRE: Insh Hall, Kincraig, Inverness-shire PH21 1NU (tel 01540-651272; fax 01540-651208; e-mail office@lochinsh.com; www.lochinsh.com). Loch Insh Watersports and skiing centre nestled in the foothills of the Cairngom Mountains in the scenic Spey Valley. Lochside Restaurant and Watersports Centre. Snowskiing December to April. Bed and Breakfast ensuite accommodation and self catering log chalets on site.

Watersports Instructors. RYA and BCU qualified, or trainee instructor standard. To work 6 days a week.

Skiing Instructors. BASI-qualified, or trainee instructor standard. To work 6 days a week.

Restaurant Staff. To work a 5 or 6 day week. Experience preferred.

Wages variable. B & L provided at a charge of up to £40 a week. Free watersports and skiing for staff. Min. period of work 3 months, with work available all year round. Non-smokers only. Overseas applicants with good spoken English welcome.

Applications to Mr Clive Freshwater, at the above address.

MONSTER ACTIVITIES: South Laggan, by Spean Bridge, Inverness-shire PH34 4EA (tel 01809-501 340 ext. Leisure; fax 01809-501 218; info@ monsteractivities.com). A multi-activity centre catering for both family and group activities situated on the Caledonian Canal, on the shores of Loch Oich.

Instructors (5) to carry out various tasks including instruction in archery, windsurfing, sailing, rafting; duties also include equipment maintenance, client reception and staff training. Wages £150 per week. Hours of work vary. Applicants must have a first aid certificate, driving licence and a qualification relevant to the sport that they are teaching, e.g. Power Boat II or III, or Raft Guide Level 2 or 3.

Applications at any time after February to Mr I. Mackinnon, Leisure Manager, at the above address.

PERTH AND KINROSS LEISURE: Company Headquarters, 2 High Street, Perth PH1 5PH (tel 01738-477907; fax 01738-477910; e-mail DMGaffney@ pkc.gov.uk). Provide leisure and community facilities throughout the Perth and Kinross area to promote development, health, fitness and wider leisure services.

Relief Leisure Assistant (Wet Facilities). Wages £4.85 per hour. RLSS pool lifeguard qualification needed.

Relief Leisure Assistant (Dry Facilities). Wages £4.85 per hour. First aid at work qualification needed.

Sports Coaches From £5-£10 per hour. Appropriate coaching certificates needed.

Hours are variable. Positions are available at variable times throughout the year, especially holiday periods, weekends and evenings. No accommodation available. Foreign applicants welcome with appropriate work permit.

Applications should be made to Diane Gaffney, Administration Manager, by letter. Interview necessary.

RAASAY OUTDOOR CENTRE: Isle of Raasay, By Kyle, Ross-shire, IV40 8PB (tel 01478-660266; fax 01478-660200; e-mail raasay.house@virgin.net). An outdoor centre located on a remote and peaceful Hebridean Island. Sailing, windsurfing, kayaking and climbing offered to clients.

Outdoor Activity Instructors (8). To work 44 hours per week between March and October. Min. period of work 1 month. Must have first aid qualifications plus one of the following: Windsurfing RYA, Sailing RYA, Kayak BCU, Abseil and Climb, Walking S.P.S.A. Wages depend on responsibility and experience; board, accommodation and activities provided at no extra cost.

Applications to Freya Rowe from March at the above address. All applicants must speak good English. An interview is required.

Voluntary Work

Conservation and the Environment

BTCV SCOTLAND: Balallan House, 24 Allan Park, Stirling FK8 2QG (tel 01786-479697; fax 01786-465359; e-mail scotland@btcv.org.uk).

BTCV Scotland is one of the UK's largest environmental conservation charities. It operates a network of local centres in, or close to, Scotland's 5 major cities. **Volunteer Officers** required to assist in a varied range of projects e.g. community groups, recycling, environmental projects, administration and residential projects. Hours of work vary, expenses are paid to volunteers. Staff are required all year round for a minimum of 3-6 months. Training is provided in skills needed such as Health and Safety or First Aid. Suitable for New Deal placements. Those over 21 with a clean driving licence held for 2 years are particularly desirable.

Applications to Peter Blackburn at the above address.

THISTLE CAMPS: The National Trust for Scotland, 28 Charlotte Square, Edinburgh EH2 4ET (tel 0131-243 9470; fax 0131-243 9593; e-mail conservationvolunteers@nts.org.uk; www.nts.org.uk).
The Charity protects and promotes Scotland's natural and cultural heritage. Thistle Camps are voluntary work projects organised by The National Trust for Scotland to help in the care and practical management of its countryside properties. Each year there are approx. 40 camps, running from March to October and lasting from one to three weeks. They are always of a **Practical Nature**, undertaking such tasks as mountain footpath improvement, habitat management, archaeology or working with crofting communities on Fair Isle (Britain's most remote inhabited island) and Iona. Volunteers must be aged over 16.

Camps are usually accommodated in a Trust basecamp or in similar hostel-type lodgings. All food is provided but volunteers are expected to help with the preparation of meals as well as general domestic tasks during the week. Participation in a camp costs from £45 (£30 for students etc), and volunteers must pay their own travel expenses to a central pick-up point. All volunteers must bring good waterproofs and sturdy footwear.

The programme for 2002 is available from January and *applications* should be made to the above address. Overseas applicants must apply by February to ensure a place.

Heritage

STRATHSPEY RAILWAY CO. LTD: Aviemore Station, Dalfaber Road, Aviemore PH22 1PY (tel 01479-810725; e-mail laurence.grant@strathspey-railway.freeserve.co.uk).
Highlands steam railway which runs for 5 miles between Aviemore and Boat of Garten. Work is being done to extend the line to Grantown-on-Spey.
Volunteer Guards, Ticket Inspectors and Booking Clerks. Volunteers are also needed to help maintain the railway and its rolling stock and locomotives. Free but very basic accommodation in sleeping car at Boat of Garten station. Hostel for members who work at Aviemore £2.50 per night. Minimum age 16. Fitness needed for some jobs. Vacancies all year.

Applications to the above address.

Physically/Mentally Disabled

BEANNACHAR: Banchory-Devenick, Aberdeen AB12 5YL. (tel 01224-869138; e-mail beannachar@talk21.com; www.beannachar.co.uk).
Beannachar is one of the Camphill communities in which vulnerable children and adults can live, learn and work with others in healthy social relationships based on mutual care and respect.
Beannachar is a training community for teenagers and young adults with learning disabilities. **Volunteers** are needed for household, workshop, garden and farm

duties during the summer, and also long-term volunteers at any time of year. Free B & L plus pocket money provided. To work long hours, 6 days a week. Min. age 19. Must have lots of enthusiasm and a positive attitude. Overseas applicants must speak fluent English. Min. work period 2 months between June and September, 1 year for long-term volunteers.

Applications at any time to Ms E.A. Phethean at the above address.

SPEYSIDE TRUST: Badaguish Outdoor Centre, Aviemore, Inverness-shire PH22 1QU (tel 01479-861285; fax 01479-861258; e-mail info@Badaguish.org; www.badaguish.org).
The Centre specialises in outdoor recreation holidays for children and adults with learning or multiple disabilities. Clients enjoy various adventure activities and 24 hour respite care in a spectacular setting.
Volunteer Care Assistants to work with people with Special Needs for 2 or more weeks from April to October. Volunteers are expected to work 10 hours a day with 2 days off a week. £30 pocket money per week plus B&L.
Seasonal Care Assistant/ Instructor. Paid post from April-October. Accommodation available at the Centre; residential work experience essential. 2 references required.

For more information and *applications* write to the above address.

YOUNG DISABLED ON HOLIDAY: Flat 4, 62 Stuart Park, Edinburgh EH12 8YE (tel 0131-339 8866).
Voluntary Workers (as many as possible) required for holidays for disabled people in the U.K. and abroad for one week throughout the summer. Each volunteer needs to help a disabled person on a one-to-one basis. Workers are expected to make a minimum contribution towards accommodation, food and trips. Preferred age group 18-35, though anyone up to the age of 40 will be considered. No previous experience required, just patience. Overseas applicants welcome.

Applications to Alison Walker at the above address.

Social and Community Schemes

BRAENDAM FAMILY HOUSE: Thornhill, Stirling FK8 3QH (tel 01786-850259; fax 01786-850738; e-mail braendam@care4free.net).
Volunteers required throughout the year to work for a minimum of 6 months at a short stay family house for families experiencing disadvantage and poverty. £30 pocket money and full board provided in return for a 40 hour week within a 2 week rota (5 days off in 14 days); most accommodation is in a single room although it may be necessary to share. Tasks include direct support to families, participating in trips and outings, domestic chores, driving, organising children's activities and play and generally responding to the needs of families.

Volunteers are entitled to holidays, use of house car and bicycles for a small charge, and access to internet/e-mail, again for a small charge. Volunteers will also have the opportunity to explore Scotland on days off. Applicants must be over 18, be willing to work long days and to cary out domestic chores and maintain enthusiasm and energy for supporting families in need. A clean driving licence would be an advantage

Applications to Brian Guidery, Co-ordinator, at the above postal or e-mail address.

EDINBURGH CYRENIANS: Norton Park, 57 Albion Road, Edinburgh EH7 5QY (tel 0131-475 2354; e-mail edinburgh.cyrenians@vigin.net; www. cyrenians.org.uk).

A professional and respected local charity, providing all kinds of practical help for homeless people since 1968. It is not a religious group and the only mission is to help homeless people.

The Cyrenian Trust runs two community houses (one in the city centre and another on an organic farm in West Lothian) that are primarily for young adults who are otherwise homeless, and who have experienced a variety of difficulties which they are seeking to overcome. Residential volunteers, of a similar age to residents, live alongside residents sharing the life and work of the community. Support and regular training is provided by non-residential staff. No experience needed.

Volunteers receive full B & L, weekly pocket money, holiday, leaving grants, and access to a time-off flat. Minimum commitment 6 months. Vacancies all year round. Overseas applicants with good working use of the English language welcome.

For further information and *application* form contact Volunteer Recruitment at the above address. Online applications are possible via website.

IONA COMMUNITY: The Iona Abbey, Isle of Iona, Argyll PA76 6SN (tel 01681-700404; fax 01681-700460; e-mail ionacomm@iona.org.uk and macion2@surfaid.org).
An ecumenical Christian Community sharing work, worship, meals and recreation with guests visiting the Macleod and Abbey centres on Iona, and Camas, the more basic outdoors centre on nearby Mull. Guests come and stay for a week to take part in the common life of work, worship and recreation.

Volunteers work in the kitchen, shop and office, help with driving, gardening, maintenance, housekeeping and with the children's and craft work activities programme.

Volunteers are needed for between 6 and 14 weeks between March and November. They receive full B & L, travelling expenses within the U.K. and pocket money of around £25 per week. They work 5¹/₂ days per week. Volunteers should be in sympathy with the Christian faith and the ideals of the Iona Community. Volunteers of 18+ are required. Overseas applicants with reasonable English welcome.

Recruitment begins in the autumn. For details and *applications* write to the Staff Co-ordinator, Iona Abbey, enclosing a stamped addressed envelope or International Reply Coupon.

Vacation Traineeships

Science, Construction and Engineering

BAE SYSTEMS (MARINE): Waterside House, Barrow, Cumbria, LA14 1AF (tel 01229-875833; fax 01229-875092).
Offers opportunities to approx. 20 students to undertake various projects within the Operations, Technical, Projects and Service departments. Applicants should be university students studying Electrical Engineering, Mechanical Engineering, Naval Architecture, Engineering with Management, Business or Manufacturing systems. Salary depends on year of study.

Placements occur in June-September in Glasgow or Barrow. No accommodation is provided. Overseas applicants are considered, but security clearance may be a problem.

Applications by March/April to Stephen Grafton.

Wales and Northern Ireland

Relative positions & sizes are not correct

Prospects for Work.

Wales. Most of the seasonal jobs in Wales are to be found in hotels, restaurants and holiday centres. The towns offering the largest number of vacancies are Aberystwyth, Brecon, Cardiff, Llangollen, Llandudno, Newport, Porthcawl, Rhyl, Rogerstone, Swansea and Tenby. If you have some knowledge of riding, or are a good group leader, there are numerous riding schools and trekking centres in more remote locations; for those not local to Wales the advantage with this work is that accommodation will normally be provided. In the resort towns rented accommodation is limited and expensive.

Most Jobcentres, including those in Llandudno and Llangollen, advise jobhunters to contact them early. Local job ads appear in the *Brecon and Radnor Express.* The best paper for jobs around Llandudno is the *North Wales Weekly News* or the *Liverpool Daily Post.* Llandudno Jobcentre usually has a high number of vacancies for staff between April and September. In and around Llangollen, try the *Evening Leader* or the *Shropshire Star.* It is worth noting that there is very little chance of finding work with accommodation provided in the Llandudno area. In Tenby *The Tenby Observer* and *The Western Telegraph* are worth looking at while

Swansea Jobcentre recommends the Workpost Job Feature which appears in Wednesday editions of *The South Wales Evening Post* and again on Saturdays.

Aberystwyth can offer a comparatively good supply of jobs – not only in pubs, hotels and restaurants, but at nearby holiday parks and caravan sites too. Rented accommodation in the town is limited since students from the local university take up most vacancies. The local *Cambrian News* carries job advertisements.

In South Wales, Newport Leisure Services usually advertises vacancies for its playscheme in March or April each year. While Newport may not have the appeal of Llangollen or Brecon, it is one of the few towns in Wales to have plenty of rentable accommodation.

Call centres often recruit temporary staff, the main centres being in Cardiff and Swansea. Local Jobcentres have details of recruitment. Large manufacturing firms which may require temporary staff include Tetra Pak (who make cardboard milk and juice cartons) in Wrexham, the Driver and Vehicle Licensing Agency in Morriston, and R.F. Brookes in Rogerstone. Apply early to these firms and contact the necessary Jobcentre to establish whether or not application forms will be available.

The Royal Welsh Show in Builth Wells in mid July provides a number of jobs for a few weeks.

Northern Ireland. Over the last decade the economy of Northern Ireland has been the fastest growing of all the UK regions with unemployment rates now lower than some regions on the mainland, and strong economic growth. In and around Belfast most vacancies are in the retail, hotel and restaurant trade. Further afield hotel work is more plentiful in the lakeland areas of Co. Fermanagh and in seaside towns such as Portrush and Newcastle. Short term relief rangers are needed at the various country parks in Northern Ireland from April-May onwards, recruitment is through the local job markets. Students may register for seasonal work with private employment agencies or Employment and Training Jobcentres which are located throughout Northern Ireland. Holiday job vacancies for specific areas are usually advertised in local newspapers, job clubs and libraries.

Business and Industry

JOHN BROWNLEE: Knockmakagan, Newtownbutler, Co. Fermanagh, Northern Ireland (tel 028-6773 8277/028-6773 8275(home) or 07909-432131).
Bottlers of Spring Water (2). National minimum wage. Free accommodation at farm. Work available all year round. Overseas applicants welcome. *Applications* to Mr John Brownlee at the above address.

Children

ACORN ADVENTURE LTD: Acorn House, 22 Worcester Street, Stourbridge DY8 1AN (tel 01384-446057; fax 01384-3788866; e-mail topstaff@ acornadventure.co.uk.). Acorn adventure is the leading provider of outdoor adventure camps for schools, youth groups and families. They operate 9 activity centres in France, Italy, Spain and the UK.
Instructors. Must hold at least Instructor status with e.g. BCU or RYA, or have passed SPA or MLTB assessment. Other nationally recognised coaching awards may be considered.
Assistant Instructors. Must be registered as training for the above award(s).
Support Staff. Maintenance and/or catering. No experience necessary.
Fully Qualified Nurse.
Please note that all staff must be available from April/May to September: full period only.

Applications and requests for an information pack should be sent to the Recruitment Department at the above address.

GRANGE TREKKING CENTRE: The Grange, Capel-y-Ffin, Abergavenny, NP7 7NP (tel 01873-890215; fax 01873-890157). Family-run guest house and trekking centre situated high in the Black Mountains.
Nanny And Mothers' Help required between April and November, wages by arrangement. Applicants should be 18+, duties include looking after 2 children between 15 months and 2¹/2 years old plus some cleaning, food preparation and waiting on tables.
Applications to Jessica Grange at the above address.

THE TREBINSHUN GROUP: Trebinshun House, near Brecon, Powys LD3 7PX (tel 01874-730653; fax 01874-730843; e-mail lizawatson@ compuserve. com). A language school in a countryside location teaching English to foreigners. Recognised by The British Council.
Social Assistants (2-4). Wages £175 per week living in. To work full-time with mornings free. Staff required from end of June to mid-August for a minimum period of 8 weeks. Must be outgoing country-lovers with sports experience. Driving licence an advantage. Duties include looking after up to 12 foreign children, with one other person including planning and supervision of a social and activity programme. No cooking or cleaning.
Applications after January to Liza Watson, at the above address.

Holiday Centres and Amusements

ANGLESEY MUSEUMS SERVICE: c/o Anglesey Heritage Gallery, Rhosmeirch. Llangefni LL77 7TW (tel 01248-724444).
Seasonal Museums Attendants to work in the museum shop, in ticketing and admissions, cleaning, security, guiding, customer care and stock control. Wages £4.30 per hour. To work from Easter until the end of September. All applicants must be available for the entire season. Min. age 18. Must speak Welsh fluently, and be a good communicator, organised and with an interest in museums and heritage.
Applications to the Heritage Education Officer at the above address before the end of February.

ANGLESEY SEA ZOO: Brynsiencyn, Anglesey LL6 6TQ (tel 01248-430411; fax 01248-430213; e-mail fishandfun@seazoo.demon.co.uk). A family run public aquarium employing 30 staff and welcoming 100,000 visitors per year.
Catering Assistants (4). Wages £4.50-£4.95 per hour; to work 35-39 hours per week. No accommodation is available. Staff required for a minimum of 2 months between March and October. Applicants should be over 16 and have relevant catering experience. A food hygiene certificate is desirable.
Applications should call or e-mail for further details and an application pack. *Applications* to Alison Lea-Wilson after January.

GREENHILL YMCA NATIONAL CENTRE: Donard Park, Newcastle, Co Down, Northern Ireland BT33 0GR (tel 028-4372 3172; fax 028-4372 6009). Situated at the foot of the Mourne Mountains, overlooking the town of Newcastle.
Instructors (20). To work up to 3 sessions per day. Experience or qualifications in one of the following is required: mountaineering, canoeing, orienteering, archery, environmental studies or working with young people on day camps. Min. age 18 but persons over age 20 preferred. Staff will be responsible for children and young

people, so vetting references as to suitability in this area will be required.

Drivers. Must be over 25 years old, reliable, safe and experienced in driving minibuses and towing trailers. An up to date clean driving licence will be required.

Domestic Hosts (5). Must be hard-working, sociable and responsible.

Cooks (3). Basic cooking and catering qualifications necessary.

All staff are given expenses of £45 a plus free B & L. Hours variable, 5 days a week in most cases. Min. period of work 6 weeks. Instructors and day camp staff must attend a staff training programme from 23 June to 30 June. The summer camp period is from 1 July to 28 August. Greenhill is a Christian Centre; applicants should therefore be supportive of its Christian ethos and promotion of the same. Applicants must speak fluent English and supply photocopies of relevant qualifications. One year Instructor posts (September-August) are also available for mature people who are active in the Christian faith.

Applications should be sent a.s.a.p. to the Volunteer Co-ordinator at the above address.

HAFAN Y MÔR HOLIDAY PARK

Bar Staff • Catering Staff • Chefs • Lifeguards • Sport & Leisure Staff
Retail Staff • Receptionists • Security Staff • Cleaners

Needed from late March to early November to work in the leisure industry. Enjoyable working environment.
Uniform and attractive staff package provided.

Applications to: Personnel, Hafan Y Môr, Pwllheli, Gwynedd LL53 6HX
tel: 01758-612112 • fax: 01766-810379
email: admin.hafanymor@bourne-leisure.co.uk

HAFAN Y MOR HOLIDAY PARK: (tel 01758-612112; fax 01766-810379; e-mail admin.hafanymore@bourne-leisure.co.uk). Part of the Bourne Leisure Group. An all action family holiday park on the picturesque Llyn Peninsula in the shadow of Snowdon.

Staff wanted for all leisure positions: Bar Staff, Catering Staff, Chefs, Lifeguards, Sport and Leisure Staff, Retail Staff, Receptionists, Security Staff, Cleaners (400 in all). To work from late March to early November. Wages in line with national minimum wage legislation, with increments according to age and experience. Uniform and an attractive staff package provided.

No qualifications are required except for Lifeguard and Chef positions as full training will be given. Recognised qualifications can be gained in most positions. Live-in accommodation available to successful applicants aged over 18.

Applications to be sent to Personnel at the above address.

PEMBROKESHIRE COAST NATIONAL PARK AUTHORITY: Winch Lane, Haverfordwest, Pembrokeshire SA61 1PY (tel 01473-764636; fax 01437-769045; e-mail PCNP@Pembrokeshirecoast.org.uk; www.pembrokeshirecoast. org.uk) A national park authority, responsible for building planning control, conservation and education regarding the environment within the national park. **Visitor Centre Assistants (2) Site Guide Assistants (2)** to work from 2-5 days per week including week-ends. Applicants must be 18 or over with good communication skills and enjoy working with the public. It may be an advantage to have knowledge of the area.

Coast Path Wardens (2) to work Monday to Friday. Applicants should have countryside skills. Main duty is maintenance of footpaths.

Car Park Attendants (2) working hours vary but will include weekends and holidays. Applicants should have good communication skills, experience of cash handling and practical skills for machine maintenance.

Summer Ranger Guide working hours vary but will include weekends and holidays. Applicants should have up to degree level qualification in Tourism/Leisure or Environmental Studies.

For all positions the wage is £4.78+ per hour. Ability to speak Welsh is desirable for all jobs. Staff are required from March/April to September. No accommodation available. Information packs will be made available in 2002 and will also be available on the website.

Applications should be sent to Alison Wood at the above address during January and February.

TRANS-WALES-TRAILS: Pengenfford, Talgarth, Brecon, Powys LD3 0EU (tel 01874-711398; fax 01874-711122; e-mail riding@transwales.co.uk www.transwales. demon.co.uk). Based at a remote farm guesthouse in the Black Mountains of S.E. Wales: specialists in horse riding holidays for international adult visitors.

General Domestic Assistants (2). £120 per week. To work approx. 40 hours a week, with 1 day off which may be carried forward. Free horse riding, and free B & L suitable for females only. Age: 18-25 years. Duties include helping in the kitchen, bedmaking and cleaning. Assistants must be smart, responsible, of high moral standard and prepared to speak English clearly to foreign guests. Min. period of work 3 months between 1 April and 30 September. Overseas applicants with college-level English welcome.

Applications during February and March to Mr and Mrs Michael Turner, Trans-Wales-Trails. Note: Only affirmative responses will be made.

WELSH CANAL HOLIDAY CRAG LTD: The Wharf, Llangollen LL20 8TA (tel/fax 01978-860702; e-mail sue@horsedrawnboats.co.uk). Horse drawn public boat trips along Llangollen canal, also motor boat trips over Pontoysyuteaguenot. There is a busy wharf cafe and gift shop alongside the canal. The cafe is open 10am-6pm, 7 days a week.

Cafe Assistants (2/3) to serve hot meals, drinks, snacks and ice cream. Wages £3.65 per hour (over 18) or £3.50 (under 18); to work full-time or part-time to suit. Must be good with people and have lots of common sense

Horse Walker (1) to lead horse along tow path for public boat trips; will be walking up to 14 miles per day. Wages £25 per day (negotiable); to work 9am-6pm. Must have experience with horses and/or boats.

Staff are required from April to October for a minimum of 1 month. Subsidised food is available for staff. Overseas applicants are welcome but must be able to speak enough English to serve in the shop.

Applications should be sent to Sue Knapp at the above address from April onwards. Foreign applicants must have a valid work permit. Interview probably necessary.

Hotels and Catering

AMBASSADOR HOTEL: Grand Promenade, Llandudno, North Wales LL30 2NR (tel 01492-876886). A family run seafront hotel in the largest resort in Wales. Known for its unspoilt Victorian image, the hotel is close to Snowdonia National Park.

Waiting Staff (2). Wages by arrangement. Good conditions and hours. Free B & L. Must be over 17 years of age. Min. work period 2 months at any time of year.
Applications to Mr D.T. Williams, Proprietor, Ambassador Hotel.

CHIMNEY CORNER HOTEL: 630 Antrim Road, Newtonabbey, Co. Antrim, N. Ireland BT36 4RH (tel 028-9084 4925; fax 028-9084 4352; e-mail info@chimneycorner.co.uk).
Waiting Staff (2), Commis Chef, Receptionist required from 1st July. All posts work 40 hours per 5 day week, with the possibility of overtime, plus accommodation and meals on top of wages. Wages vary according to age: under 21 £3.50 per hour, over 21 £4 per hour (waiting staff may also get tips). The work is mainly restaurant work and overtime may be available at the hotel's night club. Training will be given for all posts; waiting staff should have a pleasant disposition, and applicants for receptionist should have good telephone skills and a basic knowledge of computers.
To apply *contact* Brenda Crawford, Manager at the hotel.

CHRISTIAN MOUNTAIN CENTRE – PENSARN HARBOUR: Pensarn Harbour, Llanbedr, Gwynedd LL45 2HS (tel/fax 01341-241646; e-mail office@cmcpensarn.org.uk; cmcpensarn.org.uk).
House Staff (4). Wage and accommodation details on application. No qualifications necessary. To work 40 hours per week: min. period of work 3 weeks between March 1 and October 30. Applicants must speak English to a reasonable standard. The CMC is a Christian Centre and requires applicants who have a sympathy towards the faith.
Apply from November onwards to Mr R. Mayhew at the above address.

COBDENS HOTEL: Capel Curig, Snowdonia National Park, North Wales LL24 0EE (tel 01690-720 243; fax 01690-720 354; e-mail info@cobdens.co.uk; www.cobdens.co.uk). Situated in the heart of Snowdonia, Cobdens is family owned and popular with climbers and walkers.
Housekeeping/Bar/Waiting Staff (3). Live-in with good rate per hour plus free food. To work 40 hours over five days per week. Experience preferred but personality more important.
Kitchen Staff. Must have a real interest in food.
Min. period of work 6 months preferred. Staff required all year round. Work is hard and to a high standard, but good fun. Overseas applicants with a reasonable standard of English welcome.
Applications any time to the General Manager at the above address.

COURT HOTEL: Lamphey, Pembroke, Pembrokeshire SA71 5NT (tel 01646-672273; fax 01646-672480). A four star country hotel and leisure centre set in a pleasant village near the coast. Under present owner for 20 years with a friendly team of 25 staff.
General Assistants/Waiting Staff (2). £90-£160 a week.
Breakfast Cook (1). £90-£160 a week.
Gardener (1). £90-£160 a week.
All staff work 5 days a week. B & L is available at £30 a week. Hotel experience helpful. Min. work period 4 weeks, between Easter and the end of September. Some full-time positions are also available. Overseas applicants welcome.
Applications from February onwards to Mr or Mrs Lain, at The Court Hotel.

THE FEATHERS ROYAL HOTEL: Alban Square, Aberaeron, Cardiganshire, West Wales SA46 0AQ (tel 01545-571750; fax 01545-571760; e-mail emma@feathers17.freeserve.co.uk). Originally an 18th century coaching inn, the Feathers Royal Hotel is now a modern well equipped hotel with a restaurant and conference facilities.

General Assistants (4). Live-in. Flexible hours and adequate free time. Must be energetic and adaptable. Min. age 18. Min. period of work the summer vacation. Overseas applicants with good working knowledge of English welcome.

Applications (with photograph) to Miss Emma Hunter, Feathers Royal Hotel or to emma@feathers17.freeserve.co.uk.

GRANGE GUEST HOUSE: The Grange, Capel-y-ffin, Abergavenny, Gwent NP7 7NP (tel 01873-890215). A small, informal family run centre situated in a very rural area, high in the beautiful Black Mountains.

Accommodation Worker/Assistant to perform cleaning, waiting, taking 2 little girls aged 2 and 3 for a walk, gardening and customer care duties. Wages and hours negotiable, with free accommodation in a caravan with shower block. Min. period of work one month between Easter and October. Overseas applicants with good English welcome; preferable that candidates can visit for an interview, but not essential.

Applications should be directed to Jessica Griffiths from February onwards at the above address.

LION HOTEL: Y Maes, Criccieth, Gwynned LL52 0AA (tel 01766-522460; fax 01766-523075). A busy 3 star hotel centrally situated in a seaside resort.

General Assistants (Bar, Restaurant, Bedroom) (2). £3.70 per hour depending on age. To work 39 hours a week over 6 days.

Cook/Kitchen Assistant (1) Wages £3.70-£4.25 per hour depending on age and experience. Clean accommodation is available, at a price to be negotiated. Min. period of work 4 months.

Applications from 1 March to Mrs S.A. Burnett, Manageress, at the above address.

MARINER'S INN: Nolton Haven, Haverfordwest, Pembrokeshire, Dyfed SA62 3NH (tel 01437-710469). A friendly residential inn, overlooking the sea.

Bar Staff (2), Waiting Staff (3). To work 10am-2pm and 4.30-11pm, split shifts.

Chamber Staff (1). To work 10am-2pm, split shifts.

Wages from £4.50 per hour. Overtime as required, particularly on bank holidays. Min. age 18. Min. period of work 3 months from June to September. B & L is sometimes available.

Applications from Easter to Mr C. Quinlan at the Mariner's Inn.

METROPOLE HOTEL: Temple Street, LLandrindod Wells, Powys LD1 5DY (tel 01597-823700; fax 01579-824828; e-mail info@metropole.co.uk; www.metropole.co.uk). Family owned and a member of the Best Western group, The Metropole is a three star Victorian style hotel with 122 bedrooms and extensive conference and banqueting facilities.

Waiting Staff (6). Wage at National Minimum Wage level.

Commis Chef (4). Wage at National Minimum Wage level.

All staff to work 5 days per week plus overtime if necessary. Accommodation available at a cost of £19.95 per week. Min. age 16 years. Min. period of work 6 months; staff required all year round. Overseas applicants welcome. All applicants must be available for interview.

Applications any time to Mr Nichouas, Ireland General Manager, at the above address.

MIN-Y-DON HOTEL: North Parade, Llandudno LL30 2LP (tel 01492-876511; fax 01492-878169). Located on the north shore seafront, opposite the famous Victorian pier.
Room Assistants (2), Hotel Assistants (2), Dining Room Assistants (2) to work from June to October. Wages and hours by arrangement. Accommodation is available. Applicants should be under 21. Overseas applicants welcome.
Applications to the Manager at the above address.

**PORTH TOCYN HOTEL: Abersoch, Gwynedd LL53 7BU (tel 01758-713303; fax 01758-713538; e-mail porthtocyn.hotel@virgin.net; www.porth-tocyn-hotel.co.uk). A country house hotel by the sea, filled with antiques. The house has been in the family for 50 years, and has been in the Good Food Guide for over 40 years.
GENERAL ASSISTANTS (10), ASSISTANT COOKS (4). Wages guaranteed above the National Minimum Wage. To work a 4¹/₂-day week in split shifts. Free B & L and use of tennis court and swimming pool. Intelligence and sense of humour required. Cooking experience useful but not essential. Min. period of work 6 weeks between March and November:** *Applications* **from those who are able to work over Easter and/or outside the summer university vacation period welcome. Travel expenses will be paid for those able to work for short stints over Easter and the spring bank holidays.**
Applications **with s.a.e. to Mrs Fletcher-Brewer, Porth Tocyn Hotel.**

ROYAL GATE HOUSE HOTEL: North Beach, Tenby, Pembrokeshire SA70 7ET (tel 01834-842255; fax 01834-842441; e-mail royal-gatehouse@hotmail.com). Family run hotel with superb views of Tenby harbour and Carmarthen bay.
Waiting Staff (3). To work 6 days a week. Shifts 7.30-10.30am and 6-10pm, plus some lunchtimes (noon-2pm). Min. age 18. Silver service experience preferred, but not essential.
Chamber Staff (4). To work 8am-1pm, 6 days a week. Min. age 18. Experience preferred.
Bar Person (1). To work shifts of 10.30am-3pm, and 6-11pm, 6 days a week. Also shifts of 11am-7pm and 7pm until closing in the residents' bar. Min. age 18. Experience essential.
Wages by arrangement. Some accommodation is available. Period of work March to November. *Applications* to Mr G.T.R. Fry at the above address.

THE ST DAVID'S HOTEL AND SPA: Havannah Street, Cardiff CF10 5SD (tel 02920-454045; fax 02920-313075; e-mail ndavies@thestdavidshotel.com). The St David's Hotel and Spa, Wales' Premier five star hotel, is located at the waterfront of the Cardiff Bay development. One of Rocco Forte's Hotels, it offers excellent opportunities for staff development.
Waiting Staff (5), Housekeeping Staff (3), Kitchen Staff (3). Wages of £5.00 per hour.
Spa Assistants (2); £4.50 per hour.
Accommodation provided; charge to be arranged. To work five days per week. Fluent English essential.
Applications should be made to Nicola Davies at the above address. Interview required for UK residents.

TYN-Y-COED HOTEL: Capel Curig, Betws-y-Coed LL24 0EE (tel 01690-720331). A small friendly hotel in the centre of Snowdonia, which caters mainly for mountain users and tourists.

General Assistants (4). £120 per week for approx. 40 hours a week. To work 5 days per week on split shifts. Full board accommodation is included. Min. age 18.

Applications to G.F. Wainwright, Tyn-y-Coed Hotel.

Language Schools

ENGLISH STUDY CENTRE: 19-21 Uplands Crescent, Swansea, West Glamorgan SA2 0NX (tel 01792-464103; fax 01792-472303).

EFL Teachers (3-4) to teach adults or junior groups. £11-£12.50 per hour, 15 to 30 hours per week. No accommodation provided. Must be graduates with TEFL qualifications and/or experience and able to speak English to the level of a native speaker. Min. period of work three weeks between the beginning of June and the end of August.

Applications from March to Esther Richards, Principal, at the above address. Interview if possible.

UNIVERSITY OF WALES ABERYSTWYTH: Language and Learning Centre, Llandinam Building, Penglais Campus, Aberystwyth SY23 3DB (tel 01970-622545; fax 01970-622546; e-mail: language+learning@aber.ac.uk). Attractive working environment in a secure seaside location between the coast of Cardigan Bay and the Cambrian Mountains. The centre offers courses to language learners and language teachers in a warm and welcoming academic environment.

Language Tutors (6-10). £350 per week. 20 hours teaching per week, plus 16 hours social duties per month and 12 hours administration per month. Min. period of work one month between mid July and early September. B & L available. Applicants must speak English to the standard of someone who speaks it as a first language. First degree, TEFL qualifications and 3 years experience required. Interview necessary.

Applications from January 1 to Rex Berridge, Director, at the above address.

Medical

EVERYCARE: 28 Carlisle Street, Splott, Cardiff CF2 2DS (tel 02920-455300)

Care Assistants needed for ongoing positions. Wages of £4.50-£9.60 per hour, working hours to suit. Applicants must be over 18, with full driving licence, own transport and telephone.

Applications to Helen Ford, Care Manager, at the above address.

Outdoor

JOHN BROWNLEE: Knockmakagan, Newtownbutler, Co. Fermanagh, Northern Ireland (tel 028-6773 8277/028-6773 8275(home) or 07909-432131).

Fruit Pickers (4-6). Wages at piece work rates. Free accommodation at farm. Period of work September and October. Overseas applicants welcome.

Applications to Mr John Brownlee at the above address.

DAVISON CANNERS LTD: 107 Summerisland Road, Portadown, Co.Armagh, Northern Ireland BT62 1SJ (tel 028-3885 1661; fax 028-3885 2288; info@davisonfreshfood.demon.co.uk). Harvests and processes fruit for retail, catering and bakery markets, mainly in the UK and Ireland.

Fruit Pickers. Wages at piece work rates. To work five to six days a week for approximately six weeks from September until the end of October.

Accommodation is available. *Applications* to Mr Ronnie Davison at the above address.

NORTH DOWN MARQUEES LTD: 39 Ballynathnett Road, Carryduff, County Down, Northern Ireland BT8 8DL (tel 028-9081 5535; fax 028-9081 2344; e-mail northdown.marquees@virgin.net). One of the largest marquee companies in Ireland, established 20 years ago, always busy.
Marquee Erectors (10). Wages negotiable. Physically demanding work and hours can be long; applicants must be able to work under pressure and take responsibility. Positions are available from June to October. Foreign applicants welcome. No accommodation available.

Applications should be made from April onwards to Mr Sam Weir at the above address. Interview necessary, may be telephonic.

Sport

ARTHOG OUTDOOR EDUCATION CENTRE: Arthog, Gwynned LL39 1BX (tel 01341-250455; www.arthog.co.uk). A Local Education Authority run centre situated below mountains, about 1km from the sea. Fully staffed by 7 professional instructors, it takes up to 90 clients.
Outdoor Instructors. Activities include mountaineering, canoeing, sailing, walking etc. Wages according to qualifications. RYA, ML, or BCU qualifications useful, teaching certificate a bonus. Interested applicants without qualifications may be taken on, but on a voluntary basis. Work equivalent to 5 days a week, but long hours. Free board and accommodation provided. Overseas applicants considered.

Applications to Head Office at the above address.

CANTREF TREKKING CENTRE: Brecon, Powys LD3 8LR (tel 01874-665223). Situated in the Brecon Beacon mountain range. Pots of riding involved and contact with all ages.
Pony Trekking Guides (2). Wages on application. B & L available. Hours according to length of treks, with possibility of overtime. To work 6 days a week. Min. age 18. Pony Club B or BHS Stage 1, also Riding & Road Safety qualifications essential. Must be experienced rider and able to get along well with people. Period of work 1 June or 1 July to 1 September. Applicants must be prepared to work the specified length of time. Interview essential.

Applications, enclosing s.a.e., from March to M. Evans, Cantref Pony Trekking Centre.

CHRISTIAN MOUNTAIN CENTRE: Pensarn Harbour, Llanbedr, Gwynedd LL45 2HS (tel/fax 01766 512616). A 50 bedded outdoor pursuits centre set in a tidal estuary within the Snowdonia National Park.
Helpers. £25-£70 per week plus full board and accommodation. To work 40 hours per week: min. period of work 3 months between March 1 and October 30. Overseas students with a high standard of English welcome. The CMC is a Christian Centre and requires applicants who have a Christian faith.

Applications from November onwards to Mr R. Mayhew at the above address.

CLYNE FARM CENTRE: Westport Avenue, Mayals, Swansea SA3 5AR (tel 01792-403333; fax 01792-403339; e-mail info@clynefarm.com; www. clynefarm. com). A converted farm complex on the Gower Peninsula with spectacular views.

It offers a range of activities and accommodation from camping to self-catering cottages.

Activity And Horse Riding Instructors. Wages negotiable. To work 40 hours a week. Min. age 18. Min. period of work 4 weeks from June to September. Accommodation may be available, charge to be negotiated. Overseas applicants with good spoken English and eligible to work in the UK welcome. All applicants must be available for interview.

Applications from January to the Manager at the above address.

GRANGE TREKKING CENTRE: The Grange, Capel-y-ffin, Abergavenny, Gwent NP7 7NP (tel 01873-890215). A small, informal family run centre situated in a very rural area, high in the beautiful Black Mountains.

Trek Leader And Assistant Leader for a variety of work including mucking out, trek leading, tack cleaning, maintenance and dealing with customers. Some training available. Salary and hours negotiable. Free accommodation in caravan with shower block. Must be over 18 years old; first aid qualifications preferable. Also the possibility of looking after two little girls, aged 2 and 3, for a few hours a day.

Min. period of work 1 month between Easter and October. Overseas applicants with good English welcome. Preferable that candidates can attend an interview but not essential.

Applications from February onwards to Jessica Griffiths at the above address.

HIGH TREK SNOWDONIA: Tal y Waen, Deiniolen, Caernarvon, Gwynedd LL55 3NA (tel/fax 01286-871232; e-mail high.trek@virgin.net; www.hightrek. co.uk). A small company which offers guided walking holidays in Snowdonia.

Trek Assistant (1). £60 a week with free B & L. To work 5 days a week including some evenings. Duties include help with driving, group leading, domestic chores, etc. Applicants should be over 21, have a full driving licence, mountain leadership training and First Aid certificate. Must be very fit and have a strong interest in the outdoors and countryside. Should also have a flexible nature and be able to do anything from paper work to portering loads. Overseas applicants who fulfil these criteria will be considered.

Min. period of work 6 weeks between Easter and October. Priority is given to those able to work the whole season. Applicants must be available for interview.

Applications should be sent as early as possible to Mrs Mandy Whitehead, at the above address.

LAKELAND CANOE CENTRE: Castle Island, Enniskillin, Northern Ireland BT74 5HH (tel 028-6632 4250; fax 028-6632 3319). An outdoor activity centre with activities including canoeing, sailing and mountain biking.

Assistant Instructor (2), Kitchen Helper (1), Cleaner (1). Minimum period of work 3 weeks from March to October. Board and accommodation provided free of charge. Minimum age 18. Applicants must be interested in young people.

Applications from February, enclosing a photo, to Gary Mitten, Director, at the above address.

MOUNTAIN VENTURES LTD: Bryn Du, Ty Du Road, Llanberis, Gwynedd LL55 4HD (tel 01286-870454). Outdoor pursuit centre and water sports and activity centre. Provides residential packages for groups, including kayak and canoe paddling, rock climbing, abseiling and mountain walking from centres in the Snowdonia National Park.

Instructors needed: Mountain Ventures offers work opportunities as instructors to people who have appropriate qualifications and experience. There are also opportunities for assistant staff to take on work of a general nature, helping instructors and domestic staff in exchange for accommodation, food, some payment and the opportunity for some training in Snowdonia National Park during June and July, together with a group of other young people.

Applications to the above address.

PGL TRAVEL: Alton Court, Penyard Lane (874), Ross-on-Wye, Herefordshire HR9 5GL (tel 01989-767833; www.pgl.co.uk/personnel). Over 200 staff needed to assist in the running of children's activity centres in the Brecon Beacons and Black Mountains. Europe's largest provider of adventure holidays for children has offered outstanding training and work opportunities to seasonal staff for over 40 years.

Qualified Instructors in canoeing, sailing, windsurfing, pony trekking, hill walking, fencing, archery, judo, rifle shooting, fishing, motorsports, arts and crafts, drama, English language and many other activities. Min. age 18.

Group Leaders to take care of small groups of children and ensure that they get the most out of their holiday. Min. age 18. Previous experience of working with children necessary.

Pocket money from £50 per week plus full B & L. Vacancies available for short or long periods between February and October. Overseas applicants eligible to work in the UK welcome.

Requests for application forms to the Personnel Department at the above address.

RHIWIAU RIDING CENTRE: Llanfairfechan, North Wales LL33 OEH (tel 01248-680094; fax 01248-681143; e-mail rhiwiau@aol.com; www.rhiwiau.co.uk.). Residential riding holiday centre in Snowdonia National Park, catering for adults, families and unaccompanied children.

Instructor/Ride Leader to work from 8am-5.30pm, 5 days per week. Wages of £100 per week with full board provided. Must be aged over 18 and have either a BHS Preliminary Teaching or BET qualification.

Assistants to give general help in the house and organise evening activities. Wages £75 per week plus full board. To work from 8.15-10.15am, 12.30-1.30pm and 6-9.30pm, 6 days per week.

Period of work from June to September.

Applications to Ruth Hill, Proprietor, at the above address.

SHARE HOLIDAY VILLAGE: Smiths Strand, Lisnaskea, Co. Fermanagh, BT92 OEQ (tel 028-6772 2122; fax 028-6772 1893; e-mail share@dnet.co.uk). The largest activity centre in Northern Ireland. A charity dedicated to providing opportunities for able bodied and disabled people to take part in a wide range of activities together. A team of 25-30 paid staff and volunteers works with families, individuals and groups of all ages.

Outdoor Activity Instructors (6) to work 5 days plus one night a week. Applicants must be aged over 18 and have one of the following qualifications; RYA dinghy sailing instruction; BCU canoe or kayak instructor plus current first aid certificate; or RYA powerboat handling level II.

Social Programme Activity Leaders (2) to plan and run a programme of social activities including arts, drama, singing, storytelling, folk dancing etc. To work 5 days a week. Must love working with people and have plenty of different skills in arts, drama and dance.

Wages £50-£120 per week depending on qualifications plus meals and accommodation. To work from early May to the end of September/early October. *Applications* to Dawn Latimer, Director at the above address.

SNOWDONIA RIDING STABLES: Wainfawr, Caernarfon LL55 4PQ (tel 01286-650342; e-mail riding@snowdonia2000.fsnet.co.uk) A trekking centre/riding school with approximately 50 horses including dressage/event horses, young stock and liveries.

Trek Leaders (2) Work includes care of horses, yard work, trek leading and light maintenance work. Wages on application: to work approximately 40 hours per week. Applicants must be over 18 with good riding ability. Staff are required from mid July to mid September. Overseas *Applications* are welcome. Accommodation is available in self catering caravans free of charge.

Applications should be sent to Mrs R. Thomas at the above address from Spring onwards.

TAL Y FOEL RIDING CENTRE: Dwyran, Anglesey LL61 6LQ (tel 01248-430377).A friendly BHS approved centre on the shores of the Menai Straits. Facilities include indoor and outdoor menage, cross country training course, four miles of grass tracks, liveries, lessons and treks. Best Small Tourism Business in Wales 1998.

Yard Staff/Ride Leaders (4). £75 per week plus free accommodation in a caravan. To work from June to August; min. period of work 8 weeks. Must be qualified in riding and stable management. Overseas applicants who are available to attend an interview welcome.

Applications from January to Dr Judy Hutchings or Miss Kayte Lloyd Hughes at the above address.

TYN-MORFA RIDING CENTRE: Rhosneigr, Anglesey LL64 5QX (tel 01407-810072). The Riding Centre is situated on the West Coast of Anglesey at Rhosneigr within minutes of Anglesey's finest beaches. It is one of North Wales' oldest riding establishments, with beach riding a speciality.

Trek Leaders or Assistants (2) to escort rides on the beach. Wages negotiable, according to age and experience. Hours: 8am-5pm, 6 days per week. Free B & L in caravan. Applicants should be aged 18+, be able to ride well and be responsible enough to take charge of rides. Season begins mid-May.

Applications from 1 May to Mr C.P. Carnall, Tyn-Morfa Riding Centre.

Voluntary Work

Conservation and the Environment

CONSERVATION VOLUNTEERS NORTHERN IRELAND: 159 Ravenhill Road, Belfast, Northern Ireland BT6 0BP (tel 02890-645169; fax 02890-644409; e-mail CVNI@btcv.org.uk).

Conservation Volunteers Northern Ireland is part of the BTCV, which involves over 70,000 volunteers each year in environmental projects throughout Northern Ireland, England, Wales and Scotland, making it the largest practical conservation charity in the country.

Volunteers to participate in practical conservation work throughout Northern Ireland. This includes community development work and use of practical skills etc. A number of week-long Working Holidays and Weekend Breaks are organised throughout the year or for those who wish to become Volunteer Officers, a commitment of at least six months is requested; types of positions available are: weekday officer, education officer, publicity officer, local groups officer, tree nursery officer and residentials officer.

To work 6 hours a day. No experience is necessary. Minimum age 18. Board and accommodation provided for Working Holiday volunteers at a cost of £42-£82 a week; limited amount of free accommodation for volunteer officers.

Applications for Working Holidays to Maddy Kelly, and for volunteers and Volunteer Officers to Lynn McCready, at the above address, at any time of the year.

THE WILDLIFE TRUST WEST WALES: The Welsh Wildlife Centre, Cilgerran, Cardigan, SA43 2TB (tel 01239-621212; fax 01239-613211; e-mail wildlife@wtww.co.uk).
Voluntary Assistant Wardens are required for Skomer Island, a National Nature Reserve off the Welsh coast. Work involves meeting day visitors, census work, general maintenance and recording, etc. To work 7 days a week for a minimum of 1 week between Easter and 31 October. Self-catering accommodation is available free of charge. Min. age 16, and volunteers should have an interest in natural history. Overseas applicants welcome.

Applications should be sent to Mrs J. Glennerster, Islands Booking Officer, at the above address. It is advisable to contact Mrs Glennerster from September onwards to book for the following year as places go very quickly.

Heritage

CYFARTHFA CASTLE MUSEUM AND ART GALLERY: Brecon Road, Merthyr Tydfil, South Wales CF47 8RE (tel/fax 01685-723112).
A registered museum set in a regency gothic castle in 160 acres of parkland. The museum displays range from fine art to the industrial revolution.
Volunteers (2) needed around the year to assist with museum functions including documentation, cataloguing, producing text for leaflets and guides, work with schools and exhibitions. Work is normally unpaid. Applicants must provide their own accommodation, a list of local B & Bs is available on request. Should be educated to at least A level standard; would suit students wishing to pursue a career in museum, gallery or heritage work.
Applications to Mrs C. Dovey-Evans, Museums Officer at the above address.

FFESTINIOG RAILWAY COMPANY: Harbour Station, Porthmadog, Gwynedd, North Wales LL49 9NF (tel 01766-512340; fax 01766-516006; e-mail tricia.doyle@festrail.co.uk; www.festrail.co.uk).
The world's oldest passenger carrying narrow-gauge railway. 13^1/2 mile long route through Snowdonia National Park.
Volunteers are required to help in the maintenance and running of the 170-year-old railway. It is a good opportunity to meet new people and learn new skills. A wide variety of work is available in the Operating and Marketing, Commercial, Locomotive Operating, Mechanical, and the Civil Engineering departments. The Buildings, Parks and Gardens Department need skilled and unskilled assistance with improving the appearance of the station surrounds and picnic areas. Qualified and experienced electricians and builders also needed. Training is given where necessary. Min. age 16. All volunteers must be fit. Overseas applicants must speak English to the standard of that of a native.

Limited self-catering hostel accommodation is provided for regular volunteers, for which a small charge is made; food is extra. Camping space and a list of local accommodation also available.

Applications to the Volunteer Resources Manager at the above address.

WELSHPOOL AND LLANFAIR RAILWAY: The Station, Pool Road, Llanfair, Caereinon, Welshpool, Powys SY21 OSF (tel 01938-810441; fax 01938-810861).

Volunteer operated steam railway in mid-Wales. The 8-mile narrow-gauge railway between Welshpool and Llanfair Caereinion travels through the beautiful mid-Wales countryside in the delightful Banwy Valley. The leisurely atmosphere provides the perfect companion to your working holiday.

Volunteer Maintenance Staff (up to 10 at any time) for varied duties including the clearing of vegetation at any time of year. No pocket money paid, but accommodation available at cheap rates. Should be over 16, fit, healthy and enthusiastic.

Applications to the above address.

Physically/Mentally Disabled

SHARE HOLIDAY VILLAGE: Smith's Strand, Linaskea, Co. Fermanagh, Ireland BT9 0EQ (tel 028677-22122; fax 028677-21893; e-mail katie@sharevillage.org; www.sharevillage.org).

A residential outdoor activity centre for the disabled and the able bodied. Located on the shores of Upper Lough Erne. Activities such as day trips, barge trips, evening social events and a wide range of outdoor and art activities.

Share Holiday Village is looking for volunteers to work as **Carer Companions** to elderly and disabled guests who come on respite care holidays in the summer months. There are also limited places for volunteer outdoor pursuit instructors with relevant recognised qualifications e.g. RYA, BCU and First Aid Instructor Level.

Approximately 200 volunteers are required for a minimum stay of 7 days from May until September. Shared accommodation and all meals are provided as are necessary travel expenses within Northern Ireland. Min. age 18.

Applications to the Volunteer Co-ordinator at the above address.

Workcamps

UNA: International Youth Service, Welsh Centre for International Affairs, Temple of Peace, Cathays Park, Cardiff, South Glamorgan CF10 3AP (tel 029-2022 3088; e-mail unaexchange@btinternet.com; www.unaexchange.org).

Volunteers required for international voluntary projects in Wales for social, manual, playscheme and environment projects. Usually 6-8 hours work per day, 5 days per week. Must pay own travel costs but free B & L provided. Min. age 18, no qualifications required. Period of work varies according to project but usually 2-4 weeks. Camps arranged all year round. Registration fee from £50. The UNA workcamps are primarily for overseas volunteers, though there are a few places for UK workers on some camps. Volunteers resident outside the UK must apply through the workcamp organisation in their own country. (British volunteers are also sent to projects overseas: registration fee from £90.)

Project leaders are also required. They are trained over one weekend in April, pay no fee and have travel expenses reimbursed.

Applications from March to the above address enclosing a s.a.e.

Au Pair, Home Help and Paying Guest Agencies

Prospects for Work

Finding a job as a mother's help or au pair in Britain is comparatively easy and is ideally suited to overseas visitors eager to improve their English. Families taking home helps are most common in London and the South-East, but mothers returning to work have brought a steady increase in demand nationwide. The majority prefer a commitment of six months to a year, but others require help for just two or three months over the summer.

The work may involve little more than light housework, playing with the children and some simple cooking. The pay, hours and training of au pairs are not supervised by any regulatory body at present, and so while a few work long hours and are treated like a skivvy, others are given great freedom, the use of the car and *Cordon Bleu* meals. Most enjoy something between the two and find working with a family to be a positive experience.

Hours vary according to the position: au pairs work 25-30 hours per week, *demi pairs* should expect to work less than that and *au pair plus* more. Mother's helps tend to work longer hours still, and are therefore usually UK nationals (see below). While the earning potential of qualified nannies has seen a dramatic rise recently, with the weekly salary of some as high as £350, au pairs should still expect to receive pocket money of around £45 or so per week. Mother's helps and au pairs plus can expect in the region of £45-£80. Free board and lodging is included. Qualifications are rarely required (except for nannies), but babysitting experience is always useful.

Changes to the law six years ago now permit the employment of males in what has been a traditionally female trade. Undeniably, au pairs remain predominately female, however the growing number of progressive agencies taking male au pairs find that increasingly more and more families are willing to try one and are in general pleased with their decision. Kingston College in Surrey recently accepted two male students on their National Nursery Examination Board nanny training course for the first time ever.

Many agencies specialise in the recruitment of home helps, and it is important to contact several in order to compare terms. Some may charge for their services, so check beforehand. You will be asked to fill out a questionnaire and should then receive a contract laying down working conditions, hours, pay, etc. Insist on being given more choice if you are not satisfied with the family allotted to you.

Immigration: nationals of the EU and of European Economic Area Countries are free to take employment in the United Kingdom including taking up 'au pair' placements.

Nationals of any of the following countries are also permitted to work as au pairs in the UK: Andorra, Bosnia-Herzegovina, Croatia, Cyprus, Czech Republic, The Faroes, Greenland, Hungary, Macedonia, Malta, Monaco, San Marino, Slovak Republic, Slovenia, Switzerland and Turkey. Nationals of Bosnia-Herzegovina, Macedonia and Turkey must obtain a visa from their designated

British Embassy or Consulate before travelling to the United Kingdom. Some au pair agencies only deal with EEA nationals.

The Home Office lays down certain regulations regarding au pairs; they must be single and without dependants; aged 17-27; should help in the home for a maximum of 5 hours per day, with 2 free days per week; receive full board, a reasonable allowance (normally up to £45 per week) and sufficient time to attend language classes.

The au pair should produce, on arrival, a valid passport and a letter of invitation from the host family giving full details of the family and household, the duties they will be expected to undertake, the allowance they will receive and the amount of free time they will have for study and recreation.

ABBEY AU PAIRS AND NANNIES: 8 Boulnois Avenue, Parkstone, Poole, Dorset BH14 9NX (tel 01202-732922; fax 01202-466098; e-mail abbey.aupairs@virgin.net). Established in 1988, the agency places mainly girls with families around Bournemouth and Poole. Coffee mornings and language courses are arranged for au pairs.
Au Pair Placements for normal housework and childcare duties. Wages £45 per week for a 25 hour week, free accommodation. Min. period of work of 2 months. Positions are available all year round.
Applications can be made at any time to Mrs Ursula Foyle at the above address.

ACROBAT AUPAIRS AGENCY: Marion House, 62A Stockport Road, Cheadle, Cheshire SK8 2AF (tel 0161-286 6566; fax 0161-286 2122; e-mail enquiries@acrobataupairs.com; www.acrobataupairs.com). Specialist au pairs agency with opportunities to work with families in Britain and learn lanuages at a local college or university.
Demi Pairs (20) for a maximum of 2-3 hours per day plus babysitting usually 2 evenings a week. Two days will be completely free for own leisure time. Own room and meals provided plus £15 pocket money a week.
Au Pairs (70) for up to 5 hours per day with 2 days off per week. Own room and meals provided plus £45 per week. Also opportunity to have English classes.
Au Pair Plus (40) for 8 hours a day plus babysitting 2-3 evenings a week. Two days free each week. Room and meals provided free of charge plus £60 a week salary. Can attend English classes.
Nannies (20) for 8-9 hours a day. Must have NNEB qualification or similar. Salary £120-£250 per week.

All positions open for girls and boys aged17/18-27 years old. Vacancies range from 3 months to 2 years. Au Pair Plus for EC Nationals only and Nannies minimum age 18 years old.
Applications welcome from all EC Nationals and Andorra, Bosnia-Herzegovina, Croatia, Cyprus, Czech Republic, Faroe Islands, Greenland, Hungary, Liechtenstein, Macedonia, Malta, Monaco, San Marino, Slovak Republic, Slovenia, Switzerland and Turkey.

ACADEMY AU PAIR AGENCY: 42 Milsted Road, Rawham, Kent, ME8 6SU (tel 01634-310808; e-mail academy4aupairs@hotmail.com; www.academyagency. co.uk).Established for ll years and full members of REC. Staff are friendly, knowledgeable, and always available to assist in enquiries.
Au Pairs. £45 for 25 hours work per week. Must be aged between 18 and 27 with some babysitting experience. Non smokers and drivers preferred.
Applications and enquiries to the above address.

AU PAIRS PLUS: £50-£60 for a min. of 30 hours work per week. Conditions as above.

Mothers Helps. Starting at £150 per week for a 40/45 hour week, must be experienced in sole charge childcare. Must be able to produce a current CV and references.

Nannies. Min. of £200 for 40/45 hours work per week. Qualifications required, such as BTECH, NNEB, NAMCW. CV and references required.

Placements are throughout the UK from Edinburgh to the south coast of England. Work is available from mid June/early July to the beginning/mid September; min. period of work 2 months. Accommodation available at no extra charge. Overseas applicants welcome. An interview is not necessary for the au-pair positions, but may be necessary for those wishing to work as nannies.

Applications should be made enclosing an International Reply Coupon before the 1st of March to Mrs Sheehan or Mrs Spett Scivoletto at the above address.

A-ONE AU-PAIRS AND NANNIES: Suite 216, The Commercial Centre, Picket Piece, Andover, Hampshire SP11 6RU (tel 01264-332500; fax 01264-362050; e-mail info@aupairsetc.co.uk; www.aupairsetc.co.uk). This REC registered agency places au pairs and home helps; see website for details.

Au Pairs/Au Pairs Plus required for light housework and childcare 5 days per week. Wages from £45 per week for au pairs, from £60 for Au Pair Plus. Min. period of work of 2 months. Positions are available from June to September. Applicants should be 17-27 years old. Foreign applicants with work permits and acceptable spoken English welcome.

Applications should be made from March onwards to Mrs Hopwood, Proprietor, at the above address.

AU PAIR CONNECTIONS: 39 Tamarisk Road, Hedge End, Hampshire SO30 4TN (tel 01489-780438; fax 01489-692656; e-mail aupairconnect@aol.com; www.aupair-connections.co.uk). An Au Pair agency operating in Southern England; some of the loveliest locations in the UK. Good monitoring and recommended by Au Pairs and families alike.

Au Pairs/Mothers Helps (300). £45 per week for au pairs and a minimum of £60 for au pairs plus. To work 25 hours per week or more. Must have a minimum of two years childcare experience and be at least 18. Accommodation available free of charge. To work from mid June-mid September; min. period of work six weeks.

Applications from January to mid June to Denise Blighe at the above address. Note that all applicants must enclose either an IRC or a s.a.e.

THE AU-PAIR PROJECT: 27 Oakfield Road, Clifton, Bristol BS8 2AT (tel 0117-9744 779; fax 0117-9077 181; e-mail info@languageproject.co.uk). This is an agency which also has a language school and has a long experience of working with foreign students.

Au Pairs (25) To look after children and do some domestic work. Wages of £40 per week, full board and accommodation. To work 25 hours a week. Min. period of work of 4 months. Positions are available all year. Preferably aged 18-26 (those over 20 preferred), with good English and some previous experience helping with children.

Applications should be made at least 1 month before employment to Jon Wright at the above address.

A22 AUPAIRS: The Old Smithy, Fitzhead, Taunton, TA4 3JP (tel 01823-401070; fax 01823-401071).

Au Pairs (50) required in June to work 25 hours per week looking after children and carrying out light housework. Pocket money of £45 per week plus accommodation. Applicants should be aged between 17 and 27.

Applications should be made to Rebecca Haworth-Wood at the above address.

ARNECLIFFE AU PAIR AGENCY: Bwthyn Bach, Wilsill, Pateley Bridge, North Yorkshire HG3 5EB (tel 01423-712709; fax 01423-712709; e-mail arncliffeaupairs@hotmail.com). A small, family-run service, aiming to provide personal support before and during a placement.

Au Pairs needed for various families in the UK and abroad. Pocket money of £45 per week, free board and accommodation with families in exchange for light housework/childcare. To work 15 hours a week. Min. period of work of 1 week. Positions are available all year. Applicants should be 17+ and preferably have childcare experience.

Applications should be made at any time to Jayne Humphreys at the above address.

BELAF STUDY HOLIDAYS: Banner Lodge, Cherhill, Calne, Wiltshire SN11 8XR (tel 01249-812551; fax 01249-821533; belaf@aol.com). Since 1975 BELAF has been organising holiday placements for European students in carefully selected families in Southern England, London and the surrounding regions, Wiltshire, Dorset, Hampshire, Gloucestershire and Somerset.

Au Pairs (200). £40-£60 per week plus accommodation. To work 25 hours per week from mid June to late August. Min. period of work 6 weeks. Min. age 18; all applicants must speak reasonably good English. Overseas applicants welcome.

Applications from January-May to Carole Browne at the above address.

BUNTERS AU PAIR AND NANNY AGENCY: The Old Malt House, 6 Church Street, Pattishall, Towcester, Northants NN12 8NB (tel 01327-831144; fax 01327-831155; e-mail caroline@aupair-bunters.demon.co.uk).

Au Pairs. Min. £45 for 25 hours and 2 evenings work over 5 days per week. Board and lodging included. Applicants should have some childcare experience such as babysitting. Must be aged between 18-27. Staff required from May to September, min. period of work 8 weeks. Overseas applicants with some knowledge of English and valid working visas welcome.

Apply before May to Mrs Caroline Jones at the above address.

CHELTENHAM NANNIES: Wharf Office, The Wharf, Coombe Hill, Near Cheltenham, Gloucestershire GL19 4BB (tel/fax 01242-680999; e-mail nanniesc@aol.com). By matching applicants to clients carefully the agency tries its best to bring about win-win situations. They also offer pre and post placement advice and guidance.

Nannies, Proxy Parents, Maternity Nurses, Mothers' Helps, Nanny Housekeepers, Day Nursery Staff Of All Levels (around 200 per year in all) placed in the UK and overseas. Wages, dates etc. depend on the employer. Relevant experience and checkable references are essential; qualifications can be an advantage. Minimum age 18; a driving licence can be an advantage.

Applications to Lynne Shrubb, Proprietor, at the above address.

NICOLA J. CUFFE: 1 Paxton Gardens, Woodham, Surrey GU21 5TR (tel 01932-341704; fax 01932-341764).

Summer Au Pairs from June to September. Approx. £45 per week depending on family and duties. Approx. 5 hour day, 5 day week, but must be flexible. Childcare experience desirable. Age limits 18-27. Must have references.
Applications to the above address.

EDGWARE AU PAIR AGENCY: 1565 Stratford Road, Hall Green, Birmingham B289JA (tel 0121 745 6777 fax 0121 243 4200 e-mail lorraine@au-pairs4u.com www. au-pairs4u.com).
An agency established in1963 by Lorraine Bushell, who commutes regularly to her home in London).
Au Pairs placed in London and the Home Counties. Au Pairs live as family members, have their own bedroom and receive weekly pocket money. Families are available all year round. Au Pairs usually attend English language classes. Age required is 18 - 27. Basic child-care experience is essential, plus a good basic knowledge of English. Minimum stay is 6 months, maximum 12 months.
Please visit the above website or write directly to the agency for full details and an *application* form.

EURO PAIR AGENCY: 28 Derwent Avenue, Pinner, Middlesex HA5 4QT (tel 020-8421 2100; fax 020-8428 6416; e-mail europair@btinternet.com; www.euro-pair.co.uk). The agency takes great care in the selection of posts available and has a back-up service if things do not work out.
Au Pairs (50+). Wages of £60 for 5 hours work a day, five days a week, with free board and accommodation. Min. period of work of 8 weeks. Positions are available all year. Applicants should be 19+, childcare experience and driving licence helpful.
Applications should be made at any time to Mrs C. Burt at the above address. Telephone interview possibly required.

EUROYOUTH LTD: 301 Westborough Road, Westcliff, Southend-on-Sea, Essex SS0 9PT (tel 01702-341434; fax 01702-330104). Established in 1961, Euroyouth places Au Pairs, Paying Guests and School Groups, with or without language and sports courses. Au Pairs are placed throughout Britain, other positions are only for the Southend area.
Au Pair positions, all parts of the UK. Min. length of stay 3-6 months. Throughout the year.
Paying Guest/Home Stays in selected host families throughout the year in Southend, and Essex and some parts of London suburbs. Min. period of stay is 2 weeks. Sports courses are an optional extra. English language courses available in British Council recommended colleges in London for au pairs and paying guests throughout the year.
Write enclosing IRC/s.a.e. for details to Euroyouth, at the above address.

GENEVIEVE BROWNE AU PAIRS: Banner Lodge, Cherhill, Calne, Wiltshire SN11 8XR (tel 01249-812551; fax 01249-821533; e-mail belaf@aol.com).
Au Pairs. Wages from £45-£50 for 25 hours work per week with board and accommodation. Usual au pair duties including housework and childcare. Min. period of work of 4 weeks. Positions are available all year. Minimum age 18.
Applications should be made at any time to Carole Browne at the above address.

JOLAINE AU PAIR & DOMESTIC AGENCY: 18 Escot Way, Barnet, Hertfordshire EN5 3AN (tel 020-8449 1334; fax 020-8449 9183; e-mail

aupair@jolaine.prestel.co.uk; www.jolaine.com). Jolaine Agency has been successfully placing applicants in the UK and abroad since 1975 and operates a follow-up system to ensure that all applicants are happy with their stay.
Arranges **Au Pair/Plus and Mother's Help** positions in the UK throughout the year. Min. stay 6 months, max. 2 years. Payment is from £140 per week for a mother's help and £50-£70 for an au pair plus. Also arranges Paying Guest family stays in the London suburbs throughout the year, from £85 per week. Accommodation available for individuals or groups of any size. Visits, excursions, activities and classes arranged on request.
    For further information and *applications* forms write anytime enclosing s.a.e. or IRC to the above address.

LADYBIRD AU PAIRS: 5 Sandringham Road, Bromley, Kent BR1 5AR (tel/fax 020-8249 2124; e-mail ladybirdaupairs@yahoo.com).
Au pairs required to help with children and for light household chores. Wages of £45 per week for approx. 25 hours work. Board and accommodation provided. Positions are available all year; minimum period of work 3 months. Child care experience helpful.
Applications to Bussy Giwa at the above address.

MONDIAL AU PAIR AGENCY: The Old Barn, Shoreham Lane, Halstead, Sevenoaks, Kent TN14 7BV (tel 01959-533664; fax 01959-533504; e-mail mondialaupairs@aol.com; www.mondialaupairs.co.uk). Proprietor, Mrs Alison Freethy. The agency celebrated its 50th anniversary in 1999. The agency prides itself in matching applicants to families.
Applicants are placed mainly in London, Kent, Sussex and Surrey.
Applications should be made to the above address.

MONDIAL PAYING GUESTS: Four Wents Farmhouse, Goudhurst, Cranbrook, Kent TN17 2QD (tel 01580-714714; fax 01580-720202; e-mail sales@mondialtravel.co.uk).
Paying guest stays arranged with families in south east London and the Weald of Kent for groups of students/individuals. For further details *contact* Mrs S.F. Roeder at the above address.

MORTON AND DAIS: The Stores Cottage, Warings Green Road, Solihull, West Midlands BN4 6BT (tel 0121-7332433; fax 0121-2404411; e-mail nannies@waverider.co.uk). A leading Nanny agency. Organiser of children's charity events and publishers of *The Nanny Bulletin.*
Morton and Dais places UK nannies (including some men) in the UK and overseas. Minimum stay of 6-12 months, and summer nannies start in July. Nannies must be 18-28 and preferably have experience of childcare/babysitting. Nannies must have two or three childcare references and two character references. For both positions applicants should be medically fit. Personal interviews are required for Nannies. Wages are £70-£100 per week plus full board and accommodation.
    Applicants should send a s.a.e. for an application form or telephone for more information.

MUM'S ARMY LTD: The Torrs, Torrs Close, Redditch B97 4JR (tel 01527-402266; fax 01527-403990; e-mail marion@mumsarmy.u-net.com; www.mumsarmy.u-net.com)
Summer Au Pairs. £45 a week plus full board. To work minimum 25 hours a

week. Duties include childcare, household duties and some cooking. Applicants should have common sense and some experience of looking after children. Non-smokers preferred. Driving would be helpful. Period of work June to end of September. Min. period of preferably 3 months.

For *application forms* write to the above address early.

NORFOLK CARE SEARCH AGENCY: 19 London Road, Downham Market, Norfolk PE38 9BJ (tel 01366-384448; fax 01366-385226; e-mail viviennepartner@hotmail.com). Most work is based in the East Anglia region, and offers competitive salaries and good conditions for live-in staff. Country minded applicants are particularly welcome.

Childrens' Nannies And Mothers' Helps. £150-£200 a week plus full B & L. To work an 8-10 hour day. Min. age 18. Positions available all year. Staff must be based in the UK and have appropriate work permits.

Enquiries and *applications* to the above address.

QUICK AU PAIR & NANNY AGENCY 22 The Ridings, Norwich NR4 6UJ (tel 0845-345 5945; fax 01603-455144; e-mail info@quickaupair.co.uk). Agency covering the whole of the UK and Republic of Ireland. A very caring, fast and efficient au pair placement service.

Summer Au Pairs (30). Wages from £45-£50 per week, free board and accommodation. To work 25 hours a week doing light housework and childcare duties with the possibility of overtime in the school holidays. Min. period of work of 2 months. Positions are available from mid-June to mid-September. Applicants should be 17+, have childcare experience and an ability to help with light housework. Foreign applicants welcome.

Applications should be made from March onwards to Bryan Levy at the above address or to info@quickaupair.co.uk. An application form is required, along with 2 character references, 2 childcare references, a 'Dear Host' letter, 2 (smiling) photos and a letter from the family doctor.

RICHMOND & TWICKENHAM AU PAIRS: The Old Parsonage, Main Street, Barton Under Needwood, Staffordshire DE13 8AA (tel 01283-716611; fax 01283-712299; www.aupairsnationwide.co.uk). An established agency running since 1992, run by Vicki and Linda who have both been Nannies/Au Pairs. The agency places mainly French, Spanish and Danish girls, and all girls are given a second chance.

Au Pairs (500 per year). Must have childcare experience, and be happy and confident with a good command of the English language. Duties involve childcare, ironing, washing up and 2 nights babysitting a week. £45 per week plus accommodation. To work at least 25 hours per week all year round; min. period of work 2 months in the summer.

Applicants must be aged between 17-27. Overseas applicants welcome; interview is not necessary. Most au pairs are placed in south west London. Applicants are requested to fill in *applications* forms available on the company Website, as above.

SOLIHULL AU PAIR & NANNY AGENCY: 1565 Stratford Road, Hall Green, Birmingham B28 9JA (tel. 0121 733 6444: fax 0121 733 6555:e-mailsolihull@100s-aupairs.co.uk www.100s-aupairs.co.uk).

AU PAIRS placed throughout Great Britain, England, Ireland, Scotland and Wales. Au pairs must be from EU countries plus some other countries as specified by the Immigration and Nationality Department. Au pairs live with the host

family as a family member, they have their own bedroom,and board and lodging, plus an amount of pocket money each week,(approximately £40-£50) payable weekly in arrears. Male and female au pairs placed for periods of 6-12 months.
Nannies placed in top jobs in many areas including London and the West Midlands. Drivers and non smokers are always in demand. References and Police Clearance Certificates are essential.
Mother's Help positions available all over the UK and mature applicants are always in demand.
For *further details* consult the above website or write to the above address.

SUPERSTUDY UK: 1-3 Manor Parade, Sheepcote Road, Harrow HA1 2JN (tel 020-8861 5322; fax 020-8861 5169; e-mail superstudy@btinternet.com; www.superstudy.com). An English language school based in Harrow, North West London. Open all year for work and study programmes and general English courses. The most economic way to improve your English and make new friends for life.
Work And Study Students. Students spend 15 hours per week as an au pair for their host family and 15 hours per week studying at the language school. They pay only for the language course and receive free board and lodgings in return for the au-pair work. Work involves general housework and perhaps entertaining children. Students are required all year round, especially in July and August, for a minimum period of 8 weeks. EU and EEA nationals aged 19-29 with a reasonable standard of English should apply.
Applications at any time to Mrs Admira Kijac, at the above address.

UNIVERSAL AUNTS LTD: PO Box 304, London SW4 0NN (tel 020-7738 8937). Established in 1921.
House Keepers, Nannies, Mothers' Helps, etc. required, in both residential and non-residential positions. Must be available to sign on with the agency for min. of 2 months. Please note the agency does not place au pairs. *Applications* any time to Universal Aunts Ltd.

USEFUL PUBLICATIONS

GET 2002: Hobsons PLC, Bateman Street, Cambridge CB2 1LZ (tel 01223-273300; www.gethobsons.com).
A careers guide for students that lists major employers; intended mainly for those choosing a career, but also a useful resource for those looking for vacation traineeships. Normally distributed free to students, otherwise may be available for reference in careers departments or obtained from the above address.

ISCO PUBLICATIONS: 12A Princess Way, Camberley, Surrey GU15 3SP (tel 01276-21188; fax 01276-691833; e-mail info@isco.org.uk).
ISCO publishes the book *Opportunities in the 'Gap' Year* which is aimed at school leavers taking a year off before going into higher education. It gives details of paid and voluntary work, inside and outside the UK, as well as study opportunities. It also includes sections on the armed forces, expeditions and outdoor work. The booklet is available from ISCO for £5.95 plus £1 for postage within the UK.

JOB MAGAZINE: University of London Careers Service, 49-51 Gordon Square, London WC1H 0PN (www.careers.lon.ac.uk).
A weekly graduate careers magazine for London featuring part-time and vacation work as well as full-time graduate positions. A subscription costs £16 for twelve weeks, including complimentary issues of Prospects today; to subscribe send cheques payable to the University of London to the above address, call 020-7554 4530 or e-mail job.ads@careers.lon.ac.uk.

LIFETIME CAREERS PUBLISHING: 7 Ascot Court, White Horse Business Park, Trowbridge, Wiltshire BA14 0XA (tel 01225-716023).
Publishes *A Year Off ... A Year On?*. This is a guide to employment, voluntary work and working holidays for gap year students and anyone considering taking a break during their education or career. It provides information, addresses, and ideas plus a variety of accounts of personal experiences. The current edition costs £8.99; a new edition is to be published at the end of January.

PETERSON'S GUIDES: P.O. Box 67005, Laurenceville, NJ 08648-4764, USA. (www.petersons.com). Leading publishers of books on employment and education in the US.
Summer Jobs for Students 2002; ($18.95). Covers opportunities in the US in detail. Available in the UK as *Summer Jobs USA* from Vacation Work (see below).
Internships USA. ($26.95). A guide to career-related employment in the US.
Petersons are also the US distributors of *Work Your Way Around the World* ($17.95), *Summer Jobs in Britain* ($17.95) and *Teaching English Abroad* ($17.95): see under Vacation Work below for details of these titles.

RECRUITMENT UK: 24a Bristol Gardens, London W9 2JQ (tel 020-7266 4947; fax 020-7289 6562; e-mail recruitmentuk@recruitment uk.net; www. recruitmentuk.net).
A quarterly magazine aimed primarily at Australians and New Zealanders looking for work in the UK,where it is primarily distributed, but it is also available free from the above address.

TNT MAGAZINE: 14-15 Childs Place, Earls Court, London SW5 9RX (tel 020-7373 3377). A magazine available available free in London from dispensers around tube stations that is packed with job advertisements; it is principally aimed at working travellers from Australia and New Zealand, but could be useful to any job-seeker.

VACATION WORK PUBLICATIONS: 9 Park End Street, Oxford OX1 1HJ (tel 01865-241978; fax 01865-790885; www.vacationwork.co.uk). Publishes or distributes the following titles in the UK.
2002 May Supplement to Summer Jobs (£6.00). This booklet lists requirements for summer staff from employers in Britain and Abroad which arrive too late for inclusion in *Summer Jobs in Britain* and *Summer Jobs Abroad.*
Working in Tourism – The UK, Europe & Beyond (£11.95). A comprehensive guide to short and long-term work in the tourist industry.
Work Your Way Around The World (£12.95). Contains invaluable information on ways to find temporary work worldwide, both in advance and when abroad.
Teaching English Abroad (£12.95). Covers both short and long term opportunities for teaching English in Britain and abroad for both qualified and untrained teachers.
Working with the Environment (£11.95). A guide to the enormous range of possibilities for short and long term work with the environment, both in Britain and around the world.
The International Directory of Voluntary Work (£11.95). A comprehensive guide to worldwide residential and non-residential voluntary work.